LOUISIANA
DURING
WORLD WAR II

LOUISIANA DURING WORLD WAR II

Politics and Society
1939–1945

JERRY PURVIS SANSON

Louisiana State University Press
Baton Rouge

Copyright © 1999 by Louisiana State University Press
All rights reserved
Manufactured in the United States of America
First printing
08   07   06   05   04   03   02   01   00   99   5   4   3   2   1

Designer: Michele Myatt Quinn
Typeface: Granjon
Typesetter: Coghill Composition Co., Inc.
Printer and binder: Edwards Brothers, Inc.

Library of Congress Cataloging-in-Publication Data

Sanson, Jerry Purvis, 1952–

    Louisiana during World War II : politics and society, 1939–1945 /
Jerry Purvis Sanson.

        p.   cm.

    Includes bibliographical references (p.   ) and index.

    ISBN 0-8071-2308-0 (cloth : alk. paper)

    1. World War, 1939–1945—Louisiana.   2. World War, 1939–1945—
Social aspects—Louisiana.   3. Louisiana—Politics and
government—1865–1950.   4. Louisiana—Social conditions—20th
century.   I. Title.   II. Title: Louisiana during World War 2.
III. Title: Louisiana during World War two.
D769.85.L6S26   1999
976.3'062—dc21   98-51457
                                                                    CIP

To the memories of my son, Adam Sanson, and my father, Luther Sanson

Contents

Preface

Why study World War II in Louisiana? For me, the answer lies in my longstanding interest in the recent history of my native state. Louisiana's history is a fascinating story from its beginning as a French colony in 1699, but I find its twentieth-century history especially interesting. Few other states have experienced the same level of political interest and political misconduct as Louisiana, but the state also occasionally produces politicians who sincerely try to provide honest, efficient government. The state's culture is likewise unique and compelling. Even today, it reflects deep cleavage between the north, with its more typical "southern" ways, and the south, with its distinctive Latin heritage.

The World War II years are essential to an understanding of modern Louisiana. Huey P. Long established the foundation upon which much of the modern state is built, but the post-Long years 1939–1945 also brought important developments in the state. Anti-Longite politicians proved during the administrations of Sam Jones and Jimmie Davis that they also could govern the state. And Louisiana's society and economics began to develop modern characteristics during those years.

Finally, World War II brought tragic losses to the families of both my mother and my father. The Japanese executed my uncle Hayden R. Lawrence in the Philippines, and a sniper killed my uncle Eli A. Sanson just after the Battle of the Bulge. In researching this book, I wanted to reach a better understanding of the war that cost them their lives.

ACKNOWLEDGMENTS

Many people contributed to the completion of this book. I must begin by acknowledging the assistance that I received from members of the Louisiana State University History Department. The late Mark T. Carleton provided encouragement from the beginning of the project, read several versions of the manuscript, and generously shared with me his vast knowledge of Louisiana history. The late T. Harry Williams spent hours with me when I began graduate school discussing his insights into Huey Long and the Long era in Louisiana politics. John Loos provided unfailing encouragement. William Cooper and Burl Noggle read one version of the manuscript and provided useful suggestions for improving it, as did Kevin Mulcahy of the LSU Political Science Department. I am also indebted to John Tew and Brady Banta, both formerly of the LSU Measurement and Evaluation Center. Brady provided especially valuable information that helped me to understand better the intricacies of oil and gas regulation in Louisiana during the early 1940s and guided me to useful archival collections.

Many archivists and librarians across the state helped me to find sources of information that might have otherwise eluded me or taken me great amounts of time to locate. I am grateful to the many archivists who tolerated seemingly endless questions about World War II materials in their collections.

Staff members at the Louisiana State University Press were especially helpful during the publication process. Margaret Dalrymple, former editor-in-chief, helped me through the initial submission process. Sylvia Frank and John Easterly provided assistance during later revisions. I was fortunate to have Sara Anderson edit the manuscript for LSU Press. Her careful reading and editing improved it in countless ways.

Many friends, colleagues, and family members provided encouragement for this project. That list includes Garry Tisdale, Greg Gormanous,

Anna Burns, Gloria Shelby, and the late Jerry Myrick, colleagues at LSU at Alexandria; David Moreland and Richard Bier, former colleagues at LSU at Eunice; Oberia Price, former president of the Historical Association of Central Louisiana; my parents, Lois and the late Luther Sanson; other family members, including Patsy and Douglas Jenkins; Dana and Jonathan Garrett; Jason, Jill, Josh, and Justin Jenkins; Boyce Leigh and Aubrey Ryder; Bethany and Lee Ponder; and Judy, Jeff, Jacob, and Amber Crawford.

Foremost in my thoughts are my wife, Becky Ryder Sanson, and my son, Benjamin Ryan Sanson. Their love and support are the inspirations of my life.

Abbreviations Used in Notes

AJE   Allen J. Ellender Archives, Allen J. Ellender Library, Nicholls State University, Thibodaux, La.

CRS   Center for Regional Studies, Southeastern Louisiana University, Hammond, La.

DL   Archives and Manuscripts Collection, Dupre Library, University of Southwestern Louisiana, Lafayette, La.

HTML   Special Collections Division, Howard-Tilton Memorial Library, Tulane University, New Orleans, La.

LLMVC   Louisiana and Lower Mississippi Valley Collections, Louisiana State University, Baton Rouge, La.

ML   Cline Room, Magale Library, Centenary College, Shreveport, La.

RWNL   Richard W. Norton Memorial Library, Louisiana College, Pineville, La.

LOUISIANA
DURING
WORLD WAR II

Introduction

Louisiana experienced significant change between the years 1939 and 1945. Events of the six-year period of World War II affected state and national politics, the economy, and virtually every aspect of life on the Louisiana homefront.

State politics were affected most, however, not by America's involvement in the war, but by the venality of Longite politicians who in 1939 incurred the wrath of the voters by their greedy excesses. From Huey Long's death in 1935 until the exposure of the Louisiana Scandals in 1939, top officials of the Longite organization lived ostentatiously expensive lives largely financed by fraudulent or improper use of state resources. Their ambition to continue enjoying the "good life" clashed with the political ambitions of James A. Noe, who alerted federal officials to the misuse of state resources.

As a result of the subsequent federal investigation, Louisiana voters temporarily banished the Longite machine, exposed as greedy and unworthy, from control of the governor's office that it had dominated since Huey Long's election in 1928. That banishment left open the way for the anti-Longite faction of the Democratic party to prove its ability to govern Louisiana honestly and effectively.

Anti-Long forces had been out of power for eleven years, however, and thus did not have recent experience in governing the kind of state that Long and his associates had created. The anti-Longites' last hurrah before the Scandals had been their impeachment of Long in 1929, a move that he thwarted. Long and his allies proceeded to construct by parliamentary maneuver, legislative act, and executive fiat a powerful organization capable of keeping virtually all its opponents out of office. When that domination of the executive branch ended in 1939, the reformers who swept into office on the tide of voter disgust had to learn how to govern and not merely criticize the government in office. In addition, voter revulsion at the excess of the Scandals did not sweep all Longites out of positions of influence. Thus when reform governor Sam Jones sought to dismantle the highly centralized administration that Huey Long and his associates had created in Louisiana, he found a strong faction in the legislature that sought to derail his reforms at every turn. The 1940 legislature granted Jones many of his reforms because the influence of the Scandals was too recent to ignore, but during the 1942 session, Longite lawmakers regrouped and brought the governor's efforts to a virtual standstill until he outmaneuvered them by withholding funds from the New Orleans Charity Hospital. The Longites subsequently agreed to certain key measures in a special legislative session.

Another way the Longites made trouble for Jones was to muster a series of "taxpayer suits" against the new governor's reforms that nullified many of them as the courts examined their enabling legislation carefully. Therefore, while Jones perhaps proved that Louisiana could be governed honestly, the powerful Longite bloc in the legislature, inexpert drafting in the legislative process, and unfavorable judicial decisions worked together to reduce the effectiveness of his reform administration.

Jones's successor, James H. (Jimmie) Davis, favored the reform initiative in Louisiana politics during his administration from 1944 to 1948, but his soothing personality and frequent absences from the state created a different ambience between the chief executive and the legislature, which was still influenced by the Longites. When legislators in 1944 defeated his proposal to levy an additional one-cent sales tax, Davis announced that he was disappointed, but not bitter, about the rejection.

Even the limited success of the anti-Longite administrations, however, proved that both Longite and anti-Longite candidates could be elected. The resulting system of effective bifactional politics within the Democratic party gave Louisiana a political system somewhat analogous to the national two-party system, with the relatively conservative reformers (a rather anomalous concept in itself) resembling the Republicans and the more liberal Longites resembling the Democrats.

This system of effective bifactionalism that began in 1939 ended in 1960, when the race issue swept aside the old politics based on economic issues. While the bifactional era lasted, however, it gave Louisiana three reform governors (Jones, Davis, and Robert Kennon) and the same Longite governor three times—Earl Long, who carried on many of his older brother's social welfare programs without the attendant concentration of political power that Huey had achieved.

Louisiana politics also evolved on the national level during the war years. Congressional campaigns often reflected the state's bifactional division with candidates seeking the endorsement of either the Longite organization or the incumbent reform administration. Even though Longite members of Congress in the 1940 election suffered along with their allies at the state level from the exposure of the Louisiana Scandals, they were not completely eliminated from office. Six were defeated, but Longites retained two seats throughout the war—Overton Brooks's Fourth District and A. Leonard Allen's Eighth District. Moreover, Louisiana's two Longite United States senators, Allen J. Ellender and John Overton, successfully defeated reform challengers.

Congressional races generally turned on two issues: corruption within the Longite organization, and the United States war effort. Reformers frequently focused on the former issue, whereas Longites often stressed the latter in order to downplay the aura of fiscal malfeasance that clung to Longite politicians. The emphasis varied from campaign to campaign and from district to district, depending on the success of the war effort or on the personalities involved, but even in campaigns that stressed the war issue corruption always loomed as a ready weapon with which a reformer could attack a Longite opponent.

Throughout the United States during the war years, the force of Franklin Roosevelt's personality overrode all other concerns in presidential politics, and it displaced bifactionalism in Louisiana during presidential campaigns. No matter how far apart reformers and Longites stood on various other issues, they found common ground in their general support of Roosevelt's presidential campaigns.

Nevertheless, Louisiana shared with the rest of the South some rumbling of discontent with the continued urban, liberal, and racially progressive drift of Roosevelt's Democratic party. The stirring of racial equality that was a feature of the war years, and that Roosevelt's brand of New Deal democracy fostered, engendered the beginnings of unease among many southern white Democrats. The war emergency helped Roosevelt to contain the southern revolt against the party, even when he chose the eccentric Henry A. Wallace as his running mate in 1940; but by the first peacetime presidential election in 1948, President Harry Truman could no longer retain the unquestioning loyalty of the South, and Louisiana, along with three other southern states, bolted to Strom Thurmond and the States' Rights Democrats ("Dixiecrats"). Once it broke with the Democrats, Louisiana found it easier to do so again when other parties offered presidential candidates closer to its conservative ideology in national affairs.

During the war, public opinion on issues other than presidential campaigns also shifted. Sentiments of noninvolvement with the rest of the world gave way in the months between September 1939 and December 1941 to the realization that the United States' assumption of a major role in defeating the Axis, which increasingly seemed a necessity for victory, required a repudiation of earlier isolationism. Major sources of public opinion in the state adopted the theory that when the United States had rejected its international role in the League of Nations during the 1920s and 1930s, it had helped lead the world into the explosive situation that burst into World War II. Therefore, many Louisianians renounced any idea of another postwar retreat and embraced the new international organization designed to keep the peace in the post–World War II international alignment of nations.

Almost all aspects of life in Louisiana experienced wartime change. The state's educational system met the challenge of World War II on two levels, one practical and one idealistic. On the practical level, Louisiana educators provided technical training required by new workers in both industrial and agricultural pursuits made necessary by the war effort.

Schools also became major components of wartime scrap collection and war stamp sales drives, as well as registration and distribution centers for the federal government's rationing program. On the idealistic level, Louisiana education rededicated itself to the role of inculcating a healthy patriotism in its students. Patriotic themes dominated consideration of history and civics courses, and teachers also used wartime necessity to urge their students to read more, or to do well in math and science.

The Louisiana educational system achieved many of its goals during the war years even though it suffered from a shortage of teachers caused by the military draft and by higher salaries in defense industries. It also experienced change when Governor Jones and State Superintendent of Education John E. Coxe imposed their reforms. Jones included the Department of Education in his general state reorganization plan in 1940, and the department suffered along with other state agencies in the administrative chaos that resulted when the state supreme court declared the Jones plan unconstitutional. While the governor sought to liberate Louisiana education from the politicalization it had experienced under the Longites, Superintendent Coxe imposed internal reorganization to provide a professional orderliness in administration. Throughout all these challenges, however, Louisiana's Department of Education struggled to continue providing the education required in the new, threatening world situation. Higher education suffered from declining enrollments as male students joined in the war effort, but the resulting loss of income was partially offset by military training programs. Collegiate athletics suffered a temporary curtailment, but various curricula were modernized to accommodate technological advancement brought on by the war.

Louisiana's economy shared in the prosperity of the war years that obliterated the Great Depression of the 1930s by the simple law of supply and demand. Louisiana agriculture helped to meet the Allied war effort's insatiable need for food and fiber, and shared in the attendant financial gain. Major manufacturing establishments in the state likewise provided vital products, materiel, and petrochemicals to the Allied cause.

Wartime prosperity, however, had different lasting effects on the agricultural and industrial sectors in the state. Although the war introduced no major new crops to Louisiana agriculture, it accelerated mechanization in the fields because of the acute shortage of labor on American farms caused by military needs and the labor requirements of new industrialization within the state. Many farmers tried, with varying degrees of success, to remedy the labor problem by utilizing Axis prisoners of war incarcerated in the state, but even these producers came to rely on increased automation in their operations. Sugarcane agronomy led the way in mechanization, while cotton and rice production lagged behind. One significant effect of the automization of agriculture was that beginning in the late 1940s and continuing into the 1950s and 1960s, Louisiana's black population increasingly left the farming business and moved out of the South or to one of its urban areas.

Although the industrial sector partook in the wartime acceleration, basic practices in that realm generally continued along the paths already established in the state. New Orleans, with its major shipbuilding, aircraft, and other manufacturing plants, remained the state's major industrial area. Baton Rouge, Shreveport, Monroe, Alexandria, and Lake Charles continued as industrial and urban centers, while other areas of the state, even though some slightly increased their industrial production, remained marginal.

Louisianians shared in the curtailment of the quality of American life experienced by the rest of the country during the war. Shortages and rationing removed some consumer goods from store shelves and made others difficult to obtain. The population as a whole, used to deprivation during the 1930s, probably survived the shortages with more equanimity than they or their descendants would have shown had they occurred during the Age of Abundance of the 1950s and 1960s. But those individuals with money from wartime jobs found the shortages galling, for now they had money to spend after doing without during the lean years of the Depression, but found few goods to spend it on. Scarcity of gasoline and tire supplies severely hindered traditional American freedom of movement. Holiday celebrations assumed a military and patriotic tinge. Involvement in civilian defense, scrap collection drives, and war bond and stamp sales, which provided civilians with a sense of participation in the titanic struggle to rid the world of the Axis menace, replaced recreation and concern for personal affairs in the lives of many people.

Two substantial minority groups in Louisiana, blacks and women, historically denied access to full participation in society and the economy, utilized the opportunities presented by the war years to establish themselves as heirs of the full equality accorded other Americans. Both groups moved out of traditional low-paying jobs and into more lucrative jobs formerly dominated by white males now away at war. The advances made by both groups, however, proved to be only a shaky beginning on the road to true equality. With the advent of peace, many women retreated to traditional roles, and blacks had to endure the white backlash of the 1950s and beyond, but the experiences sown by the war in both cases lay ready as a foundation for the struggles to achieve equality that began in earnest during the 1960s.

So Louisiana changed significantly during World War II. Politics, the economy, and society were recognizably different in 1945 from what they had been in 1939. Many of the changes, however, were only bare beginnings. The old state was often still visible underneath the layers of change. This book chronicles the important years of World War II, with the change that occurred amid the continuity that remained during that period in the history of the Bayou State.

1

The Legacy of Huey Long and His Associates

The New Year's holiday in 1939 ushered in the last year of a trying decade that witnessed the near collapse of the American economic system. Presidents Herbert Hoover and Franklin Roosevelt each had struggled to cure the system's ills, but economic want still haunted the country.

American attention, focused primarily on domestic problems during the 1930s, expanded to include foreign developments when German chancellor Adolf Hitler ordered a dawn invasion of Poland on September 1, 1939. Britain and France abandoned their accommodating policy toward Hitler and declared war on Germany. Although many Americans hoped that the conflict would be contained in Europe and that the United States would remain uninvolved, President Roosevelt nevertheless assisted Britain and France as much as possible throughout 1940–41 and prepared the United States to defend itself. The country entered the war in December, 1941, when negotiations with the Japanese over conflicting interests in the Pacific Basin failed to achieve results, and Japan launched a surprise attack on American military installations in Hawaii.

The United States' participation in the war led to changes in Louisiana: its Depression-ravaged economy improved because of an influx of federal money, and the people adjusted to life in a modern age of grave threats to national security. The most significant change in Louisiana politics during the war years, however, arose out of the simple greed of the state's elected officials. In 1939, that greed led to the temporary downfall of the dominant power in state politics, the Longite faction of the Democratic party created by Huey P. Long and, since his assassination in 1935, led by his political heirs. From the 1939 scandals originated a new political order—effective bifactionalism—in which both Longite and anti-Longite Democrats were competitive in statewide elections.

Louisiana's ruling political organization from 1928 until 1939 was the creation of one man, Huey Pierce Long, Jr., who shaped the state's politics to meet his own demands. His virtual dictatorship of the state reshaped both the form and the substance of Louisiana politics.

Huey Long pitched his campaigns to Louisiana's masses who were discontented with the ruling faction dominated by the Regular Democratic Organization of New Orleans. The RDO, "Old Regulars," or "Ring," as the association was variously called, together with upstate planters, composed a tight oligarchy that controlled the state from the 1880s until 1928. During those decades, successful gubernatorial candidates generally obtained victory by winning the support of the Old Regular/planter alliance. Huey Long, in contrast, spoke directly to the ordinary people, and with their support, he rose from an obscure Winn Parish boyhood to the Louisiana Railroad Commission, the governor's office, and the United States Senate.[1]

Long was born August 30, 1893, near the small, north-central town of Winnfield, seat of Winn Parish. During the 1890s, the parish was strongly Populist, providing the Populist candidate for governor in 1892. Following a visit by Socialist presidential candidate Eugene V. Debs in 1908, many Winn voters supported Socialists and even elected some to parish offices.[2] This poor, agrarian, radical environment in which Huey Long matured seems to have influenced him deeply.

By 1918, Long concluded that the oligarchy had exploited Louisiana's

1. T. Harry Williams, *Romance and Realism in Southern Politics* (Baton Rouge, 1966), 67, 69; T. Harry Williams, *Huey Long* (New York, 1969), 4.

2. Williams, *Huey Long,* 13, 17, 23; Arthur M. Schlesinger, Jr., *The Politics of Upheaval* (Boston, 1960), 43; William Ivy Hair, *The Kingfish and His Realm: The Life and Times of Huey P. Long* (Baton Rouge, 1991), 24–30; Reinhard H. Luthin, *American Demagogues: Twentieth Century* (Boston, 1954), 239; Alan Brinkley, *Voices of Protest: Huey Long, Father Coughlin, and the Great Depression* (New York, 1982), 10–12.

resources for too many years, a conclusion that led him to run for the Third (North Louisiana) District seat on the Railroad Commission. He realized that the commission, which regulated pipelines and utilities as well as railroad rates and practices, offered a platform from which an ambitious young politician could launch a successful career. Besides, the Louisiana Constitution stipulated no minimum age for Railroad Commission members, and Long was only twenty-four years old, too young for most state offices.[3] The commission, soon to be renamed the Public Service Commission, therefore served as an ideal beginning for Long's career.

Long made himself the people's champion on the commission, successfully challenging public utilities and railroads and bringing some rates down. He believed that fulfillment of his campaign promises created an important distinction between him and other politicians: "I would describe a demagogue as a politician who don't keep his promise. On that basis, I'm the first man to have power in Loozyanna who ain't a demagogue."[4] Moreover, he could not afford to forget the voters. He planned to run for higher office, and he needed their continuing support.

In 1924, Long ran a vigorous race for governor against Old Regular candidate Henry L. Fuqua and Lieutenant Governor Hewitt Bouanchaud, but finished third in the first Democratic primary. Even though he lost, Long became better known statewide, and began the groundwork for his next gubernatorial campaign immediately after his defeat.[5]

In 1928 he again faced two opponents—incumbent Oramel H. Simpson, who had become governor upon Fuqua's death in 1926, and Congressman Riley J. Wilson. The main issues of the campaign were Long's

3. Williams, *Huey Long,* 119–21; Schlesinger, *Politics of Upheaval,* 51; Hair, *The Kingfish and His Realm,* 86–87; Luthin, *American Demagogues,* 239; Earl Long, "Last of the Red-Hot Poppas" (Baton Rouge, 1961), phonograph recording.

4. Williams, *Huey Long,* 4–5; Schlesinger, *Politics of Upheaval,* 45; Forrest Davis, *Huey Long: A Candid Biography* (New York, 1935), 38; Monroe Lee Billington, *The Political South in the Twentieth Century* (New York, 1975), 43; Daniel M. Robison, "From Tillman to Long: Some Striking Leaders of the Rural South," *Journal of Southern History* 3 (August 1937): 303.

5. Williams, *Huey Long,* 191–213; Hair, *The Kingfish and His Realm,* 123–38.

proposals to improve living conditions in Louisiana: toll-free bridges, state-owned "free" school textbooks, construction of modern roads, improved state social services, and opposition to Old Regular and corporate rule. Wilson and Simpson maintained that Long represented a Communist attempt to take over the state, but their tactic failed. Long won the Democratic nomination when Wilson and the Old Regulars chose not to continue the struggle into the second Democratic primary.[6] Democratic nomination was then tantamount to election in Louisiana because the impotent state Republican party rarely entered candidates in general elections.

Long's administration continued Louisiana's lengthy tradition of powerful governors who aggregated influence through practice as well as through constitutional provision.[7] Once in office, he fully developed the powers inherent in the Louisiana governor's control of such crucial matters as budget formulation, selection of legislative officers, patronage, and the granting of state contracts.

Despite efforts by the old political establishment to neutralize him, Long immediately began to place his adherents in positions of power in the legislature. He obtained control of patronage with which to reward loyal followers when he appointed friends to chair the highway commission, the board of health, and the conservation commission. In the legislature, he often served as his own floor leader, rallying his troops and issuing orders on key bills. He pushed through a bond issue for sorely needed hard-surfaced roads, which upset conservatives whose political beliefs led them to recoil from public indebtedness. He financed his new "free" schoolbooks program with increased severance taxes.[8]

Long hoped to establish his programs while his opponents were still in

6. Williams, *Huey Long,* 244–81; Harnett T. Kane, *Louisiana Hayride: The American Rehearsal for Dictatorship* (1941; reprint, Gretna, La., 1971), 13–35.

7. Ed Renwick, "The Governor," in *Louisiana Politics: Festival in a Labyrinth,* ed. James A. Bolner (Baton Rouge, 1982), 75, 77; Edwin W. Edwards, "The Role of the Governor in Louisiana Politics: An Historical Analysis," *Louisiana History* 15 (spring 1974): 115.

8. Williams, *Huey Long,* 230–311; Brinkley, *Voices of Protest,* 22–24; Hodding Carter, "Huey Long: American Dictator," in *The Aspirin Age, 1919–1941,* ed. Isabel Leighton (New York, 1949), 349–50.

disarray after the election, but anti-Longite strength rebounded in March 1929 when the legislature met in special session to consider a tax he had proposed on refining oil in Louisiana. Instead of acting on the new governor's recommendation, his opponents rallied enough support in the house of representatives to impeach him. He prevented his trial by persuading fifteen senators (one more than enough to block the two-thirds vote necessary to convict him) to sign a "round robin" pledge not to vote to convict him because the impeachment charges were invalid.[9]

Long's impeachment increased his determination to obtain control of the state. He spent the remainder of his life acquiring enough power to prevent other challenges to his position and his program.[10]

While still consolidating his position in Louisiana, Long ran for the United States Senate, to which he was elected in 1930, and in which he assumed his seat in 1932. The delay resulted from Long's refusal to resign the governorship and leave Louisiana in the hands of Lieutenant Governor Paul Cyr, who was now his political enemy. Long claimed the Senate seat only after Cyr had himself sworn in as governor to replace Long, maintaining that Long could not be both governor and senator, and that Long's Senate term had begun with the new session of Congress even though Long had not claimed his seat. Cyr's futile attempt to assume the governorship allowed Long to have Cyr removed from office, thereby allowing state senate president Alvin O. King, a Longite, to become governor until the 1932 campaign, when Huey engineered the election of the pliant Oscar K. "O.K." Allen, one of his boyhood friends from Winn Parish.

Other senators looked upon Long as just another southern demagogue and considered his frequent absences and repudiation of committee assignments as attempts to avoid the hard work of the Senate. When he appeared on the Senate floor, many of his colleagues regarded his vitupera-

9. Williams, *Huey Long*, 298, 347–419; Carter, "Huey Long," 350–51; Kane, *Louisiana Hayride*, 70–76; Russell Long, remarks, War and Politics Symposium, Louisiana State University, Baton Rouge, Louisiana, April 27, 1979, typescript copy, author's collection; Russell Long, interview by Gus Weill, Louisiana Public Broadcasting, January 9, 1984.

10. Williams, *Huey Long*, 409–10; Hair, *The Kingfish and His Realm*, 178–88; Carter, "Huey Long," 351.

tive personal attacks and prolonged filibusters as grandstand plays designed to advertise his ideas on a national stage.[11]

Following his U.S. Senate race in 1930, Long consolidated his hold on Louisiana. The Old Regulars began defecting to him when New Orleans business and political leaders realized that they had to cooperate in order to maintain state funding for the city. In 1934, two years after he had moved to the Senate, he dominated a series of special sessions of the state legislature that approved laws stripping the opposition of virtually all its few remaining sources of support.[12]

As senator, Long also made his presence felt on the national level, demonstrating his ability to attract votes outside Louisiana by helping to elect Hattie Caraway from Arkansas to the U.S. Senate in 1932. His greatest failure in national politics was his inability to come to terms with President Roosevelt. He supported Roosevelt's quest for the presidency in 1932, but broke with him after concluding that the New Deal would not thoroughly reform the American economy. That opposition led him to create the Share Our Wealth movement, his alternative to the New Deal. By 1935, Huey Long not only stood unquestionably at the helm of Louisiana, but was also considering a campaign for the presidency itself.[13]

11. Williams, *Huey Long,* 559–60; Schlesinger, *Politics of Upheaval,* 53; Brinkley, *Voices of Protest,* 74–77; Hair, *The Kingfish and His Realm,* 234–38, 267–70; Allan P. Sindler, *Huey Long's Louisiana: State Politics, 1920–1952* (Baltimore, 1956), 83; Harry S. Truman, *Memoirs of Harry S. Truman,* Vol. 1: *Year of Decisions* (Garden City, N.Y., 1953), 145–46; Merle Miller, *Plain Speaking: An Oral Biography of Harry S. Truman* (New York, 1974), 161.

12. Williams, *Huey Long,* 481, 738–40; Billington, *The Political South,* 73–74.

13. Williams, *Huey Long,* 481, 738–40; Brinkley, *Voices of Protest,* 68–69; Henry M. Christman, ed., *Kingfish to America: Share Our Wealth, Selected Senatorial Papers of Huey P. Long* (New York, 1985), 29–68; David Malone, *Hattie and Huey: An Arkansas Tour* (Fayetteville, Ark., 1989); Sheldon Marcus, *Father Coughlin: The Tumultuous Life of the Priest of the Little Flower* (Boston, 1973), 84–85; Earl Long, "Last of the Red-Hot Poppas"; Robert E. Snyder, "Huey Long and the Presidential Election of 1936," *Louisiana History* 16 (spring 1975): 117–44; Michael Kurtz, "Earl Long's Political Relations with the City of New Orleans," *Louisiana History* 10 (summer 1969): 242; Alan Brinkley, "Huey Long, the Share Our Wealth Movement, and the Limits of Depression Dissidence," *Louisiana History* 22 (spring 1981): 131–32; Glen Jeansonne, "Challenge to the New Deal: Huey P. Long and the Redistribution of National Wealth," *Louisiana History* 21 (fall 1980): 332.

Speculation about a possible Long presidential candidacy in the 1936 election ended abruptly when he was shot in Baton Rouge on September 8, 1935, while managing yet another special session of the legislature. His assailant was a young Baton Rouge physician, Carl A. Weiss, who evidently committed the murder because Long was attempting to gerrymander out of office Weiss's father-in-law, state judge Benjamin Pavy.[14]

Long died two days later. Share Our Wealth leader Reverend Gerald L. K. Smith provided a eulogy. Long's beloved Louisiana State University band played his theme song, "Every Man a King," transposed into a minor key to be his dirge, and his body was laid to rest on the grounds of the towering capitol he had built.[15]

The Longite organization in late 1935 still held numerous political assets, among them the governorship and its array of powers, and the memory of Huey Long with which to appeal for votes from people enjoying the increased state services he had provided. The organization also stood atop an environment rife with opportunities for corruption. Long had almost obliterated the checks and balances of the democratic process with his concentration of power and his domination of the legislature. Writer Hamilton Basso observed Long's heirs and accurately predicted how events would soon unfold: "From now on the boys who own the cow get the cream, every ounce of it, and the skimmed milk as well." Huey Long himself had recognized the opportunities for graft created by his machine's tight control of the state. He observed on occasion, "If those

14. Williams, *Huey Long,* 859–76; Luthin, *American Demagogues,* 270; Hermann B. Deutsch, *The Huey Long Murder Case* (Garden City, N.Y., 1963), 29–135; David H. Zinnman, *The Day Huey Long Was Shot: September 8, 1935* (New York, 1963), 113–18, 183–92.

15. *In Memoriam: Funeral Oration Delivered over the Grave of Huey Pierce Long By Gerald L. K. Smith, September 12, 1935* (New Orleans, 1935); Glen Jeansonne, "Partisan Parson: An Oral History Account of the Louisiana Years of Gerald L. K. Smith," *Louisiana History* 23 (spring 1982): 153; Glen Jeansonne, *Gerald L. K. Smith, Minister of Hate* (New Haven, Conn., 1988), 41; Anne Price, *To Commemorate the 50th Anniversary of the Louisiana State Capitol, 1932–1982* (Baton Rouge, 1982), 22; Dawson Corley, "Huey's Capitol Idea," *Louisiana Life* (January/February 1982): 74; Castro Carazo, interview by T. Harry Williams, March 26, 1961, T. Harry Williams Papers, LLMVC.

fellows ever try to use the powers I've given them without me to hold them down, they'll land in the penitentiary."[16]

A contemporary news magazine divided Long's political heirs into two groups: "insiders" working behind the scenes to keep the machine running smoothly, and "outsiders"—the vote-getting political front for the machine. "Insiders" included Seymour Weiss, who administered the organization's money and tax payments, and Conservation Commissioner Robert Maestri. "Outsiders" included Public Service Commissioner Wade O. Martin, Sr., state senator James A. "Jimmie" Noe, and state representative Allen Ellender. No one in either group had an undisputed claim to Long's mantle. Instead, the day after Long died they pledged to follow Governor Allen's lead when he called a caucus to agree upon a slate of candidates for the next year's campaign for statewide offices.[17]

The Longites eventually agreed on a ticket for the 1936 campaign headed by New Orleans Appeals Court judge Richard W. Leche for governor and Earl K. Long for lieutenant governor. Leche handily defeated the anti-Longite candidate, attorney Cleveland Dear of Alexandria, in an election that Perry Howard described as "the peak of the Long surge that had scattered the Bourbon Democrats into disarray."[18]

The new administration established itself as the true heir of Huey Long by continuing programs of public works and public assistance. But Longites in high positions also stole money from the state, the top leaders clothing themselves in the trappings of wealth. One student of this period of Louisiana politics observed, "Huey liked money but loved power; 'Governor Dick' [Leche], on the other hand, liked power but loved

16. Carter, "Huey Long," 357; Sindler, *Huey Long's Louisiana*, 128; Jeansonne, *Gerald L. K. Smith*, 42–43; Hamilton Basso, "The Death and Legacy of Huey Long," *New Republic*, January 1, 1936, 218.

17. "Mourners, Heirs, Foes," *Time*, September 28, 1935; Zinnman, *The Day Huey Long Was Shot*, 189–90; Kane, *Louisiana Hayride*, 153; "Schism Among Long's Political Heirs," *Literary Digest*, September 28, 1935.

18. Carter, "Huey Long," 357–58; Kane, *Louisiana Hayride*, 159–62; Perry H. Howard, *Political Tendencies in Louisiana*, rev. ed. (Baton Rouge, 1971), 263; John T. Hood, Jr., "History of Courts of Appeal in Louisiana," *Louisiana Law Review* (April 1961): 552.

money."[19] Leche's administration came to an ignominious end in 1939 largely because of action by disgruntled former Longite Jimmie Noe.

Noe had broken with the Longites because they failed to nominate him for governor in 1936. In 1937 he began collecting affidavits from state employees reporting thefts in state government and sending them to the United States Justice Department, because he had no faith in state courts subservient to the Long organization. Justice Department lawyers dismissed the affidavits as nonsubstantial, and Noe responded by adding photographers to his staff of researchers, but their early pictures proved useless because none showed a theft that unquestionably involved state property.[20]

Noe's luck changed on June 7, 1939, when the telephone in his Monroe home rang before daylight. Hicks Batts of the Louisiana State University construction department reported that a truck loaded with window frames was leaving a workshop on campus bound for the construction site of a house in Metairie owned by James McLachlan, an associate of Governor Leche. Noe quickly relayed this information to the city editor of the *New Orleans States,* his friend F. Edward Hebert. Hebert assigned reporter Meigs O. Frost and photographer Wilfred D'Aquin to accompany Ray Hufft, station manager of Noe's New Orleans radio station WNOE, to the construction site. They followed the truck to the McLachlan housesite. D'Aquin and Hufft crawled through a vacant lot and took photographs under the cover of high weeds. The truck bore no identifying marks, and the rear license plate was smeared with mud, but photo-

19. Alva Johnston, "Louisiana Revolution," *Saturday Evening Post,* May 11, 1940; Davy Brooks, "A Turn of Events: Earl Long and the Louisiana Gubernatorial Elections of 1940 and 1948," *Southern Historian,* spring 1984, 38.

20. Kane, *Louisiana Hayride,* 267; George E. Simmons, "Crusading Newspapers in Louisiana," *Journalism Quarterly,* December 1939, 325–26; Elmer L. Irey and William J. Slocum, *The Tax Dodgers: The Inside Story of the T-Man's War with America's Political and Underworld Hoodlums* (New York, 1949), 98–99, 101; F. Edward Hebert and John McMillan, *"Last of the Titans": The Life and Times of Congressman F. Edward Hebert of Louisiana* (Lafayette, La., 1976), 118–20; Betty Marie Field, "The Politics of the New Deal in Louisiana" (Ph.D. diss., Tulane University, 1973), 397.

graphs of the front of the truck revealed license numbers that *States* researchers traced to LSU.[21]

The *States*'s subsequent page-one article carefully detailed the episode and caused quite a sensation. Leche attempted to explain away the apparent wrongdoing, declaring that the sale of LSU products to individuals was not unusual and citing the public sale of LSU dairy products as an example. He also maintained that university workers constructed the window frames while otherwise unemployed, and that the McLachlans purchased the materials and paid the workers.[22] Such efforts at smoothing over the corruption, however, proved ultimately ineffective.

In addition to Noe's private investigation that led to the *States* revelations, United States Treasury Department officials also had kept a watchful eye on the Longites since a 1937 settlement of income tax claims against them. In 1938, Rufus W. Fontenot, collector of internal revenue at New Orleans, convinced Elmer Irey of the Bureau of Internal Revenue in Washington to resume an active investigation of Louisiana's politicos. By mid-1939 special agent James M. Cooner found that LSU president James M. Smith had spent sums of money far in excess of his salary.[23] Irregularities at LSU proved to be only the tip of a system of corruption unequaled in Louisiana history.

Even Louisianians, inured to venality in their state officials, were aghast at the federal discoveries. J. J. Fournet, president of the Louisiana Police Jury Association, observed that "men in public life, in too many instances, are unable to resist successfully always the evil influences of a money-mad age, and are selling our people down the river." The board of directors of the Shreveport chamber of commerce called on President Roosevelt, Congress, and the attorney general of the United States to con-

21. Hebert and McMillan, *"Last of the Titans,"* 123–24; Kane, *Louisiana Hayride,* 267–68.

22. Hebert and McMillan, *"Last of the Titans,"* 126–27; Kane, *Louisiana Hayride,* 269–70; Alva Johnston, "The Camera Trapped Them," *Saturday Evening Post,* June 15, 1940, 22; New Orleans *States,* June 13–15, 1939.

23. Irey and Slocum, *The Tax Dodgers,* 99–100; Hebert and McMillan, *"Last of the Titans,"* 126; Kane, *Louisiana Hayride,* 275–79; Field, "The Politics of the New Deal," 398–99.

duct a thorough investigation to uncover "every misdeed affecting the good State of Louisiana." Other Louisianians expressed their disgust in diverse ways. A correspondent using the pseudonym "John Gauthier" wrote to Hammond attorney James H. Morrison, "They have stole even the stink from the pole cat." The Scandals inspired one Louisiana poet to compose the following doggerel:

> Sing a song of monkey money
> Pocket full of swag
> Four and twenty blackguards
> Caught in a bag
> And when the bag was opened
> They all began to moan
> 'Headed for Atlanta
> But not there alone.'[24]

Atlanta, Georgia, was the site of a major federal prison.

The federal government quickly launched an investigation in Louisiana directed by O. John Rogge, chief of the Justice Department's criminal division. Rogge intended to prosecute errant state officials on charges of income tax evasion. He found, however, that most machine leaders dutifully reported their income, from whatever source, just to prevent the sort of indictments that he envisioned. As Rufus Fontenot informed Elmer Irey, "All we did [in the 1937 tax evasion cases] was to teach 'em to cut Uncle Sam in on their graft."[25]

Rogge discovered, however, that the officials were vulnerable on other charges. He prosecuted LSU president Smith, Seymour Weiss, and three

24. Kane, *Louisiana Hayride,* 264; Hebert and McMillan, *"Last of the Titans,"* 124; J. J. Fournet, "A Message from President Fournet," *Louisiana Police Jury Review,* April 1939, 3; Minutes of the Meeting of the Board of Directors of the Shreveport Chamber of Commerce, July 13, 1939 (Microform Room, Troy H. Middleton Library, Louisiana State University, Baton Rouge); "John Gauthier" to James H. Morrison, August 6, 1939, and poem, n.d., James H. Morrison Collection, CRS.

25. Irey and Slocum, *The Tax Dodgers,* 99; Kane, *Louisiana Hayride,* 335–37; Field, "The Politics of the New Deal," 400; *Times-Picayune,* June 26, 28, 1939. (Note: Louisiana newspapers are identified with city of publication in the bibliography of this book.)

others for mail fraud because the check for seventy-five thousand dollars that they had received in a corrupt arrangement (the Bienville Hotel case in which the university paid twice for the building's furnishings) was mailed from a bank in New Orleans to a bank in Baton Rouge for redemption after it was deposited. The court held that this use of the mail to defraud the state resulted directly from one of the defendants cashing the check, and all were convicted.[26]

The most notorious of the Scandals trials occurred in June, 1940, when Governor Leche went to court. He was charged with participating in several illegal arrangements, but his trial focused on a kickback scheme with an Alexandria automobile dealer named George Younger. Leche denied receiving any money from the Younger truck deal, but admitted under Rogge's relentless questioning that he netted $67,000 in an oil deal with Seymour Weiss, and that his $75,000 St. Tammany Parish home cost him personally only $10,000. Leche also admitted that he owned an $11,000 yacht bought with Conservation Department funds and presented to him as a gift from "friends," and that the sale of Huey Long's old newspaper, the *Progress,* brought him a profit of $215,000.[27]

Leche received support from his friends in organized labor among other Longite groups. A pro-Leche booklet circulated in 1941 asked, "Why is Labor's Best Friend Being Crucified in Louisiana?" and answered, "The Demagogues Want Him Incarcerated. Ten Years Imprisonment on a Technicality. Political Vengeance Was Satisfied." Many Louisianians, however, agreed with a caustic couplet published in the *Louisiana Bumble Bee*: "Tokens here and shakedowns there/Has made Brother Dick a millionaire."[28]

Leche was convicted and sentenced to ten years' imprisonment. He entered the Atlanta federal penitentiary on December 31, 1941. Following a disbarment trial during which he again denied any involvement in the

26. Alva Johnston, "They Sent a Letter," *Saturday Evening Post,* June 22, 1940, 29.

27. Irey and Slocum, *The Tax Dodgers,* 111; Kane, *Louisiana Hayride,* 333; *Times-Picayune,* June 12, 1940.

28. Michael J. Cousins, ed., *Organized Labor's Tribute to the Record of Governor Richard W. Leche: The Record Speaks for Itself* (New Orleans, 1941), John B. Fournet Papers, LLMVC; *Louisiana Bumble Bee,* n.d., clipping in Richard W. Leche Papers, LLMVC.

Younger deal, the Louisiana State Bar Association disbarred him. He remained in prison until June 27, 1945. Upon his release, the United States attorney in New Orleans, Herbert W. Christenberry, announced that the government had dropped two of its remaining charges against him. He was never tried on any other charge and in 1953 received a full pardon from President Harry S. Truman.[29]

LSU's Smith was tried in state court and entered the Louisiana State Penitentiary at Angola on November 18, 1939. The pardon board recommended a commutation of Smith's sentence on November 14, 1944, and Angola warden D. D. Bayer recommended a "double good time" early release. The following April 3, Governor Jimmie Davis announced that he had released Smith and commuted his sentence to time already served. Smith returned to Angola in 1946 as director of rehabilitation and filled that post until his death in June 1949. He reformed the prison's work policies and instituted a screening program to direct prisoners into jobs that would prepare them for legitimate occupations. The effectiveness of his work, however, was limited by a lack of official support.[30]

In a statement issued just before he entered prison, Richard Leche remarked, "I am happy that . . . the vast improvements attained during my administration will long outlast the ten years I am about to serve for an offense which I never committed." Investigation of the record, however, reveals that Leche's administration achieved only a mixed success in "vast improvements." It did continue some traditional Longite construction and state service programs, but while members of the administration enriched themselves at state expense, they neglected to provide adequate facilities or services for many of the most unfortunate of Louisiana's citi-

29. *Times-Picayune,* June 12, 1940; *Shreveport Journal,* November 14, 1941; *Town Talk,* December 30, 1941, March 17, 1943, June 28, 1945; *Louisiana State Bar Association v. Richard W. Leche,* Supreme Court of Louisiana No. 35,352, Fournet Papers; *Morning Advocate,* June 29, 1945; *States,* May 23, June 28–29, 1945; *Times-Picayune,* January 24, 1953; Field, "Politics of the New Deal," 403.

30. Mark T. Carleton, *Politics and Punishment: The History of the Louisiana State Penal System* (Baton Rouge, 1971), 135, 148–49; *Item,* November 20, 1939, November 5, 1945, January 17, February 21, 1946; *Morning Advocate,* November 15, 1944, April 4, 6, 1945, January 18, 1946.

zens—residents in the state mental hospitals and inmates of the state prisons.[31]

A thorough investigation of Central Louisiana State Hospital in Pineville and the East Louisiana State Hospital at Jackson, conducted by state supervisor of public funds Jerome Hayes in 1941, revealed that at Central between December 1938 and November 1940 some "employees" carried on the payroll performed no work; some purchases occurred without public bids; and nonindigent patients owed the state over ten thousand dollars. During that period, administrators discontinued athletic contests for the patients, who were housed in old buildings equipped with improperly maintained fire extinguishers. Trash blocked fire escapes, and helpless and elderly patients lived in third-floor rooms. Hayes's investigation found patient care as inadequate as the physical facilities at both hospitals. A 1978 study of this period of mental health care in Louisiana concurred, calling the administration of the facility at Jackson "an abomination." Agricultural land became weedlots, the orchards lay abandoned, fields were rented out and equipment sold. Recreation for patients was discontinued. The tennis courts deteriorated. Even the simple recreation provided by reading rooms and organized walks disappeared. As at Central, fire fighting equipment was not in good repair and officials conducted no fire drills.[32]

Just as Louisiana's mental patients were mistreated, so were its convicts. Huey Long had established his machine's penal administration when he hired Robert L. "Tighty" Himes as general manager of the Louisiana State Penitentiary in 1931. Long endeavored to maintain the prison as cheaply as possible, and his successors continued his policy. By 1940 their goals for the prison included keeping the prisoners securely behind bars and making the prison "as light a burden on the tax-payers as possible." They made no mention of reform or rehabilitation. Concentration on discipline and control led to beatings administered by guards to prisoners.[33]

31. Richard Lawrence Gordon, "The Development of Louisiana's Public Mental Health Institutions, 1735–1940," vol. 2 (Ph.D. diss., Louisiana State University, 1978), 438–41.
32. *Ibid.*
33. Carleton, *Politics and Punishment,* 126–34; *States,* June 25, 1941.

Even though the Long machine often presented itself as the friend of the common people of Louisiana, obviously certain groups were excluded from its friendship, often for practical political reasons. The mental patients and prisoners did not vote, and relatively few members of the general voting population witnessed conditions in the mental hospitals or the prison. Money spent on highways and public buildings was much more visible and worth more politically.

During late 1939, the Scandals overshadowed any other shortcomings of the Leche administration. The breaking of the Scandals story just as Louisiana began the 1939–40 gubernatorial campaign added to the normal factional stridency of the state's political landscape. In addition, the vibrant campaign style of such 1940 candidates as Earl Long and James H. Morrison produced a rowdy campaign even by Louisiana standards.

2

The Creation of Effective Bifactionalism

Louisiana's 1939–40 gubernatorial campaign was a turning point in the state's politics. Before Sam Jones's victory in February 1940 over Earl Long, anti-Longite Democrats were an ineffectual minority protesting political and fiscal abuses within state government. While Huey Long's election to the governorship in 1928 had spawned a sharply polarized political system in which recognizable Longite and anti-Longite factions within the Democratic party vied for control, it was Jones's election that proved that reformers within the party could carry the anti-Long banner and still win a statewide election. This effective bifactionalism ushered in by the 1940 contest continued for two decades. During the next five hard-fought state campaigns, both factions were viable contenders for capturing control of state government. The anti-Longites elected two successive governors during those years: Jimmie Davis followed Jones in 1944, and Robert Kennon won in 1952. The Longites elected Earl Long in 1948 and 1956.

The Louisiana Scandals dominated the 1939–40 contest. Other issues arose before the first Democratic primary in January 1940—the beginning of World War II abroad, military records of the candidates during World War I, continued apparent corruption in government, and, eventually, the race question—but the primary issue remained the Long machine's systematic looting of state resources during Richard Leche's administration.

The Longite gubernatorial candidate, Huey Long's younger brother

Earl Kemp Long, inherited the political fallout caused by the corruption issue. Machine leaders had selected Earl to run for lieutenant governor in the 1936 election because of his last name and his close kinship to the martyred Huey. In 1939 they chose him as their candidate for governor largely by default.

Earl Long learned fundamental rules and tactics of politics beginning in 1918 when he assisted Huey in the latter's campaign for railroad commissioner. Following study at Loyola University, Earl was admitted to the Louisiana bar. In 1928, following Huey's election as governor, Earl became attorney for the state inheritance tax collector in New Orleans, a plum that allowed him to spend much of his time in Baton Rouge performing political odd jobs for Huey.[1]

The brothers did not always see eye to eye, though. In 1932, Earl asked Huey to support him for governor and Huey refused. He also declined to support Earl for lieutenant governor. Nevertheless, Earl ran a futile campaign for that post against Huey's candidate, state senator John B. Fournet.[2]

Bitter feelings caused by the rift surfaced during investigations conducted by the United States Senate into alleged improprieties in John H. Overton's election to that body in 1932. Earl testified that Huey had stolen votes during an election in 1930 and that he gave and took bribes. After his break with Huey, Earl lost his state job but became Louisiana counsel for a New Deal agency, the Home Owners' Loan Corporation. By 1934, the two had reconciled, and together helped elect Fournet to the Louisiana Supreme Court. Earl resumed state employment as counsel to

1. Richard B. McCaughan, *Socks on a Rooster: Louisiana's Earl K. Long* (Baton Rouge, 1967), 14; G. Dupre Litton, *The Wizard of Winnfield* (New York, 1982), 15; Margaret Dixon, "Governor Earl K. Long," *Morning Advocate,* May 9, 1948, magazine section, 7; Williams, *Huey Long,* 315–16.

2. McCaughan, *Socks on a Rooster,* 39–40; Litton, *The Wizard of Winnfield,* 13–14; Huey P. Long, *Every Man a King: The Autobiography of Huey P. Long* (New Orleans, 1933), 260–62; Russell B. Long, interview by Gus Weill, Louisiana Public Broadcasting, January 9, 1984.

the State Tax Commission. The brothers continued on amicable terms until Huey's death in 1935.[3]

Following his return to favor, Earl could not be ignored by the Long machine leaders who met to choose a ticket for the 1936 election, even though some were uneasy about his forceful personality, and others remembered the Overton hearings during which they thought Earl had betrayed Huey. They therefore declined to nominate him for governor, choosing instead the more polished and urbane Richard Leche, but Earl was offered the second spot on the ticket.[4]

Earl Long remained in the background from 1936 until 1939 while the dapper Leche and his associates ran the state and filled their bank accounts. The question of Earl's involvement in the Scandals remains unsolved. If he was not involved in the corruption, why did he not report it or move more forcefully against it in 1939? The answer probably lies in his political ambition. Earl knew that he could not win the governorship without the support of either Leche or the Longite machine led by Robert Maestri. Because he did not wish to lose either of these potential sources of support, Earl kept quiet about whatever he knew of the corruption. Moreover, the fact that Earl himself was a top member of the administration should not be overlooked. It would have been difficult and politically unwise for him to expose his associates. It is also possible that he had used his own office "for personal gain and that he received graft from federal funds," as Michael Kurtz and Morgan Peoples maintain in their biography of him. If so, his reluctance to help expose the Scandals becomes even more understandable.[5]

Even though Earl Long was not convicted for any offense arising from the Scandals, he was indicted along with four other officials for allegedly

3. McCaughan, *Socks on a Rooster,* 39–40, 42–54, 57, 270–82; Litton, *The Wizard of Winnfield,* 13–14; Stan Opotowsky, *The Longs of Louisiana* (New York, 1960), 139; Russell B. Long, Weill interview, January 9, 1984.

4. McCaughan, *Socks on a Rooster,* 57–58; Litton, *The Wizard of Winnfield,* 15; Kane, *Louisiana Hayride,* 154.

5. Michael L. Kurtz and Morgan D. Peoples, *Earl K. Long: The Saga of Uncle Earl and Louisiana Politics* (Baton Rouge, 1990), 99–102.

ordering that ten people employed by the New Orleans dock board be paid whether or not they appeared for work. The indictment was later quashed because it was improperly worded, and the case was not revived. Nevertheless, Long had to defend himself for the rest of his political life from charges that he had profited at state expense during his term as lieutenant governor. The effect on the voters caused by the aura of corruption surrounding Earl Long is illustrated by a letter Mrs. Mary Flogel wrote to James H. Morrison in 1939: "Its a lots of voters around here [Tunica] certainly dont want Earl long for Governor becaus he was with the crowed when they were doing the Stealing & wouldnt open his mouth untile they were caught."[6]

Just after the *States* printed the McLachlan window frame story and the investigation into James Monroe Smith's personal finances began, rumors circulated in Louisiana and in Washington, D.C., that Governor Leche planned to resign from office. Leche maintained that his health no longer permitted him to carry out his duties, but many people in Louisiana suspected that he hoped to fade quietly into the background without further involvement in the Scandals. Leche apparently did have problems with chronic arthritis. In letters he received early in 1939, months before any public hint of the Scandals, his correspondents either mentioned his poor health or sent hopes that he was feeling better. Also, Leche told an interviewer in February 1939 that he suffered "a million shooting pains" in his legs and was recently incapacitated because of them.[7]

On June 26, 1939, Leche resigned and issued a declaration that he was no longer governor. He undoubtedly breathed a sigh of relief as he com-

6. Sindler, *Huey Long's Louisiana,* 145; *Times-Picayune,* July 30, 1939, July 24, 26, August 8, 1940; *Times-Picayune/New Orleans States,* July 28, 1940; *Morning Advocate,* October 3, December 12, 1940; "New Light on Earl's Record," radio address by Congressman James Domengeaux, typescript copy, William Walter Jones Collection of the Papers of Sam Houston Jones, HTML; Mrs. Mary Flogel to James H. Morrison, December 10, 1939, Morrison Collection, CRS.

7. Governor Albert B. (Happy) Chandler to Richard Leche, January 18, 1939, W. W. Cunningham to Leche, January 29, 1939, Earle Christenberry to Leche, February 14, 1939, E. A. Conway, Sr., to Leche, March 9, 1939, clipping from *New York Journal and American,* February 25, 1939, all in Richard W. Leche Papers, LLMVC.

mented, "It's all yours now, Earl." The new governor in his first official statement characteristically captured the mood of the Louisiana public and announced that his new administration would take as its motto a text from the book of Proverbs: "Better a little with righteousness than great riches without right." "That's a significant statement," an anonymous observer remarked.[8]

Earl Long quickly settled into the governorship and began his campaign to retain the office, but he was ultimately defeated by Lake Charles attorney Sam Houston Jones. Jones was born on July 15, 1897, near the small town of Merryville, in rural Beauregard Parish in southwest Louisiana. The physical surroundings of his childhood were not substantially different from those of Huey and Earl Long in Winn Parish at about the same time. One study of Louisiana's political culture categorizes Beauregard as not in character a southwestern parish, but rather the most southwesterly of "North Louisiana" parishes.[9]

Jones's earliest political training came from his father. When Jones was three, the family had moved to the small town of DeRidder in north-central Beauregard Parish, where his father served on the town's board of councilmen and as mayor. During World War I, the elder Jones served on the local draft board and board of health, and capped his political career as Beauregard Parish clerk of court, leaving that post in 1928. He initially supported Huey Long, but after Long began forging his powerful hold on the state he looked upon his early Longism as a great personal mistake.[10]

Sam Jones remarked during the 1970s that he was "practically born in a courthouse." He began his public career during World War I as clerk of the draft board in Beauregard Parish. Army service from 1917 until 1919

8. McCaughan, *Socks on a Rooster,* 65; *Times-Picayune,* June 23, 25, 27–28, 1939.

9. Denny Daugherty, "From Log Cabin to Governor's Mansion" (senior thesis, Louisiana State University, 1970), 16–17; Sam Jones to Denny Daugherty, July 22, 1970, Dennis Daugherty Collection, LLMVC; David M. Landry and Joseph B. Parker, "The Louisiana Political Culture," in *Louisiana Politics,* ed. Bolner, 3; Bob Angers, Jr., "Sam Houston Jones, Reform Governor," *Acadiana Profile,* October/November 1971, 6.

10. Daugherty, "From Log Cabin to Governor's Mansion," 16–20; Jones to Daugherty, July 22, 1970, Daugherty Collection.

interrupted his career, but in 1920 he became his father's deputy clerk of court, and in 1921 was the youngest delegate to the Louisiana constitutional convention. He became an attorney in 1922 and less than one year later received an appointment from Governor John M. Parker to fill an unexpired term as city judge of DeRidder. In 1924 he became an assistant district attorney for the five parishes of southwest Louisiana, even though the new job required him to move to Lake Charles.[11] Believing that active opposition to the powerful Long machine was useless, the younger Jones left political life the same year as his father, 1928.

When the Scandals story broke, Jones was a successful Lake Charles lawyer, bound by commitments to his wife, Louise Gambrel Jones, and his partners to stay out of politics. In early August 1939, however, a committee of prominent anti-Longites led by Prescott Foster, son of former governor Murphy J. Foster, visited Jones to try to persuade him to run for governor. In addition to this show of support, as state commander of the American Legion Jones had created a network of personal contacts and acquaintances that he could utilize in a political campaign.[12]

While Jones rejected initial entreaties to enter the race, he gave his permission when Foster asked whether his group could talk to his law partners. Subsequently, both the partners and Mrs. Jones (to whom the group also talked) encouraged him to make the race. His old friend Vance Plauché exhorted: "There are times when we have to risk everything for the right. This is one of them." Fearing retaliation from the Longites, Jones did not declare for the governorship lightly. He waited until at least

11. Daugherty, "From Log Cabin to Governor's Mansion," 16–20; Jones to Daugherty, July 22, 1970, Daugherty Collection; Maj. Gen. E. S. Adams to Allen J. Ellender, February 3, 1940, Allen J. Ellender Papers, AJE; *Roster, Members and Officers, Constitutional Convention, State of Louisiana, of 1921* . . . (Baton Rouge, 1921), 5, 10, 15; "Louisiana's Governor-Elect," *Louisiana Police Jury Review,* April 1940, 14; Angers, "Sam Houston Jones," 6.

12. Daugherty, "From Log Cabin to Governor's Mansion," 21–22; Sam Houston Jones, interview by Dennis "Denny" Daugherty, May 6, 1970, tape recording, and Jones to Daugherty, July 22, 1970, Daugherty Collection; Sam Jones, interview by James M. Godfrey, February 1977, LSU Oral History Collection; Angers, "Sam Houston Jones," 6; Roland Boatner Howell, Sr., *Louisiana Sugar Plantations, Mardi Gras and Huey P. Long: Reminiscences of Roland Boatner Howell, Sr.* (Baton Rouge, 1969), 168.

one of the accused received a prison sentence before he made a final commitment. And before tossing his hat into the ring the day after the Bienville Hotel case ended in September 1939, he made preparations to move to Houston, Texas, to continue his law practice there if he lost the election.[13]

After overcoming his initial hesitation, Jones waged a vigorous and ultimately successful campaign focused on his pledge to restore much-needed "Common Honesty" (his campaign slogan) to Louisiana government, for, as he cogently reminded voters, "We are seeing the result of the lack of it in Louisiana affairs today."[14]

Even though he dissociated himself from the corruption that accompanied the Longite administrations, Jones promised that he would continue to provide popular social programs. He and most other conservative anti-Longite reformers knew they could not propose "turning back the clock" to reinstate old-guard Bourbon practices of governing and still hope to win elections in post–Huey Long Louisiana.

Besides Long and Jones, three other candidates campaigned in the first Democratic primary, including former governor Jimmie Noe, who had, as detailed in the previous chapter, been instrumental in exposing the scandals. The West Point, Kentucky, native was born in 1893, and had begun his political career in his adopted state as a Longite. Elected to the state senate in 1932 from Ouachita Parish, he was serving as senate president-pro-tempore when Governor Oscar Allen died in 1936. As there was no lieutenant governor owing to John Fournet's election to the state supreme court, Noe became governor. Although his term lasted only four months, the feel of the office suited him, and he used the time to establish the foundations for a later campaign. During his brief tenure, Noe opened the governor's mansion to Huey's country people and further courted their favor by naming Huey's widow to complete her husband's unexpired U.S. Senate term.[15]

13. Daugherty, "From Log Cabin to Governor's Mansion," 25–27; Kane, *Louisiana Hayride*, 347.

14. *Item,* September 21, 1939.

15. Robert Sobel and John Raimo, eds., *Biographical Directory of the Governors of the United States, 1789–1978. Volume II: Iowa–Missouri* (Westport, Conn., 1978), 585; Sindler,

After 1936, when the Longite machine disappointed him by not making him its candidate for a full term as governor, Noe devoted himself to his personal businesses—oil and gas leases, real estate, and radio station WNOE in New Orleans—and to his personal vendetta against Richard Leche. By 1939, he was again serving in the state senate and launched his new gubernatorial campaign from that post. His political career both inside and outside the Long camp was reflected in his first Democratic primary campaign. He had broken with the machine after the 1936 disappointment and could expect no help from it, but neither was he fully accepted by the reformers because of his previous close ties to the Longites. He pitched his campaign appeals to the Huey Long voter who was disgusted with the corruption of the post-Huey machine. Longites counterattacked Noe for supposed irregularities committed while amassing his wealth. Earl Long, for example, declared on numerous occasions during the campaign that Noe had been on the "Crooks To Look Out For" list of the United States Post Office since the 1920s.[16] Despite his awkward position, Noe ran a strong third in the first primary and helped to elect Jones in the second primary.

James Hobson Morrison was the fourth candidate in the race. Morrison was an attorney in Hammond whose legal career included work for various groups of strawberry farmers in the Florida parishes, and he hoped to capitalize on his "friend of the small farmer" image in his campaign. Morrison later recalled that he really did not have much chance to win the governorship in 1940, but the race allowed him to express his contempt for the corruption rampant in public office: "[the election] gave me a chance to show what I had—the courage of my convictions."[17]

Morrison's campaign was easily the flashiest of any candidate in the contest, outstripping even that of Earl Long. The centerpiece of Morrison's appeal was his fiery stage presence: on some occasions he called Earl Long a "slimy little stooge" and shared the stage with a monkey named

Huey Long's Louisiana, 142; Kane, *Louisiana Hayride,* 155, 191–92; *Times-Picayune,* March 19, 1940.

16. Kane, *Louisiana Hayride,* 431; Sindler, *Huey Long's Louisiana,* 269.

17. *Congressional Directory,* 78th Cong., 1st sess., 1942, 43; James H. Morrison, interview by author, May 13, 1982.

"Earl Long" until the beast went mad. (Morrison commented that he must have called the monkey by that name once too often.) His most colorful innovation was "Jimmy Morrison's Convict Parade," a group of his farmer friends who volunteered to appear on floats depicting state officials dressed in convict garb in the act of looting the state.[18]

Despite a shoestring budget that forced him to collect money at each rally to move the convict parade to the next stop, Morrison's sideshow proved to be a popular adjunct to his campaign. Its appearance on Canal Street drew a crowd estimated to be larger than that of the Rex Mardi Gras parade. A correspondent from Winnfield wrote to Morrison, "When you visit this section, we certainly expect your parade." Another correspondent wrote that his family enjoyed the parade "even better than [the] 'Gang Busters' [radio] program." With the convict parade, Morrison solved a persistent problem in politics: how does a minor candidate attract public notice? His answer included the surface fun-and-games of the parade—as he said, "If you didn't make a flamboyant campaign, you might as well stay home"—but after the entertainment attracted a crowd, Morrison made hard-hitting speeches to present his ideas to his audience. Moreover, the parade was undoubtedly a graphic reinforcement of the Scandals stories appearing each day. Its effect on a poorly educated Louisiana electorate should not be underestimated simply because Morrison finished a distant fourth in the first primary. He declined to endorse either Earl Long or Sam Jones in the second primary.[19]

The fifth and most minor candidate in the first primary was Vincent Moseley, an Opelousas lawyer. Moseley's campaign can be accurately described as fiercely independent (he described his effort as "not supported by any coterie or any close corporation of capitalistic capons") and passionately anti-Long. He often appeared to be running as much against Huey as against Earl Long, remarking of the Kingfish that "his was the master mind, and he the master evil."[20] The Longites considered Moseley

18. Morrison, interview by author, May 13, 1982.

19. B. W. Bailey to James H. Morrison, November 2, 1939, Frank B. Beadle to Morrison, January 5, 1940, Morrison Collection; Kane, *Louisiana Hayride,* 438–39; *Times-Picayune,* September 30, 1939.

20. Sindler, *Huey Long's Louisiana,* 142.

a minor nuisance. The other candidates generally ignored him unless he made a direct personal attack on one of them that they felt compelled to refute. Otherwise, outside the urban press, Moseley's campaign received scant attention.

Other politicians throughout the state had announced their intention to run for the governorship but dropped out of the race before the first primary. Among them were former public service commissioner and irrepressible Cajun politician Dudley LeBlanc, Shreveport mayor Sam Caldwell, and State Treasurer Andrew P. "Pat" Tugwell.[21]

Tugwell had been Earl Long's most vocal critic during the early weeks of the campaign. He attacked Long first about so-called "de-duct" money taken without permission by the state machine from state employees' paychecks to finance political activities. He began his attack with a letter to John M. Fush, assistant to the general manager of the New Orleans dock board, asking whether it was true that New Orleans mayor Robert Maestri had custody of the funds derived from the payroll deductions. Fush replied that Maestri had "nothing whatsoever" to do with the deduction funds. The next day, Tugwell quoted from a speech Leche made on May 24, 1938, in which he disclaimed handling any money from the deductions: "Dr. O'Hara [Joseph A. O'Hara, president of the state board of health] is president of it [the Louisiana Democratic Association, political front for the deduction money], Mayor Maestri and Mr. Fush are treasurers of it." Tugwell commented that in light of Leche's speech, "Mayor Maestri's denial regarding the shakedown fund is far from satisfactory."[22]

Tugwell's persistent investigation brought LDA finances under increased public scrutiny. On July 10, Dr. O'Hara and Fush revealed that they were indeed the custodians of the deduct fund collected by the LDA. Fush, though, declared that he was "too busy" to show Tugwell any of the organization's records, but they would be open for his inspection if O'Hara approved. O'Hara refused to permit anyone to see the LDA rec-

21. *Item-Tribune,* September 10, 1939; Vincent Moseley to W. Scott Heywood, August 11, 1941, Jennings-Heywood Oil Syndicate Records, LLMVC; Kane, *Louisiana Hayride,* 428–29.

22. *Times-Picayune,* July 6–7, 1939.

ords and emerged as a staunch defender of the deduct system, commenting that the funds "are just like the dues of almost any other organization of its kind," without explaining which other states, parties, or factions had an "organization of its kind," which subsisted on forced contributions from public employees. He admitted, however, that LDA funds were indeed the deduct dollars from state paychecks. When asked if Governor Long had made any move to change LDA financing, O'Hara replied, "No, not that I've heard of."[23]

O'Hara was correct. Upon taking office, Earl Long began tidying up the sloppy payroll procedures of the Leche administration by halting the practice of carrying employees on the payroll of one department even though they worked in another department. But he had not taken action against the deducts, even though Noe made public the sworn affidavit of James S. Allain (former clerk in the Louisiana State Automobile License Bureau office in New Orleans), which revealed that Hubert Haydell, chief clerk in his office, had cashed his $100 payroll check each month and returned $95 to him without mentioning where the other $5 went. Furthermore, Frank S. Perilloux, eighth ward leader for the LDA in New Orleans and chief inspector for the dock board, stated that contributions equal to 5 percent of their salary were expected of state employees, and added that he collected an additional 1 percent for the local organization because local units received none of the "five percent money." Even though Governor Long intimated that the deducts would be discontinued, he did nothing to stop them, and the LDA continued to take money from state employees.[24]

Administration officials realized, however, that the public mood demanded that they change their methods of collection. State employees reported in early August 1939, that "sources which experience has taught them to respect" assured them that no more deductions would be taken from their salaries in the immediate future. One employee added, though, that "we have been told to save our money because, when things quiet down, they will expect us to pay in a lump sum the equivalent of

23. *Ibid.*, July 11, 1939.
24. *Ibid.*, June 29, July 14, 21, 24, 1939.

deductions not taken out of our pay." Governor Long announced on August 9 that no further deductions would be taken from state employees, and responded angrily to reports that employees would be assessed later.[25]

LDA leaders subsequently devised a "voluntary contribution" plan to replace the straight deduct. Workers at Charity Hospital in New Orleans first reported the new system. They would be "permitted to contribute" to Long's campaign, but hospital officials had assured them that no one would lose employment for refusing to do so. Several workers reported a refinement of the old system: the "voluntary contributions" would be accepted from them after they cashed their paychecks, not before, and in a building set aside from the main hospital. Even though Governor Long steadfastly maintained that contributions "will never be collected on a fixed percent while I am governor," and that if any state worker was unable or unwilling to contribute, or had experienced a recent family illness, "he or she won't be allowed to contribute," Charity Hospital workers in New Orleans nonetheless found envelopes marked for their "voluntary contribution" included with their mid-November paychecks. State police and highway department workers also received strong hints to make the "voluntary contributions." Employees of the State Employment Service Perdido Street office in New Orleans received a form letter in December addressed to Governor Long with which they were to send their contribution "in recognition of your integrity and outstanding record of accomplishments and to aid you in some small measure in your great fight to secure for Louisiana four more years of the good government that you inaugurated when you became governor."[26]

State employee assessments to help finance Long's campaign particularly incensed his opponents because the practice allowed Longites to tap into a rich source of political contributions. Tugwell, Jones, Noe, and Morrison repeatedly referred to the practice when reciting their litany of

25. Bill Attel to "Gentlemen," August 7, 1939, Morrison Collection; *Times-Picayune*, August 8–9, 1939.

26. *Times-Picayune*, November 15–16, 1939; *States*, November 10, 15, 17, December 18, 1939; *Item*, November 15, 28, 1939; Stella O'Connor, "The Charity Hospital at New Orleans: An Administrative and Financial History, 1736–1941," *Louisiana Historical Quarterly* 31 (January 1948): 90.

abuses practiced by the Long regime. Reform opinion was best typified in two editorials that appeared in the *New Orleans States*. The first portrayed a Long machine comprised of politicians who treated the poor with callous disregard "unless the poor bow down and worship them and give up in many instances part of their pay by means of the nefarious deduct system." More directly, the *States* reminded its readers that given the administration's record, every state employee who received one of the "voluntary contribution" envelopes and failed to respond "would soon be regarded as inefficient, defiant or not possessing the requisite qualities to hold a job."[27]

Having created a fundamental and enduring campaign issue with his investigations into the deduct system, Tugwell next focused his attention on suspicious activities of the Louisiana Conservation Department. He first questioned an arrangement by which the Longwood Oil and Gas Company received a permit to produce an extraordinarily large amount of gas from two wells in the Cotton Valley oil and gas field in Webster Parish. The permit was ostensibly for the purpose of conducting an experiment on recycling distillate gas in the field, but Tugwell charged that the extra gas was not recycled. He compared the Longwood permit to one issued to the Ohio Oil Company for a similar experiment in the same field. The Ohio permit was limited to a period of thirty days while the Longwood permit was issued for an unlimited period.[28]

Tugwell discovered other irregularities in the Conservation Department. The department had received $350,000 during the previous legislative session to build a new geology building at Louisiana State University, but campus records showed only $275,000 received. Governor Long held a hasty conference with university officials and Conservation Commissioner William O. Rankin, and shortly afterwards LSU received the remainder of the money. Tugwell next charged that many Louisiana companies dealing in oil field supplies and equipment were compelled to

27. *States,* November 9, 17, 1939.

28. Brady Michael Banta, "The Regulation and Conservation of Petroleum Resources in Louisiana, 1901–1940" (Ph.D. diss., Louisiana State University, 1981), 458–59; *Times-Picayune,* July 12–13, 1939.

obtain merchandise through the Maxwell Supply Company, which kept
10 percent of the total amount of the order even though it provided essentially no service. Other firms transported, stored, and delivered the equipment. Tugwell identified C. A. Morvant of Thibodaux as the registered
agent of the Maxwell Company in Louisiana. Morvant also happened to
be chief attorney for the Department of Conservation. Morvant admitted
that he was the company's agent, but maintained that no one was compelled to order through the Maxwell firm.[29]

Governor Long initially declined to make any personnel changes in
the Conservation Department, but as the political attacks mounted he
removed Commissioner Rankin and appointed state senator Ernest S.
Clements in his place. Clements knew little about the oil business in Louisiana and freely admitted so, but pledged to obtain the best advice possible from experts in the field. Some Louisiana oil men looked hopefully to
his pledge to run the department without political favors. Rankin was
eventually jailed for using Conservation Department funds to purchase a
yacht for Governor Leche, then was sentenced to an additional five years
for his participation in the Longwood arrangement.[30]

The oil and gas business arrangements of erstwhile reformer James A.
Noe also received criticism. On August 23, 1939, the Ouachita Parish
grand jury indicted W. D. Dark and L. J. Melton, respectively manager
and field agent of the Louisiana Conservation Department in northeast
Louisiana, charging them with bribery in connection with the flow of gas
wells in the area. Dark and Melton admitted their guilt but maintained
that the principal beneficiaries of the arrangement were the people who
had bribed them. The indictments stated that the defendants had received $2,250 from the J. and H. Gas Company to permit it to acidize
twelve wells and thus increase production. James A. Noe was listed as
president and general manager of J. and H., and incorporation papers for
the company listed Noe and Harold Wood as joint stockholders. Noe
quickly explained, "Since the beginning of the Dick Leche–Earl Long

29. *Times-Picayune,* July 14, 19, 25, 28, 30, 1939.

30. *Ibid.*, July 25, 1939; W. Scott Heywood to Mr. and Mrs. Gene Heywood, August 2,
1939, Jennings-Heywood Records; Banta, "Conservation of Petroleum Resources," 459.

administration, the independent oil and gas operators in this area have had to pay tribute to the indicted representatives of this vicious political machine," and added that the grand jury had examined all the evidence and had not indicted him. Governor Long responded that "Noe used to run the conservation department" in Monroe, and that if he had nothing to hide, he should have reported the shakedowns instead of unlawfully paying them. Melton added that acidization of Noe's wells was a direct violation of a 1936 agreement among oil men in the region to refrain from using acid in their wells because its continued application caused an intrusion of salt water into the field, thus ruining it for further production. Melton also stated that Noe had not explained why he paid the two agents $666.66 in 1937 not to report him for producing excess gas from two of his wells. The money Noe called a "shakedown," Long machine representatives maintained, was in fact a bribe he paid to needy department officials who allowed him to operate his wells illegally. The *Progress,* the administration newspaper, thereafter often caricatured Noe in cartoons as the mother of two children: plump, well-dressed "Shakedown," whom he acknowledged; and skinny, bedraggled "Bribe," whom he sought to disown. Regarding the language play of the episode, the *Item* commented that the logic in the "Bribery-Shakedown" incident was "more lengthy than convincing."[31]

In the gubernatorial campaign, Longites correctly considered Noe and Jones to be their most formidable opponents, and concentrated most of their attacks on them. The anti-Noe assault focused on convincing the public that he had not earned his considerable wealth honestly and that he had betrayed Huey Long when he broke with the machine in 1936. Earl Long, for example, in one speech told his audience, "This Jimmie Noe has made plenty of money out of oil and gas when he was governor, taking it away from the school children of this state."[32]

The anti-Jones facet of the attack sought to portray Jones as a conservative corporation lawyer who would turn back the clock by taking away

31. *Times-Picayune,* August 24–25, 1939; *Item,* September 12, 17, 1939; *Progress,* various issues, August 1939–January 1940; Banta, "Conservation of Petroleum Resources," 455–58.
32. *Times-Picayune,* September 5, 1939.

the state facilities and services that Longism had provided for the people. The *Progress* exclaimed that "Stuck-up Sam Jones, the High Sassiety Kid, of Lake Charles is to receive $100,000 for himself to run for governor of Louisiana as the candidate of the corporate interests." Long charged that Jones represented fifty corporations in his legal practice, a number that the *Progress* reduced to forty-three. The governor rousingly warned Jones that "the people are not ready to turn this government over to the corporate interests."[33]

Later during the heated campaign, Earl Long coined a description that became infamous in Louisiana politics and haunted Jones throughout his political life: "High Hat Sam Jones, the High Society Kid, the High-Kicking, High and Mighty Snide Sam, the guy that pumps perfume under his arms." U.S. senator Allen J. Ellender, speaking in Long's behalf, told an audience that "the opposition" wanted to turn the state back over to the "big boys who haven't forgotten that the present regime made them turn over $8,000,000 in severance taxes, $3,500,000 in corporation franchise taxes, and $5,500,000 per year in income tax."[34] Presumably the "big boys" were now out for revenge.

In response, Jones repeatedly stressed his humble beginnings in rural Beauregard Parish and reminded voters that even though his law practice included corporate clients, he accepted only "honest" cases, corporate or otherwise, and moreover, he had been a member of the same law firm as former governor Alvin O. King, whom Huey Long had made governor during his fight with Paul Cyr. He also remarked that he had recently won a large judgement for some southwestern Louisiana rice farmers who had sued a milling corporation. In Gueydan, Jones warned his audience that the administration would tell them that he was against free school books, homestead exemptions, the right to vote freely, and old-age pensions, but he cited an article printed in the *DeRidder Enterprise* in 1920, in which he advocated those measures. Speaking to a carpenter's union, Jones advocated labor's right to organize, strike, and picket. He also incorporated some of Huey's social welfare philosophy into his plat-

---

33. *Ibid.*, September 21, 1939; *Progress,* September 15, October 7, 1939.
34. Kane, *Louisiana Hayride,* 434–35; *Item,* November 17, 1939.

form: $3 automobile licenses, salary increases for teachers, and $30 monthly "old-age" pensions. His most effective rebuttal to the "High Hat" charge was his "My pappy was for Huey" phrase, repeated endlessly on the campaign trail. But he failed to mention his father's eventual disillusionment with the Kingfish.[35]

The charges and countercharges of both sides were briefly pushed from the front pages of state newspapers during early September 1939. International relations in Europe had steadily worsened after Adolf Hitler's rise to power as German chancellor in 1933, and war erupted when Hitler ordered his armored columns to invade Poland during the early hours of September 1. England and France subsequently launched a futile effort to save Poland, and World War II spread across the European continent. The mood on the opposite side of the Atlantic, both in the United States as a whole and in Louisiana, was at first one of reluctance to envision any possibility of American involvement in the spreading war. But the outbreak immediately made the candidates' World War I army records primary campaign topics as they sought to prove their patriotism. The only major candidate without a war record was Earl Long. Noe hastened to attack Long as a "slacker," remarking on Armistice Day that "when the armistice was signed, a warrant was out for Earl Long's arrest as a draft dodger."[36]

Noe also sought to draw parallels between the Long machine in Louisiana and Nazi Germany, characterizing the incumbent administration as "a political machine as evil and debauched as Adolf Hitler, Europe's madman." James Morrison joined the fray when he charged that the Louisiana administration even provided aid to Hitler by producing oil in excess of the allowable under the Connolly "Hot Oil" Act and selling the excess oil to Nazi Germany to be refined into airplane fuel. Pressing the

35. *Times-Picayune,* October 1, 3, 5, 15–16, 26, 1939; Kurtz and Peoples, *Earl K. Long,* 105.

36. Jerry Purvis Sanson, "North Louisiana Press Opinion and the Beginning of World War II," *North Louisiana Historical Association Journal,* fall 1980, 33–36; James MacGregor Burns, *Roosevelt: The Soldier of Freedom* (New York, 1970), 37, 41, 43; Robert Dallek, *Franklin D. Roosevelt and American Foreign Policy, 1932–1945* (Oxford, 1979), 201, 228; *Times-Picayune,* November 12, 1939.

same "Nazification" idea still further, Sam Jones declared that the Long machine had attempted to "Hitlerize" the schoolchildren of the state when State Superintendent of Education T. H. Harris suggested to school principals that if they could only afford one newspaper for their school, that paper should be the *Progress*.[37]

Earl Long defended himself against charges of disloyalty to his country. He explained that during World War I he had been living in Browns-ville, Texas, selling baking powder for $100 per month plus expenses. With that money, he helped provide for a sister in Colorado suffering from tuberculosis and another widowed sister studying at the State Normal College at Natchitoches in hopes of one day supporting her children as a teacher. His draft board placed him in Class II, which provided only temporary exemptions until the local board's supply of Class I registrants was exhausted. Earl could be placed in this classification only by a strained interpretation of its first provision, which provided exemptions for registrants with both wife and children, or who were the fathers of motherless children, where the family was not solely dependent upon the registrant's labor for support because "reasonably certain sources of support" were available. Actually, Earl's situation could have more easily placed him in Class III, Section A, providing exemption for a registrant who was the main support of children not his own issue, or Section C, a registrant with a helpless brother or sister, regardless of age, mainly dependent on his labor for support. In any event, Huey had ultimately offered to support their sisters, and Earl had reported promptly for induction, but by that time was told that an armistice was so close at hand that if he had a job, he need not enlist.[38]

Long's explanation did nothing to defuse the opposing attacks. Noe remarked that he did not understand "how Earl Long . . . can stand between American flags and ask the people of Louisiana to elect him governor," and charged that Long moved to Texas during the war not to pursue his career, but to escape the Winn Parish draft board. The *States*

37. *Ibid.*, September 10, November 4, December 19, 1939; *States,* December 19, 1939.
38. *The Classification Process, Special Monograph No. 5. Volume 1: Selective Service System* (Washington, D.C., 1950), 22–23; *Times-Picayune,* November 13, 1939.

taunted the governor with a series of editorial cartoons deriding his supposed draft dodging, and commented that "Earl Long did not fight for anything in 1917–18, except for a few dollars in commissions."[39]

Long sought to deflect criticism by belittling Sam Jones's military experience, claiming that his wartime duties consisted of tending livestock at Camp Beauregard, north of Alexandria. The *Progress* dubbed him "Mule Nurse Sam." Jones had in fact spent his World War I army days in Louisiana and so was vulnerable to criticism. He had originally been a clerk of the Beauregard Parish draft board, but he had taken that job only with the understanding that he would join the army reserves and be subject to call at any time. He was soon called into the army and applied for admission to the Army Artillery Officers Training School, but the armistice became effective before he received his appointment.[40]

The candidate who tried the hardest for veteran support was Jimmie Noe, who maintained that his overseas service gave him a special rapport with that group. Noe's campaign network encompassed veterans' organizations throughout the state, including the "Jackson Brigade," charged with keeping the New Orleans vote count honest. Following his defeat in the first Democratic primary, Noe directed the brigade's efforts toward protecting the interests of fellow veteran Sam Jones.

Despite the sudden timeliness of the candidates' World War I army records—or in Long's case, the absence of same—the dominant issue of the campaign remained the corruption of the incumbent administration. Jones continued to stress his "Common Honesty" theme, charging that even "if Earl Long was deaf, dumb, and blind . . . he should have known that something was rotten in Louisiana." He observed that "everybody in the state—even the big majority of the jobholders," now wanted to clean up Louisiana, and predicted that the organized reformers only had to ensure that public sentiment was accurately counted at the polls for him to win. In a particularly vitriolic speech broadcast over New Orleans radio

39. *Item,* October 9, 1939; *Item-Tribune,* November 12, 1939; *States,* February 9, 13, 17, 1940.

40. *Progress,* February 16, 1940; Sam Jones to Denny Daugherty, July 22, 1970, Daugherty Collection; Maj. Gen. E. S. Adams to Allen J. Ellender, February 3, 1940, Ellender Papers; Angers, "Sam Houston Jones," 6, 12; *States,* January 15, 1945.

station WDSU, he charged, "The ancient Huns of the Old World were not so barbarous in their treatment of their enemies as these people have been in the treatment of those who elected and trusted them."[41]

Former U.S. senator Joseph Ransdell, whom Huey had defeated in the 1930 senate race, endorsed Jones, as did the state's major newspapers, as well as citizen groups with such names as the Fearless Democrats, the Citizens' Voluntary Committee of Louisiana, the Louisiana Association for Clean Government, and the People's League (chaired by young New Orleans attorney T. Hale Boggs). The Catholic church establishment joined in the general revulsion at the rampant corruption but carefully avoided any appearance of factional alliance. In February 1940, Archbishop Francis Rummel of New Orleans called on citizens to correct and atone "for all the public scandal, ugly crimes, flagrant injustices, slanders . . . which have during the past eight months poisoned our atmosphere . . . humiliating our state before the nation." The *Catholic Herald* newspaper added its hopes that "the shock of the recent revelations of scandals instill[s] a firm resolution in the people to cherish the franchise of freedom before it is too late" and remarked of Rummel's comment about politics that "those of the priesthood should counsel and encourage the people to the performance of their duty, to an honest use of their American birthright, the Ballot."[42]

Earl Long and his allies countered the barrage of criticism with the political means at their disposal, legal, illegal, and questionable. The governor was an effective stump speaker, amply able to conduct his own defense, but even he called upon the eloquent Gerald L. K. Smith to join him on the stage. He also called upon Huey's widow, Rose, to attend a few rallies and ask the audience to vote for him. Illegally, state trucks and employees continued distributing the *Progress*. Questionably, Dr. E. L. Sanderson, superintendent of the Shreveport Charity Hospital, sent a form letter to the parents of student nurses studying at the facility, asking

41. *Item,* September 21, October 5, 16, 20, 1939.

42. *Times-Picayune,* November 24, 1939; *Shreveport Times,* January 7, 1940; *Item,* November 29, 1939, January 3, February 19, 1940; *Catholic Herald,* February 15, 1940; Howell, *Louisiana Sugar Plantations,* 169.

them to support Long. Again illegally, state workers glued Earl Long posters to the Orleans civil court building on Royal Street while city officials refused permission to Jones and Morrison workers to place their political posters on public buildings already bearing Long posters. Civil sheriff Louis Knopf would not allow Noe workers to photocopy Orleans Parish poll lists so they could carefully check for fraudulent names, even though state law declared that the records of registrars of voters were open to inspection by the public and that copies of the records could be made as long as the process did not interfere with business in the registrar's office.[43]

The effect of the Scandals and the continued anti-Long effort to focus the campaign on corruption became apparent in December 1939, when George Gallup began releasing the results of a poll his American Institute of Public Opinion had conducted that month. A sample of 2,500 Louisianians revealed that Long and Jones were running statistically even with 34 percent of the straw vote. Noe received 20 percent of the vote, Morrison 10 percent, and Moseley 2 percent. These findings indicated severe erosion of Longite support in the time since Leche's rout of Cleveland Dear in 1936. Even more ominously for the Longites, poll results predicted that a Jones-Long second primary would result in Jones receiving 58 percent of the vote and Long 42 percent.[44]

The pollsters also asked other questions that revealed a lack of confidence in state government. When asked, "Do you think elections in Louisiana in recent years have been honestly conducted?" Louisiana voters responded: honest—25 percent, dishonest—60 percent, no opinion—15 percent. Asked, "Do you think that if the present state administration is returned to office next year it will 'clean house' in state government?" those polled responded: yes—30 percent, no—51 percent, no opinion—19 percent. Asked, "Do you think that state courts are honest?" they re-

43. *Times-Picayune,* January 4, February 8, 1940; *Progress,* February 16, 1940; *Item,* November 16, December 20, 1939; *States,* November 6, December 4–5, 21, 1939; Coleman Lindsey, *Elections in Louisiana* (Baton Rouge, 1940), 21; Earl Long circular, January 14, 1940, Ellender Papers.

44. George Gallup and Saul Forbes Rae, *The Pulse of Democracy* (New York, 1940), 156–58; *Item-Tribune,* December 17, 1939; *Times-Picayune,* December 24, 1939.

sponded: yes—36 percent, no—40 percent, no opinion—24 percent. Despite the opinions revealed in these numbers, a fourth question substantiated the enduring legend of the Kingfish. Asked, "Taking everything into consideration, do you think that Huey P. Long was a bad or good influence in Louisiana?" Louisianians responded: good—55 percent, bad—22 percent, both—14 percent, no opinion—9 percent.[45]

Even beyond these statistics, however, the Gallup pollsters made a chilling empirical assessment of Louisiana's political culture: "The Institute has never found, in any state, on any question, such widespread reluctance to speak and such guardedness in replies." The pollsters found fear of expressing an opinion more common in the poorer sections of the state, and more common in men than in women, though some women interviewed alone made such comments as, "My husband has told me not to talk to anybody about state politics." Overall, one person in five indicated a reluctance to talk for fear of political or personal reprisal. Their fears were not unjustified. When told that some respondents thought Huey Long had been a bad influence on the state, one man replied, "I wish you'd show me the ones that says he was a bad influence! I'll report 'em tomorrow and they'll sure lose their jobs fast."[46]

Candidate reactions to the poll results are understandable. Long thought the poll "ridiculous." The *Progress* charged that the Gallup organization came to Louisiana solely to rig the election, and in an attempt to discredit the results made the racial slur that the Gallup team included "a Harlem nigger in a double-breasted suit." Noe and Moseley had no comment; Morrison instructed his followers to "pay no attention to this poll." Jones's forces, however, used the results to their advantage. In a circular bearing the results, Jones rhetorically told Long, "It may not be that you are beaten—but you are at least found out."[47]

The political threat to the machine revealed in the Gallup poll results helped lead to increased Longite use of racism, an issue that Longites had

45. Gallup and Rae, *The Pulse of Democracy,* 156–58; Kane, *Louisiana Hayride,* 440; Sindler, *Huey Long's Louisiana,* 115–16; *Item,* December 20, 22, 1939.

46. *Item-Tribune,* December 17, 1939.

47. Sam Jones circular, December 20, 1939, James B. Aswell and Family Papers, LLMVC; Hebert and McMillan, *"Last of the Titans,"* 145.

previously avoided in favor of class-based campaign appeals. When Dudley LeBlanc withdrew as a candidate in October 1939, all sides hoped to inherit his support. Louisiana political folk wisdom held that LeBlanc strongly controlled 5,000 to 6,000 Cajun and black votes, a significant number in a close election. LeBlanc endorsed Jones on October 25 and thus inspired a racist attack on the Jones camp. The *Progress* printed a picture of two black children holding Jones signs and literature, and noted that black support came along with LeBlanc's endorsement.[48]

As the campaign neared the first Democratic primary, U.S. senator Ellender led the new racial offensive. Speaking at Earl Long's final New Orleans rally, he asserted that federal prosecutor O. John Rogge had come to Louisiana charged by the Justice Department with establishing the right of properly qualified blacks to vote in the election, and dared Rogge to do his duty. The next day Ellender declared that "if you people don't watch out, in 10 or 15 years the federal government will be in charge of all your elections and the darkies will be voting." He offered hope to those who feared black participation in the political process, and took comfort from the observation that there were "too many good white citizens in Louisiana who remember the carpetbag days, when Negroes voted and held office, to permit any federal interference in state affairs." Earl Long did not join in this blast. During Ellender's offensive, he satisfied himself with calling the opposition candidates "filth chunkers and brow beaters" and declaring that "I have been carrying on like Huey P. Long, Oscar Allen, Jesus Christ, and God Almighty would have me do."[49]

Despite the Long machine's efforts, in the first primary Earl Long received only a plurality of the vote—226,385, compared to Jones's 154,936,

48. *Item,* October 26, 1939; Floyd Martin Clay, *Coozan Dudley LeBlanc: From Huey Long to Hadacol* (Gretna, La., 1973), 132–33; Trent Angers, "The Three Faces of Dudley LeBlanc," *Acadiana Profile,* second quarter 1977, 47–48, 58; C. A. Shaw to David C. Pipes, October 2, 1940, Pipes to R. H. Chadwick, September 26, 1940, David C. Pipes Papers, LLMVC; *Progress,* December 22, 1939.

49. *Times-Picayune,* January 14–15, 1940; Kane, *Louisiana Hayride,* 446–47; Thomas A. Becnel, *Senator Allen Ellender of Louisiana: A Biography* (Baton Rouge, 1995), 99–100; Earl K. Long to W. Scott Heywood, December 11, 1939, Jennings-Heywood Collection.

Noe's 116,564, Morrison's 48,243, and Moseley's 7,595. The governor carried only nine parishes and failed to win nomination outright as he had often boasted that he would do.

For the second Democratic primary, the *Progress* continued its blatantly racist appeal for votes. In the last edition published before election day, the newspaper reprinted excerpts of the February 10, 1940, issues of the *Louisiana Weekly,* which it identified as the "largest Negro newspaper in the South," and the *Sepia Socialite,* described as the "No. 2 Negro newspaper in New Orleans." The sole purpose of these reprints was to appeal to the racism of white voters. A passage quoted from the *Louisiana Weekly* describing the voting process during the first primary portrayed the Long machine and its allies as staunch defenders of white supremacy. Slyly attacking the opponents' war records, the *Progress* further quoted from the *Louisiana Weekly* that "another advantage that the Negro who fought in World War No. 1 has is the comradeship of Mr. Jones and Senator Noe. The sterling qualities possessed by these gentlemen will permeate down throughout the past system giving impetus to . . . the birth of enfranchisement."[50]

The *Progress*'s editorial comment about the black newspapers' endorsement of Jones included more racist rhetoric. "This Negro 'society newspaper' attacks Governor Long for not letting the Negroes vote in the Democratic primaries and praises Sam Jones. . . . 'We are against Earl Long because he takes the stand that the Democratic primary is a white man's election' says this Sam Jones Negro newspaper. The *Sepia Socialite* says that 'Sam Jones is the white hope of the black man.' "[51]

Even though Jones and Noe ignored most of these attacks, many reformers condemned the Long machine for this ugly phase of the campaign. The *Item* editorialized, "We can't recall in 35 years any political faction that has departed so far from decency to raise the race-issue among Democrats, or even so-called Democrats, in this state," while the *States* commented that "the Maestri-Leche-Long machine has stooped to foul means of any sorts in the effort to win this election, but the most

50. *Progress,* February 16, 1940.
51. *Ibid.*

venal and contemptible plot it has yet engineered was its clumsy attempt to promote race animosity and class strife." A statement by James E. Wilkins, president of the New Orleans branch of the National Association for the Advancement of Colored People, raised a pertinent question about the entire episode: why did the Long machine choose this time to raise the race issue?[52]

Louisiana voting rolls in 1939 reflected approximately four decades of systematic disfranchisement beginning with the 1898 constitution. White Democrats denied suffrage to most potential black voters in the state as well as to many poor whites. In 1940, only 886 black voters were registered in the entire state, constituting .1 percent of the total registration. It was not until 1944 that the first blacks since disfranchisement in the early 1900s registered to vote in Rapides Parish, and Tangipahoa Parish assistant registrar of voters Merle S. Weigel reported to her soldier-husband in the same year that no blacks had registered there. (It was not until 1964 that every parish in Louisiana had at least one black voter.)[53] Nevertheless, the Long machine used the threat of a fictitious black vote to capitalize on the ingrained fears and prejudices of the white voters.

A full account of the *Louisiana Weekly* and *Sepia Socialite* articles reveals a trail of greed and misplaced zeal. *Louisiana Weekly* editor C. C. Dejoie, Jr., stated in an affidavit that James B. LaFourche brought to him the articles he published favorable to Sam Jones and that LaFourche paid for their inclusion in the newspaper. He identified LaFourche as a black man who performed odd jobs for the New Orleans Police Department and also for "a lawyer known to support the administration." LaFourche later issued his own affidavit stating that he wrote and sold the articles to the two newspapers in an effort to make money. He had learned that Long supporters wanted to buy 450,000 copies of a black newspaper carrying an article asking O. John Rogge to help blacks obtain the vote and suggesting that Jones and Noe were willing to assist him. With an eye on

52. *Item,* February 14, 1940; *States,* February 27, 1940; *Item,* February 16, 1940.

53. Howard, *Political Tendencies in Louisiana,* 422; Riley E. Baker, "Negro Voter Registration in Louisiana, 1879–1964," *Louisiana Studies,* winter 1965, 335, 338; *Alexandria Daily Town Talk,* August 8, 1944; Merle S. Weigel to H. S. Weigel, August 11, 1944, H. S. Weigel and Family Papers, LLMVC.

the projected sale, LaFourche penned the article and arranged with one of the papers to receive a two-cent royalty on the sale of each copy above the normal circulation. The Long machine subsequently purchased extra copies of the newspaper issues carrying LaFourche's articles, but when he heard them misrepresented in a radio address, he went to Jones's headquarters and agreed not to write any more of them, commenting that "my only idea was to agitate for civil rights of Negroes with an increased circulation of the papers out of which I would realize a profit."[54] Even though simple commercial greed lay behind the publication of the articles, the Long machine nonetheless bore responsibility for injecting the race issue into the campaign.

The major event affecting the outcome of the second Democratic primary occurred when Noe endorsed Jones "1000 percent" and actively campaigned for his election. Jones warmly welcomed Noe's support, but the *Progress* detected a "deal" in the Jones-Noe agreement. The newspaper charged that Noe received $150,000 for his endorsement, and cartoons appearing in the paper showed Noe clutching a money bag labeled "$150,000" and dressed in a "Mark Hanna" suit covered with dollar signs. In fact, Jones and Noe had reached an agreement, but not exclusively for money. Instead, their arrangement stipulated that the Jones organization would pay Noe's campaign expenses and, ironically, that 50 percent of state patronage jobs would be reserved for Noe's supporters, despite Jones's promise to create an effective civil service presumably based on merit rather than political allegiance. Refusing to endorse either Long or Jones, Morrison announced that he was "going fishing" on election day. Moseley also did not participate in the second primary.[55]

The second primary alliance of Jones and Noe proved too powerful for Earl Long to overcome. Even the threat of massed troops could not sway

54. *Item,* February 14, 16, 1940.

55. *Progress,* January 19, 1940; *Times-Picayune,* January 20, 25, 1940; Hermann B. Deutsch, "New Orleans Politics: The Greatest Free Show on Earth," in *The Past as Prelude: New Orleans, 1718–1968,* ed. Hodding Carter et al. (New Orleans: Tulane University, 1968), 329; Howell, *Louisiana Sugar Plantations,* 170–71; Kane, *Louisiana Hayride,* 443–44; Kurtz and Peoples, *Earl K. Long,* 109; Mrs. Louise Jones to author, August 4, 1982; Hebert and McMillan, *"Last of the Titans,"* 149.

voters to mark their ballots in his favor. On the eve of the voting, Governor Long ordered the Louisiana National Guard to be ready to move in case of disorder at the polls. In 19 cities throughout the state, 3,500 men were on call on election day. To counter this threat and also any attempted vote stealing in the election, Noe enlisted more volunteers in his Jackson Brigade.[56]

Earl Long lost the Democratic nomination for governor when the voters in the second primary gave him 261,790 votes (48.2 percent) compared to Jones's 282,470 (51.8 percent), but Long was not yet ready to retire to his Winn Parish farm. The governor attempted to obtain a lesser state office after the death of incumbent secretary of state E. A. Conway on February 18, 1940. Conway had defeated reform candidate James Gremillion in the first primary for the Democratic nomination, but died just before the second primary. Long appointed E. A. Conway, Jr., to fill the remainder of his father's term, and several candidates emerged for the regular term to be filled in the general election. The leading contenders for the post were Long and Conway, Jr.[57]

The Longite-dominated Democratic state central committee that had been elected in 1936 selected Long as their nominee, but reform members of the new committee elected in 1940 maintained that they should be the ones to determine the nominee. Sam Jones reached a settlement with Wade O. Martin, Sr., chairman of the 1936 committee, in which Martin agreed to call his committee into session again to replace Long with a nominee more compatible with the governor-elect. The settlement was successful, and the 1936 committee switched their nomination to Gremillion. The 1940 committee affirmed that action the same day.[58]

Earl Long immediately appealed to District Court Judge James D. Womack for a court order blocking Gremillion's certification as the legal candidate in the general election, but Jones forces blocked this maneuver

56. *Times-Picayune,* February 13, 20, 1940; *Item,* February 9, 1940; *States,* February 9, 1940.

57. *Times-Picayune,* February 23, 1940; *Item,* February 19, 1940; Alexander Heard and Donald Strong, *Southern Primaries and Elections, 1920–1949* (University, Ala., 1950), 71.

58. *Times-Picayune,* February 23, 25, 28, March 3, 1940; *Morning Advocate,* March 1, 1940.

by filing a petition for application of writs with the Louisiana Supreme Court asking that Womack be relieved of all jurisdiction in the struggle. The high court agreed that district courts did not have jurisdiction in such cases and later dismissed Long's suit, stating that he had no legal basis for contesting Gremillion's nomination.[59] The Supreme Court ruling thus marked the end of Long's hope of remaining in office in 1940.

The campaign of 1940 was over at last. Jones still faced token opposition in the general election from Republican William Tuttle of New Orleans, but did not bother to campaign against him. The minuscule Louisiana Republican party was split into two warring factions, and the Democratic nomination was still tantamount to election. Even without further campaigning, Jones amassed 225,841 votes to Tuttle's 1,367, lending a final stamp of authority to the vigorous reform movement now ready to do battle with the Longite machine.[60]

Reform-minded commentators throughout the state and nation hailed Jones's victory as a triumph for democratic principles of government. Jones, however, saw his election not as a final victory, but only as a beginning. He commented after the second Democratic primary, "We have got to restore decent, democratic government and enact legislation that will prevent the recurrence of debauchery, corruption and dictatorship that has characterized Louisiana in recent years," and reminded the people in his inaugural address that "once again yours is the dictatorship, the dictatorship of the whole people over the men who serve them, the only kind of dictatorship that a Democracy can abide."[61]

59. *Times-Picayune,* March 3, 8–9, 13–14, 1940.

60. Jack Bass and Walter DeVries, *The Transformation of Southern Politics: Social Change and Political Consequence since 1945* (New York, 1976), 166–67; Perry H. Howard, "Louisiana Resistance and Change," in *The Changing Politics of the South,* ed. William C. Havard (Baton Rouge, 1972), 561–66; Howard, *Political Tendencies,* 386–89; *States,* January 31, 1940; *Times-Picayune/New Orleans States,* March 24, 1940; *Official Journal of the House of Representatives of the State of Louisiana at the Tenth Regular Session of the Legislature* (Baton Rouge, 1940), 10–11.

61. Sam Jones Inaugural Address, Aswell Papers; Tom Dutton, "Sam Houston Jones: Louisiana's Liberator," *Christian Science Monitor Magazine,* April 27, 1940; James C. Crown, "Louisiana's David," *New York Times Magazine,* March 3, 1940; Alva Johnston, "Louisiana Revolution," *Saturday Evening Post,* May 11, 1940; "The Whole People," *Aca-*

Even though he acknowledged his debt to Noe and to the reformers who had aided him from the beginning of the campaign, Jones also noted the help he had received from Louisiana's women voters: "It can safely be said that a good many thousands of wives of state and city officials voted against their own husbands who drew their pay from the political payrolls." With the secret ballot, of course, his estimate is unverifiable, but it echoes the sentiments of organized reform women's groups and of Mrs. James A. Noe, who stumped for her husband in the first primary and Jones in the second primary.[62]

While the reformers exulted in their victory, the Longites consoled each other and tried to understand what had gone wrong. T. H. Harris, defeated Longite candidate for re-election as state superintendent of education, stated blandly that the Long slate had lost because the votes of the candidates who had been eliminated in the first primary went to their opponents in the second primary. Privately, however, he seems to have revealed his true feelings by describing the anti-Longites as "incompetent," "utterly lacking in efficiency," and "surrounded by sinister influences."[63]

Jennings oil businessman W. Scott Heywood, who campaigned for Long in the first primary, concluded that Long had lost because he was "double-crossed by the school teachers, the bus drivers, and the truck owners," because Jones had promised a fee of three dollars per year for automobile licenses, a 50 percent reduction in the fee for truck licenses, and 12 months' pay for school teachers, even though Long had maintained that the state could not afford such favors. Long himself provided the most fitting epitaph for his 1939–1940 campaign when he wrote eight years later, "They charged me with being politically and personally dishonest, and there was no way on earth, at that time, for me to prove that their contemptible accusations were untrue."[64]

---

diana Profile (October/November 1971): 6; *Times-Picayune,* February 22, 1940; *Shreveport Times,* February 12, 1940; Jones to Denny Daugherty, July 22, 1970, Daugherty Collection.

62. Jones to Denny Daugherty, July 22, 1970, and Jones, interview by Daugherty, May 6, 1970, Daugherty Collection.

63. William J. "Bill" Dodd, *Peapatch Politics: The Earl Long Era in Louisiana Politics* (Baton Rouge, 1991), 250.

64. W. Scott Heywood to Gene B. Heywood, February 27, 1940, Jennings-Heywood

As Long's ally Ellender surveyed the political situation after the election, he looked forward to a friendlier political climate in the future. "Right now sentiment is swinging the Jones way, but I predict that the people will soon wake up and realize their mistake."[65] The Long machine thus lay in wait for Sam Jones. Its articulate spokesmen still sat in the national and state legislatures and in parish courthouses and city halls throughout the state. Jones began his administration in a state filled with expectation. The reformers expected a vigorous assault on the abuses of the previous administrations; the Longites expected Jones, despite his campaign promises, to turn back the clock to a pre–Huey Long time, obliterate state services, and thereby lose his thin margin of support.

Sam Jones's victory in the 1939–1940 election, while important because it established effective bifactionalism in Louisiana, was incomplete. Jones had no sweeping mandate from the voters. Even with the help given his campaign by the revelation of the Scandals, he had still received only a slim victory in the crucial second primary.[66]

Brief analysis of the results of that primary, the election that most clearly revealed the Long/anti-Long cleavage, shows that Longism remained strong in its traditional home base in the north Louisiana hills. Earl Long carried 14 of the 27 north Louisiana parishes. Eleven of those parishes gave him at least 53.3 percent of their vote. Moreover, southwest Louisiana, Sam Jones's home territory, also voted heavily Longite, with Allen Parish giving Long 57.4 percent of its vote and Jones's native Beauregard Parish split almost evenly (50.1 percent Long, 49.1 percent Jones). Only in his adopted Calcasieu Parish (55.9 percent to 44.1 per cent) and neighboring Jefferson Davis (60.3 to 39.7) did Jones fare well in his home region.

The reformers found much more support in south Louisiana. Jones swept the twenty-four south Louisiana parishes with the exception of Or-

Records; T. H. Harris, *The Memoirs of T. H. Harris, State Superintendent of Public Education in Louisiana, 1908–1940* (Baton Rouge, 1963), 191; Earl K. Long to John B. Fournet, Fournet Papers.

65. Allen J. Ellender to Donald A. Draughon, March 5, 1940, Ellender Papers.
66. Perry H. Howard, *Political Tendencies,* 264.

leans, St. Bernard, and Plaquemines, which voted for Long as a result of alliances between the Longites and Old Regulars in Orleans and because of the staunch support of political boss Leander Perez in Plaquemines and St. Bernard. Long carried the fourth "Longite" south Louisiana parish, St. James, by only five votes. In addition, south Louisiana contained six of the sixteen parishes statewide giving Long the lowest percentage of their votes.

The Florida parishes, also in the southern half of the state, remained a center of anti-Longism, with Long carrying only Washington Parish. The two bastions of reform sentiment in this region were East Feliciana, which voted for Jones 61.1 percent to 38.9 percent, and East Baton Rouge, 65.9 percent for Jones, 34.1 percent for Long.

A survey of the 1940 Longite vote also reveals that the faction continued to maintain stronger support in rural rather than urban areas. Louisiana then had six parishes that either were urban or contained one of the state's largest cities. Earl Long carried only one of these, boss-controlled Orleans, by 55.3 percent to Jones's 44.7 percent. Jones carried the other five: East Baton Rouge and Calcasieu by the totals noted above; Rapides by 57.6 percent to 42.4 percent; Ouachita by 62.5 percent to 37.5 percent; and Caddo by 66.9 percent to 33.1 percent. Perhaps more significantly, Jones also carried the nascent "bedroom suburbs" of New Orleans— Jefferson Parish by 56.8 percent to 43.2 percent and St. Tammany by 53 percent to 47 percent.

Despite the large number of parishes he carried, however, Jones still won the election only narrowly, carrying eight of his forty-one parishes by a 5 percent or less margin of victory. Furthermore, he failed to carry all the members of his ticket into state office. Reformers won in the races for attorney general, superintendent of public education, and secretary of state, while independent reformer A. P. Tugwell retained the treasurer's office, and Longite holdovers remained as registrar of state lands and commissioner of agriculture.

More important, Jones's supporters did not win a majority of seats in the legislature. One estimate divided the house of representatives into 61 or 62 "independent" members and 38 or 39 Longites, and the senate into 24 Jones supporters compared to 15 for Long. This estimate was probably generous to Jones, as other observers found as few as 7 senators and 14 representatives prominently aligned with him. Jones later claimed at most 35 supporters in the house and 15 in the senate.[67] Jones, therefore, was not able to act independently and tear the Long machine "leaf from twig" as he had promised during the campaign. Because of his partial victory, he was forced to compromise on some of his measures in order to establish any of his reform program. His election indicated a temporary popularity of reform in Louisiana, but in its narrowness it bore the seeds of an uneasy tenure in office.

67. *Morning Advocate,* February 22, 1940; *States,* May 13, 1940; Jones, interview by Daugherty, May 6, 1970, Daugherty Collection.

3

Sam Jones and the Beginning of Reform

Following his second-primary victory in February 1940, Sam Jones traveled to Tucson, Arizona, for a vacation. He could not rest for long, however, because he had to begin planning his administration. In an attempt to discredit the High Hat label bestowed upon him by Earl Long, he announced that his inauguration would be conducted "in the most democratic way possible." He specifically sought to dispel the "corporation lawyer" image Long had attached to him by making his first speech as governor-elect to a state Federation of Labor convention in Shreveport. He promised to appoint a "real labor man" as labor commissioner and recommended that union leaders continue their work to improve the economic condition of their members, but also warned his listeners that labor's legitimate work could best be continued outside politics.[1]

Inauguration day, May 14, 1940, was busy for the new governor. Festivities began at 9:00 A.M. with a parade from his Heidelberg Hotel headquarters in downtown Baton Rouge to the inaugural site at the Louisiana State University football stadium. The formal ceremony began at noon as Louisiana chief justice Charles P. O'Neill administered the oath of office. In his address, Jones paid homage to the Scandals investigators, cautioned his followers not to expect a free disbursement of public jobs, promised

1. *Times-Picayune,* February 29, March 4, 29, 1940; *Times-Picayune/New Orleans States,* March 31, 1940; *Town Talk,* April 4, 1940.

that the state police would no longer be used as political instruments, pledged to destroy completely all vestiges of the Long machine and repair its damage to political democracy in Louisiana, and, finally, contrasted the hopelessness of the European situation with the favorable events in Louisiana. The audience interrupted his speech with cheers and applause and, when he concluded with a fervent "God Bless Louisiana," gave him a standing ovation.[2]

Afternoon festivities included a public barbecue and block dances in front of the LSU Memorial Tower, on the old and new capitol grounds, and in Victory Park; revelers at all locations could buy souvenir top hats and perfume bottles. Informal dances at the LSU gymnasium and field house and at the American Legion Community Club concluded the day's public events. Governor and Mrs. Jones then retired to the executive mansion for a buffet supper with close friends and relatives. Former governor and defeated candidate Long was absent from all inaugural activities.[3]

Sam Jones became Louisiana's chief executive at a threatening time in European affairs. On his inauguration day, German troops broke through French lines at Sedan, while the Netherlands surrendered to the Germans that same evening. In Washington, President Roosevelt worked on a message to Congress requesting extraordinary defense funds. Within one month of Jones's swearing in, Antwerp fell to German onslaught, the Allied debacle at Dunkirk occurred, Italy entered the war against France and England, and Paris fell to the Nazis.[4]

The events of the war in Europe caused concern in Louisiana, but attention nevertheless focused on events in Baton Rouge. Sam Jones began his first day in office by driving himself to the capitol. His first visitor was his friend Vance Plauché, and many politicians followed, including James A. Noe. Jones spent most of the day politicking: he shook hands with ordinary citizens, held his first gubernatorial press conference, and ap-

2. *Morning Advocate,* May 14–15, 1940; *States,* May 14, 1940; Sam Jones Inaugural Address, May 14, 1940, Aswell Papers. LLMVC.

3. *Morning Advocate,* May 15, 1940.

4. *Times-Picayune,* May 14–15, 1940; *States,* May 14, 1940; *Morning Advocate,* May 14–15, 1940; *Town Talk,* May 14, 17, 20 30, June 9, 13, 1940.

pointed Steve Alford as superintendent of state police and F. Edward Hebert as his personal representative in Washington, D.C. The latter
appointment stemmed from his fear that the Longite Louisiana Congressional delegation would not adequately represent his interests, and besides, the governor's office had always maintained a representative in
Washington. The new governor also signed Executive Order No. 1,
which forbade state department heads from collecting "deducts" from the
salary of their employees and directed any employee approached for a deduct to report the incident promptly. This order was especially important
as a symbolic act—the reformer sweeping aside vestiges of corruption. Finally, Jones hosted an afternoon reception for legislators and then worked
past midnight outlining administration bills.[5]

Although he had no mandate with which to persuade legislators to follow his lead, Jones secured important legislative leadership posts for his
followers and allies. Several candidates announced their intention to seek
the post of speaker of the house, but Norman S. Bauer of St. Mary Parish
emerged as the governor's choice. Frank B. Ellis of Covington became
senate president pro tempore. Jones's allies also claimed important committee posts: Joe T. Cawthorn, a Noe associate, chaired the Senate Finance Committee; pro-Jones senators James Bailey, W. D. Cotton, and
Grove Stafford chaired senate judiciary committees; and Lionel Ott, a
Jones man from New Orleans, chaired the Affairs of New Orleans Committee. In the house, important leadership posts likewise went to Jones
men: Rules (A. C. Petitjean), Ways and Means (H. H. Huckabay), Judiciary (Arthur C. Watson and Lester Bordelon; the third judiciary chair
went to Old Regular Frank Stitch).[6]

The governor called on legislators to help him carry out his pledges to

5. *Morning Advocate,* May 14, 1940; *Times-Picayune,* May 16, 1940; Hebert and McMillan, *"Last of the Titans,"* 153; Roman Heleniak, *Soldiers of the Law: Louisiana State Police*
(Topeka, Kans., 1980), 50–51.

6. *Morning Advocate,* February 22, 1940; *States,* May 13, 1940; *Times-Picayune,* February
29, 1940; *Times-Picayune/New Orleans States,* April 7, 1940; *Morning Advocate,* April 30,
1940; *Town Talk,* April 8, 30, 1940; Denny Daugherty, "From Log Cabin to Governor's
Mansion," 48–49; Sam Jones, interview by Daugherty, May 6, 1970, Daugherty Collection,
LLMVC.

reform Louisiana, and he won two early skirmishes on his anti-corruption pledges, even though one victory came through default. On May 21, 1940, Representative deLesseps S. Morrison of New Orleans introduced a resolution declaring vacant the seat of Representative Chester Wooten of Plaquemines Parish because Wooten had served as parish registrar of voters until September 22, 1939, and the state constitution clearly stated that no parish registrar could be elected or appointed to any office for twelve months after vacating the registrar's office. Wooten represented the bailiwick of the pro-Long political boss Leander H. Perez, and his expulsion became a test of strength for the two sides. The expulsion resolution deadlocked the Committee on Elections, but Wooten resigned rather than face possible expulsion. Jones thus indirectly obtained his objective. He was more clearly successful in ousting state bank examiner Jasper S. Brock, who kept the payroll records of the infamous Louisiana Debt Moratorium Commission that Longites used to reward friendly legislators. The final vote to remove Brock was decisive, passing 79–17 in the house and 31–6 in the senate. Jones's new bank examiner found that legislators had collected $296,987 in debt moratorium commission salaries during the past four years.[7]

Jones's success in these early maneuvers and in his subsequent passage of bills implementing a large part of his campaign platform can be attributed to several circumstances. Allan Sindler traces much of the success to a working arrangement reached by Jones and Robert Maestri shortly after the second Democratic primary. Maestri recognized that New Orleans needed continued state fiscal assistance, and that his own domination of New Orleans resulted in large part from legislation that could be undone in Baton Rouge. The Old Regular delegation therefore agreed to support many of Jones's key reform bills in return for favors from the state government. Ever the political realists, the Old Regulars recognized the direction of the political wind and accommodated themselves to it, pledging to support the governor "in every constructive move he made for the benefit and welfare of our beloved state and its people."[8]

    7. *Times-Picayune,* May 21–23, 28–29, 1940.
    8. Sindler, *Huey Long's Louisiana,* 162–63; New Orleans *Item,* May 10, 1940.

Jones subsequently declared that he had been successful in the 1940 legislative session not because of an arrangement with Maestri but because the public's anti-Long, anti-corruption sentiment was so strong that few legislators chose to challenge it. He also maintained that some Longites voted with him in order to placate him and obtain patronage jobs for their followers. In reality, both of these considerations influenced decision making in the 1940 legislative session. Robert Maestri and Sam Jones were shrewd politicians who realized that both would benefit from a political compromise, and so they designed a temporary truce that both could accept. Jones, however, always claimed there was a limit to how far he could compromise: "The important thing," he said later, "is getting your program through without sacrificing your principles."[9]

Jones was eager to begin carrying out his campaign pledge to reform Louisiana. He had to govern, however, with a legislature in which many of his supporters were political neophytes, inexperienced in the procedure of governing and unfamiliar with the political accommodations necessary to accomplish their objectives. The result of this situation was the introduction of 1,430 bills, only 481 of which became law, partially because of the inexperience and excessive optimism of administration leaders in both branches of government.[10]

Even so, Jones managed at the outset of his administration to fulfill part of his platform immediately. The heart of his effort included his determination to dismantle the concentration of power and resultant opportunities for corruption created by the Longites and to reorganize the government into a manageable system. His record of accomplishment in these areas is mixed. Some of his reforms were successful, while others proved to be temporary or ineffective.

Much of Jones's lasting success occurred in his fight to repeal numerous laws, some dating back to Huey Long's administration, that allowed the state government to dominate local governments. Both the Louisiana

9. Jones, interview by Daugherty, May 6, 1970; Jones, interview by Godfrey, February 1977; LSU Oral History Collection; *Times-Picayune,* August 8, 1940.

10. James Bugea, Carlos Lazarus, and William T. Pegues, "The Louisiana Legislation of 1940," *Louisiana Law Review,* November 1940, 98.

Police Jury Association and the Louisiana Municipal Association eagerly sought the repeal of such measures. Shreveport mayor Sam Caldwell noted at the 1940 LMA convention that the absence of home rule in municipal governments led to morale and control problems. If an employee knew that his job was a state appointment, Caldwell asked, how were municipal officials to ensure that he did not to neglect his work?[11]

The major legislation concerning local revenue approved at the 1940 regular session was Act 70, which restored full authority to municipalities and parishes to impose taxes and license fees without legislative approval. Jones had little trouble with this repeal, which originated in the Senate where it passed with a 30–6 vote. The proposal passed the House unanimously.[12]

Municipalities of 12,500 or more people also received authorization to install and operate parking meters on their streets, provided that they called an election after a three-month trial period to decide whether the meters should remain. Alexandria, which was soon swamped by vehicles from nearby army camps, was one of the first major Louisiana cities to experiment with parking meters, not so much for revenue as to control traffic in its congested downtown. Another measure authorized local governments to donate or otherwise transfer land to the United States for national defense purposes, especially for the maintenance or construction of waterways.[13]

Jones also sought the creation of a state crime commission, comprised of the governor, the executive counsel to the governor, and the attorney

11. "Rights Restored to Police Juries," *Louisiana Police Jury Review*, April 1941, 27; S. S. Caldwell, "Address," *Louisiana Municipal Review*, May–June 1940, 7.

12. *Acts Passed by the Legislature of the State of Louisiana at the Regular Session, 1940* (Baton Rouge, 1940), 383; *Official Journal of the Proceedings of the House of Representatives of the State of Louisiana at the Tenth Regular Session, 1940* (Baton Rouge, 1940), 1631; *Calendar of the House of Representatives of the State of Louisiana at the Tenth Regular Session . . . 1940* (Baton Rouge, 1940), 507; *Official Journal of the Proceedings of the Senate . . . at the Tenth Regular Session . . . 1940* (Baton Rouge, 1940), 493; *Senate Calendar 1940 of the State of Louisiana, Tenth Regular Session . . .* (Baton Rouge, 1940), 65.

13. *Acts Passed by the Legislature, 1940,* 392, 441; *Town Talk,* August 16, 1941, January 22, 1942.

general, to pursue people who had stolen property or money. The agency was to exist for four years with an appropriation of $1 million. Jones hoped to recover at least $4 million. The bill was introduced in the house on June 3, and after unsuccessful attempts by Representative James E. Bolin to reduce the appropriation to $250,000 and Representative Lloyd Hendrick to instead form a legislative commission, the bill passed the house on June 19 with an 87–7 vote, most of the nay votes being cast by rural north Louisiana Longites. The bill passed the senate on July 4, by a 32–4 vote, with opposition from a combination of north and south Louisiana senators.[14]

Despite the frequency with which former legislatures granted extraordinary powers to governors, some Longite legislators feared that the crime commission gave too much power to the governor; one called it the "Hitleristic, dictatorial, tyrannical crime commission." Conversely, reformers applauded the new gubernatorial authority. The Longites, however, chose not to criticize the purpose of the crime commission, but attacked the legality of its appropriations.[15]

Their challenge came in the form of a lawsuit filed in the 19th Judicial District Court of Judge James D. Womack in Baton Rouge. Womack, a Longite, issued a preliminary injunction against the Crime Commission on June 21, 1941, prohibiting it from expending funds because, he said, it had no legal source of revenue. The legislation provided financing from state funds not otherwise appropriated, but at the time all funds were earmarked.[16] Judge Womack viewed this as ground for beginning hearings into the legality of the funding plan.

These hearings led to a sharp exchange between Jones and Womack over the limits of executive privilege in Louisiana. Womack subpoenaed Jones to testify about the Crime Commission bill, and Jones, in turn,

14. *Proceedings of the House, 1940*, 1055–57; *House Calendar, 1940*, 251; *Proceedings of the Senate, 1940*, 403–404; *Senate Calendar, 1940*, 1779–80; *Times-Picayune*, June 3, 13, 1940; *States*, June 3, 1940.

15. *Morning Advocate*, September 9, 1940.

16. Louisiana Crime Commission, *Report to the Legislature* (May 11, 1942); *Harold G. Falkenstein Et Al. v. Sam Houston Jones, Governor, Member of Commission Created by Act 13 of 1940*, Supreme Court of Louisiana No. 36, 416, Fournet Papers, LLMVC.

asked the Louisiana Supreme Court to issue a writ prohibiting Womack from forcing his appearance. The governor surrounded himself with state troopers and announced that he would not be taken from his duties by "frivolous efforts of a few demagogues and enemies of good government." The supreme court acted in Womack's favor, declining to revoke the restraining order against the Crime Commission and denying Jones's request that he not be forced to appear in court.[17]

Jones, however, had no intention of honoring the subpoena. He cited as precedent Thomas Jefferson's refusal to appear in court during his years as president. If Jones were to appear in every political suit brought against the state, he maintained, he would have no time to attend to his duties as governor. Besides, he added, the attorney general had issued the opinion that "I am not amenable to subpoenas." Although Womack was ready neither to recognize Jones's claim nor to establish executive immunity in Louisiana, he declined to reissue a subpoena for Jones, thus neglecting to force the controversy to a conclusion. Instead, he issued a ringing statement reiterating his belief in judicial supremacy over the executive: "In the event I signed an order compelling his attendance and it became . . . my personal duty to serve that order, I would bring him into court regardless of the consequences."[18]

On July 14, Womack ruled that the appropriation plan for the Crime Commission was defective and issued an injunction to replace his temporary restraining order. The Louisiana Supreme Court upheld Womack's ruling on appeal by the state and in a later ruling held that the commission's authority to institute lawsuits was unconstitutional.[19] As a result of these court decisions, Sam Jones's crime commission perished.

Jones similarly lost a bid to reorganize the 179 divisions of state government. The nationally known consulting firm Griffenhagen & Associates modeled a reorganization plan on arrangements already in effect in Virginia, Illinois, New York, Massachusetts, Ohio, and Minnesota. The

17. *Morning Advocate,* July 3, 8, 1941.

18. *Ibid.,* July 11, 1941; Sam Jones to J. D. Womack, June 28, 1941, Jones Collection, HTML.

19. *Morning Advocate,* July 11, 15, August 3, 1941; *Item,* December 1, 1941; Louisiana Crime Commission, *Report* (May 11, 1942); *Falkenstein v. Jones.*

administration used that model to produce a reorganization bill that consolidated state government into twenty departments: Revenue, Treasury, Finance, State, Education, Occupational Standards, State Lands, Agriculture, Labor, Banking, Public Service, Public Welfare, Institutions, Public Safety, Highways, Public Works, Conservation, Minerals, Military Affairs, and Independent Establishments. The bill also created an executive cabinet, comprised of the department heads, the governor, and his executive counsel and special assistants, which was to coordinate governmental affairs.[20]

The key to the plan was the Finance Department, divided into bureaus for the budget, accounts and control, purchases and property control, buildings, local governments, and administrative services. In addition, a new fiscal code proposed in a companion bill buttressed the Finance Department's central role in administration. The fiscal code empowered the Finance Department to develop preliminary budgets for all other state departments, supervise all expenditures, and make all purchases, while the treasurer continued as custodian of all state funds, disbursing officer, and supervisor of state investments. The state auditor examined all state accounts and reported any unauthorized or illegal transactions to the legislature. In addition, the fiscal code provided for a new finance board comprised of three members appointed by the governor that would approve all rules in the Finance Department, especially those governing selection of depositories for state funds and incurring debt. The board could also investigate any department operations.[21]

Introduction of the companion reorganization and fiscal code bills engendered a storm of protest from the Longites. Representative Wilbur T. McCain of Grant Parish complained that the bills were too long (the reorganization bill alone ran to more than one hundred pages), and that legis-

20. *Morning Advocate,* May 1, June 2, 1940; *Proceedings of the House, 1940,* 1245–41; *Acts Passed by the Legislature, 1940,* 220; Charles S. Hyneman, "Political and Administrative Reform in the 1940 Legislature," *Louisiana Law Review,* November 1940, 147; Mortimer Barr, "The Louisiana Public Service Commission" (Master's thesis, Louisiana State University, 1941), 102–103.

21. *Morning Advocate,* June 2, 1940; *Proceedings of the House, 1940,* 1242–45; *Acts Passed by the Legislature, 1940,* 288.

lators had to vote on them without sufficient time for proper consideration. Representative C. O. Webb of Red River Parish added, "I have read [these bills] twice and all I could get was a headache. I defy any member of this House to say truthfully that he knows what these bills mean." Other legislators, however, thought that they knew exactly what the bills meant—Teutonic dictatorship on the Nazi model. Senator Ernest Clements asserted that Griffenhagen was "an emissary of Adolph [*sic*] Hitler," and reported that "in the cafe the other day, I saw one of Griffenhagen's associates and he had the map of Germany written all over his face." Moreover, the Griffenhagen plan represented "an attempt in a most dictatorial manner through the governor to take charge of our state." If the reorganization passed, Clements worried, "we will have a combination of Fascism, Naziism and Bolshevism that will be known as the Jones Four Year Plan."[22]

Senator Frank Ellis defended the reorganization, reminding Clements that "it is as necessary for the government to adjust itself to progress and social change as for individuals to become adjusted." The governor defended his plan as "the heart and core of reformation in Louisiana" and noted that "the administration is not 30 days old yet, but we have seen the restoration of democracy and abolition of dictatorship."[23]

Opposition notwithstanding, the reorganization bill (Act 47) passed the house with an 89–2 vote and the senate with a 35–3 vote, as Clements persuaded two others to vote with him. The companion fiscal code bill (Act 48) passed by similar margins: 87–1 in the House and 36–1 (Clements's nay) in the Senate.[24]

Since the reorganization bill was a constitutional amendment, it required ratification in the November 1940 general election. Longites waged a strenuous campaign against the amendment, but the voters approved it 140,543 to 113,876. Jones proceeded to establish the new governmental order in Louisiana, but his efforts ultimately came to nothing.

22. *Times-Picayune*, June 11, 24, 28, 1940.

23. *States*, June 13, 18, 1940.

24. *Acts Passed by the Legislature, 1940*, 220–28; *Proceedings of the House, 1940*, 1242–51; *House Calendar, 1940*, 248, 258–59; *Proceedings of the Senate, 1940*, 1604–1605; *Senate Calendar, 1940*, 400, 410; *Times-Picayune*, July 3, 1940.

The reorganization and fiscal code acts faced the same gauntlet as the Crime Commission had: the 19th district courtroom of J. D. Womack.[25]

Six Louisiana taxpayers filed suit in Womack's court contending that the Reorganization Act was unconstitutional on three grounds: first, it violated the fundamental principles of the republican form of government guaranteed by the state and federal constitutions because it concentrated power in the governor's office; second, the legislature failed to designate the specific election at which the amendment was to be submitted to the voters as required in Article 21, Section 1 of the state constitution; and third, the statute as presented to the voters also violated the same article and section of the constitution which required "when more than one amendment has been submitted at the same election, they shall be so submitted as to enable the electors to vote on each amendment separately."[26]

Womack and the Louisiana Supreme Court both dismissed the plaintiff's first contention, the higher court noting that enforcement of the constitutional guarantee of a republican form of government was a political question over which the courts have no jurisdiction. Both courts agreed, however, that the reorganization was invalid because of sloppy procedure. They invalidated the amendment on two points—the legislature failed to specify the date on which the amendment was to be submitted to the voters, and the act should have been submitted as at least two separate amendments (a practice dating from the 1879 constitution and its stipulation that acts of the legislature must deal with one subject only). In this, the courts supported the plaintiffs' contention that a voter might want to approve reorganization of one department of state government but not approve reorganization of another and could not do so under the amendment.[27]

The complex decision from the high court left Governor Jones in an unusual situation. The murky majority opinion written by Justice Wynne G. Rogers appeared to rule that while the enactment of the reorganiza-

25. *Times-Picayune,* August 16, 1940; *Morning Advocate,* November 3, 14, 1940.

26. *Morning Advocate,* July 1, 1941; *States,* July 1, 1941.

27. James D. Womack, *The Griffenhagen-Jones Reorganization Amendment: The Decision Rendered by a Competent, Honest and Courageous Judge Holding the Scheme Flagrantly Unconstitutional* (n.p., n.d.), 2–23; *Morning Advocate,* July 1, 1941; *States,* July 1, 1941.

tion had been completed improperly and was thus unconstitutional, the enabling acts relating to it and the fiscal code were not unconstitutional.

Jones questioned the court's authority to declare an amendment unconstitutional, and admitted that his administration had no alternative plan for reorganization. The supreme court anticipated Jones's challenge, and in its opinion cited the *American and English Encyclopedia of Law*: "The courts have full power to declare that an amendment to the constitution has not been properly adopted, even though it has been so declared by the political department of the state," and further cited the *Miller v. Johnson* decision noted in the *Lawyers' Reports Annotated,* which declared that "the question of lawful adoption of an amendment to the constitution is a judicial question."[28]

Jones began a public campaign to restore state reorganization. He portrayed the decision publicly as an assumption of judicial power unprecedented in Louisiana. Earl Long and Ernest Clements refuted his contentions. The administration, meanwhile, asked the supreme court to rehear the case, or, failing that, to issue a clarification of its controversial ruling. As the state awaited the outcome of the request, house speaker Norman Bauer hinted that if the court denied the rehearing, Jones might call the legislature into special session either to repass the reorganization or to call a constitutional convention to write the reorganization into the organic law of the state.[29]

In the end, neither happened. In 1942 the supreme court invalidated the reorganization act. Jones salvaged some of his plan when the 1942 legislature recreated the Departments of Public Works, Finance, and Occupational Standards, but generally the state government reverted to its pre-1940 organization. Careless drafting of legislation on the part of the reformers thus rendered their attempt to reorganize the state administration vulnerable to nullification.[30]

The governor was more successful in his efforts to establish a classified

28. *Morning Advocate,* July 1, 1941.

29. *Ibid.,* July 16–17, 1941.

30. *Ibid.,* July 1–2, 4, 16–17, 23, 30, 1941; *Report of the Committee to Consider Changes in the Powers, Duties, and Responsibilities of the Governor,* May 11, 1966, E-12.

state civil service system. Jones appointed prominent New Orleans attorney Charles E. Dunbar, Jr., who had been crusading for institution of the merit system since Governor John M. Parker's administration, to chair a committee to draft civil service bills for the state and for New Orleans. Dunbar's committee responded with two separate bills modeled after the civil service laws of the federal government and other states.[31]

The bills were introduced in 1940 with the governor's blessing. The administration also proposed a constitutional amendment that provided that civil service legislation could not be amended or repealed by any subsequent legislature except by a two-thirds vote of both houses. Therefore, while the civil service bills did not face the November hurdle of popular ratification, their protecting amendment did. The bills originated in the House, where they passed by wide margins following surprisingly mild debate, and then passed the senate after the defeat of several proposed diluting amendments, thus becoming Act 171 (New Orleans) and Act 172 (state) of the 1940 regular session of the legislature.[32]

The state bill created the Louisiana Civil Service Commission, which was composed of five members appointed by the governor for staggered six-year terms. Lists of potential appointees were provided by the presidents of five colleges: LSU (public), Tulane University (private), Loyola University (Catholic), Centenary College (Methodist), and Louisiana College (Baptist). Dunbar and his associates assumed that future governors could be hostile to civil service and therefore built several safeguards into the system. If a governor failed to appoint a member to a vacancy on the commission within six months of its occurrence, for example, the person whose name appeared first on the list submitted by the college president who had recommended the member whose seat had been vacated automatically became a full member of the commission. The bill also authorized the commission to select and appoint a state director of personnel

---

31. L. Vaughn Howard, "Civil Service Development in Louisiana," in *Tulane Studies in Political Science* (New Orleans, 1956), 75–76.

32. Hyneman, "Political and Administrative Reform," 15–16; Howard, "Civil Service Development," 75–76; *Acts Passed by the Legislature, 1940,* 687–729; *Proceedings of the House, 1940,* 833–34; *House Calendar, 1940,* 220–23; *Times-Picayune,* June 12, 15, July 5, 1940; *States,* June 14, 1940.

from a list prepared by a special examining committee of three persons skilled in personnel management. The act brought under the control of the classified civil service most of the employees of executive departments and agencies except the offices of the governor, the attorney general, and the crime commission. Entrance into the civil service was to be by "truly competitive" examinations. The exception to this requirement was that current Louisiana employees had to pass noncompetitive examinations proving their minimum competence, after which they were "blanketed in" under civil service protection. In a direct response to the Long machine's "deducts" and forced *Progress* subscriptions, the act forbade the use of political pressure for employment or promotion and also forbade employees to pay "any assessment, subscription, or contribution for any political organization or purpose." The law was not to become effective until July 1, 1942 (and the legislature later delayed the effective date to January 1, 1943), thus allowing time for the commission members and the personnel director to be appointed and the tests designed.[33] Critics charged that Jones postponed the implementation so that he could fill state payrolls with his supporters before instituting the competitive examinations, but such an accusation is unsupportable, since any new government program requires time for initial implementation.

The other administration-sponsored civil service bill applied only to cities with a population in excess of 100,000, such as New Orleans. This measure established a separate commission and provided that all current city employees would be blanketed in on July 1, 1942, without an examination, a concession to Mayor Maestri and members of the New Orleans legislative delegation who threatened to oppose civil service if the test requirement was not dropped. Thinking the bill could not be enacted without their support, the reformers agreed to this concession, which made meaningful implementation of civil service in New Orleans a matter of employee attrition.[34]

33. *Acts Passed by the Legislature, 1940,* 687; Hyneman, "Political and Administrative Reform," 16–22; Howard, "Civil Service Development," 77–79; Department of State Civil Service, Report (1943–1944) (Baton Rouge, 1945), 18–20.

34. Howard, "Civil Service Development," 79–80, 92; Sindler, *Huey Long's Louisiana,* 157; Edward F. Haas, "New Orleans on the Half-Shell: The Maestri Era, 1936–1946,"

The voters approved the protection amendment by more than 9,000 votes in the November 1940 election, and six days later Jones appointed the first Civil Service Commission. The commission survived a taxpayer suit when District Judge Charles A. Holcombe ruled in December 1941 that plaintiff O. Dolan Ricks (a Longite former deputy fire marshal) was not directly affected by the provisions of the act and could therefore properly contest only the constitutionality of the act and not the expenditure of general revenue funds to pay for its operation, which his suit questioned.[35]

A third civil service act passed by the 1940 legislature provided protection to municipal firemen and policemen in cities with more than 16,000 people. This bill did not have administration backing, and Jones vetoed it when it reached his desk. He subsequently reconsidered and signed it into law. The court ruling in *State v. Junkin* (1907), he said, provided that as long as a bill remained in the governor's possession, it was subject to consideration, and he had never filed his veto with the secretary of state.[36]

Civil service in Louisiana, as enacted by the Jones administration, proved to be temporary. In the 1948 extraordinary session of the legislature, newly elected governor Earl Long mustered a two-thirds vote that destroyed civil service except with respect to employees of the social security agencies (where the federal government required it). State civil service did not return to Louisiana until Governor Robert Kennon's administration in 1952.[37]

Governor Jones's reformation of Louisiana's electoral procedures bet-

Louisiana History 12 (summer 1972): 298; Edward F. Haas, *DeLesseps S. Morrison and the Image of Reform: New Orleans Politics, 1946–1961* (Baton Rouge, 1974), 21; Joseph B. Parker, *The Morrison Era: Reform Politics in New Orleans* (Gretna, La., 1974), 59–60.

35. *Item,* November 8, 1940; *Morning Advocate,* November 14, 1940; *Times-Picayune,* December 9, 1941; *States,* March 30, 1942; *O. Dolan Ricks v. Department of State Civil Service, Et Al.,* Supreme Court of Louisiana No. 36,529, Fournet Papers.

36. Howard, "Civil Service Development," 81–83; Bugea, Lazarus, and Pegues, "The Louisiana Legislation of 1940," 99.

37. Howard, "Civil Service Development," 108–09; Sindler, *Huey Long's Louisiana,* 243; Michael Kurtz, "Government By the Civics Book: The Administration of Robert F. Kennon, 1952–1956," *North Louisiana Historical Association Journal,* spring/summer 1981, 56.

ter survived judicial and political challenges. The legislature approved administration bills prohibiting any state office from increasing its number of employees in the six months preceding a gubernatorial election; prohibiting any person from allowing his or her name to be carried on a state, parish, or municipal payroll for services not rendered; prohibiting political advertisements on public property; prohibiting any employee of the state or any of its political subdivisions making two hundred dollars or less per month to contribute to political campaigns either directly or indirectly; providing that illiterate voters could obtain help from poll commissioners only if they produced an affidavit certifying their inability to read; and providing that parish registrars of voters must have their records available for public inspection for part of each day.[38]

Act 84, authorizing the use of voting machines in primary and general elections, and making their use mandatory in all municipalities with populations above 150,000 (New Orleans), caused a great legal and political battle. Even though the measure passed the legislature with little difficulty, it faced both judicial challenges and resistance by New Orleans officials reluctant to implement a reform that would make vote manipulation more difficult. In June 1941 the state bought 435 machines for New Orleans. The city was to repay the state one-half the cost over the next several years. O. Dolan Ricks (the same man who challenged the civil service act), represented by attorney Charles Rivet of New Orleans—who had been special assistant attorney general and revenue department attorney in former Longite administrations—quickly challenged the funding arrangement. Ricks alleged that the board created to supervise purchase of the machines had no power to incur debt and asked that the purchase be prevented. Judge J. D. Womack agreed that the board had exceeded its authority in contracting the debt and issued a temporary order restraining the state treasurer from spending any money for the machines.[39]

38. *Acts Passed by the Legislature, 1940,* 14, 377, 832, 1141, 1197; Sindler, *Huey Long's Louisiana,* 155–56; *States,* May 30, June 4, 1940; *Times-Picayune,* May 17, June 12, 14, 19, 28, July 10, 1940; *Times-Picayune/New Orleans States,* July 7, 1940.

39. *Acts Passed by the Legislature, 1940,* 406; *States,* May 21, 1940; *Morning Advocate,* June 11, 22, July 9, August 14, 1941; *Times-Picayune,* June 13, 1940, August 15, September 26, December 2, 23, 1941; *Town Talk,* September 23, 1941; *Item,* December 1, 1941.

More trouble for the voting machines occurred in August 1941 when Adam J. Falkenstein (brother of Harold G. Falkenstein, who had challenged the crime commission) filed a suit seeking to prevent state treasurer Andrew P. Tugwell from withholding funds due New Orleans to offset homestead exemptions. Falkenstein's contention was that if the state subsidy were withheld, then the city might not grant his exemption because it would need the money to purchase the machines. His suit was dismissed, however, because he had received full homestead exemption on his New Orleans property in 1941 and had thus paid no taxes. A third suit against the voting machine act was filed by Lafayette policeman Alphonse Peck, who maintained that the act unlawfully required the state to pay one-half the cost of New Orleans voting machines but did not provide similar help for any other municipality. Judge Womack decided that Act 84 was invalid, "a striking and glaring example of loosely written, hastily prepared and ill-considered legislation," and prohibited the state and the city from acquiring the machines. The state supreme court, however, overruled Womack in the Peck case and found Act 84 legal.[40]

The battle was not over, however, as resistance to implementing the act surfaced in the New Orleans Commission Council. Mayor Maestri informed the governor that the city could not pay its share of the cost because the money was not available in the 1941 budget. Jones replied that the Commission Council had amended budgets before to pay for unforeseen expenses. Meanwhile, the Citizens' Voluntary Committee of Louisiana, a civic group, offered to arrange a loan to the city, although city attorney Francis P. Burns quickly ruled this move illegal. Subsequently, the Optimist Club, the Woman Citizens' Union, the People's League, the Citizens' Voluntary Committee, and the Louisiana League of War Veterans joined with the New Orleans Junior Chamber of Commerce to support a subscription drive to raise the money. Additionally, the Woman Citizens' Union picketed city hall to remind the administration that citizens demanded voting machines. (Maestri warily eyed the pickets as he passed

40. *States,* May 21, 1940; *Morning Advocate,* June 11, 22, July 9, August 14, 1941; *Times-Picayune,* June 13, 1940, August 15, September 26, December 2, 23, 1941; *Town Talk,* September 23, 1941; *Item,* December 1, 1941.

by, but said only, "Keep up the good work.") The Commission Council finally voted in September to set aside money in the 1942 budget to pay for the voting machines.[41]

Other measures approved by the 1940 legislature dealt with more mundane aspects of governing: taxes, education, and housing. To fulfill a Jones campaign pledge, Representatives deLesseps S. Morrison and Welborn Jack introduced a sales tax repeal bill. The bill specified no termination date for the tax because the authors expected the Ways and Means Committee to fit the repeal into a general tax reorganization and not leave the state without sufficient revenue. Senator Joe Cawthorn simultaneously introduced a senate bill for repeal, but his bill provided a specific termination date of October 1, 1940. The Ways and Means Committee decided on December 31, 1940, as the termination date to be inserted in the house bill, thus removing the chief obstacle to its passage. Subsequent repeal of the sales tax, along with the voters' decision not to ratify a constitutional amendment increasing income tax rates, set the stage for further conflict between Jones and the Longites during the 1942 legislative session.[42]

Jones's entire new tax package, introduced in early June, included increases on liquor and tobacco products, income, and gasoline, extension of the severance tax, and imposition of a distribution tax on natural gas. The new liquor taxes provided for increases on liquor and on still and sparkling wines, and in fees for saloon permits and package house permits. Beer, however, escaped the upward revision completely. The tobacco tax increased the rate on cigars and cigarettes, with one-third of that revenue earmarked for the general fund and two-thirds dedicated to the public school fund.[43]

41. *Times-Picayune,* August 15, 20–21, 28, September 3, 4, 6, October 4, 11, 1941; *Town Talk,* August 21, 25, 28, 1941; Haas, "New Orleans on the Half-Shell," 302; Haas, *DeLesseps S. Morrison,* 21.

42. *States,* May 15, June 17, 1940; *Times-Picayune,* May 16, 1940; *Acts Passed by the Legislature, 1940,* 402; Edward J. Gay, Jr., "Louisiana Housing Legislature, Urban and Rural," *Louisiana Municipal Review,* January/February 1941, 9–11.

43. *Morning Advocate,* June 3, 1940; *Times-Picayune,* June 3, 1940; M. G. Dakin, "Louisiana Tax Legislation of 1940," *Louisiana Law Review,* November 1940, 74–76.

Adjustments to the severance tax included extensions to tax pulpwood, distillate, casing head gasoline, and natural gasoline, while tax rates on previously taxed oil increased. The package also included a tax on the gathering of natural gas—a temporary measure, the administration said, to help the government liquidate the huge Longite public debt, meet the state's emergency financial needs caused by repeal of other taxes, and continue state public assistance programs.[44]

Even though administration critics attempted to portray Jones as a friend of the rich and the corporations, his tax package also proposed raising income taxes and tightening loopholes in the gift tax. The proposed rates taxed incomes at the rate of 2 percent on the first $4,000 in excess of credits, 4 percent on the next $4,000, and 6 percent on income above $8,000. The old Longite rates had been 2 percent on the first $10,000; 4 percent on the next $40,000, and 6 percent on all above $50,000. In addition, corporate income tax increased from 4 percent to 6 percent and applied to all taxable new income without the $3,000 exemption allowed by the Longites. Individuals and corporations alike faced a 5 percent surtax on net income in excess of $5,000 resulting from sales of unimproved land, sale of mineral rights or oil royalties, or lease of land for oil exploration. The gift tax provision closed the loophole by which an individual could save taxes by spreading large cash gifts over several years. Under the new tax, the amount paid would be the same whether the gift was made in one year or in several years.[45]

While the governor's sales tax repeal successfully passed the legislature, the income tax increases, which had to be framed as a constitutional amendment because prevailing rates were written into that document, failed to win approval in the November election. This failure created a dire problem with which Jones wrestled until 1942: how to fund a $154,002,641.58 biennial budget without a major source of revenue he had anticipated.[46] It also created the opportunity for Longites to humiliate him during the 1942 session of the legislature.

44. *Times-Picayune,* June 3, 1940; Dakin, "Louisiana Tax Legislation of 1940," 74–76.

45. *Times-Picayune,* June 3, 1940; Dakin, "Louisiana Tax Legislation of 1940," 55–60.

46. *Times-Picayune,* June 18, 1940; *Morning Advocate,* November 3, 1940.

Education bills approved by the 1940 legislature provided improved benefits for teachers and public school funding at unprecedented levels. Teachers received ten days of paid leave per school year for illness or emergency, sabbatical leaves in all parishes, and the establishment of a teachers' retirement system. With Jones's urging the legislature dedicated the severance tax revenues to public education with the goal of providing a maximum of $20 per educable child, and also reserved a portion of the tobacco tax revenue for education. Teachers received slight pay increases: the average white teacher's annual salary rose to $1,331.88, while the average black teacher's annual salary was less than half that—$558.81. Requirements for teacher certification were tightened, and a bachelor's degree replaced the sketchy college training course as the minimum requirement. The primary criticism of the 1940 education legislation was that it did not accomplish enough. Representative William J. Dodd, an Allen Parish teacher and president of the Louisiana Teachers' Association, pointed out that even with the pay raise, the average Louisiana teacher received only $83 per month after taxes. He also criticized Jones and Superintendent John E. Coxe because they had not supported a bill to extend Louisiana's high school requirement for graduation from eleven to twelve years.[47]

Overall, Governor Jones was well pleased with his first legislative session. It was, he said, a legislature that "cannot be bought, bull-dozed or browbeaten." He reported to the people that he had worked with the legislature, but emphatically reminded them that he had "never appeared on the floor of either House and . . . never appeared before any committee," a pointed reference to his Longite predecessors. The people, he said, were now free of political dictatorship.[48] Subsequent taxpayer suits, of course, eventually dampened his optimism.

---

47. *Times-Picayune,* June 26–27, 1940; "Legislation of 1940," *Louisiana Schools,* September 1940, 22–23; "Address by President W. J. Dodd," *Louisiana Schools,* November 1941, 4; Charles E. Sutton, Charles L. Foxworth, and Robert E. Hearn, *Louisiana's Story of Public Education* (Ruston, La., 1971), 10–11; Minns Sledge Robertson, *Public Education in Louisiana after 1898* (Baton Rouge, 1952), 149–53; Charles E. Weimer, "John Easterly Coxe, Louisiana Educator" (Ed.D. diss., Louisiana State University, 1974), 23.

48. *Times-Picayune,* June 13, July 12, 1940.

Another reality he came upon only after the legislative session had ended was that even the best intentions for good government did not protect him from problems with patronage. He often appointed businessmen to government positions: sugar planter W. Prescott Foster of St. Mary Parish became chairman, and Alexandria produce merchant Martin L. Close and Franklin Parish planter/businessman W. E. Gilbert members, of the state highway commission. New Orleans engineer Frank Grevemberg became business manager of executive buildings; independent oil operator B. A. Hardey of Shreveport became conservation commissioner, while another Shreveport oil man, Charlton H. Lyons, became president of the board of supervisors of elections for Caddo Parish.[49] Jones experienced relatively little resistance to these appointments, but the agreement by which his camp had agreed to share state patronage equally with James A. Noe's supporters slowly came unraveled, and as it did, Jones gained a foe as implacably anti-Jones as he had been anti-Longite. Moreover, Noe took many of his supporters into an anti-Jones camp.

Governor Jones had shrewdly not begun a serious redistribution of state jobs until the 1940 legislative session neared adjournment, thereby retaining the votes resulting from a promise or even a hint of a state job for a legislator's favored supporter. He and Noe, however, held several meetings in Baton Rouge during which they discussed patronage. Noe denied rumors that he and Jones had failed to reach an early agreement. After the legislative session, competition for state jobs began as rumors raced across the state that "Long men" were to be purged from state payrolls and replaced by men loyal to Sam Jones. Hundreds of people— hopeful Jones supporters, legislators, and Noe—converged on the state capitol and the executive mansion during late July 1940 for a series of patronage meetings.[50]

The governor's original plan for the distribution of state patronage was complex. All job changes under this plan were to follow recommen-

49. *Town Talk,* May 4, 1940; "Major Hardey Looks Ahead at the 'Golden Age of Louisiana,'" *Louisiana Conservation Review,* spring 1940, 7; Sam Jones to Charlton H. Lyons, Sr., October 16, 1942, Lyons Papers, LLMVC.

50. *Morning Advocate,* May 17–18, 1940; *Times-Picayune,* July 26, 1940.

dation of his allies on the parish level. He also hoped to arrange for a representative in each congressional district to smooth over problems that might arise and to forward recommendations of job seekers to any department with an opening. Several legislators complained that the plan had no place for them except that they were given a final veto over job offers in their districts. That meant, they said, that when someone received a job, he or she would feel indebted to the Jones organization, but when someone failed to receive a job, he or she would blame the legislator. In his public announcement of the plan, Jones reiterated his simple wish that people appointed to jobs be required to be qualified for the tasks involved. Jones planned a major turnover to begin August 1, when the state composed its new payrolls.[51]

In this political atmosphere, jockeying for control of patronage brought together strange bedfellows. Orleans assessor James E. Comisky and property commissioner Joseph P. Skelley met with Jones and Noe to obtain Old Regular input into selection of state workers in New Orleans. In exchange, they agreed to support Jones-Noe candidates in city elections. Remnants of the Leche-Long administration, meanwhile, announced formation of the American Democratic Association led by George W. Flynn, who had worked in Earl Long's campaign headquarters, to seek votes from people who opposed the Jones–Noe–Old Regular alliance.[52]

In spite of his careful planning, Jones's guidelines to distribute patronage through the district representative system failed as Noe's forces protested their lack of influence in the selection process. Noe, however, at this point remained publicly loyal, and the administration formulated a new plan that allowed him to establish his own parish committees to be consulted on patronage distribution. Jones also announced a new "high command" comprised of Vance Plauché and Francis Whitehead, both former members of his campaign team, and Charles E. McKenzie, Noe's campaign manager, to consider all requests for patronage.[53]

---

51. *Times-Picayune,* July 26–27, 1940; *Item,* July 17, 1940.
52. *Times-Picayune,* July 30–31, 1940; *Times-Picayune/New Orleans States,* July 28, 1940.
53. *Times-Picayune,* July 13–August 2, 1940.

Jones's hope that the new arrangement would quell disputes was short-lived. In December 1940, Jones and Noe met again, and neither was satisfied with the outcome of their conference. Noe remarked with restrained understatement that "we haven't been so very well pleased with what we've been getting," but added that "we hope things will get better." He adamantly rejected a suggestion to solve the problem by merging his organization with Jones's. Jones ruefully remarked, "I guess this will be going on up to 1944." Following the meeting, Jones leaders unveiled a third patronage plan, in which Jones and Noe would each appoint three members to a patronage committee. A member from each side would then contact state department heads and discuss patronage with them.[54]

The new arrangement failed to satisfy Noe. Ill tempers flared again at patronage conferences in the spring of 1941, and the conflict fueled rumors of an impending Jones-Noe split. Noe termed his April 7, 1941, meeting with Jones "highly unsatisfactory." His organization, meanwhile, began to crack apart over patronage. Five of his New Orleans ward leaders did not attend a meeting of his city organization because they believed that total amalgamation of the Noe and Jones camps was the essential requirement for full participation in patronage. They also wondered if Noe's determination to hold his inner circle together showed his dedication to political ideals or, rather, his "ambitions for personal political advancement," that is, his intention to run for the United States Senate seat held by Allen J. Ellender. Noe held that he would continue to fight for the complete independence of his organization, but that he would also go on supporting "every constructive move" Jones made.[55]

On April 17, however, Noe left Baton Rouge, saying that the governor had not responded to his request to meet with New Orleans Noe leaders about patronage. That same day, three Noe leaders in the city became co-leaders of their wards in the Jones organization. Noe hurriedly sought and received Jones's assurances that the defections would have no effect on Noe followers who had received state jobs yet remained loyal to Noe. He reiterated, though, that "we haven't been treated right, either in the

54. *Morning Advocate,* December 17, 22, 1940.
55. *Ibid.,* April 8–9, 1941.

country or the city," and threatened to devise his own plan to distribute jobs.[56]

Rapidly becoming disillusioned with the controversy, Noe angrily charged that even though he favored civil service, he suspected that the Jones camp was maneuvering to install its followers in state jobs and blanket them in under the new civil service legislation. The final break occurred after Noe charged on May 14, 1941, that Jones was erecting a new dictatorship. He claimed that the governor planted spies in Noe organization meetings and then fired from state jobs Noe supporters who would not join his organization, or who spoke against him. "This is nothing more than dictatorship dressed up in silk stockings and under a new name," Noe fumed.[57]

Even though the bitter split cost Jones some of the support with which he had established his reform program at the beginning of his administration, it was not as costly as it might appear at first glance, because Noe's status as an asset was soon to be vastly diminished. In late 1940 he had been indicted by a federal grand jury for income tax evasion allegedly committed in 1935 by the Win or Lose Oil Corporation, whose profits Noe (who had served as president), Seymour Weiss, Oscar K. Allen, and Huey Long (the last two secretly) had shared. Following a tearful court appearance, Noe was acquitted on all counts, but his statewide political influence was waning. He announced on several later occasions that he planned to run for governor or United States senator, but his only real campaign for an important state post, his ill-fated 1959–60 gubernatorial candidacy in Earl Long's bizarre attempt to retain political power, ended in a crushing defeat.[58]

The alliance of convenience that had been forged between Jones and Noe seemed almost destined to disintegrate. They were, after all, unlikely allies. Jones's need for Noe's help was most acute during the second primary campaign in 1940, and thus he might have agreed to provide more

56. *Ibid.,* April 17–18, 1941.

57. *Ibid.,* May 15, 1941.

58. *Morning Advocate,* July 12, August 17, 1941, April 12, 1942; *Times-Picayune/New Orleans States,* April 12, 1942; Glen S. Jeansonne, *Race, Religion and Politics: The Louisiana Gubernatorial Elections of 1959–60* (Lafayette, La., 1977), 31–32.

patronage than reality later allowed him to supply to Noe's supporters. In addition, the normal pressure exerted on a governor to reward his loyal supporters made it difficult to keep the bargain.

Not all Jones's time during his first two years as governor was occupied by formulating or defending reform plans or attempting to pacify Noe. The unfolding European war caused a boom in defense industries throughout the United States, and Jones traveled to Washington, D.C., to ask President Roosevelt "for anything and everything that will help Louisiana." New defense stations, he said, expansion of present army, navy, and marine organizations, opening of airplane factories—anything that would bring money into Louisiana—would be considered: "If there any federal funds to be got, I am going to do my darndest to get them."[59]

Jones also proposed that the Southern Governors' Conference sponsor a study of all states to determine the resources that each could contribute to national defense, and called for a Southern Defense Council, comprised of one representative appointed by each southern governor. He was not ready, however, to gear Louisiana's economy solely to defense. He announced that Louisiana would join in the "Balanced Prosperity" program, a ten-year effort sponsored by the conference to establish a diverse economy in the region.[60]

As Jones worked tirelessly to attract federal dollars to Louisiana, he established himself as a staunch advocate of improving United States's relations with Latin America, a favorite project of President Roosevelt. Jones's efforts stemmed from his pragmatic attempts to reestablish New Orleans as the premier port connecting the Upper Mississippi Valley to the outside world, especially to Latin America. He further envisioned New Orleans as the "air hub of America," connecting the Mississippi Valley and South America, and pledged his administration to fostering better understanding among all the Americas. He proposed increased study of Spanish and Portuguese at LSU to ease communication problems, advocated an exchange student program, and encouraged citizens of all Amer-

59. *Times-Picayune,* June 3, 1940.

60. *Times-Picayune,* June 3, 4, 11, 19, September 24, 1940; *Morning Advocate,* February 16, May 9, 1941.

ican countries to visit other countries so that nonrepresentative nationals in foreign lands would not discredit the entire citizenship of their country. In the aftermath of the grueling campaign to win approval of his constitutional amendments in the fall 1940 general election, Jones set an example by vacationing in several Caribbean countries. He also chaired the five-member committee formed by the Southern Governors' Conference to promote trade, defense preparedness, and friendship with Latin America.[61]

Perhaps Jones's most flamboyant diplomatic effort in this regard occurred in July 1941 when the "Greater Louisiana Special Train" carried a group of prominent Louisianians to Mexico City to promote trade between Louisiana and Mexico. Legal challenges to his reform plans kept the governor in Baton Rouge, but Mrs. Jones and agriculture commissioner Harry D. Wilson led the delegation in his place.[62]

Marked as they were by a mix of successes and failures, Governor Jones's first two years in office would prove to be the easier half of his governorship. His break with Noe and his lack of a strong political base in the legislature led to additional problems. The 1940 session of the legislature had been difficult for him. The 1942 sessions were worse.

61. *Times-Picayune/New Orleans States,* August 4, 1940; *Times-Picayune,* August 7, 1940; *Morning World,* September 17, 1940; *Morning Advocate,* November 23, 1940; *Town Talk,* December 11, 1940; A. E. Pradillo, "Louisiana's Governor 'Sells' Middle West," *New Orleans Port Record,* October 1943, 9–10; Willard Range, *Franklin D. Roosevelt's World Order* (Athens, Ga., 1959), 52–66; Gary Arnold Bolding, "Efforts to Develop New Orleans as a World Trade Center," (Master's thesis, Louisiana State University, 1966), 62–64.

62. *Morning Advocate,* July 10, 1941; *Greater Louisiana Special Train* (n.p., n.d.), Justin E. Wilson to W. Scott Heywood, June 28, 1941, Heywood to Harry D. Wilson, June 30, 1941, Heywood to Sam Jones, June 30, 1941, Jones to Heywood, July 2, 1941, all in Jennings-Heywood Oil Syndicate Records, LLMVC.

4

The Continuing Struggle for Reform

Louisiana politics began 1942 with the Democratic primary for mayor of New Orleans. Anti-Longite attention had first focused on freshman U.S. representative F. Edward Hebert. Hebert, however, had no interest in the office, so some reformers chose as their candidate former Old Regular congressman Paul H. Maloney, whom T. Hale Boggs had defeated in 1940. Governor Jones briefly considered supporting Maloney, but purists among the governor's supporters dissuaded him from making the endorsement. The Old Regulars, however, promised to support Maloney for Congress in the 1942 fall election in exchange for his withdrawal from the mayor's race, an arrangement he accepted. The reformers then turned to attorney Herve Racivitch, a veteran of Jones's gubernatorial campaign, while the Old Regulars backed incumbent Robert Maestri. Two minor candidates, Shirley G. Wimberly and John T. Knoop, entered the race as independent Democrats who attacked Maestri as the close ally of the "thieving" Long machine and Racivitch as the candidate of a new reform machine.[1]

Sam Jones did not enthusiastically follow his faction in supporting Racivitch, evidently because he hoped to continue the working relation-

1. Haas, *DeLesseps S. Morrison,* 14–15, 21–22; Parker, *The Morrison Era,* 60; Hebert and McMillan, *"Last of the Titans,"* 164–65; Kurtz and Peoples, *Earl K. Long,* 84–86; *Times-Picayune,* September 16, 18–19, October 2, 11, December 16, 18, 1941; *Times-Picayune/New Orleans States,* November 16, 1941; *Item,* July 31, 1941; *Morning Advocate,* August 1–2, 1941; *States,* December 18, 1941.

ship with Maestri that had enabled some of his proposals to pass the 1940 legislature. He apparently had also agreed with the Old Regulars to divide offices in the New Orleans area, and part of that arrangement prevented him from intervening directly in the 1942 mayoral election. He accompanied Racivitch to a New Orleans dinner commemorating the Louisiana Purchase, but his speech that night included only general allusions to the mayor's race. Again in New Orleans for a program commemorating the 127th anniversary of the Battle of New Orleans, he refrained from endorsing Racivitch.[2]

Jones's disaffected former ally, James A. Noe, had already announced his intention to run for Allen J. Ellender's U.S. Senate seat in 1942 or for governor in 1944, and used the 1942 mayor's race to shore up his support by endorsing Maestri. The mayor replied that he was "happy" to accept the support.[3]

Noe, however, had unwittingly created a split within his New Orleans organization. Twelve ward leaders opposed the Maestri endorsement. Their leader asserted that they stood by the original intent of the Noe organization "to bring an end to the Maestri-Leche-Long dictatorship." James D. McNeill, chair of the Noe city caucus, charged that they had received state jobs in exchange for their defection. Noe added, "I am still Kingfish of the Noe lodge," and proclaimed that "we are 100 per cent with Bob Maestri in this fight."[4]

Maestri and the Old Regulars cited improvements in city finances made since 1936 as their primary theme. Racivitch's campaign hoped to undermine those accomplishments by focusing on Maestri's ties to the Longites. Reformers thought that they had uncovered a new deduct scheme when they announced that city employees were buying tickets to a "lotto party" to benefit Maestri's campaign, but the sponsoring Old

2. *Times-Picayune/New Orleans States,* December 21, 1941; *Times-Picayune,* September 22, 1941, January 9, 30, 1942.

3. *Morning Advocate,* October 5, 1940, July 16, 1941, January 17, 1942; *Times-Picayune,* January 3, 1942.

4. *Times-Picayune/New Orleans States,* January 4, 1942; *Morning Advocate,* January 17, 1942; *Times-Picayune,* January 6, 8, 16, 21, 23, 28–29, 1942.

Regular ward leaders explained that the proceeds "are to be used for baskets for poor families and for no other purpose."[5]

Charges of corruption, past or present, failed to bring a reform victory in New Orleans. Maestri received 76,008 votes to Racivitch's 49,762, Wimberley's 11,029, and Knoop's 788. Sam Jones noted that the Old Regulars carried 3,000 fewer votes for Maestri in the city than they had carried for Earl Long in the governor's race two years previously, but the reformers could take little other comfort in the election. Governor Jones soon canceled the general election as state law required if the Democratic candidates were unopposed and the deadline for qualifying had passed with no other party candidates in contention. He attempted to console Racivitch by appointing him attorney to collect delinquent taxes in Orleans Parish.[6]

The 1942 mayoral campaign proved to be only the preliminary bout to the major political battles of the year: the regular and extraordinary sessions of the legislature. Governor Jones's main problem was the voters' rejection of a constitutional amendment raising income taxes to replace some of the revenue lost by sales tax repeal in 1940. Immediately after the income tax amendment failed, he received authority from the state board of liquidation to poll the legislature for permission to borrow up to $5 million in case of a shortfall to tide the state over until he could call a special legislative session to address the situation. Prompt action was necessary because state treasurer Tugwell announced in November 1940 that the state could run out of money and have an $8 million deficit by March or April 1941. Despite Jones's attempts to establish an efficient administration, at the end of 1940 the state faced a biennial deficit of $14 million, chiefly caused by legislatively-distributed public largesse, continued borrowing, and Jones's inability to implement his administrative and fiscal controls because of successful Longite lawsuits. Also, the governor's split with Noe caused Noe's fiery young protégé, state senator Joe T. Cawthorn of DeSoto Parish, to become one of Jones's most ardent and vocal critics. The state's dire fiscal condition became apparent in early 1941,

5. *Times-Picayune,* September 20–21, October 10, 12, 1942.

6. *Ibid.,* January 28–29, February 1, March 31, 1942; *Morning Advocate,* May 16, 1942.

when New Orleans' Charity Hospital closed two floors, thus eliminating 497 patient beds.[7]

During early 1942, Jones asked his department heads both to adapt their agencies to the war effort and to address the state's economic problems. His guidelines included returning to the state treasury as much of the current appropriations "as humanly possible," not replacing personnel called into military service, eliminating nonessential services, and cultivating all available state land for food and fuel. These attempted savings, however, did not obliterate the deficit. State finance officers estimated in 1942 that the 1940 legislature had increased state expenditures for schools, hospitals, and public assistance by about $8 million per year, while state income had increased by only about $5 million. The state would therefore require at least $3 million to relieve the existing deficit, an additional $4 million for each of the next two years to prevent a recurring deficit, and about $3 million more to fund built-in increases in salaries, materials, and other expenses. Jones blamed the problems on the failure of the 1940 income tax amendment and the state's bonded indebtedness from the Long-Allen-Leche era, but Senator Cawthorn charged instead that "waste and inefficiency" since 1940 had led to the current situation.[8]

The 1942 regular session of the legislature, which opened in May, was dominated by problems concerning both Louisiana's role in the war and its fiscal condition. Bifactional wrangling often affected constructive debate. The first skirmish of the session occurred in a vote to replace the late J. Martin Hamley as secretary of the senate. The administration initially supported William Gladney of New Orleans for the post, but abandoned him for the more popular Robert A. Gilbert of Napoleonville, brother of the late Longite senator Philip Gilbert. Staunch anti-Jones senators led by Cawthorn nominated former Acadia Parish representative N. Smith Hoffpauir. The two sides agreed on a compromise of Gilbert for secretary

7. Sindler, *Huey Long's Louisiana,* 169–70; *Morning Advocate,* November 20, 30, December 8, 12, 1940, February 20, March 3, 13, May 26–27, June 7, 12, 28, August 11, 1941; *Town Talk,* December 20, 1940, August 27, 1941.

8. *Shreveport Times,* January 10, February 11, 1942; *States,* March 21, 1942; *Morning Advocate,* April 9, 29, 1942; *Item,* May 14, 1942.

and Hoffpauir for assistant secretary. Lieutenant Governor Marc Mouton ruled that the two appointments were separate and had to be considered separately. Cawthorn retorted that the senate could make its own rules, and a 20–19 vote sustained him. The senate then elected Gilbert and Hoffpauir by the same 20–19 vote.[9]

The vote revealed an additional problem for Jones. His ally from the 1940 session, President pro tempore Frank B. Ellis, voted against the administration. Ellis maintained that he had not abandoned Jones but was merely exercising his right to make independent decisions. Jones's opponents, though, counted Ellis as one of their own, or at least now expected him to vote with them more than against them. Jones later remarked that Ellis had "sold out to Maestri."[10]

Governor Jones, in his opening remarks to the legislature, called for measures to provide for Louisiana's role in the war effort, to solve problems created by invalidation of some of his 1940 reforms, and to finance necessary and beneficial government activities. His desired war measures included mundane proposals regulating blackouts, penalties for anyone trespassing in or attempting to sabotage a war industry, and election reforms allowing servicemen to register and vote absentee, providing leaves of absence to servicemen in state employ, and permitting servicemen to run for public office absentee. With regard to the reorganization problem, his proposal included legislative recognition of the departments of government not invalidated by the adverse court decisions on the constitutional amendments. Administration fiscal proposals provided no detailed plan to raise revenue. Jones had already stated that it was the legislature's role to provide money necessary to fund state government, and thus issued general platitudes about reducing appropriations and appealing to unnamed additional revenue sources in order to balance the budget.[11]

Longite opposition to the governor and his programs coalesced around

9. *States,* May 7, 11, 1942; *Morning Advocate,* May 8, 10, 12, 1942; *Item,* May 12, 1942.

10. Sam Jones, interview by Daugherty, May 6, 1970, Daugherty Collection, LLMVC.

11. *Morning Advocate,* May 13, 1942; *States,* May 13, 1942; *Shreveport Journal,* May 13, 1942.

Robert Maestri, who during legislative sessions rented the house in Baton Rouge belonging to Longite registrar of state lands Lucille May Grace to serve as a convenient political and entertainment headquarters. Reformers tried but failed to pass resolutions asking Maestri to leave the city and to stop his attempts to influence legislators. Bills stripping the New Orleans mayor's office of extraordinary powers granted at the expense of the commission council during the Leche administration also failed.[12]

Reformers were more successful in passing measures to facilitate Louisiana's participation in the war effort. Pertaining directly to military issues were acts that provided for "forces of Louisiana" other than the National Guard to serve outside the state and to pursue enemies of the state into other states with reciprocity agreements. Other legislation authorized the governor to order practice blackouts, radio silences, and other precautionary measures. Act 117 stipulated that anyone on any harbor, ship, or navigable waters or on land within two hundred feet of a navigable stream must have a valid identification and approval by the Coast Guard. Act 242 made it unlawful to encourage violence, sabotage, or disloyalty to the United States or Louisiana, or to give information on military secrets, operations, or plans of defense, and Act 290 prohibited employment of known enemy aliens or conscientious objectors. Legislation relating to stateside support of the war effort included measures designed to protect war industries in the state. The legislature made trespassing illegal on any premises engaged in defense activities, established the crime of sabotage, and provided prison terms for those convicted of tampering with or intentionally damaging public or private property engaged in war production, or intentionally producing faulty articles destined for war or defense of the United States. The Louisiana Commission of Labor received limited authorization to dispense with some labor laws for six-month periods for businesses producing goods under army or navy contracts, while the director of highways could close or restrict civilian use of any highway or street used in the war effort. To conserve gasoline and tires, a new law decreed that most service stations be closed between mid-

---

12. *Morning Advocate,* May 15, 19–20, 1942; *Item,* May 19–20, June 2, 16, 1942; *States,* May 19–20, 1942.

night Saturday and midnight Sunday. Five percent of the stations, chosen by lot every three months, would remain open for emergencies. The legislators authorized the governor to grant leaves of absence to appointed officials and notaries public who joined or were drafted into the armed services. To facilitate participation in the federal government's war bond program, businesses chartered under state law were allowed to issue U.S. Government obligations. The state, police juries, school boards, and municipalities were authorized to invest surplus funds in series E, F, and G war bonds, and state and parish employees were allowed to purchase series E bonds through payroll deductions.[13]

While there was usually widespread agreement on necessary wartime measures, not all proposals enjoyed bifactional support. Governor Jones's plan for an all-volunteer state guard, for example, drew heavy Longite fire. Representative deLesseps Morrison introduced the bill in the house, and the original version included provisions for drafting men if not enough volunteers emerged to fill the ranks. Representative William J. Dodd of Allen Parish stated that he favored creating the guard, but opposed creating a "buzzard roost" of deadheads on the state payroll. Why not, he asked, rely strictly on volunteers? Adjutant General Raymond H. Fleming of the Louisiana National Guard was initially concerned that the State Guard would infringe on his command, but eventually supported the bill and supplied the new military units with arms and uniforms and helped to establish standards for officers. The governor himself even made a rare appearance before a legislative committee to testify for the disputed bill.[14]

Most wartime measures passed the legislature easily. The bill allowing pursuit of "enemies of the state," for example, passed the house of representatives with an 83–6 vote, and three of the nays saw fit to include a rare "Explanation of Vote" in the house *Journal*. Beatrice Moore, W. O.

13. *Acts Passed by the Legislature of the State of Louisiana at the Regular Session, 1942,* passim; Frances Perkins to Sam Jones, June 13, 1942, Jones Collection, HTML.

14. *Item,* May 21, June 4–5, 19, 1942; *States,* June 2, 1942; *Morning Advocate,* June 5, 1942; *Town Talk,* July 18, 1942; W. Scott Heywood to Neal Whisenhunt, July 6, 1942, Jennings-Heywood Oil Syndicate Records, LLMVC; Major General Raymond Fleming to Sam Jones, September 15, 18, 22, 25, 1942, Jones Collection.

Noble, and T. C. Brister said that they opposed the bill, not because it had originated with the administration, but because they thought the Federal Bureau of Investigation and other federal agencies could better handle interstate troubles. When it finally came to a vote, the state guard bill also passed by a wide margin, 85–5.[15]

Other laws the governor pushed through the 1942 legislature were designed to salvage part of his government reorganization that had been struck down by the state supreme court. The administration crafted a package of bills, each of which created and provided for the continued operation of one state department (Public Welfare, Occupational Standards, Labor, Public Safety, Institutions, Highway, and Finance), administered by a director whom the governor would appoint. Another bill established a new fiscal code. While the entire reorganization package faced opposition, the proposed fiscal code drew the strongest Longite ire. It passed the senate by a slim 20–18 margin, with Senator Cawthorn in strong opposition. Jones later vetoed the bills creating the Public Welfare and Labor Departments, remarking that he had concluded that laws already in existence sufficiently established them.[16]

The newly-created civil service also faced stiff challenges. Representative Moseman Simoneaux of New Orleans, a Maestri ally, introduced a resolution suspending civil service in New Orleans until after the 1944 regular session of the legislature (at which time the Longites hoped to control the governorship again). A coalition of rural legislators introduced a similar resolution to delay implementation of state civil service. Longites sought to achieve the desired delay by resolution in an attempt to circumvent the governor's veto power.[17]

---

15. *Official Journal of the Proceedings of the House of Representatives . . . at the Eleventh Regular Session . . . 1942,* 495–96. Unfortunately, the *Senate Journal* for this session is virtually inaccessible because the complete *Senate Calendar* was never published. The fragmentary calendar only covers the first four weeks of the session and is incomplete even for that short period. Some House bills that the Senate considered during that time are not listed in the fragment.

16. *States,* May 25, June 3, July 13, 1942; *Item,* June 3, 1942; *Morning Advocate,* June 13, 1942.

17. *Morning Advocate,* June 1, 1942; *States,* June 5, 1942.

Reformers rallied to rescue civil service. In the house, they beat back an attempt by Representative A. D. Flowers of LaSalle Parish to reduce appropriations for the institution by about $83,000 in its first year and $71,000 in its second year. In time, the governor agreed to delay implementation of New Orleans civil service—ostensibly because the administrative apparatus was not yet in place—and also agreed to postpone implementation of state civil service in order to avoid additional factional animosity. The delay, however, was not as long as the Longites originally desired. Civil service was delayed from July 1, 1942 (original implementation date) to January 1, 1943, instead of July 1, 1944, as the Longites had wished.[18]

The chief battle (and the most important stalemate) between the two factions occurred over Jones's budget and taxes. He submitted two budget bills, an "A" budget maintaining approximately the current spending levels, and a "B" budget with reduced appropriations. The A budget called for the state spending $152,654,467.15 over the next biennium (fiscal years 1942–43 and 1943–44) and included projected revenues from a sales tax and a natural gas tax. The B budget provided for the spending of $133,178,365.29 over the biennium without new sales tax revenue. Budget Director James I. Smith explained to the legislature that adoption of the B budget would require removing 4,000 patients from state hospitals, dropping 2,400 students from state colleges and 700 from trade schools, removing 19,000 recipients from welfare rolls, closing some health units, and losing countless dollars in federal matching funds. The governor, for his part, reiterated his belief that it was the legislature's proper task to determine budget appropriations and warned that he would veto all appropriations for which sufficient revenue was unavailable.[19]

Moreover, Jones cautioned legislators of impending major deficits in state expenditures—$9,647,462.86 by the end of the 1942–43 fiscal year, and $9,989,831.27 by the close of the 1943–44 fiscal year—unless they provided additional funds for "the present services of our state agencies

18. *Morning Advocate,* June 7, July 15, 1942; *States,* June 25, July 1, 15, 1942; Sindler, *Huey Long's Louisiana,* 172.

19. *Times-Picayune,* May 19, 1942; *Item,* May 19, 1942; *States,* May 21, 1942.

which have been authorized by you." But both the house and the senate ignored his warnings and established a budget of approximately $175 million for the biennium, approximately $25 million above the governor's most optimistic proposals.[20] The legislature would have seemed less irresponsible had it provided sufficient revenue to fund its appropriations. Whenever the opportunity arose, however, factional politics overrode any consideration of fiscal responsibility.

Representative Paul F. Stinson of Jackson Parish, a Jones ally, introduced a 2 percent state sales tax bill on wholesalers to help alleviate the budget problems. Opposition to Stinson's bill emerged immediately from all sides: Longites, reformers, and business groups. The *States* described the wholesale tax as a "camouflaged sales tax" and called on the administration to present its case of need, ask for a statewide sales tax, "and try to fool no one." A delegation of merchants led by the New Orleans Association of Commerce and Young Men's Business Club (friendly to Jones since 1939), called the proposal "unfair, impracticable, and unworkable," primarily because the bill did not require that retailers pass along the increased cost of the tax to their customers. The businessmen thought that the Office of Price Administration, a federal wartime agency, would object to increased retail prices resulting from the wholesale tax. Subsequently, the house Ways and Means Committee dropped the wholesale sales tax in favor of a retail sales tax. The new proposal called for a 1 percent sales tax on all retail purchases from 13 cents to 62 cents and 2 percent on sales above 62 cents, with exemptions for gasoline, natural gas, and water. The committee attempted to make the tax more acceptable by labeling it a "War Emergency Tax" and limiting its term to two years.[21]

Battle lines appeared almost immediately. James A. Noe and Senators Cawthorn and Clements reminded the house Ways and Means Committee that Jones had promised to end the sales tax. Jones replied that even though he did not favor a sales tax, it was now a necessary evil: "I would rather defend my support of the sales tax than explain closed hospitals and hungry old people, and bankrupt local governments, and unbalanced

---

20. *States,* May 26, June 22, 29, 1942.
21. *States,* May 12, 28, June 5–6, 9, 1942; *Item,* June 1, 4–5, 9, 1942.

budgets, and underpaid teachers, and impassable roads." Superintendent of Education Coxe urged school board members, parish superintendents and supervisors, and school principals to support the sales tax and its proposed $2,135,000 increase in school funds. As a result of that recommendation, forty parish superintendents endorsed the tax.[22]

The house debated the sales tax for a stormy four hours. Representative Theo Cangelosi of East Baton Rouge Parish warned that the people favored retrenchment, not excessive taxation. Representative James E. Bolin of Webster Parish appeared in his army lieutenant's uniform to argue against the tax, telling fellow legislators that they should "leave as much money with the people as we can to pay federal war taxes and to buy war bonds and stamps." Pro-Jones representatives appealed to benefits of the tax: $20 per educable child for public schools, regular equalization fund payments, regular contributions to the teacher retirement fund, additional old-age pension funds, and added revenue for hospitals. The house approved the sales tax on June 17, 1942, by a vote of 51 yeas to 43 nays.[23]

The thin margin by which the bill passed the house, where it had a friendly presiding officer, did not augur well for it in the senate. Jones lobbied the senators as he had the representatives, calling the tax "a grim necessity." Despite his entreaties, the senate disposed of the sales tax on June 24 in a complex bit of parliamentary maneuvering. The senate first voted 21–17 to postpone indefinitely (and thus kill) the bill. Senator Grove Stafford, a Jones floor leader from Rapides Parish who voted against the indefinite postponement, announced that he wished to switch his vote to the prevailing side so that he could give notice of reconsideration and bring the bill back before the senate the next day. Senator Cawthorn maintained that Stafford was out of order, but Lieutenant Governor Marc Mouton ruled that he could change his vote and give notice of reconsideration. Cawthorn moved to suspend the rules in order to revert to the bill so that he could move it be laid on the table (again effectively killing it). Mouton denied Cawthorn's motion to suspend the rules,

22. *Morning Advocate,* June 12, 16, 1942; *States,* June 13, 16, 1942; *Item,* June 17, 1942.
23. *States,* June 17–18, 1942; *Item,* June 18, 1942; *Morning Advocate,* June 18, 1942.

but Cawthorn asked for a vote and carried the motion by 20 yeas to 18 nays. With the rules thus suspended, Cawthorn made another motion to table the bill and carried it, thereby killing the sales tax for the 1942 regular session.[24]

Political maneuvering aside, Louisiana still faced the problem of its looming deficits. The house passed new revenue bills adjusting income tax rates, and the senate talked of reviving the wholesale sales tax, but the only major piece of revenue legislation passed by both chambers was the gas-gathering tax, estimated to raise about $1.5 million per year. Jones announced that he had failed to win the support of the Old Regulars, so his wartime tax program was dead. The governor now had one option: vetoing sufficient items to balance the budget. An independent citizen's committee investigating state finances reported that the 1942 legislature had appropriated $8 million to $11 million in excess of estimated revenue for 1942–43 and between $7 million and $9 million in excess for 1943–44.[25] The governor clearly faced a difficult task.

The performance of the rebellious 1942 legislature underscores Longite political duplicity. They assumed the mantle of "fiscal integrity" and reiterated their compassion for the "common man" by defeating the taxes proposed by the reformers. At the same time, they expected their own programs to be financed. When the legislature adjourned, it therefore left the governor as the scapegoat who had to reduce state expenditures by eliminating desirable programs.

The Longites were generally pleased as the legislature adjourned sine die on July 9, 1942. They had delayed, though not obliterated, civil service, they had forced Sam Jones to endorse a distasteful sales tax in violation of his campaign pledge and then brought him to his knees by failing to pass it, and had custom-tailored a campaign issue to use against the reformers in 1944: "Where is your health care? Where are your schools?" The Longites, however, had underestimated the governor's willingness to take a political gamble in order to balance the budget.[26]

24. *Morning Advocate,* June 21, 1942; *States,* June 24, 1942.

25. *Acts Passed by the Legislature, Regular Session, 1942,* 80; *States,* June 26, July 3, 6, August 7, 1942; *Morning Advocate,* July 6, 1942; *Town Talk,* July 8, 1942.

26. Glen Jeansonne, *Leander Perez, Boss of the Delta* (Baton Rouge, 1977), 124.

To that end, and to create pressure on legislators to provide the revenue needed for state services, Jones vetoed both necessary and popular programs. The vetoes resulted in, among other cutbacks, approximately 11,000 families leaving the relief rolls, a $342,000 reduction in the appropriations for Louisiana State University, the loss of $2 million to aid unemployables not covered by federal programs, and the loss of $1 million for the teachers' retirement system. And Jones's biggest gamble of all was his veto of the $6.5 million biennial maintenance appropriation for the New Orleans Charity Hospital.[27]

Charity Hospital had experienced difficulties even before it was caught in the bifactional conflict. By June 23, 1942, it had lost to the armed services 80 resident physicians, 93 nurses, 38 junior interns, and 49 members of the visiting staff. Hospital officials feared that in case of serious emergency, the remaining staff would be unable to provide adequate medical service.[28]

In an effort to overturn Jones's veto, Longites resorted to their familiar tactic of filing a lawsuit. New Orleans attorney Alfred O. Danziger, represented by attorneys Leander Perez, George M. Wallace, and Wade O. Martin, Jr., filed suit in Judge J. D. Womack's court seeking to block the veto because it prevented payment on the state's $800,000 indebtedness for the hospital, of which Danziger held two bonds. The administration asked the Louisiana supreme court to dismiss the suit because Womack's court lacked jurisdiction in the case, but that court declined. Womack declared Jones's veto unconstitutional on two grounds: it canceled the obligation of contract and it should have been returned to the legislature for action prior to adjournment. The state then appealed Womack's ruling in the supreme court. The appeal was granted and both sides were directed to submit briefs on September 4, at which time the court would set a date for hearing the injunction. This action effectively nullified Womack's decision, because the court on the same day announced its summer recess, meaning that the case could not be heard until October, weeks after the

---

27. *Morning Advocate,* July 11, 13, 1942; *States,* July 11, 1942.
28. *States,* June 23, 27, 1942.

September date set for the closing of Charity Hospital unless it received its funding.[29]

The obvious answer to the state's fiscal problems appeared to lie in a special legislative session. The governor, however, was reluctant to incur additional expense unless he obtained reasonable assurance of success. "It would be a waste of the state's money to have a special session that would result in a cat and dog fight," he remarked. On July 26, sixteen senators urged him to call a special session empowered to raise money for all curtailed state services, not just those at Charity Hospital. A vacillating Senator Ellis called for a session to provide funds for the hospital, but remained opposed to the sales tax. He suggested instead a transfer scheme by which a surplus in the Confederate pension fund could be used as the foundation of a bond issue to pay for programs for the aged and needy, thus freeing money in the general fund for use for the hospital. The Young Men's Business Club of New Orleans also appealed for relief for the hospital.[30]

Jones continued to seek assurances that the special session would not be called in vain. In mid-August, he informed Mayor Maestri that he was contemplating a call for the session and asked the mayor to meet with him to discuss ways of raising enough revenue to keep Charity Hospital open and other state services functioning. Maestri, queried by reporters, testily denied receiving Jones's invitation, declared that he did "not propose to be dictated to by his excellency," and maintained that he had no more influence in the legislature than did any other mayor in the state. He also announced, however, that "several of my friends" had confided that they would vote for any tax necessary to raise revenue except a sales tax.[31]

Meanwhile, Old Regular floor leaders Frank Stitch of the house and J. Aubry Gaiennie of the senate met with the governor and informed him that they would consider anything other than a sales tax. The participants

29. *Morning Advocate,* July 28, 1942; *States,* July 31, August 1, 6, 10, 12, 14–15, 1942; *Item,* August 15, 1942.

30. *States,* July 7, 27, August 10, 14, 1942; *Item,* August 13, 1942.

31. *States,* August 16, 18, 1942; *Morning Advocate,* August 17, 1942; *Morning Advocate,* August 20, 1942.

in this meeting declined to disclose the proposals discussed, but political insiders reported that the primary topic had been a 1.5 percent sales tax and an alternate 1 percent sales tax with increased additional taxes. Stitch and Gaiennie favored the latter proposal. Some Longites questioned the need for a special session before the September congressional primaries, but the governor called the session for August 20, 1942. His call authorized consideration of various revenue measures that the legislators wished to propose.[32]

Jones recommended that the legislature focus on the 1.5 percent retail sales tax, and Representatives Bonnie Baker of East Baton Rouge Parish and H. H. Huckabay of Caddo Parish introduced a bill in the House establishing such a tax. Representative W. O. Noble of Richland Parish and Senator Cawthorn introduced the major Longite alternative to the sales tax, bills that would fund Charity Hospital by cutting all other state expenditures by 30 percent. Administration leaders saw this move as the political ploy it was intended to be: though the hospital would remain open, Longites could campaign throughout the state against Jones, telling the people he had handled the state's funds so badly that services to them had had to be reduced.[33]

The house passed the 1.5 percent sales tax by a 51–33 vote, but only after adding an amendment providing that if the people approved a proposed increased income tax amendment in the November election, the sales tax would expire. The house Ways and Means Committee concurrently ruled unfavorably on six revenue bills (a 1 cent soft drink tax, an increased common carrier tax, and an increased gas-gathering tax, among others) introduced by anti-Jones members as substitutes for the sales tax.[34]

Debate on the bill caused open warfare in the senate. The melee began when Senator Dudley LeBlanc roundly attacked the governor. Representative Fred J. Heintz of St. Tammany Parish exchanged words with LeBlanc and invited him outside the Senate chamber to continue the ar-

32. *States,* August 18–20, 1942; *Item,* August 18–20, 1942; *Morning Advocate,* August 20, 1942.

33. *Morning Advocate,* August 21, 24, 1942; *States,* August 21–22, 24, 1942.

34. *States,* August 24–26, 1942; *Morning Advocate,* August 25, 1942; *Acts Passed by the Legislature of the State of Louisiana at the Extraordinary Session, 1942,* 6, 28.

gument. Both men began swinging, and other senators immediately joined the fracas. Representatives seated in the gallery vaulted the low railing onto the floor. Shouts arose to call the police, and Lieutenant Governor Marc Mouton pled for order. His mild admonition went unheeded as one legislator grabbed a brass cuspidor and bandied it about before he was disarmed. The members finally returned to order, but anger continued to seethe within the chamber. Adjournment was accompanied by fistfights between spectators. Senator Cawthorn and state police superintendent Steve Alford began a fight in the corridor just outside the governor's office, but friends quickly separated them. The *New Orleans States* commented that many of the legislators were "young enough to hurl bombs at Hitler and Hirohito" and added that if their performance in the fight was any indication, "many of them should make good commandos."[35]

Earlier on the day of the melee, former governor Noe had signaled a break in Longite opposition to the sales tax when he testified to the senate Finance Committee that he favored the tax, but only as a last resort to keep the hospitals open and to provide state services to the poor, sick, blind, and insane. He also assured the senators that he would remove the sales tax after he was elected governor in 1944.[36]

Despite Maestri's earlier protests that he had no extraordinary influence in the legislature, final negotiations to break the impasse occurred in his Heidelberg Hotel room at a meeting of Old Regulars, the New Orleans legislative delegation, and rural Longites. Senator Grove Stafford almost disrupted their agreement when he objected to dedicating $1,750,000 of the proposed revenue to parish police juries. Nevertheless, the senate passed an amended version of the house sales tax (the senate would only support a 1 percent levy) with a 20–15 vote following a complex session filled with parliamentary points of order. The house concurred in the senate amendment the next day, thus giving Jones a source of revenue expected to yield about $6 million every two years.[37]

35. *Morning Advocate,* August 26, 1942; *States,* August 26, 1942.

36. *Morning Advocate,* August 26, 1942; *States,* August 26, 1942.

37. *States,* August 27–29, 1942; *Item,* August 27–28, 1942; *Official Journal of the Proceedings of the House of Representatives . . . at the Seventeenth Extraordinary Session . . . 1942,*

Typically, neither Jones nor Maestri could resist making political capital out of the results of the special session. Jones exulted that the opposition "has taken a political shellacking and they know it," and hoped that after the congressional primary "we can all settle down and give the people a breathing spell from partisan politics." Maestri, on the other hand, reminded Louisianians that Jones had originally considered a higher sales tax but that "the resistance of the city delegation and their country friends resulted in reducing this tax to 1 percent," with a proportionate saving to the voters.[38]

Even though the new sales tax began generating revenue at midnight on August 31 (after the legislature had given its final approval on August 29), Charity Hospital's troubles did not end instantly. Hospital superintendent Dr. Oliver P. Daly announced that while the infusion of revenue would allow an expansion of the hospital's capacity, it would not be possible to use all 3,300 beds until after the war because of the shortage of doctors, nurses, and other staff members.[39]

The records of the 1942 legislative sessions reveal that despite national and state calls for setting politics aside for the duration of the war, combative bifactionalism continued in Louisiana. If Sam Jones was correct in his later assessment that in 1940 the Longites were convinced that they had the votes to do as they pleased, but decided to cooperate with him in hopes of a share of the patronage, then by 1942 that prospect and its attendant spirit of cooperation was gone. Moreover, the rural Longites were even more resistant to rapprochement with Jones than were the Old Regulars. Senator Clements of Allen Parish, for example, was one of the fifteen senators who voted against the resuscitated sales tax in the extraordinary session, even after Cawthorn had abandoned his opposition to it. Clements also cast the lone dissenting vote against creating a war emergency revenue fund, which would channel sales tax receipts into the hospital, welfare, and school funds. Both sides went through the motions of

---

40–41; *House Calendar, Seventeenth Extraordinary Session, 1942,* 1–2; *Official Journal of the Proceedings of the Senate . . . at the Seventeenth Extraordinary Session . . . 1942,* 116–30.

   38. *Morning Advocate,* August 30, 1942.

   39. *States,* August 31, 1942; *Item,* August 31, 1942.

appealing for unity, but neither was willing to neglect its concerns. Each looked forward to the 1944 state campaign and attempted to establish a strong foundation for its appeal to the voters.

With Louisiana's fiscal problems solved more or less to his satisfaction, Sam Jones faced one more major challenge to his control of the state before the end of his administration—the infamous "little war" of 1943. The problem began when Plaquemines Parish sheriff L. D. Dauterive died on June 1, 1943. According to Jones and Attorney General Eugene Stanley, the constitution provided that when an official died with less than one year left to serve, the governor could appoint a successor to fill the office until the next regular election. The next election in this case was the statewide general election to be held on April 18, 1944 (thirty days after which the governor could issue a commission to the newly elected official). Jones and Stanley thus assumed that the governor was authorized to appoint Dauterive's successor. Plaquemines district attorney Leander Perez, a Longite since Huey's day and undisputed boss of the parish, thought otherwise. Dauterive, he claimed, had not filed his oath of office until June 14, 1940, so his term lasted until June 14, 1944, more than one year past his death. Therefore, Perez concluded, the constitution did not empower Jones to appoint a successor, but instead required him to call a special election to fill the vacancy. Perez's strained interpretation stemmed from his fear that Jones planned to appoint a sheriff who would oppose Perez and make for a difficult situation. It was also in direct contradiction of the terms of Perez's original appointment to public office as district judge in 1919; a dispute over that appointment had established the legality of the less-than-a-year appointment schedule.[40]

Perez had Plaquemines coroner Benjamin R. Slater sworn in as acting sheriff on June 2. According to the state constitution, however, Slater could only assume the sheriff's civil duties. Jones, after a frantic search for an anti-Perez man willing to challenge the boss, appointed Walter Blaize

---

40. Jeansonne, *Leander Perez,* 127–28; James Conaway, *Judge: The Life and Times of Leander Perez* (New York, 1973), 66; Robert Sherrill, *Gothic Politics in the Deep South: Stars of the New Confederacy* (New York, 1968), 15–16; Harnett T. Kane, *Deep Delta Country* (New York, 1944), 210; *Morning Advocate,* June 12, 1942.

as sheriff. Blaize, a Buras automobile repair shop owner, was a noted anti-Perez man who possessed the courage to run repeatedly on an anti-Perez platform and to experience defeat after defeat. Predictably, Slater refused to relinquish the office to Blaize, and Perez barricaded the courthouse at Pointe à la Hache.[41]

Jones, meanwhile, gathered a force of State Guardsmen in Baton Rouge, evidently hoping to frighten Perez into submission with an implied threat of invasion. But instead of being frightened, the pugnacious Perez gathered his own army. Evoking one of the new wartime laws that authorized local officials to call upon citizens to quell a public emergency, he created the Plaquemines Wartime Emergency Patrol, ostensibly to guard the parish coastline from German submarine attack, but in reality to keep Walter Blaize and the State Guard away from the courthouse.[42]

Confrontation seemed likely as the protagonists drew their armies around them, but the first clash occurred in court. (The little war was to generate numerous cases filed in various state and federal courts.) Jones initially filed a friendly suit against the supervisor of public funds and the collector of revenue, claiming that they had refused to yield their roles as temporary Plaquemines tax collectors to Blaize. This move allowed the administration to establish the legality of the governor's action in a district court other than the Plaquemines–St. Bernard district, which Perez dominated. Despite Perez's arguments that the Plaquemines deputy tax collector had never surrendered tax records to the state officials and therefore they could not have been expected to turn them over to Blaize, the Baton Rouge district court on June 18 ruled that Blaize's appointment was valid. To lend an additional stamp of authority to the decision, the defendants appealed the district court decision to the Louisiana Supreme Court, which upheld the lower court ruling on July 13.[43]

41. Jeansonne, *Leander Perez,* 128–29; Conaway, *Judge,* 66; *Morning Advocate,* June 12, 1943; *Times-Picayune,* June 12, 1943.

42. Jeansonne, *Leander Perez,* 130; Conaway, *Judge,* 66–67; *Times-Picayune,* June 9–11, 1943.

43. Jeansonne, *Leander Perez,* 131–32; *Morning Advocate,* July 15, 17, 1943; *Walter J. Blaize v. Jerome A. Hayes, Supervisor of Public Funds, Et Al.,* Supreme Court of Louisiana No. 37,190, Fournet Papers, LLMVC.

Blaize's legal right to the Plaquemines sheriff's post proved to be easier to obtain than physical possession of the office. His initial foray to Pointe à la Hache ended at the northern parish line, where he saw a group of deputies stopping vehicles at Braithwaite and inspecting occupants' identification before allowing them to enter the parish. Perez had the highway to Pointe à la Hache blocked in front of his house and traffic diverted through his yard, where he stationed his guards to detain undesirables. Blaize announced that he would not attempt to force his possession of the sheriff's office. "We're working on something else" was his evasive comment.[44]

In due time, Blaize and Jones had to resort to outright invasion. On October 8, 1943, by refusing Perez's application for a rehearing of its July 13 decision, the state supreme court effectively reiterated its decision that Blaize legally possessed the office. On October 9, Jones declared martial law in Plaquemines Parish and directed State Guard commander Brigadier General Thomas F. Porter to install Blaize in office. Perez obtained a restraining order from "his" district judge Albert Estopinal, Jr., prohibiting the Guard from installing Blaize, but it proved to be useless. The Guard gathered at Camp Pontchartrain in Orleans Parish, and Perez made last-minute preparations to repel them. One Plaquemines deputy reported that the courthouse was "bristling with machine guns" but also added significantly, "we don't have the men to shoot them if the going gets tough."[45]

The State Guard rolled into Plaquemines Parish early on the morning of October 9, 1943. They met only three pockets of resistance: several deputies met them at Braithwaite and attempted to serve Estopinal's court order, but they were arrested and the court order torn up; the highway before Perez's home was blocked by oil field equipment, which had to be removed; and oyster shells blocked the highway at the outskirts of Pointe à la Hache. As the caravan approached the courthouse, Perez and his followers abandoned the building after looting the sheriff's office and fled

44. Jeansonne, *Leander Perez,* 133–34; *Morning Advocate,* June 12, July 15, 1943.

45. Jeansonne, *Leander Perez,* 134; *Morning Advocate,* October 8–9, 1943; *Times-Picayune,* October 8–9, 1943.

on a ferry to the middle of the Mississippi River. Slater himself refused to leave the office and had to be carried from the building before Blaize could be installed in the wrecked room. One Slater deputy remarked that the lack of office equipment really did not matter because "I give Blaize two weeks in office. Then he will have to call the State Guard again."[46]

Threats of continued violence proved to be groundless. Blaize, the State Guard, and newspaper reporters who accompanied them had to cope with harassment from local citizens who spoke, whistled, sang into, or turned the crank on their old-fashioned telephones, thus disrupting contact with the outside world. A blackout left the courthouse without electricity while nearby residential customers continued receiving power, but no act of violence occurred.[47]

Jones and Porter soon removed all but a token two Guardsmen and one officer from Pointe à la Hache. Even though a surface quiet prevailed, Blaize was not effective as sheriff. He soon located missing tax records left behind in a locked courthouse safe, but made only desultory efforts to collect taxes. Meanwhile, Perez continued his battle against the state, filing as many as fifteen lawsuits at one time. The administration, in turn, fought back with lawsuits of its own, and filed impeachment proceedings against Perez and Estopinal.[48]

Louisiana's "little war" occurred against the backdrop of the 1943 statewide primary election campaign. In Plaquemines Parish, both Slater and Blaize qualified to run for sheriff. Not surprisingly, Slater, with Perez's help, defeated Blaize by an overwhelming margin, but his election did not end the controversy. It was not until October 4, 1944, that the state supreme court dismissed charges of conspiracy to commit murder brought against Jones and Attorney General Stanley, fraud charges against Stanley, and the impeachment proceedings against Perez and Es-

46. Jeansonne, *Leander Perez,* 135–36; Conaway, *Judge,* 72–76; *Morning Advocate,* October 10, 1943; *Times-Picayune/New Orleans States,* October 10, 1943.

47. Jeansonne, *Leander Perez,* 137–38; *Morning Advocate,* October 11–12, 16, 1943.

48. Jeansonne, *Leander Perez,* 137–40; *Morning Advocate,* October 16, November 1, 18, 1943; *Benjamin R. Slater v. Walter J. Blaize Et Al.,* Supreme Court of Louisiana No. 37,237, *Benjamin R. Slater v. Walter J. Blaize,* Supreme Court of Louisiana No. 37,341, Fournet Papers; *Congressional Record,* 78th Cong., 1st sess., 1943, vol. 89, pt. 12: A4598–A4600.

topinal. Most of these charges were dropped because of lack of evidence or because the points of law upon which they were based were moot since Jones, Stanley, and Blaize were now out of office. Even these dismissals did not end litigation in the case, however. On October 9, 1944, former Plaquemines deputy Joseph Cappielo sued Jones, Stanley, and eight others in federal court for injuries he allegedly suffered at the hand of the State Guard during the invasion. The final decision in the "little war" cases occurred on February 7, 1945, when the Fifth Circuit Court of Appeals in New Orleans upheld federal district judge Adrian J. Caillouet's dismissal of the suit for lack of jurisdiction.[49]

The Plaquemines incident was a reprehensible waste of precious fuel and manpower during wartime, but it should also be interpreted as part of the larger theme in Louisiana politics of continued bifactionalism. The thread of bitter division ran through Jones's administration, especially from 1942 on. The unnamed "oppositionist" senator who remarked during the 1942 regular session, "We don't expect to get bills we really want. . . . We're just concentrating on keeping Jones from getting what he wants," accurately summarized the situation. The reluctance of the 1942 regular-session legislators to pass the sales tax while increasing state expenditures stemmed not only from their philosophical opposition to a regressive sales tax (even though many of them had supported Leche's sales tax in 1936), but also from the Longites' desire to put Jones in an uncomfortable position. The bitter last-ditch stand by country Longites against the sales tax in the 1942 extraordinary session likewise revealed a continued bifactionalism. Then the "little war" exploded across the news reports of the state as a major challenge to Sam Jones. He won the battle, installing Walter Blaize as sheriff, but he lost the war. Leander Perez reestablished an iron control over Plaquemines Parish that was never successfully challenged until his death in 1969.[50]

As his administration drew to a close in early 1944, Sam Jones judged that he achieved much success. He had fulfilled, he said, 43 of 45 cam-

49. *Morning Advocate,* October 10, 1944, February 8, 1945.
50. *Item,* June 26, 1942; *Morning Advocate,* October 16, 1943; Jeansonne, *Leander Perez,* 141; Kane, *Deep Delta Country,* 213; Sherrill, *Gothic Politics,* 17.

paign promises made in 1939, and had failed to eliminate the sales tax and to provide old-age pensions at the level he anticipated only because of Longite obstructionism. In fact, Jones left a mixed legacy. As Allan Sindler observes, many of the reformers, expecting a renewal of John M. Parker's holy war against machine politics, stood aghast as they witnessed Jones reaching understandings with Noe and Maestri as needed to implement his reforms. At the same time, Jones disappointed Longites by not mindlessly assaulting Longism's social services, as they had expected.[51]

Perhaps it required the shock of Huey Long to focus conservative Louisiana's attention on poor people's problems, but Jones aptly demonstrated that by 1940–44, conservative Louisiana had learned its lesson. He fully realized by 1940 that it was not possible in Louisiana for an anti-Longite gubernatorial candidate to campaign openly and sincerely against public services and expect to be elected. This practical realization marked a new maturity and political realism in the anti-Long ranks. No longer would conservatives propose dismantling Long's social programs. By the early 1940s, Huey Long's philosophy of providing social services had become so institutionalized that debate no longer focused on whether the state should provide them, but instead on how much money it should spend on them. Even so, the reformers were still not as comfortable as the Longites in spending large sums of money on many of Long's favorite programs. "My pappy was for Huey," Jones reminded the voters, but it was not until he was in office that the anti-Long reformers had a chance to prove their ability to provide many of Longism's services without the accompanying corruption and dictatorial political apparatus.

Sam Jones learned much about politics during his four years as governor: the necessity of forming alliances with people not normally considered allies, the demands for patronage, the frustration of being unable to save a legislative program from defeat, and the desertion of friends. He remarked on inauguration day in 1944 that "all of the saints were not in my political faction, and all of the sinners were not in the opposing fac-

51. *Shreveport Times,* December 11, 1943; *Morning Advocate,* December 11, 14, 1943; *Sam Jones Report to the People,* December, 1943; Barney Krebs to "Mr. Healy," n.d., deLesseps Story Morrison Papers, HTML.

tion." Despite his setbacks, however, Jones provided a "progressive conservatism" that Sindler accurately maintains "became impressed upon large numbers of voters . . . as a reasonable alternative to the buccaneering liberalism of the Longs."[52]

Since 1898, Louisiana's constitutions had forbidden the governor to succeed himself. As Jones therefore prepared to leave office and return to his Lake Charles law practice, anti-Longites sought a candidate to take up the reform banner, while Longites regrouped for a strong attempt to grasp again the levers of power.

52. Sindler, *Huey Long's Louisiana,* 177–80; *Shreveport Times,* May 10, 1944.

5

The Emergence of Jimmie Davis

Speculation about the 1943–44 gubernatorial campaign in Louisiana focused on two questions: would the anti-Longites retain state government offices they had won in 1940, and would United States involvement in World War II have an effect on the campaign?

Sam Jones did not openly endorse a successor to carry on his reforms. Instead, he broadcast a series of ten radio addresses in December 1943 underscoring the benefits provided by his anti-Longite administration. Even though he wanted a reformer to follow him into office, Jones's political principles would not allow him to name a successor. Such activity would contribute to the appearance of his building a political machine, an image that he, arch foe of Huey Long's machine, could not afford.[1]

Even though Jones did not publicly involve himself in the campaign, it was an open secret throughout Louisiana that he wanted Public Service Commissioner Jimmie Davis of Shreveport to succeed him despite his misgivings about Davis's ability to govern the state. He was "not a good candidate," Jones later recalled of Davis, "but he was a good campaigner."[2]

The governor sent two emissaries, Prescott Foster and Louisiana high-

---

1. *Morning Advocate,* March 10, 1944; Sam Jones to Denny Daugherty, July 22, 1970, Daugherty Collection, LLMVC; *Sam Jones Report to the People,* 1943.

2. Sam Jones, interview by Godfrey, February 1977, LSU Oral History Collection.

way department director D. Y. Smith, to Shreveport to discuss a possible candidacy with Davis, but Davis declined to see them because he did not want a higher office. Soon after, however, Davis attended a Public Service Commission meeting in Baton Rouge, and Lee Laycock, clerk of the house of representatives, persuaded him to meet with the governor. During their informal meeting, Jones told Davis that he was in favor of Davis's becoming a candidate. Davis, however, remained reluctant to run for governor, fearing the potential for scandal associated with the oil business and for unpopularity if he decided to supersede local officials and prosecute gamblers in the state. He feared that he had too little experience with the oil business to understand its complexities and could thus enmesh himself unwittingly in improper agreements. He also recognized the popularity of gambling, especially in south Louisiana. Jones reassured Davis that the Mineral Board insulated the governor from the oil business, and as for gambling, "I guess the best thing on that subject is just to let [local officials] handle their own business," a statement that reveals Jones's acceptance of political reality and the "art of the possible" in reforming Louisiana.[3]

The fundamental reason behind Jones's lack of public support for Davis remains unclear. Gus Weill maintains (based on Davis's recollection) that Davis told the reformers at a meeting at the governor's mansion that he would not accept their offers to campaign for him because "I don't believe the people will go for the show of a lot of power." Jones, however, maintained that the decision was his and that he refrained from campaigning because he had no plans to construct a machine. The important specters overhanging both interpretations are those of the Longite machine and its Louisiana Scandals of 1939. The deep impression made by the Scandals on Louisiana politics is amply illustrated by the determination of Jones and Davis to avoid any hint of connection to a powerful political organization. The Scandals made it imperative that they avoid the appearance of machine tactics. In addition, Jones's failure to endorse Davis, as Allan Sindler explains, allowed Davis to attract cross-factional

---

3. Gus Weill, *You Are My Sunshine: The Jimmie Davis Story* (Waco, Tex., 1977), 61–63.

support that might not have been possible had he publicly enjoyed strong support from Jones.[4]

Davis, one of eleven children, was born sometime around the beginning of the twentieth century. His birth was not recorded. His father was a tenant farmer in the tiny community of Beech Springs in rural Jackson Parish. The area shared many traits with neighboring Winn Parish. Both locales were inhabited by heavily Anglo-Saxon Protestant populations wresting a living from the inferior hill soil. "We were the same kind of people as those at Winnfield," Davis later wrote. "My Dad farmed—cotton . . . peanuts, corn, hay, and watermelons."[5]

Davis graduated from Beech Springs High School in 1920 and from Louisiana College, a small Baptist institution in Pineville, in 1924. He returned to Beech Springs High as a teacher and coach for two years before entering Louisiana State University, from which he received a master of education degree in 1927.[6]

Following his LSU graduation, Davis taught social studies at Dodd College, a Baptist women's school in Shreveport, and began a professional music career, writing country songs and performing on Shreveport radio station KWKH for five dollars per week. His regional success led to recording contracts with nationally known labels. Early hits included "Nobody's Darling But Mine," recorded in 1934, and "You Are My Sunshine," recorded in 1939. The latter became his signature song for the remainder of his public life. Davis's entertainment career introduced him in nontraditional ways to Louisiana voters. In 1944 Merle Weigel of Amite wrote to her soldier-husband, "What do you think about Jimmie

4. *Ibid.,* 64; *Morning Advocate,* March 10, 1944; Jones to Daugherty, July 22, 1970; Sindler, *Huey Long's Louisiana,* 182–83.

5. Weill, *You Are My Sunshine,* 8–10; Jimmie Davis, "Country Music Is Part of the People," *Louisiana Heritage,* summer 1969, 17; Sobel and Raimo, *Biographical Directory of the Governors of the United States,* vol. 2, 588.

6. Weill, *You Are My Sunshine,* 35–36; *Shreveport Times,* May 9, 1944; Morgan Peoples, "The Sunshine Governor from Jackson Parish" (paper presented to the Louisiana Historical Association Annual Convention, March 25, 1983); *The Pine Knot* (Louisiana College, 1924), Keatchie-Mt. Lebanon Collection, RWNL; Jimmie Davis, televised interview by Gus Weill, Louisiana Public Broadcasting, April 9, 1984.

Davis for our Governor?" and added, "The first time I ever heard him was on a 'Juke Box' at Felders."[7]

Davis entered public office in 1929, as clerk of the Shreveport city court. In 1938 he defeated two opponents, one backed by the Longites, to become Shreveport's Public Safety Commissioner. During this campaign he discovered the effectiveness of using his band to attract a crowd, a tactic he used to good advantage during the 1943–44 governor's race. Davis also made use of his singing ability to sell Shreveport on public safety. His talks on traffic safety to schoolchildren included his renditions of several ballads.[8]

In 1942, he began a movie career in the musical *Strictly in the Groove*. That appearance led to other roles, usually as the leading man's best friend in "B" western films. Also in 1942, he defeated Longite John S. Patton for the Louisiana Public Service Commission Third District seat. By 1943, therefore, when the reformers were casting about for a gubernatorial candidate, they found that Jimmie Davis was widely known through his entertaining, was not only electable but also had defeated two Longites, and possessed a personality and soothing campaign style that kept him from accumulating many political scars.[9]

Davis's statement of his candidacy revealed that he planned to run a harmonizing campaign. He called for the retention of "all constructive legislation of all past administrations," including Longite programs such as adequate old-age pensions, free school books, continued road construction, and access to health care. He also endorsed reform programs for civil service and proper accounting of state finances.[10]

7. Weill, *You Are My Sunshine,* 47–49; Davis, "Country Music Is Part of the People," 16–17; Peoples, "The Sunshine Governor"; S. A. Wilkins, "Dodd College: A Brief History," *North Louisiana Historical Association Journal,* summer 1980, 29–30; Jimmie Davis, interview by Weill, Louisiana Public Broadcasting, April 16, 1984; Merle Weigel to H. S. Weigel, March 3, 1944, Weigel Papers, LLMVC.

8. Weill, *You Are My Sunshine,* 49, 54–55; *Morning Advocate,* September 12, 1943; *Louisiana Municipal Review,* March–April 1941, 61.

9. Weill, *You Are My Sunshine,* 57–60; *Times-Picayune,* April 8, 1943; *Morning Advocate,* December 28, 1943.

10. *Morning Advocate,* August 29, September 12, 1943; *Times-Picayune/New Orleans States,* September 12, 1943; *Shreveport Times,* September 12, 1943.

Davis's efforts to be noncontroversial should not be confused with neutrality. He recalled in 1983 that the strength of Huey Long's dictatorship and the Louisiana Scandals had convinced him that Louisiana needed four more years of reform. He had hoped, however, to transcend faction: "We had a lot of dissension," he said in 1983. "I wanted to get those people together. I said I didn't care if they were Long or anti-Long . . . I wanted them to be a Davis man"—a remark that brought to mind his pledge of 1943, "I shall do all in my power to bury the hates and distrusts of the past and raise the curtain that will let in the sunshine of Louisiana's future greatness."[11]

The Longites, meanwhile, splintered as they tried to select their candidate for governor. James A. Noe announced in January 1943 that he planned to run, but he withdrew from the race when his campaign failed to attract adequate support.[12]

The major split within Longite ranks occurred between the New Orleans Old Regulars and the country Longites from north Louisiana. To combat the Old Regulars, the country Longites created the Louisiana Democratic Organization (LDO) at a conference held at Hotel Bentley in Alexandria in February 1943. The LDO was distinct from the established Longite Louisiana Democratic Association (LDA), which had essentially merged with the Old Regulars after Sam Jones won the governorship. The LDO was also strongly anti-Jones, but its primary purpose was to outmuscle the Old Regulars and obtain the Longite gubernatorial nomination for a candidate from outside New Orleans. Alexandria businessman J. A. Blackman, LDO chair for the Eighth Congressional District, maintained that the Longites had to nominate either James A. Noe, Earl Long, or Ernest Clements for governor.[13]

None of these three, however, commanded enough support to claim the nomination. Long enjoyed support from state employees thrown out of office by the reformers and from rural areas. Labor leaders preferred

11. *Morning Advocate,* September 12, 1943; *Town Talk,* May 22, 1983.

12. *Morning Advocate,* January 14, September 19, 1943; *Town Talk,* September 18, 1943; *Times-Picayune,* September 19, 1943.

13. *Morning Advocate,* June 14, 1943; *Shreveport Times,* July 29, 1943; *Town Talk,* August 23, 1943.

Clements. Noe's candidacy had attracted inadequate support to obtain the nomination. Maestri and the Old Regulars thus held a key bloc of power with respect to the of Longite nomination.[14]

Maestri kept his own counsel as delegations of Longites sought some sign of Old Regular preference. Michael Kurtz and Morgan Peoples maintain that the mayor thought it better to support a losing candidate for governor than to elevate Earl Long to a post from which he would have the power to destroy Maestri just as Huey had destroyed Mayor T. Semmes Walmsley.[15]

The LDO endorsed Long in early September after he agreed to support the organization's platform, which included planks calling for the abolition of unnecessary state departments (especially the new Finance Department), a twelve-month pay plan for schoolteachers, a retirement system for teachers after thirty years' service, an increase in old-age pensions to thirty dollars per month, the lowering of the voting age in state elections to eighteen, and the organization of a constitutional convention "to remedy ills and defects in our present system of laws." Many of these initiatives, including the education and voting-age reforms, resembled planks in a platform that Long had been promulgating since March.[16] His influence within the LDO was undeniable.

As he opened his campaign for the Democratic nomination with a statewide radio address, Long sought to attract a key element in the reform coalition when he assured businessmen that his experience as a lawyer, farmer, and livestock producer qualified him to understand their needs. He tried to quell immediately any doubts about his honesty: "I have yet to find any man who could point the finger of suspicion at me for breach of the public trust." He dismissed the Jones administration as "one of the saddest failures in the history of Louisiana," warned that Jimmie Davis would "turn this state government back to Sam Jones and his henchmen for the next four years," and called Davis a "banjo-picking song and dance man."[17]

14. *Town Talk,* August 24, 1943.

15. Kurtz and Peoples, *Earl K. Long,* 119–20.

16. *Morning Advocate,* March 28, 1943; *Town Talk,* August 24, September 6, 1943.

17. *Morning Advocate,* September 15, 1943; *Times-Picayune,* September 15, 1943; *States,* September 15, 1943.

The confusion within the Longites faction over which candidate to support increased when U.S. senator Allen J. Ellender announced on September 15, 1943, that he was "seriously considering" running for governor at the behest of Longites who thought that only he could unite the faction. Ellender insisted on one nonnegotiable provision: all other Longites must withdraw from the race so that he could concentrate on attacking the reformers.[18]

Rumors circulated in New Orleans that the Old Regulars had decided to support Ellender for governor and Ernest Clements for lieutenant governor, but Ellender encountered trouble on two fronts. Other Longites refused to withdraw from the race, and William L. Donnels, editor of the state labor newspaper, announced that organized labor was "unalterably opposed" to him. "If the Old Regulars endorse Ellender," he said, "we will work for his defeat. If he runs for governor, we'll snow him under." Donnels attended an Old Regular caucus and delivered a resolution, passed at a labor rally, calling on Ellender to stay in Washington.[19]

Ellender's estrangement from organized labor apparently stemmed from his dislike of labor leaders, whom he considered to be dictatorial. Moreover, he had voted for the Smith-Connally (War Labor Disputes) Act in 1943, which authorized presidential seizure of war plants on strike, thus further incurring the wrath of labor unions.[20]

The collapse of Ellender's boomlet left Earl Long and the Old Regulars contending for control of the nomination. On September 20, it was rumored in New Orleans that they had agreed to create a virtual "co-governorship." The terms provided that Long would abandon his gubernatorial aspirations in exchange for Old Regular support for him as lieutenant governor on a ticket led by Lewis Morgan of St. Tammany Parish; in re-

18. *Morning Advocate,* September 16, 22, 1943; *States,* September 21, 1943; *Times-Picayune,* September 21, 1943; *Town Talk,* September 21, 1943.

19. *States,* September 29, October 1, 1943; *Times-Picayune,* October 1, 1943; Thomas A. Becnel, *Labor, Church, and the Sugar Establishment: Louisiana, 1887–1976* (Baton Rouge, 1980), 24–27.

20. Becnel, *Labor, Church, and the Sugar Establishment,* 24–27; Becnel, *Senator Allen Ellender,* 122–23, 126.

turn, Long would receive control of all state jobs and state government activities north of Alexandria.[21]

Besides Morgan for governor and Long for lieutenant governor, the Longite ticket included Wade O. Martin, Jr., for secretary of state, Joe T. Cawthorn for attorney general, E. J. Bourg for state auditor, John B. Daigle for state treasurer, Lucille May Grace for registrar of state lands, Harry D. Wilson for commissioner of agriculture, and Lether Frazar for superintendent of education. Long's demotion to second place on the ticket bruised his ego and caused difficulties later in the campaign.[22]

Lewis Morgan was a sixty-seven-year-old St. Tammany Parish native who graduated from Tulane University, served on the parish school board, in the Louisiana house of representatives, and as district attorney for St. Tammany and Washington Parishes. He served as Louisiana's Sixth District United States representative from 1912 until 1917, when he retired to private law practice. He returned to state government in 1929 as counsel for the Highway Commission and had represented LSU during the Scandals investigation.[23]

Both Morgan's age and a heart condition made him vulnerable to charges that he was weak and ineffectual. In addition, some of Earl Long's friends supported their hero for lieutenant governor but deserted Morgan. Long later maintained that the ticket would have been successful at the polls if only the Longites had tapped him to run for governor rather than relegating him to the second spot.

Morgan and Davis were the major candidates in the race, but other candidates joined the fray. Sixth District U.S. representative James H. Morrison had announced his candidacy in August. This campaign was not as colorful as his 1939–40 effort. There was no Convict Parade this time; Morrison offered instead a "Victory Parade," a pale copy that lacked the vitality and timeliness of the original. Louisianians, Morrison

21. *States,* September 21, 1943.

22. *States,* October 23, 1943; *Morning Advocate,* October 26, 28, 1943; *Times-Picayune,* October 28, 1943.

23. *Town Talk,* August 27, 1943; *Morning Advocate,* August 28, October 17, 26, 1943; *Times-Picayune/New Orleans States,* October 17, 1943; *States,* October 23–24, 1943; *Times-Picayune,* October 28, 1943.

thought, wanted neither Jones's reforms nor a return to Longite control, but instead desired "new blood, youth, aggressiveness, and ability to get the job done." After losing in the first Democratic primary, he endorsed Morgan in the second.[24]

The fourth major candidate for the Democratic nomination was Shreveport mayor Sam S. Caldwell. Caldwell, a three-term mayor, focused on a promise to "return home rule to every parish and to every city in the state," freeing them "from domination from Baton Rouge." He also maintained that he wanted to unite all political factions, even though Earl Long labeled him a "trial balloon for Sam Jones." (Caldwell's reply: "I have no time to waste on dead politicians nor ammunition to waste on chattering sparrows.") Caldwell eventually formed a ticket with state senator Frank B. Ellis as the candidate for lieutenant governor.[25]

The first primary in January 1944 also saw four minor candidates: state senators Ernest Clements and Dudley LeBlanc, Opelousas lawyer Vincent Moseley, and editor of the *Amite News Digest,* Lee Lanier. These candidates spent most of their time trying to prove that they were serious contenders.[26]

The campaign began in earnest in late September. Sam Caldwell launched his campaign on the 30th with promises for a strong system of public health, aid to farmers, education and employment for returning servicemen, conservation of the state's water resources, and twelve-month pay for public school teachers.[27]

Davis opened his run two weeks later with a state-wide radio address in which he proclaimed that "until the [world] war is won, there can be no other vital issue," but also went on to outline his plans for Louisiana's future. He proposed bringing marginal farmland into food production,

24. *Morning Advocate,* April 29, August 15, December 7, 1943; *Times-Picayune/New Orleans States,* October 22, 1943; James H. Morrison, interview by author, May 13, 1982.

25. *Shreveport Times,* July 29, August 1, October 26, 1943; *Morning Advocate,* July 29–30, 1943; *States,* October 25, 1943.

26. *Times-Picayune,* September 23, October 22, December 16, 1943, January 5, 1944; *Shreveport Times,* September 23, 1943, January 16, 1944; *Morning Advocate,* October 30, December 22, 1943, January 16, 1944.

27. *Morning Advocate,* October 1, 1943.

while at the same time calling for increased industrialization to ease the state's economic dependence on agriculture. He reiterated his political independence, promised to conduct a "positive" campaign, and closed with a rendition of "You Are My Sunshine," a practice that became a standard feature of his campaign appearances.[28]

Davis also broadened his ticket's appeal in October when Iberia Parish insurance agent J. Emile Verret signed on as the candidate for lieutenant governor. Davis, recognizing his weakness as a north Louisiana Protestant in Catholic south Louisiana, sought a running mate from the southern part of the state. Davis in this instance followed the example of Sam Jones. Jones had been a native of Beauregard Parish, which is geographically but not culturally in south Louisiana, and had chosen Lafayette physician Marc Mouton as his running mate in 1939 to bolster his appeal in the French areas of the state, and subsequently retained Verret in the role in his unsuccessful 1948 campaign for the governorship.[29]

Verret undoubtedly increased Davis's chances of carrying south Louisiana. He was born on a farm at Loureauville, near New Iberia on September 13, 1886, and graduated from Southwestern Louisiana Institute (now the University of Southwestern Louisiana). He had worked as an assistant overseer and store clerk, invested in sugarcane land and a sugar mill, and then entered the insurance business. He obtained his political experience on the Iberia Parish School Board to which he was elected in 1912. He became president of the board in 1914 and held that post until 1944. In addition, he was president of the Louisiana School Boards Association in 1942, giving him a network of political contacts throughout the state.[30]

28. *Town Talk,* October 15, 1943; *Shreveport Times,* October 15, 1943; *Morning Advocate,* October 15, 1943.

29. "Speech Delivered by Governor James H. Davis, Rotary Banquet, Held June 6, 1945," transcript, "Address" (1943), transcript, and "Biography of J. Emile Verret, Candidate for Lieutenant-Governor on the Sam Jones Ticket" (1948), J. Emile Verret Papers, DL.

30. "Biography of J. Emile Verret, Lieutenant-Governor of Louisiana, 1944–1948," typescript, Verret Papers; *Shreveport Times,* October 30, 1943; *Times-Picayune,* January 26, 1944.

Davis completed a bobtailed ticket in late October. His slate included himself, Verret, Fred LeBlanc of Baton Rouge for attorney general, and James Gremillion of Crowley for secretary of state. Davis then spent November spreading his "You Are My Sunshine" philosophy in a campaign that was part political rally and part north Louisiana tent revival. He called for less state government interference with local governments and pledged a comprehensive program to conserve the state's exhaustible natural resources. The latter program was an old favorite of Sam Jones, who had envisioned a vast industrial boom in post-war Louisiana fueled by cheap natural gas. Davis also promised to provide college programs or trade school training to returning war veterans, wholeheartedly endorsed civil service, and adopted Jones's proposals to develop Louisiana as the "air hub of the two Americas."[31]

In a self-professed role as peacemaker, Davis acknowledged that Louisianians appreciated improvements in the state, no matter whose administration instituted them. He therefore incorporated some Longite measures into his campaign: more adequate old-age pensions, increased services for the poor and dependent, and creation of a preventive medicine program. He couched the last proposal in economic terms. It cost the state less, he said, to keep a poor person well than to treat an illness. No matter how he presented these proposals, though, their inclusion in his platform showed how entrenched the Longite philosophy of state services was in Louisiana. Even as he promised state benefits, however, Davis acknowledged that the scarcity of goods and manpower caused by the war necessarily limited the services he expected his administration to provide. I could "promise you the moon with a fence around it," he told an audience in Sunset, but "I wouldn't do that . . . because my policy on promises has always been 'if you can't fulfill them, don't make them.' "[32]

Davis also cast his campaign as a crusade. He wanted, he said, to make the governor and the citizens of the state into "good friends." When asked why his band appeared with him on the political stage, Davis re-

31. *Times-Picayune,* November 3, 15, 18, 1943; *Morning Advocate,* November 16, 18, 28, 1943; *Town Talk,* November 17, 1943.

32. *Town Talk,* November 17, 1943; *Morning Advocate,* November 19, 29, 1943.

plied, "We always found [at Beech Springs] that people who liked to gather around the organ or music box and sing [were good friends] and that's what the people of Louisiana want to be with their governor—good friends." He repeated many times that "our meetings are friendly and happy. We are trying to spread sunshine and good will as we go along."[33]

While Jimmie Davis administered soothing homilies to the voters, Lewis Morgan spent November combatting rumors about his ill health and attempting to reduce the bitterness engendered by the bruising fight for the Longite nomination. He opened the Longite campaign in Baton Rouge on November 3 with a speech in which he promised a "sane and economical" administration, no use of state power to harass individuals, and freedom of parishes from state control. Serious injuries incurred when a heater exploded in his Covington home soon removed him temporarily from campaigning, and the Longite ticket embarked on a tour of the state without him.[34]

James A. Noe's appearance at Longite rallies in Monroe and West Monroe revived the issue of the Scandals. The *New Orleans States* recounted charges hurled between Long and Noe during the 1939–40 campaign and asked, "If Earl Long is what Jimmy Noe said he was, why does Mr. Noe support him? If Mr. Noe is the kind of character Earl Long said he was, why does he accept his support?" An even more relevant question, the *States* mused, was "why Mr. Morgan as head of the Maestri ticket accepts the support of either of them."[35]

U.S. senator John Overton partially answered this question early in 1944 when he announced that he had been "stabbed in the back" by his Longite friends. According to Overton, Noe had abandoned his 1943–44 gubernatorial candidacy in exchange for a place for his protégé, Joe Cawthorn, on the ticket and promises by Long and the Old Regulars to abandon Overton and support Noe in the 1944 U.S. Senate race. The breach between Overton and the other Longites was healed before the second Democratic primary and caused only a minor stir in the cam-

33. *Morning Advocate,* November 20, 1943; *Times-Picayune,* November 10, 1943.
34. *Morning Advocate,* November 4, 1943; *Times-Picayune,* November 8, 1943.
35. *States,* November 9, 1943.

paign, but it revealed the probable cause for Noe's withdrawal of his candidacy.[36]

Morgan returned to active campaigning on November 11, declaring that his health was good, that he was able to serve "every single moment of a four year term," and that he was not merely a "stalking horse" for Earl Long. He stressed the importance of his governmental experience during wartime and asked, "When, before, has maturity . . . been a matter which one must attempt to excuse, to vindicate, to live down?"[37]

Morgan unveiled a typically Longite platform of public services in late November. In the area of health care, he proposed well-equipped trailers to provide free dental care, free ambulance service in each parish, traveling tuberculosis-screening clinics, and an improved system of charity hospitals. For general economic and educational improvement, he called for additional work scholarships for students, a trade school in every parish, increased pay for school bus drivers and teachers, rebuilding of farm-to-market roads, improving main highways, hiring Louisiana natives for state jobs, and providing thirty-dollar monthly old-age pensions. Patriotic, conservation, and good-government plans included lending every effort toward winning the war, reclaiming wastelands, stocking streams regularly with fish, teaching reforestation in high schools and colleges, and instituting civil service.[38]

Sam Caldwell attempted to tie his campaign to the war effort in November with a proposed "Louisiana Charter," inspired by the Atlantic Charter agreement between President Franklin Roosevelt and British prime minister Winston Churchill. The Louisiana Charter, he said, would include "freedom from graft and corruption, political bosses, from those who could exploit our state for selfish gain, from inefficiency, waste, extravagance, punitive and vindictive legislation, bigotry, intolerance, bureaucrats, and dictators or control from whatever source it may come." He received several major newspaper endorsements during the month.[39]

36. *Morning Advocate,* January 6, February 16, 1944; *Shreveport Times,* January 6, 1944.

37. *States,* November 12, 26, 1943; *Shreveport Times,* November 12, 1943; *Morning Advocate,* November 28, 1943.

38. *Times-Picayune,* November 28, 1943.

39. *Shreveport Times,* November 5, 7, 28, 1943; *Times-Picayune,* November 5, 11, 1943; *States,* November 5, 1943; Sindler, *Huey Long's Louisiana,* 183–84.

James Morrison's early campaign focused on two themes: establishing himself as the only true Huey Long man in the race and protecting himself from charges of corruption. Forget Morgan and Davis, both products of machine politics, he said, and elect me, because "it is my hope to fight the battle for the people, just as Huey did."[40]

Morrison had to fight charges of his own political impropriety because of electioneering letters he inserted in the *Congressional Record,* then mailed to Louisiana voters using his congressional frank. One letter stressed his support of President Roosevelt, and another recounted the "thousands" of mistakes in family allotment checks received from servicemen that he helped to correct and also cases in which he tried to help worried family members locate a missing or wounded serviceman. He also inserted letters directed to "Dear Fellow Elected Officials" and "Dear School Bus Driver," as well as his response to a letter of inquiry (obviously contrived) from Alfred Bateman, manager of the Ascension Farmers' Cooperative Association, in which Morrison detailed forty ways in which he had helped his district or the state.[41]

Postal officials announced before the first primary that Morrison was within his rights to insert material in the *Congressional Record* and then frank it to his state. Morrison, they added, used his own funds to pay the duplication costs for the copies mailed to Louisiana.[42] Even though he was cleared of any improper behavior, the investigation provided an aura of questionable ethics that his opponents exploited.

Ernest Clements began his campaign by attacking Morgan and Davis as "hand picked" candidates and urging voters to "show the Maestri and Jones gangs in New Orleans that the people in the country don't want them to hand-pick candidates and cram them down your throats." He also unveiled a decidedly rural Longite platform calling for extensions of mail and school bus routes, restocking of lakes and woods with wildlife,

40. *Morning Advocate,* November 20, 1943; *States,* November 22, 1943; *Shreveport Times,* November 28, 1943.

41. *Congressional Record,* 78th Cong., 2d sess., 1944, vol. 90, pt. 10: A3267, A3348–49, A3598; *Times-Picayune,* November 18, 1943, January 8, 1944.

42. *States,* December 31, 1943.

protection of trappers and fishermen, as well as pensions and "rehabilitation" for needy World War II veterans.[43]

In a series of north Louisiana speeches during early December, Caldwell attacked Davis on the grounds that his singing career added nothing to his political experience. "Do the people of Louisiana want to become the laughing stock of other states?" he asked. "If so, all they must do is to elect a crooner of sweet nothings to the highest and most dignified office within their gift." Or, as he said more bitingly later, "If we must have an entertainer to lead us in these [perilous times], then let's send to Hollywood and get a good one."[44]

Davis, meanwhile, continued his relaxed campaign style and received the endorsement of several New Orleans newspapers. An appearance in Shreveport in early December included a brief recapitulation of his life, general suggestions for various improvements needed in the state, a comment that if the constantly warring peoples of Europe would "gather 'round the organ, take the old fiddle down from the fireplace and sing a while, there would be less trouble in the world," and a music program interspersed with political comments. He sang one of his songs entitled "Live and Let Live" and remarked that the attitude suggested by the lyrics "would be a good policy for any governor."[45]

Davis's campaign received a boost during late December when Theodore Hotard, president of the Orleans Parish School Board, and Samuel J. Boylan, tax assessor for the Fifth Municipal District (Algiers), both members of the Old Regular faction, bolted the Morgan ticket to support him. A *Times-Picayune* editorial applauded their action, reminded readers about the Scandals, and called the Old Regular endorsement of Morgan and Long "a flat defiance of the public will and the public interest."[46]

Not all went well for Davis, however. The *Shreveport Times* attacked him as "Absentee Ace" Davis, recounting excessive absences from

43. *States,* November 15, 25, 1943; *Times-Picayune,* November 15, 1943.

44. *Shreveport Times,* December 9, 1943; *Morning Advocate,* December 11, 1943.

45. *Times-Picayune/New Orleans States,* December 5, 1943; *Shreveport Times,* December 15, 1943.

46. *Times-Picayune/New Orleans States,* December 26, 1943; *Times-Picayune,* December 27, 1943.

Shreveport city commission council meetings when he was commissioner of public safety. "He didn't have much time at home those days," the newspaper noted, "what with going east to make juke box records, eyeing Hollywood, and keeping the old hill-billy band tuned up for 'come election time.' "[47]

Sam Caldwell charged that speeches attributed to Davis in newspapers were "but figments of the imagination of his roving press agent." Caldwell reported that one of his friends attended a Davis rally during which the candidate acted as master of ceremonies, sang, and mumbled a few "inaudible words." Caldwell's friend was surprised to read in the next day's newspapers that Davis had "discussed reforestation and the lumber industry in the manner of an expert."[48]

Caldwell's accessory, the *Shreveport Times,* immediately joined in the attack. The newspaper charged that Davis's press agents filed reports that he made wide-ranging erudite speeches on various subjects, when, in fact, he had not done so. The newspaper also disclosed that wartime shortages of gasoline, tires, and manpower created the opportunity for misrepresentation by causing newspapers that normally assigned reporters to travel with each major candidate to rely instead on reports wired in by the candidate's organization. The *Times* reported later that because of its revelation of fraudulent reports from the Davis camp, the Associated Press no longer quoted his reports directly.[49]

The charges that Davis or his agents recounted more complete speeches than he actually made were probably true. During the 1947–48 gubernatorial campaign Dave McGuire reported to candidate Sam Jones that the *Times-Picayune* refused to take "road quotes" from candidates "because they were so badly burned by phony reporting during the 1944 Davis campaign."[50]

The Longite ticket achieved a rare unity during December. Morgan reiterated his campaign pledges in speeches throughout the state and

47. *Shreveport Times,* December 8, 1943.

48. *Morning Advocate,* December 10, 1943.

49. *Shreveport Times,* December 17, 29, 1943.

50. Dave McGuire to Sam Jones, October 27, 1947, deLesseps Story Morrison Papers, HTML.

promised full support to civil service. He also attacked Sam Jones, remarking that the governor had created a surplus in the state treasury by neglecting the needs of the people and repairs to state roads and buildings. He also charged that some anti-Longites told state employees to "put Davis over if you want to hold your jobs."[51]

Lieutenant-governor candidate Long appeared with Morgan throughout the month and joined his attacks on the reformers, calling on voters to reject the "Jones-Davis do-nothing" ticket and return liberal government to the state. He also charged that one of Davis's contracts required him to be in Hollywood for several months each year and that Louisiana would have only a part-time governor if voters elected him. He joined in the accusations that Davis did not deliver the speeches credited to him and added that the speeches attributed to Davis were actually written by Sam Jones's publicity agents.[52]

New Orleans mayor Robert Maestri limited his role to speaking at Longite rallies in the city and in Algiers, where he commanded some political support and so was not likely to stir up resentment from rural Longite voters. Maestri maintained that some legislation claimed by the reformers had actually been passed with the help of the Old Regulars. Even though he confined his campaign appearances to his New Orleans base, Maestri had to defend himself against anti-Longite charges that he was trying to establish himself as dictator by endorsing Morgan.[53]

James Morrison and anti-Longites attacked Morgan during the final weeks of the campaign. Morrison stressed that Morgan, "a fine old gentleman," was nevertheless, "71 years old with a weak heart and bad health." The *Shreveport Times* charged that Morgan's pledge to build a vocational school in every parish was designed to provide work for his friends who were building contractors. The *Times-Picayune* dredged up the Scandals yet again, intimating that even though "so far as we know,

51. *Morning Advocate,* December 2, 7, 11–12, 1943; *Shreveport Times,* December 12, 1943.

52. *Morning Advocate,* December 2, 5, 11–12, 1943; *Shreveport Times,* December 12, 22, 1943.

53. *Item,* December 13, 1943; *States,* December 23, 1943; *Times-Picayune,* January 13, 1944.

he was not personally involved," he was a Longite and thus guilty by association: "he continued to occupy a luxurious rumble seat on the state machine until Louisiana voters junked it."[54]

Jimmie Davis retained his "sunshine" campaign image throughout the first primary, and continued to stress his political independence. During the last days of the campaign, however, Shirley Wimberly, a Longite former member of the State Tax Commission, raised a new and potentially damaging issue when he called upon Davis to defend himself against rumors that he had written and recorded songs with serial numbers 60836AB and 60837AB on the Decca Records label, namely "Bed Bug Blues" and "High-Geared Mama." "To say that these songs are suggestive, indecent, and vile," Wimberly judged, "would be a decided understatement. They were obviously designed for the entertainment of the denizens of the lowest dives and dens of iniquity." The East Baton Rouge Morgan Committee added that not only had Davis recorded those two songs, but he had also written and performed other equally risqué tunes entitled "High-Geared Daddy," "Honkey-Tonk Blues," "Mama's Getting Hot," "Papa's Getting Cold," and "Shirt Tail Blues." A political advertisement the committee placed in the *Morning Advocate* held that the words to these songs were "unprintable, but suffice it to say that they glorify the 'Bottom' or red light district in Shreveport which ran wide open while Jimmie Davis was Commissioner of Public Safety."[55]

James Morrison joined in the attack on Davis, who, he said, "has no political record that can be seen [but has] several obscene records that no decent people would like to hear." Morrison and the Longites, however, found it difficult to portray as "obscene" a man who had so successfully cultivated the image of "sunshine, peace, and harmony" as had Jimmie Davis. Morrison played "Red Nightgown Blues," another of Davis's records, at a Shreveport rally and his audience began dancing to the music. Morrison became enraged, broke the record, and exclaimed, "Elect him if

54. *Shreveport Times,* December 15, 17, 1943; *Times-Picayune,* December 18, 1943.

55. *Morning Advocate,* January 16, 1944; Weill, *You Are My Sunshine,* 68–69; Gary Mills and Grady McWhiney, "Jimmie Davis as a Figure of Continuity in Country Music" (paper presented to the Louisiana Historical Association Annual Convention, March 25, 1983).

you want him!" Earl Long, faring no better, played "Bed Bug Blues" for a group of ministers, expecting to hear comments of shock and outrage, but instead, heard thankful expressions that even though Davis "used to be on the wrong side of the fence . . . now he's seen the light! Thank the Lord!"[56]

Governor Jones, in an election-eve broadcast, still declined to endorse Davis, but he did remind voters of Louisiana's sordid past and indicated that he preferred a reformer to follow him into office: ". . . Every single gain you the people have made over these years [of my administration] can be wiped out in a period of five months after the next governor takes office, and I tell you that at least some of the candidates for the office would like to do that very thing."[57]

Perry H. Howard maintains that the 1943–44 election was the first of a "new competitive Louisiana politics" in which first Democratic primaries became "sorting out contests as increasingly more candidates . . . vied for a position in the runoff." While Howard's observation is accurate, the 1943–44 election also remained firmly in the bifactional tradition of the recent past. The two leading candidates in the first primary were Jimmie Davis (34.9 percent of the vote) and Lewis Morgan (27.5 percent). Davis received 167,343 votes and scored a plurality in 34 parishes, while Morgan received 131,682 votes and achieved a plurality in 11 parishes.[58]

Even though reformers took comfort in Davis's lead over Morgan, the first primary returns revealed cause for concern. The combined total of those candidates campaigning in the Longite tradition (Morgan, Morrison, Clements, LeBlanc) was 56.1 percent of the vote, while the combined reform total (Davis, Caldwell, Lanier, Moseley) equaled only 43.9 percent. Moreover, reformers trailed badly in several of the races for lesser state offices. Longite registrar of state lands Lucille May Grace and Commissioner of Agriculture Harry D. Wilson won re-election.[59] These results showed that the taxpayer suits and legislative opposition to Sam

56. Weill, *You Are My Sunshine,* 68–69.

57. *Times-Picayune,* January 18, 1944; *Shreveport Times,* January 18, 1944.

58. Howard, *Political Tendencies in Louisiana,* 269–70; *Item,* January 26, 1944.

59. Howard, *Political Tendencies in Louisiana,* 270; *Item,* January 26, 1944.

Jones's program had not been the last gasp of a beaten faction. Instead, Longism, discredited and battered four years earlier, had bounded back. Reformers faced a difficult battle to preserve their control of the government.

Morgan collected more endorsements than Davis for the second primary. Clements endorsed Morgan, as did Lanier, Morrison, and Moseley, who announced his endorsement of a split ticket of Morgan and Verret. Sam Caldwell remained neutral, as did the north Louisiana newspapers that had supported him. Only Dudley LeBlanc endorsed Davis.[60]

Reformers experienced a setback on January 26, when James A. Gremillion, the incumbent secretary of state for whom they had fought so hard against Earl Long's backdoor attempt to stay in public office in 1940, withdrew from his second primary contest, leaving his Longite opponent, Wade O. Martin, Jr., as the Democratic nominee. In response to Gremillion's defection, Davis's campaign manager, W. H. Talbot, referred vaguely to "a huge slush fund" used by the Longites to regain control of the state and its natural resources. Davis was able to offset the loss with endorsements from incumbents Superintendent of Education John E. Coxe and Treasurer A. P. Tugwell, and he added them to his ticket.[61]

Longites likewise experienced difficulties during the second primary campaign. The trouble stemmed from a quirky provision of the 1921 constitution establishing that if there were no second primary for governor, either because a candidate was nominated in the first primary or because one of the candidates selected for the second primary withdrew from that race, then there would be no second primary for any other state office. The candidate with the highest number of votes in each of the lesser statewide races would be the Democratic nominee. Soon after the first primary, some Longites realized that if Morgan withdrew from the race, they would lose the governorship but would control powerful, though

60. *Item*, February 19, January 29, 1944; *Morning Advocate*, February 19, January 22, 1944; *Shreveport Times*, January 22, 1944; *Times-Picayune/New Orleans States*, January 30, 1944.

61. *Times-Picayune*, January 22, February 4, 1944; *Item*, January 27, 1944; *Morning Advocate*, January 29, 1944.

lesser, state offices. Despite that realization, the Old Regulars on January 20 announced that they would continue to support Morgan.[62]

Other Longites, however, apparently tried to sabotage Morgan's campaign. Morgan announced on January 21 that he intended to stay in the race, even though rumors suggested that he would withdraw. Scarcely a week later, he announced that "a political friend" was negotiating with Jimmie Davis forces to end the race quickly. On February 1, after a speech in Lafayette, Morgan replied, "Yes, that's right" when asked whether Earl Long was the political friend negotiating with Davis.[63]

Morgan's comment split Longite ranks. Lucille May Grace and Wade O. Martin, Jr. proclaimed that they would "stick by Lewis Morgan" through his "darkest hour" filled with "terrific sabotage." Earl Long denied any knowledge of Morgan's allegation: "You can tell 'em I expressed utter surprise," he told a *Times-Picayune* reporter. Mayor Maestri declined to comment on the subject. Mrs. Grace's side of the story appears in a letter she wrote to Bill Dodd on March 17, 1944, which he included in his book on Louisiana politics. She maintained that Earl Long, Lether Frazar, and Joe Cawthorn agreed to sacrifice Morgan in order to secure their own elections, and that she opposed their "deliberate sellout." Dodd maintained that the ulterior motive of Mrs. Grace and other Longites opposed to Lewis Morgan withdrawing from the race was their wish to deny the lieutenant governor's chair to Earl Long.[64] The situation might not have been so confusing had Louisiana election law not allowed voters to cast separate ballots for governor and lieutenant governor. Because it did, it was possible for the right combination of factional support to elect Davis and Long to the top state offices.

Former judge James D. Womack dropped a bombshell into Longite ranks during an address broadcast over WNOE and WDSU radio on February 4. He claimed that he had attended a Longite conference at the Monteleone Hotel in New Orleans on January 25 at which Earl Long had

62. *Shreveport Times,* January 21, 1944.

63. *Times-Picayune,* January 22, February 1–2, 1944; *Morning Advocate,* February 2, 1944.

64. *Times-Picayune,* February 2–3, 1944; Dodd, *Peapatch Politics,* 233–34.

announced that John Fred Odom, E. A. Stephens, and Wade Garnier from the reform camp had requested a meeting with him. Long obtained Maestri's permission for the meeting, and then heard the reformers' proposition: Morgan would be "prevented" from continuing the second primary, thus electing Davis and the leading candidate in each of the other races. In exchange for Longite derailment of Morgan's campaign, Davis would go to Hollywood six months following his inauguration to make movies, leaving Earl Long in charge as acting governor. Davis would also resign his office eight months before the 1948 primary, thus giving Long the perquisites of the incumbency to use in a campaign for the governorship in that election. In addition, Womack said, Long reported that both Davis and Sam Jones had promised to support his 1948 bid for the governorship. When he repeated his story during a speech broadcast over WJBO radio in Baton Rouge the night after his New Orleans broadcast, Womack changed the site of the political meeting he attended on January 25 from the Monteleone to the Roosevelt Hotel, but the other details were the same.[65]

The principals named in Womack's speech immediately issued hot denials: Davis—"I have never had a political conference with Earl Long in my life"; Stephens—"unqualifiedly untrue"; Odom—"preposterous and untrue"; Long—"nonsense." Long also paid Davis an uncharacteristic compliment during the episode. Davis, he said, told "the absolute truth" when he denied the alleged negotiations.[66]

The accuracy of Womack's fantastic charges cannot be completely determined. The absurdity ("giddiest absurdity," the *Item* characterized it) of the political shenanigans he outlined, however, undermines his credibility. It is difficult to imagine the reformers willingly yielding control of the state to Earl Long six months after Davis's inauguration. It is virtually impossible to imagine Sam Jones agreeing to support Earl Long for governor in 1948. It is possible, however, that Womack's charge stemmed from knowledge of another meeting that had in fact occurred. Earl Long

65. *Times-Picayune,* February 5, 1944; *Item,* February 5, 1944; *Morning Advocate,* February 6, 1944.

66. *Times-Picayune,* February 5, 1944; *Item,* February 7, 1944.

admitted that he had met with a group of men whom he "presumed to represent Davis," but that they only sought to establish the basis for a smooth administration in case he and Davis were elected to office.[67]

The breach in Longite ranks was only papered over. On February 19, Morgan asked an audience to vote for "every solitary man" on his ticket. Joe Cawthorn announced in Gonzales on February 20 that "we've all joined hands . . . we'll never split again." But Morgan and Long did not appear together until their closing New Orleans rally.[68]

When the second primary finally took place, Jimmie Davis received the Democratic nomination, with 251,228 votes (54 percent of the total) to Morgan's 217,915. Moreover, reform candidates swept into all contested state offices: Verret for lieutenant governor, LeBlanc for attorney general, Tugwell for treasurer, and Coxe for superintendent of education.[69] The Republicans did not nominate candidates for the general election.

Observation of the 1944 second Democratic primary results reveals that while Davis added to the number of parishes voting anti-Longite in north Louisiana compared to the 1940 results, he lost some of the southern and Florida parishes that Sam Jones had carried. Davis's native Jackson Parish, East and West Carroll, Franklin, and Concordia Parishes joined the ranks of the reformers in 1944, while Grant and Caldwell left the reformers and voted for Lewis Morgan. Beauregard joined Calcasieu and Jefferson Davis Parishes in southwest Louisiana in voting for Davis, but Allen and Cameron Parishes remained Longite. Acadia and St. Martin Parishes in south Louisiana voted for Morgan by comfortable margins, but Davis carried St. Bernard, which had voted for Earl Long in 1940. Morgan's lifelong association with the Florida Parishes allowed him to erode anti-Longite strength there. St. Tammany, Tangipahoa, and Livingston Parishes all voted for him in 1944. Nevertheless, with the continued exception of New Orleans, Davis held most of the urban areas of the state for the reformers. East Baton Rouge, Calcasieu, Rapides, Ouachita, and Caddo Parishes all voted for him.

67. *Item,* February 7, 1944; *Morning Advocate,* February 7, 1944; *Town Talk,* February 7, 1944.

68. *Morning Advocate,* February 20–21, 1944.

69. Howard, *Political Tendencies in Louisiana,* p. 271; *Morning Advocate,* March 8, 1944.

The election results pleased the reformers. Sam Jones remarked that Davis's victory demonstrated that his own election had not been merely a "flash in the pan." The 1940 campaign, he said, "was won by the flame of spontaneous revolt against shocking scandal." The 1944 reform victory, in contrast, "was brought about by the unspectacular but deliberate determination of the people to continue clean, independent government." Former U.S. representative Hale Boggs congratulated Emile Verret on his victory over Earl Long: "In defeating him you have earned the everlasting gratitude of the people of Louisiana." State representative deLesseps Morrison, a thoroughgoing reformer then on army duty overseas, wrote to his mother, "Thank God, we are through with Joe Cawthorn, Earl Long, and the like."[70]

In contrast to the 1939–40 campaign, the 1943–44 contest was tame. Even the war, which dominated so much of American life, failed to ignite Louisiana's political agenda. One of the few noticeable effects of the war on the campaign was gas rationing, which caused the candidates some transportation problems even though federal officials in Washington, D.C., had empowered local ration boards to issue special gasoline allotments to the candidates.[71]

The war entered the political debate only in two minor themes. First, calls came from various sources requesting that the candidates observe the seriousness of the conflict by conducting a campaign without the ballyhoo, innuendo, distortion, and lies usually present in Louisiana campaigns (admonitions that went unheeded). Second, both Davis and Morgan pledged to provide "rehabilitation" and jobs for the returning servicemen and servicewomen. Although many people throughout the country were increasingly concerned that battle-hardened veterans might wreak havoc after their return, either because of psychological disorders

70. *Morning Advocate,* March 1, April 29, 1944; deLesseps S. Morrison to Anita O. Morrison, March 12, 1944, Morrison Papers; Hale Boggs to Emile Verret, March 6, 1944, Verret Papers.

71. *Times-Picayune,* September 16, 1943; W. Scott Heywood to Prentiss M. Brown, October 4, 1943, Jennings-Heywood Collection, LLMVC.

or by turning their military training to criminal uses, this issue never achieved major importance in the campaign.[72]

Jimmie Davis's official election to Louisiana's highest office on April 18, 1944, gave reformers another four years to govern the state. In the general election, he was unopposed and the turnout was typically low. Governor and Mrs. Jones invited the Davises to move into the governor's mansion on May 1 so that they could become accustomed to their new quarters and to simplify the logistics of inauguration day. Davis, however, when asked whether he endorsed all of Jones's reform program, replied, "I never take stock in anybody's politics except my own."[73]

Davis's inauguration was simpler than Sam Jones's 1940 extravaganza and much simpler than Earl Long's wild celebration was to be in 1948. Gasoline and tire rationing reduced the crowd at Davis's ceremony to an estimated 10,000 people, compared with the approximately 100,000 who witnessed Jones's inauguration. He was sworn in on the capitol steps, and there were no ceremonial balls. Following the inaugural speech, Governor and Mrs. Davis held an open house at the governor's mansion.[74]

Jimmie Davis translated his "peace and harmony" campaign into administrative reality. He endorsed incumbent house speaker Norman Bauer of St. Mary Parish for re-election, and reformer Grove Stafford of Rapides Parish for Senate president-pro-tempore. He announced, typically, that his endorsements did not downgrade the qualifications of any other candidates for the posts. He revealed to the Orleans delegation of lawmakers that he had no "must" legislation, but that he expected widespread support for his "non-political" program that included renewal of the sales tax, reenactment of the gas-gathering tax, and division of the Conservation Department into two agencies—one for wildlife and one for minerals. The initial success of his effort to establish concord was revealed in a public letter from Longite secretary of state Wade O. Martin,

72. *Morning Advocate,* August 19, 21, 1943; "Address" (1943), Verret Collection; Joseph C. Goulden, *The Best Years, 1945–1950* (New York, 1976), 37–51.

73. *Morning Advocate,* April 16, 25, 1944.

74. *Morning Advocate,* April 19, May 7, 10, 1944; *Item,* May 9, 1944; *Shreveport Times,* May 10, 1944.

Jr., to Davis pledging his "active support, co-operation, and assistance in every matter which shall have for its purpose the advancement and improvement of the state of Louisiana."[75]

When the legislature convened on May 8, 1944, the Old Regulars announced that they would "play ball" with Davis, and nominated no candidates for house speaker or senate president pro tempore. Reformers hoped that the state's political climate had improved. The *Morning Advocate* commented, "[We] believe that, in a manner of speaking, the sun will shine in Louisiana for the next four years."[76]

The legislature heard the new governor's plans for the state on May 15. He spoke in general terms about the need for improved flood control, highways, hospitals, and penal institutions, but reminded legislators that "these needs must continue to yield to the greater needs of war."[77]

Davis thus urged legislators to endure a period of austerity until the war ended, but he nonetheless submitted a budget with expenditures of $197,768,787.26 for the 1944–45 biennium ($15.5 million above Sam Jones's 1942–43 budget). State fiscal officers anticipated income for the two-year period to be approximately $42 million less than the proposed expenditures. The original estimates of the deficit, however, did not include approximately $16 million in revenue to be realized if the legislature reenacted the sales tax, and approximately $3.5 million in additional revenue from Davis's proposed reenactment of the gas-gathering tax. Neither had the officers considered the possibility of reducing the deficit by using part of the $12.5 million surplus left in the state treasury by Sam Jones.[78]

Davis described the executive budget (actually prepared by the executive department before he took office) as "considerably out of balance" and called upon legislators to cut appropriations "where necessary to pro-

75. *Morning Advocate*, May 2, 6, 1944; *States*, May 4, 1944; *Item*, May 6, 1944.

76. *Morning Advocate*, May 8, 1944; *Item*, May 8, 1944.

77. *Address by Governor Jimmie H. Davis Before the Joint Session of the Legislature, May 15, 1944* (Baton Rouge, 1944), 2, 6; *Shreveport Times*, May 16, 1944.

78. *Item*, May 16, 1944; *Morning Advocate*, May 16, 1944; Sindler, *Huey Long's Louisiana*, 191.

vide an economical and balanced budget." Expenditures, he said, "must be kept within the means of the state to pay."[79]

Davis further favored renewing two taxes that could generate enough income to reduce the deficit considerably. Renewal of the one-cent sales tax, he said, had not been a campaign pledge, "but after study from every angle, I believe it is necessary." The house approved the measure with a 94–0 vote with no debate. The senate passed the bill as well, and Davis signed it into law.[80]

Renewal of the gas-gathering tax, however, roused the ire of natural gas producers. They maintained that they had accepted the tax in 1940 because Sam Jones assured them that it would be in effect for only two years and that he desperately needed it to reduce the state debt. Then in 1942 they had agreed to an extension of the tax for two additional years to help ease the state's financial crunch, and had received a distinct pledge from the Jones administration that the tax would not extend beyond 1944. Davis's spokesmen replied that he was not responsible for a pledge made by the previous administration, and that it was as important for him to balance the budget as it had been for Sam Jones. The legislature ultimately did renew the tax.[81]

The peace-and-harmony façade of the legislative session, however, crumbled in bitter debate about other issues. The administration proposed to remove the Education Department from politics by appointing rather than electing its superintendent. The bill caused sharp debate between legislators who called it a reasonable reform and those who saw it as a dangerous concentration of power in the hands of the governor. The latter group succeeded in disposing of the measure. Davis also failed when he endorsed a proposal to "freeze" most of the treasury surplus by investing it in war bonds. Legislators preferred to keep the surplus liquid, even though the wartime scarcity of construction materials limited its use.[82]

79. *Item,* May 23, 1944; *Morning Advocate,* June 5, 1944.

80. *Morning Advocate,* May 30, June 13, 1944; *Item,* May 30, 1944; *Shreveport Times,* May 31, 1944; *Acts Passed by the Legislature of the State of Louisiana at the Regular Session, 1944,* 138.

81. *Item,* May 16, 1944; *Acts Passed by the Legislature, 1944,* 354–60.

82. *Item,* June 13, 1944; Sindler, *Huey Long's Louisiana,* 191.

Davis received his severest rebuff from the legislature when he proposed an additional one-cent retail sales tax. The governor and other supporters of the proposal, including state treasurer Tugwell, urged the legislature to approve the additional tax to help veterans after the war. They recognized the long-overdue need for construction and repair of roads, hospitals, and mental institutions, as well as other projects demanding large outlays of money. Just when the end of the war would make such construction projects possible, the supporters reasoned, Louisiana's economy would enter a slump because of the sudden reductions in military and industrial spending. James I. Smith, Davis's executive counsel, explained to the legislators that they could raise the money that would be needed for such projects, which in turn would create jobs for returning servicemen, in either of two ways: they could issue state bonds when the war ended, or they could impose the new one-cent sales tax now and save the revenue for postwar projects.[83]

Davis asserted that "since it is for the soldiers, I think we can all agree to be for it," but the fresh sales tax drew a storm of protest. E. H. "Lige" Williams, president of the Louisiana Federation of Labor, called the appeal to patriotism a "transparent mockery." The New Orleans legislative delegation opposed the tax because residents of the city already paid a high sales tax (a two-cent city tax and a one-cent state tax); the added cent would push their sales taxes to an unacceptable level. Opposition also arose from reformers, some of whom thought the additional levy unnecessary because of the large surplus generated by the state sales tax instituted in 1942.[84]

After a prolonged debate before packed galleries, the house voted against the additional sales tax 48–47. Davis expressed his disappointment that the state would not be collecting additional revenue from the money then circulating in Louisiana but, characteristically, also announced that he was not bitter about the defeat.[85]

83. *Item,* June 15, 1944; Sindler, *Huey Long's Louisiana,* 192.

84. *Item,* June 15, 22, 1944; *States,* June 26, 1944.

85. *States,* June 28, 1944; *Shreveport Times,* June 29, 1944; *Morning Advocate,* June 29, 1944.

As the legislative session unfolded, the reformers found that Davis was indeed not another Sam Jones. While Jones's belief in an "unbossed" legislature led him normally to refrain from attending sessions to lobby in behalf of his bills, sometimes to the detriment of his program, he worked behind the scenes to build coalitions of support for his initiatives. Davis, however, provided little legislative leadership, overt or otherwise. Without direction from the governor, legislative sessions during his administration often disintegrated into a welter of confused efforts and cross-purposes within the reform faction.

The administration's position on many issues became so unclear during the 1944 session that Davis was prompted to hold a series of caucuses with legislators to emphasize which bills had administration support, but these sessions did not stop the flow of criticism directed at him for his lack of guidance. One representative remarked that there was a vast difference between an independent legislature and a disorganized legislature. Furthermore, legislators not invited to the early caucuses were incensed at being omitted. As Representative A. R. deNux reported, his constituents in Avoyelles Parish held that "you're not representing us if you're not called in to decide on what's going to be done in the legislature."[86]

Criticism of Davis's lackadaisical leadership also came from within the reform faction. The *Item* described the "secret caucuses" as "bizarre" and called upon Davis to "express himself to the Assembly in messages or personal addresses." Veteran New Orleans political journalist Hermann B. Deutsch observed that in the house of representatives the members "are not merely independent, they are unorganized. And between those two terms yawns a tremendous difference."[87]

At the closing meeting of the legislature, concord prevailed once again. Governor Davis attended the house session, harmonized with the representatives on several songs, and rendered a solo performance of "It Makes

86. *States,* June 9, 1944; *Morning Advocate,* June 16, 19–20, 1944; *Shreveport Times,* June 20, 1944; *Item,* June 20, 1944.

87. *Item,* June 19, 1944.

No Difference Now." Representative Leonard Santos of New Orleans released two pigeons labeled "Peace" and "Harmony" in the chamber.[88]

Upon closing, the legislature left the governor with a seriously unbalanced budget, but Davis vetoed $15 million in appropriations to bring expenditures into line. His two major vetoes eliminated $5 million each to have been paid from the general appropriations fund for state drainage programs and highway construction. By July 12, Treasurer Tugwell announced that with Davis's vetoes, he projected a $1 million budget surplus for the next biennium.[89]

Projections of the surplus kept Davis from calling a special legislative session to reconsider imposition of the additional one-cent state retail sales tax. Speculation about the extraordinary session had begun when the regular session rejected the tax, and as legislators considered the idea after the regular session ended, some of them decided the proposal to stockpile revenue with the additional tax had merit. Representative Drayton Boucher of Spring Hill announced that "my people and other members of the Legislature from my district are in favor of the bill." By early September, however, the administration had abandoned all thoughts of calling the special session. A "high unnamed administration source" gave no official reason, but the *Item* pointed out that according to Treasurer Tugwell's records, during the first two months of the new fiscal year (July and August 1944), the state received $12,021,761.98 in total revenue, compared with $10,375,318.71 during the same two months of the previous fiscal year, and that the previous year had produced a $12.5 million surplus. Administration leaders thus felt great reluctance at the prospect of attempting to sell a tax increase when the state expected a healthy surplus from available revenues. Davis announced on February 14, 1945, that he would call no special session "until the end of the European war was in sight."[90]

Between the end of the regular legislative session in July 1944 and the

88. *Ibid.*; *Morning Advocate,* July 7, 1944; Sindler, *Huey Long's Louisiana,* 196–97.

89. *Morning Advocate,* July 8, 11–12, 1944.

90. *States,* February 7, 15, August 17, 1944; *Item,* September 7, 1944; Sindler, *Huey Long's Louisiana,* 192.

end of World War II in September 1945, Davis remained busy governing the state and participating in the war effort. He met with President Roosevelt and then with President Truman, talking politics and asking them to retain Louisiana's war production plants and military training camps during the postwar years. Back at home, he attempted by executive order to halt "floggings or other mistreatment" of prisoners at the state penitentiary. Sam Jones had issued a similar order, but prison officials had apparently ignored it. Davis's order was to meet a similar fate, and flogging of state prisoners continued into the 1950s. Around the South, Davis and his band made public appearances at war bond sales rallies, and made an eight-state "postwar business tour" to persuade businessmen to build commercial establishments in Louisiana. Nor, incidentally, did he forget his entertainment career during these busy months; he and singer Tex Ritter completed the score for a musical comedy entitled *Start Cheering*.[91]

Shortly after the end of the war, Davis called his promised postwar extraordinary session of the legislature. This short session quickly approved bills providing for the expenditure of $16.5 million: $7.5 million to match federal funds for construction of highways and bridges, $4 million to the Department of Highways for the construction or improvement of roads and bridges not included in the state highway system or the federal aid system, and $5 million to the Department of Public Works for developing undrained or partially drained marsh, swamp, and overflow lands.[92]

The war years proved to be the most peaceful and harmonious of Davis's administration. In the 1946 regular session of the legislature, he became embroiled in attempts to restrict organized labor's power when he vetoed a "right to work" bill outlawing union shops, calling the measure "an interference with the right of collective bargaining." Also in 1946 and again in 1947, Davis's (and Sam Jones's) "conservationist" policy of restricting exports of natural gas from Louisiana came under heavy fire from legislators ready to exploit the state's resources for short-term gain.[93]

91. *Morning Advocate,* September 7, December 2, 1944, May 12, June 1, 1945; *States,* May 16, 1945; Weill, *You Are My Sunshine,* 73–74; Carleton, *Politics and Punishment,* 144.

92. *Morning Advocate,* October 12–13, 1945; *Acts Passed by the Legislature of the State of Louisiana at the Extraordinary Session, 1945,* 5–7.

93. Sindler, *Huey Long's Louisiana,* 195–96; Weill, *You Are My Sunshine,* 75–77.

Despite these setbacks, Jimmie Davis's first administration, as Allan Sindler notes, was more than the "do-nothing" void in Louisiana politics that the Longites (on purpose) and Sam Jones (unwittingly) branded it. Sindler observes that Davis's reputation later suffered from Jones's campaign tactics during the 1948 gubernatorial race, when Jones focused on the 1939 Scandals and his own term in office, and thus acquiesced in Earl Long's contention that Davis had presided over a "do-nothing" administration. In its time, however, the Davis administration provided a friendly atmosphere for continued reform, even though Davis himself was not an ardent or aggressive reformer.[94]

Davis, then, was partially successful in his efforts to establish peace and harmony in Louisiana, but bifactionalism did not disappear. His lack of legislative leadership allowed new coalitions of Longites and reformers to form around specific proposals. The appearance of harmony was nurtured by the plentiful supply of money in the state treasury. This surplus, along with the dearth of construction materials caused by the war, necessarily limited the conflict over state funding for legislators' pet projects. In addition, the most visible factional symbols in the state, Sam Jones and Earl Long, either of whose opponents could be enraged merely by the mention of their names, were both out of office during Davis's administration. Their reappearance in the 1948 election caused a rerun of the 1939–40 slugfest, this version a bitter struggle that ended in Long's sweeping victory.

Davis's initial retirement from politics lasted from 1948 until 1960, when he was elected to a second term as governor. His third campaign for the office ended in failure in 1972, and he retired permanently from politics to devote himself to his entertainment career, which by then consisted almost exclusively of performing and recording gospel music.

Reformers in Louisiana have always experienced difficulty obtaining political power and the opportunity to improve the state that it entails. Beginning with Luther Hall's administration in 1912, reform-minded politicians have been unable to control the governor's office for two successive terms, with only one exception. The surprise in the state's political

94. Sindler, *Huey Long's Louisiana,* 190–91, 196–99.

history during the 1940s was not that Earl Long devastated Sam Jones in 1948, but rather that Jimmie Davis had been able to defeat a Longite resurgence in 1944. The irony in the reformers' great accomplishment in 1944 was that they had elected a man who did not share equally in their zeal to create a new order in the state. The reformers knew what they wanted in 1944, but Davis's administration did not provide it.

6

Bifactionalism and National Politics

Louisiana's participation in national politics during the early 1940s reflected both the state's bifactionalism and its concern about vital issues raised by World War II. Longite and anti-Longite candidates contested for seats in Congress as well as for local and state offices. The state was more unified in the two wartime presidential elections, but even then, President Franklin Roosevelt's quest in 1940 for an unprecedented third term, combined with his choice of Henry A. Wallace for vice president, caused defections from Democratic ranks. Although Louisiana did not abandon the party in 1940 or 1944, the two wartime campaigns revealed increasing discontent, shared by the rest of the South, with Roosevelt's "Grand Coalition," which included organized labor, intellectuals, and blacks. The discontent was to blossom into full rebellion in the 1948 presidential election.[1]

In 1940, Georgia commissioner of agriculture Tom Linder wrote and circulated to his colleagues in other southern states an essay that revealed emerging restiveness in the region. Linder wrote that "the nefarious practices begun by Abraham Lincoln are now being carried into completion by Roosevelt and the New Deal party." He suggested that the South boycott the Democratic National Convention and nominate its own presi-

1. Robert A. Garson, *The Democratic Party and the Politics of Sectionalism, 1941–1948* (Baton Rouge, 1974), 1–30.

dential candidate, who would then hold the balance of power between the "New Deal and the Republicans."[2]

Besides southern concern with liberal tendencies within the national Democratic party, two other issues entered into the 1940 presidential election: should Franklin Roosevelt be granted a third term as president, and how realistic were Roosevelt's plans to defend the country without directly involving American soldiers in the world war?[3]

The third-term issue split the national Democratic party as Vice President John Nance Garner, Postmaster General James A. Farley, and conservative U.S. senator Millard Tydings of Maryland each wanted the nomination. Roosevelt nevertheless won the candidacy on the first ballot at the party convention in Chicago. A contrived demonstration at that meeting allowed the president to note coyly in his acceptance speech that even though he did not want to run for a third term, the overseas conflict made it imperative that he "not reject the call of the party to run" and, if elected, "the call of the country to serve."[4]

Louisiana's support for Roosevelt in 1940 was not evident early in the year. In April, Governor Jones met with prospective candidate Farley at Shreveport, as Farley awaited a train connection to Jackson, Mississippi. Jones, however, disclaimed any endorsement of Farley for the nomination.[5]

Louisiana's bifactional division intruded into the national scene during the state party convention held in early June 1940 for the purpose of choosing delegates to the Democratic National Convention. The meeting became rowdy when Senator Ellender stepped up to the podium to move

2. Tom Linder to Harry D. Wilson, [1940], William Walter Jones Collection, HTML.

3. Garson, *The Democratic Party,* 13; Robert E. Burke, "Election of 1940," in *The Coming to Power: Critical Presidential Elections in American History,* ed. Arthur M. Schlesinger, Jr. (New York, 1972), 360–63.

4. Burke, "Election of 1940," 369–73; Geoffrey Perret, *Days of Sadness, Years of Triumph: The American People, 1939–1945* (New York, 1973), 48–50; *Public Papers and Addresses of Franklin D. Roosevelt,* 1940 vol., *War—And Aid to Democracies* (New York, 1941), 293–303.

5. *Times-Picayune,* April 5, 1940.

that Louisiana's delegates vote for Roosevelt's third nomination. State convention attendees, dominated by the reform faction, had booed Ellender as he entered the building, and as he stood to address the convention a chorus of boos again echoed through the room.[6]

While the attendees thus expressed their resentment at the Long machine by humiliating its representative, they did not want Roosevelt to think their repudiation of Ellender was also a repudiation of him. After Ellender resumed his seat on the floor of the convention, a resolution was unanimously adopted that the action not be construed as a reflection upon the president. They declined, however, to instruct Louisiana's delegates to the national convention to vote for Roosevelt, preferring instead to keep them uncommitted.[7]

At the national convention, the uncommitted delegates decided to support O. John Rogge for the presidential nomination on the first ballot and then switch to Roosevelt on later ballots. This arrangement resulted partially from their wish to honor the federal investigator who had exposed the Louisiana Scandals. They also wanted to apply political pressure to Roosevelt to include in the Democratic platform a plank they had proposed favoring strong protection of the American sugar industry. Rogge, however, quickly instructed the delegates not to vote for him. He had "cleaned up the state through a desire for justice," he told them, and not for political acclaim.[8]

Great disappointment settled over many national convention delegates when Roosevelt endorsed for the vice presidential nomination Secretary of Agriculture Henry A. Wallace, the bête noire of Louisiana sugar interests. Louisiana delegate Jared Y. Sanders, Jr., a member of the resolutions committee, tried to persuade that committee to adopt a strong resolution in favor of domestic sugar production. He marshaled support among delegates from Florida and from sugar beet–producing states, but ran into opposition from Wallace supporters, who maintained that the Sanders

6. *States,* June 5, 1940; Becnel, *Senator Allen Ellender,* 103.

7. *Times-Picayune,* June 5, 1940; *States,* June 5, 1940; "Resolution," June 4, 1940, Ellender Papers, AJE.

8. *States,* July 15, 17, 1940.

proposal would threaten international agreements establishing sugar production levels. Wallace himself told Sanders that the proposed resolution might "upset our foreign policy regarding Cuba, and seriously affect the economic life of Hawaii, the Philippines, and Puerto Rico." Sanders replied that one-third of Louisiana was directly affected by the sugar policy and that "it's more important for us not to upset the domestic economy of the United States." Moreover, he said, peacetime international agreements may no longer be valid in a world at war. Now was the time, Sanders argued, to produce all necessary food in increased volume.[9]

Despite Sanders's valiant efforts, the Democratic platform contained only a general agricultural plank; the party pledged "to safeguard the farmer's foreign market and expand his domestic market for all domestic crops."[10] Although this generously worded plank promised nothing specific for the protection of sugar, it did enable the Louisiana delegation to support Roosevelt's nomination in good faith. They remembered Wallace's personal opposition, though, and cast about for an alternative candidate for the vice presidency.

Governor Jones, who led the opposition to Wallace within the Louisiana delegation, informed Roosevelt's convention leaders, Harry Hopkins and Senators James F. Byrnes of South Carolina and Pat Harrison of Mississippi, that Wallace's nomination would "split the party wide open in the state." The Louisiana delegates selected for their endorsement Assistant Secretary of War Louis Johnson, a University of Virginia classmate of Prescott Foster and American Legion friend of Sam Jones. They agreed to support Congressman Sam Rayburn of Texas or Speaker of the House William B. Bankhead of Alabama if Johnson withdrew. Even though Wallace had only recently converted from Republicanism to the Democratic party, he won the vice presidential nomination on the first ballot, but in a relatively close vote.[11]

Louisiana delegates headed home from Chicago displeased with Wal-

9. *Item,* July 16, 1940; *States,* July 18, 1940; *Item-Tribune,* July 21, 1940.

10. *Item,* July 18, 1940.

11. *States,* July 18, 1940; Burke, "Election of 1940," 369–75; Bernard F. Donohoe, *Private Plans and Public Dangers: The Story of FDR's Third Nomination* (Notre Dame, Ind., 1965), 174–77.

lace's nomination. Jones announced that he was against Wallace "1000 percent." One irate Louisiana delegate, storming out of the convention, demanded of Washington columnist George Allen, "Name me one, just one, man [who wanted Wallace]." Allen replied, "Brother, that I can do—and that one man was Roosevelt."[12]

After the convention, some Louisiana delegates reported dissatisfaction with aspects of the meeting other than the Wallace nomination. John Caffery, a south Louisiana sugar planter, revealed that he had planned to speak in favor of a proposed anti–third term plank, but when the plank was debated, convention chairman Alben Barkley refused to recognize those delegates wishing to support it. Caffery reported that anti–third term sentiment had been strong in the Louisiana delegation until it became apparent that Roosevelt would be nominated. While most Louisiana delegates believed that the state would support the president, Caffery announced that he supported Republican candidate Wendell Willkie, and predicted the largest Republican vote in Louisiana's Third Congressional District (the heart of the sugar-growing area) since Reconstruction.[13]

Similarly disgruntled with the Roosevelt-Wallace ticket, the American Sugar Cane League in New Orleans led an effort to detach voters from their historic Democratic ties. Charles A. Farwell, chair of the league's education committee, called Wallace "the worst enemy Louisiana sugar ever had," and announced, "I'm voting for Willkie." Farwell recited a litany of complaints against the Democrats: in 1932 Roosevelt had promised not to lower United States tariff rates when a reduction would hurt a domestic crop, but had then lowered the tariff on Cuban sugar from two dollars to ninety cents per ton; in 1936, the administration had promised production of as much sugar as the market could absorb plus creation of a reserve supply, then in 1937 had promulgated a new sugar act with continued crop quotas; Wallace, while he was secretary of agriculture, had made a speech in 1934 in Ruston, Louisiana, during which he called sugar

12. *Town Talk,* July 18, 1940; Donohoe, *Private Plans,* 177–78.
13. *Item,* July 19, 1940; *States,* July 19, 1940.

"an inefficient industry," and commented, "I would not kill it outright. . . . But I would expose it gradually [to the world market]."[14]

Not surprisingly, some sugar planters concluded that they must support the Republicans. Allen Ramsey Wurtele, a New Roads planter and businessman, announced his plans to run as a Republican for Louisiana's Sixth Congressional seat. "Democracy is escaping from the United States under the Roosevelt dictatorship," Wurtele warned. "Unless the Republicans take over this country immediately, democracy is ended for us." Republicans also entered the First, Second, and Third District races, but most withdrew before election time. Only David Pipes in the Third District remained in the campaign. John P. Conway, Joseph O. Schwartz, and Wurtele withdrew from the First, Second, and Sixth District races, respectively.[15]

The tiny band of Louisiana Republicans welcomed the defecting Democrats. The state's delegation to the 1940 Republican National Convention in Philadelphia split into two groups. For the presidential nomination, one faction supported New York district attorney Thomas E. Dewey, while the other favored Ohio senator Robert A. Taft. A fabricated attempt to nominate utilities executive Wendell Willkie stampeded the convention, however. After Dewey withdrew and climbed on the Willkie bandwagon in response to Ohio governor John W. Bricker's call for a unanimous nomination, the Louisiana delegation supported Taft.[16] Nevertheless, Louisiana Republicans were comfortable with Willkie as the candidate, and worked for his election.

That effort included New Orleans attorney John E. Jackson's joining Willkie's advisory council in Washington, D.C., and local Republicans creating political associations, called Jeffersonian Democratic Clubs, to attract disgruntled Democrats. These organizations were part of Willkie's attempt to attract southern Democratic support and were organized in all

14. *States,* July 20, 1940.

15. *Ibid.,* July 22, 1940.

16. *Times-Picayune,* June 25, 1940; *States,* July 8, 1940; Warren Moscow, *Roosevelt and Willkie* (Englewood Cliffs, N.J., 1968), 104.

of the southern states. Republicans had to attract Democratic voters if Willkie was to have any hope for success in the South; Louisiana, for example, in October 1940 recorded a total of 702,545 voters—700,727 Democrats, 1,573 Republicans, 242 Independents, and 3 Socialists.[17]

Many prominent Louisiana Democrats, even those opposed to Wallace, did not join the Willkie boomlet. Governor Jones announced, "I am a Democrat. We fight out our fights in the family," and gave the Roosevelt-Wallace ticket his "complete endorsement." Louisiana Democratic Central Committee chairman Frank J. Looney of Shreveport announced that any Democrat who bolted the party to join the Jeffersonian Democratic clubs and boost Willkie's candidacy would forfeit the right to vote in all future Democratic primaries.[18]

The Roosevelt administration supplied loyal Democrats in Louisiana with statistics to refute the sugar interests' claim that New Deal farm policy had hurt the domestic sugar industry. Undersecretary of Agriculture Paul Appleby wrote to Sam Jones that Secretary Wallace helped to increase mainland sugar area base quotas in the 1937 Sugar Act from 160,000 to 420,000 tons, and helped to provide conditional payments to Louisiana farmers who violated child employment provisions of the act. In addition, Appleby said that Wallace had never ordered Louisiana sugar farmers to plow up any of their crop, as had been done in other New Deal crop reduction programs. Appleby's information, however, was incorrect. The USDA ordered Louisiana sugar farmers to plow up portions of the 1939 crop.[19]

Disaffection among sugar planters was not the only criticism Roosevelt experienced in Louisiana. His experiments in New Deal social programs and his strengthening alliance with urban and labor groups at the expense of agriculture also left some Democrats disillusioned. W. Scott Heywood

17. *Item,* July 10, 31, 1940; *States,* August 2, 1940; Donald Bruce Johnson, *The Republican Party and Wendell Willkie* (Urbana, Ill., 1960), 134; Alden L. Powell, "Your Democracy Is in Your Hands," *Louisiana Municipal Review,* September–October 1941, 146.

18. *States,* August 5, 1940; *Town Talk,* August 13, 1940; *Morning Advocate,* October 19, 1940.

19. Paul Appleby to Sam Jones, September 19, 1940, Jones Collection; Becnel, *Labor, Church, and the Sugar Establishment,* 74.

wrote to his son in 1940 that Willkie was "just as good a democrat and probably more of a democrat than Roosevelt." In addition, he objected to Roosevelt's support of "Ma Perkins," Secretary of Labor Frances Perkins. Nor did he approve of the president's "allowing his wife [Eleanor] to be popping off the way she has been doing."[20]

By the time of the American political conventions during the summer of 1940, Adolf Hitler's armies had swept through the Low Countries and into Paris. Because of his astounding success, experience in military preparedness and foreign policy became an issue in the presidential election. Indeed, Roosevelt expressed to the Democratic convention his wish to retire from the presidency, but indicated he would be amenable to a draft if the delegates wanted a candidate with his experience. Willkie had no experience in foreign affairs, a shortcoming stressed by Sam Jones in speeches against the Republican nominee, speeches that at the same time praised Roosevelt's preparedness efforts.[21]

The Willkie boomlet in Louisiana proved to be less successful than the sugar interests and traditional Republicans had hoped. A Gallup poll published on November 4, 1940, revealed that Roosevelt still commanded much support in Louisiana—82 percent compared to 18 percent for Willkie. The president's support in Louisiana was less than that found in Mississippi, but was equal to that in Arkansas, and more than that in Texas.[22]

Roosevelt's supporters not only answered polls but also turned out to vote on election day, giving him 319,751 ballots to Willkie's 52,241. Even the sugar-producing areas of Louisiana backed the president. The group labeled by Perry Howard the South Louisiana Bayou voters went 84 percent for Roosevelt, while those he calls the South Louisiana Planters were 83 percent in favor of him, thus encompassing the state's major sugar parishes. This outcome resulted from many sugarcane growers having re-

20. Hubert H. Humphrey, *The Political Philosophy of the New Deal* (Baton Rouge, 1970), 23–29; Robert Rutland, *The Democrats from Jefferson to Carter* (Baton Rouge, 1979), 197; W. Scott Heywood to Gene B. Heywood, August 14, 1940, Jennings-Heywood Oil Syndicate Records, LLMVC.

21. Sam Jones, interview by Daugherty, May 6, 1970, tape recording, Daugherty Collection, LLMVC; Sam Jones, "Address" [1940], Aswell Papers, LLMVC.

22. *Item,* November 4, 1940.

turned to the Democratic fold after the 1940 suspension of domestic sugar quotas by Senate Joint Resolution 225, which provided that a grower could harvest all of his domestic quota plus twenty-five additional acres without losing benefits. Ultimately, then, the President's popularity was not seriously threatened by the sugar planters' disillusionment. The comment of Harold H. Young, the political strategist who headed Roosevelt's campaign in the Dallas–Fort Worth area, "Nobody's for FDR except small voices—the people," was also true in Louisiana.[23] Willkie's vote total, however, does reflect substantial defection by Democrats, considering that fewer than 1,600 Louisiana voters were registered Republicans.

Obviously, not all Louisianians were ready to abandon the Democratic party. J. F. McDougall wrote a letter to the editor of the *New Orleans States* in May 1942 full of glowing praise for the president: "God has proved that He loves us and the things we are fighting for . . . by giving us a great leader, our beloved President Franklin D. Roosevelt." Ellender urged the U.S. Senate to designate Roosevelt as "supreme leader" of the Allied war effort during the summer of 1942. New Orleans industrialist Andrew Jackson Higgins said in a national radio speech in May 1943 that if the war lasted until 1944, Roosevelt should be reelected because "this war is not time for discord." By then, Higgins also recognized the economic benefit Louisiana reaped from the war, since he alone employed some twenty thousand people at seven New Orleans plants that produced war goods. In April 1944 the Louisiana State Federation of Labor urged Roosevelt to accept the Democratic party nomination for a fourth time.[24]

As usual, Louisiana's main bout during the 1944 election occurred within the Democratic party, although the Republicans opened the campaign more organized than they had been in the past. The state's delegation to the Republican National Convention in Chicago unanimously voted for the eventual nominee, Dewey of New York, and Louisiana Re-

23. Moscow, *Roosevelt and Willkie,* 189; Howard, *Political Tendencies in Louisiana,* 299; Becnel, *Labor, Church, and the Sugar Establishment,* 74–75; Robert A. Caro, *The Years of Lyndon Johnson: The Path to Power* (New York, 1982), 581.

24. *States,* May 5, 1942; *Shreveport Journal,* June 24, 1942; *Morning Advocate,* April 9, 1943, April 5, 1944; *Town Talk,* May 17, 1943; Jack B. McGuire, "Andrew Jackson Higgins Plays Presidential Politics," *Louisiana History* 15 (summer 1974): 274–75.

publican national committeeman John E. Jackson of New Orleans issued a statement that "the people of Louisiana, as well as the rest of the South, are tired of the New Deal, and I believe [they] will go along with the Republican ticket."[25] Republican politics remained the sideshow in Louisiana, however, while the Democrats dominated the midway.

Far from being a united front, the Democrats felt rumblings of discontent from the South throughout 1943. Jones and Georgia governor Ellis Arnall called for an end to Solid South politics, so that both parties would have to solicit the region's electoral votes. And when the Democratic National Committee asked for campaign funds, Francis J. Whitehead, Assistant Secretary of the Louisiana Democratic Central Committee, replied that such requests would probably go unheeded, "unless the Democrats soon straighten out their politics respecting the South." Louisiana senator John Overton joined the protest by flatly denouncing a fourth term for President Roosevelt, noting his fear that "we will be plagued in years to come for our present actions."[26]

Governor Jones reflected the frustration of many southerners in an article, "Will Dixie Bolt the New Deal?" published in the March 6, 1943, issue of the *Saturday Evening Post*. He argued that Roosevelt, despite his lengthy residence at his "Little White House" at Warm Springs, Georgia, knew little about the South, and that New Deal economic policies "continued to kick an already prostrate South in the face." Roosevelt's administration had denied the South its share of public investments and perpetuated the railroad freight rate disparity that penalized the region. Moreover, Roosevelt had shown sympathy for the emerging struggle for civil rights. Therefore, Jones suggested, it was time for the Solid South to abandon its blind allegiance to the Democratic party.[27]

The election year of 1944 brought no end to the incipient southern rebellion in Louisiana. Forty Democratic leaders from South Carolina, Mississippi, Texas, Louisiana, and Florida met in Shreveport about one

25. *Shreveport Times,* June 26, 1944; *States,* June 29, 1944.

26. *Town Talk,* March 26, June 17, 19, 1943; *Shreveport Times,* July 9, 1943.

27. Sam H. Jones, "Will Dixie Bolt the New Deal?" *Saturday Evening Post,* March 6, 1943, 20–21, 42, 45; Garson, *The Democratic Party,* 95.

month before the national convention opened in June. The disgruntled delegates agreed "to drive the New Deal, the CIO Communists and negroes out of control of the Democratic party and restore state's rights." They hoped to create a 100-vote bloc of delegates to the national convention who were opposed to Roosevelt's renomination.[28]

As the national convention got underway, Sam Jones announced that an informal poll of Louisiana delegates revealed strong support for conservative senator Harry Byrd of Virginia for president, and that "we will join with other Southern states in opposing the nomination of Mr. Wallace for vice-president." Delegates from the state's Old Regular faction, however, were not so sure that Louisiana should abandon the president. Typically, they held that Roosevelt's nomination was certain, even with the threatened southern revolt, and that Louisiana should protect its interests by staying with the winner.[29]

When the Louisiana delegates met to decide whom to support for president, the insurgents carried the day. Committeeman Henry Clay Sevier, an avowed foe of Roosevelt and the New Deal, moved that Louisiana endorse Harry Byrd. Before Sevier's motion came to a vote, Old Regular James Comisky of New Orleans made a substitute motion to endorse Roosevelt, which lost by a 14–6 margin. Sevier's original motion then carried on a 16–4 vote. Under the unit rule all 22 of Louisiana's votes (two delegates were absent from the caucus) therefore went to Senator Byrd. The caucus also approved a resolution presented by visitor Wright Morrow of Texas that opposed "with all vigor" any platform plank favoring social equality between the races or anti–poll tax legislation, and advocated the right of states to manage their domestic affairs without federal government interference.[30]

Even though he experienced these and other defections on the southern front, Roosevelt easily garnered his fourth nomination. He received 1,176 votes on the first ballot, compared with 89 votes for Byrd (Louisiana, Mississippi, and Virginia), and 1 vote for James A. Farley. Louisi-

28. *Shreveport Times,* June 10, 1944; *Morning Advocate,* June 10, 1944.

29. *States,* July 18, 1944.

30. *Item,* July 19, 1944; *Morning Advocate,* July 19, 1944.

ana's state standard did not join the exuberant victory demonstration on the convention floor, because one of the anti-Roosevelt delegates had tied it tightly in place to deny any Roosevelt enthusiast unauthorized use of it during the demonstration. The Mississippi and Texas standards were similarly tied in place.[31]

Following the nomination, attention turned to Roosevelt's vice presidential selection. The president personally supported Wallace, but bowed to the wishes of leading urban party bosses who believed Wallace to be a poor choice because of the South's opposition to him. Following their advice, Roosevelt chose U.S. senator Harry S. Truman of Missouri.[32]

Walter Sillers, chairman of the Mississippi delegation, George Butler of Texas, and Louisiana's John Fred Odom attempted to start a stampede toward Sam Jones for the nomination. Jones received promises of support from five other states, but advised a caucus of those states to focus their efforts on a man who could obtain more national support than he. The Louisiana delegation, in order to defeat Wallace, ended up voting unanimously to support Truman to the bitter end. Truman won the nomination on the second ballot.[33]

Truman's nomination removed some of the bluster from the southern rebellion. Late in the convention, Sam Jones remarked that "the defeat of the radical Easterners" had been the major accomplishment in Chicago. Had it not been for the South, "the Democratic nominee for vice president would not have been Senator Truman, but would have been a man who brazenly flouted the traditions of the South." Many southerners felt similarly comfortable with Truman, grandson of slaveholders, because of his border-state origins. Their desperate attempt to nominate "anybody but Wallace," however, had caused them to overlook Truman's support of the New Deal, and his exposure to the problems of urban and minority

31. *Item*, July 21, 1944; *Morning Advocate*, July 21, 1944.

32. Garson, *The Democratic Party*, 119–22; Miller, *Plain Speaking*, 189; Cabell Phillips, *The Truman Presidency: The History of a Triumphant Succession* (New York, 1966), 44; Alonzo L. Hamby, *Beyond the New Deal: Harry S. Truman and American Liberalism* (New York, 1973), 32, 41.

33. *States*, July 19–21, 1944; Garson, *The Democratic Party*, 122; Phillips, *The Truman Presidency*, 47.

groups in Kansas City. Truman, while not an ardent liberal, was more moderate than most of the South. Southerners would eventually feel betrayed when he supported liberal causes during his presidency, especially the desegregation of the armed forces and the renewal of the Fair Employment Practices Commission.[34]

Even with Truman on the ticket, not all Louisiana Democrats supported Roosevelt in 1944. Irving L. Lyons wrote to the *States*, "I am enough of an optimist to believe that this country has not degenerated to the point where we have only one leader measuring up to the demands of the times, critical though they may be." The Southern Anti–New Deal Association, headquartered in Shreveport, attacked Sidney Hillman, one of the founders of the Congress of Industrial Organizations and its National Political Action Committee and a Roosevelt adviser: "Today we have the foreign-born Hillman pulling the strings in the campaign to re-elect Roosevelt and the New Deal." J. T. Powell, a New Orleans attorney, formed the Democratic Committee in Favor of Dewey, which instructed Democrats how to cast a vote for Dewey for president and Democratic candidates for the other offices.[35]

The Democrats' gravest challenge in Louisiana was the refusal of some of the state's Democratic electors to sign a pledge to vote for Roosevelt and Truman, as requested by the Democratic State Central Committee. Most Democratic electors had accepted the ticket after Truman's nomination, but the State Central Committee replaced seven electors in October because four had resigned rather than sign the pledge. Three others also refused to sign, but hoped to retain their posts. These three, E. Wales Brown of Shreveport, Bronier Thibault of Donaldsonville, and George Billeaud of Broussard, filed suit seeking to overturn their dismissal, but the Nineteenth Judicial District Court and the First Circuit Court of Appeals upheld the committee's action, citing the Louisiana Supreme Court ruling in the 1940 *Earl K. Long v. Wade O. Martin, Sr.* case,

34. *States,* July 22, 1944; *Morning Advocate,* July 22, 1944; Miller, *Plain Speaking,* 79–80; Hamby, *Beyond the New Deal,* 41–56; Alonzo L. Hamby, "The Liberals, Truman, and FDR as Symbol and Myth," *Journal of American History* 56 (March 1970): 859–67; Jonathan Daniels, *The Man of Independence* (New York, 1950), 234.

35. *States,* July 25, 1944; *Town Talk,* October 18, November 4, 1944.

which upheld the State Central Committee's right to determine Democratic nominees. The state supreme court declined to hear this subsequent case.[36]

Senator Truman brought the Democratic campaign to New Orleans in mid-October. He toured the city waterfront and addressed the Mississippi Valley Flood Control Association. When asked about Democratic chances in the election, he confidently replied, "All a Southerner has to do is read the speeches of Dewey and they will be all right." Furthermore, he indicated his belief that the continuation of the war provided a strong incentive to vote for the incumbent president: "I don't think people interested in winning the war will take the chance of upsetting the cordial relations with our allies and losing any more of our young men." He also remarked later that people "just never did trust" Dewey. "He had a moustache, for one thing, and since in those days, during the war, people were aware of Hitler, that moustache didn't do him any good."[37]

Truman's expectations for Democratic success were correct for Louisiana. The party ticket carried the state, and all ten of the state's electors voted for Roosevelt.[38]

Nevertheless, it is significant that Dewey received 15,509 more votes than had Willkie in 1940. In fact, the Republicans increased their vote in Louisiana in every presidential election from 1932 to 1948. In 1932, Roosevelt received 249,418 votes to Herbert Hoover's 18,863; in 1936, the totals were Roosevelt—292,894, Alf Landon—36,791; in 1940, Roosevelt—319,751, Wendell Willkie—52,446; in 1944, Roosevelt—281,564, Dewey—67,750; and in 1948, Harry Truman—136,344, Strom Thurmond—204,290, Thomas Dewey—72,657, and Henry Wallace—3,035. These totals reflect the Democratic percentage's fall from 92.8 percent in 1932 to 32.7 percent in 1948.[39]

36. *Morning Advocate,* September 28, October 14–15, 1944; *States,* October 7, 17, 1944; *Town Talk,* October 8, 1944.

37. *States,* October 14–15, 1944; Truman, *Memoirs,* vol. 1, 193; Miller, *Plain Speaking,* 188.

38. *Morning Advocate,* December 19, 1944.

39. Milburn Calhoun, ed., *Louisiana Almanac, 1995–96* (Gretna, La., 1995), 457; Stella Z. Theodoulou, *The Louisiana Republican Party, 1948–1984: The Building of a State Political Party* (New Orleans, 1985), 14.

The threat of the previous summer to withhold Louisiana contributions from Democratic coffers never became a reality. A congressional committee examining campaign expenditures in April 1945 found that Louisianians had contributed some $40,000 to Roosevelt's campaign. Interestingly, one-half that amount came from industrialist Andrew J. Higgins, recipient of millions of dollars worth of war contracts, and his family.[40]

Congressional elections held in Louisiana during World War II lived up to the state's reputation for spirited politics. In 1940, Governor Jones hoped the reformers could defeat all the incumbent Longite members of Congress, whom he thought no longer represented the will of the people.[41] He endorsed reform candidates in most races, and campaigned for his own "reform slate" of candidates. The reform effort was not entirely successful. Longite representatives Overton Brooks (Fourth District), Newt Mills (Fifth District), and A. Leonard Allen (Eighth District) were all reelected.

Two of the bitterest campaigns for Louisiana's congressional seats during 1940 occurred in the First and Second Districts, in and around New Orleans. The campaign opened when First District Representative Joachim O. Fernandez and Second District Representative Paul H. Maloney, both Longite allies, qualified to run for reelection. The reformers quickly fielded their own candidates: New Orleans attorneys Herve Racivitch in the First District and T. Hale Boggs in the Second, both of whom were veterans of Jones's gubernatorial campaign.[42]

In the First District, clear bifactionalism was clouded when *New Orleans States* city editor F. Edward Hebert entered the campaign. Hebert's friend, James A. Noe, had asked him in 1940 to begin planning a campaign for mayor of New Orleans in 1942. Hebert did not want that office, but agreed to run for Congress in 1940. One of his motives seems to have been his realization that even if he served only one term, the lifetime ac-

40. *Morning Advocate,* May 1, 1945; McGuire, "Andrew Jackson Higgins," 174–75.
41. *Town Talk,* July 2, 1940.
42. *Times-Picayune,* July 12, 15, 1940.

cess to the House floor accorded former members would provide him with a priceless news source when he returned to journalism.[43]

Hebert built a strong coalition of support through his association with Noe. Jones, Noe, and Old Regular leader George Montgomery reached an agreement that divided offices in the New Orleans area: Jones-Noe reform forces agreed not to oppose incumbent judges seeking reelection in the area and not to interfere directly in the 1942 New Orleans mayor's race in exchange for the Old Regulars' promise to support Jones-Noe candidates in the 1940 First and Second Congressional Districts, the First and Second Public Service Commission Districts, the Orleans Parish School Board, and Orleans Parish Juvenile Court.[44] This agreement, however, did not take into consideration the private ambition of the incumbent members of Congress.

In spite of that neglect, the Old Regulars and the reformers continued their loose alliance throughout the campaign. New Orleans mayor Maestri announced to an Old Regular caucus on August 22 that "we're all Jones boys now," and instructed the Old Regular leaders to "get out in [your] wards and work hard" for the Jones-Noe candidates. In return for this endorsement, several reform candidates for the Civil District Court withdrew from their campaigns.[45]

The association between Jones and Maestri, however, did not please all reformers. George Piazza, an independent candidate in the District A Civil District Court race, refused to withdraw. "You cannot have honest courts," he announced, "when you allow political organizations to name your judges."[46]

Despite its unpopularity in some corners, Jones's deal with the Old Regulars ensured Hebert's election in the First District race. Any candidate in New Orleans with support from Jones, Noe, and Maestri had little to fear, even from an incumbent congressman. Fernandez received the

43. Hebert and McMillan, *"Last of the Titans,"* 152–53.

44. *Times-Picayune,* July 16, 18, 1940; Hebert and McMillan, *"Last of the Titans,"* 153–54.

45. *Times-Picayune,* August 13, 1940.

46. *Ibid.*

support of organized labor groups, but the principal endorsements in New Orleans went to his opponent.[47]

Hebert and Fernandez virtually ignored Racivitch and campaigned against each other. Hebert called for a national two-ocean navy, an adequate army, a "first-rate air force," federal aid for Louisiana to stimulate industry, and a new outlet from New Orleans to the Gulf of Mexico to facilitate movement of wartime supplies and commerce. He also made sure to tie Fernandez inextricably to the Longite machine: "[Fernandez is one of] the diehards who can't understand the writing on the wall. They can't believe that after twelve years of plunderbund they have been counted out by the free and independent people of the state."[48]

Fernandez, fighting back, characterized Hebert as an enemy of labor and called his platform "pure, simple, unadulterated political fakery." The incumbent also read aloud on the stump letters of support from U.S. House speaker William Bankhead and House Democratic leader Sam Rayburn, and cited his memberships in the House Appropriations Committee and its Naval Appropriations Subcommittee as reasons why voters should reelect him.[49]

The concurrent Second District race began in confusion and ended in disappointment for its incumbent. Some anti-Longites, remembering that Paul Maloney occasionally supported reform, initially wanted to endorse him. Their wishes, however, ran counter to the ambitions of New Orleans attorney Hale Boggs. While administration leaders hoped that Boggs would run for the Public Service Commission, he preferred to run for Congress, and George Montgomery's indication of Old Regular willingness to drop Maloney opened the way for a Boggs candidacy in 1940.[50]

After Maloney realized the strength of his opposition, he declared that

47. Hebert and McMillan, *"Last of the Titans,"* 158; *Times-Picayune/New Orleans States,* August 4, 1940.

48. Hebert and McMillan, *"Last of the Titans,"* 159; *Times-Picayune,* August 13, 1940.

49. Hebert and McMillan, *"Last of the Titans,"* 157–61; *Times-Picayune,* August 15, 1940; *Congressional Record,* 76th Cong., 3d sess., 1940, vol. 86, pt. 17: 5526.

50. Hebert and McMillan, *"Last of the Titans,"* 154; Lindy Boggs, letter to author, February 28, 1984; *Times-Picayune,* August 9, 1940; John R. Kemp, ed., *Martin Behrman of New Orleans: Memoirs of a City Boss* (Baton Rouge, 1977), 335–41.

he would withdraw from the race. Loss of Old Regular support, he said, "would in effect strip my candidacy . . . of election machinery." Almost immediately after he made his announcement, however, he began to have second thoughts. Perhaps one reason was a newspaper advertisement run by an anti-Jones organization named the "Friends of Honest, Efficient Government," which called upon Second District voters to reelect Maloney because "we believe we are not asking too much when we seek to elect our Congressional representative without interference from any political machine."[51]

Maloney responded by choosing to rejoin the campaign, even though the Senate had quickly confirmed him as collector of internal revenue for the New Orleans district when President Roosevelt nominated him on August 8 (upon the recommendation of Longite senators John Overton and Allen Ellender). Boggs commented on Maloney's vacillation that "no man can be a serious candidate if he cannot make up his mind whether or not he is in the race."[52]

Boggs proceeded to attack Maloney for his Longite ties. In one campaign address, the challenger noted the dangerous world situation in which the United States found itself and asked his audience, "Isn't it a dangerous thing to have representing us as our Congressman a man who has expressed so much sympathy, tolerance, and understanding of Dictatorship?"[53]

Maloney struck back with an attack on Boggs for alleged leftist activities during his days as a student at Tulane University. "T. Hale Boggs Exposed!" proclaimed one Maloney leaflet, which charged that Boggs had joined the American Student Union in 1937 while studying at Tulane. According to the leaflet, the union promoted the pacifist "Oxford Pledge" by which members promised not to fight for the United States either in a defensive or an offensive war. "Think of an organization that tells red-blooded American men that you shall not fight in defense of the United

---

51. *Times-Picayune,* July 20, 25, 1940; *Times-Picayune/New Orleans States,* July 21, 1940.

52. *Times-Picayune,* August 9, 13–15, 17, 1940.

53. *Ibid.,* July 21, 1940; T. Hale Boggs, "Address" [1940], T. Hale Boggs Papers, HTML.

States of America," the text read. Imagine that if the United States is invaded, "you must stand cowardly by while your wives, mothers, sweethearts, and sisters fall helpless prey to the wild desires of human beasts."[54]

Another Maloney leaflet asked pointedly, "Shall It Be Americanism and Maloney or Communism and Boggs?" This leaflet contained the "information" that the "Dies Committee" (the House Unamerican Activities Committee) had labeled the American Student Union "one of the eleven Border Patrols of the Communist Party," and called Boggs "a disciple of the bristle-mustached Stalin."[55]

Boggs flatly denied the charges, saying he had never been a member of the American Student Union. He noted that he had chaired the student union building committee at Tulane and suggested that Maloney might have confused the two "student unions." "I have ever been ready and willing . . . to take up arms to defend the United States of America," he concluded. He also presented statements by Tulane president Rufus Harris and Law School dean Paul Brosman affirming that he had never been involved in any "subversive movements while at Tulane."[56]

Both candidates for the Second District seat supported strong national defense. Maloney furnished statements from other members of Congress urging his reelection because Congress needed his experience during the world crisis. Boggs in turn downplayed Maloney's experience. After France fell to the Nazis in June 1940, an event that sent a sudden chill through the United States, he belittled the supposed advantage of government experience: "For years France left her destiny in the hands of old men who were re-elected year after year, and where is France today but under the dictator's yoke?"[57] Boggs, with his combined reform/Old Regular support, swept into office in the Democratic primary in September 1940. He received 33,636 votes to Maloney's 25,590.

54. "T. Hale Boggs Exposed!" [1940], Boggs Papers.

55. "Shall It Be Americanism and Maloney or Communism and Boggs?" [1940], Ellender Papers.

56. Boggs, "Address" [1940], Rufus Harris Statement, Paul Brosman Statement, Boggs Papers.

57. "What National Leaders in Congress Say about Paul H. Maloney" [1940], Boggs, "Address," Boggs Papers.

The equally spirited contest in the Third District occurred in the general election. James Domengeaux, with Governor Jones's endorsement, defeated incumbent Robert L. Mouton in the September primary, but faced David W. Pipes, a Democrat-turned-Republican because of Henry Wallace, in the general election. Domengeaux had been Sam Jones's campaign manager in the Third District. Pipes was a sugar planter who had gained a national reputation during the 1920s when he obtained seed stalks of Mosaic disease–resistant P.O.J. cane from the Dutch East Java Experiment Station and grew enough of this variety to supply the American Sugar Cane League with seed stalks for distribution to other areas.[58]

The Third District, surrounding Lafayette in south-central Louisiana, contained much sugar-producing country, and the antipathy felt by some sugar planters about the Democratic vice presidential nomination spilled over into the congressional campaign. Domengeaux found himself in legal trouble after he assaulted state senator Dudley LeBlanc when LeBlanc compared him to Wallace. Domengeaux paid a twenty-five-dollar fine, stating that he was willing to pay the cost of the satisfaction he received from physically attacking a man who had equated him with Wallace.[59]

The Democrats could not safely count on a Third District victory. In 1914 the voters had elected Progressive W. P. Martin of Thibodaux to Congress over his Democratic opponent because of their displeasure with President Woodrow Wilson's sugar policy. Martin subsequently served in Congress until April 6, 1929, when he died after his election to an eighth term.

Third District voters with sugar interests who were disillusioned not only with Henry Wallace in particular, but also with the generally leftward drift of the Democratic party, tended to support Pipes, who had indicated the depth of his own dissatisfaction by switching from Democrat to Republican on July 17 and announcing his intention to run for the seat. U. S. G. Pettycrew wrote to Pipes, "I saw in the news that you was a *real*

58. *Times-Picayune,* August 2, 1940; Stuart O. Landry to Dr. Rufus C. Harris, May 20, 1940, David W. Pipes Papers, LLMVC.

59. *Town Talk,* July 22, 1940; *Shreveport Journal,* July 23, 1940.

Democrat and not a New Dealer." Jules Godchaux wrote that "a vote for the Republican candidates is the most effective way to register our protest." Pipes thus enjoyed protest support as a viable Republican candidate.[60]

Pipes waged his campaign more against Henry Wallace than against James Domengeaux. He opened his quest on September 15, remarking that the Louisiana sugar industry had withstood plant disease, insects, frost, flood, and drought, but that it "can better face all these than the prospect of four more years of Henry Wallace."[61]

Domengeaux and his supporters responded with appeals to Third District voters to remain loyal to the Democratic party in spite of Wallace. The rooster, not the donkey, is the symbol of the Louisiana Democratic Party, and at Abbeville, Sam Jones urged voters to "stamp the rooster from tip of beak to end of claws." Lieutenant Governor Marc Mouton urged Cajun voters, "Allons faire le vieux coq crier" (Let's make the old rooster crow.) They hoped these pleas for party loyalty would help defeat the new Republican.[62]

In speeches, Domengeaux attacked Pipes as a tool of the sugar establishment, and charged that he worked laborers in his sugarcane fields for long hours at low wages. The Democrat also pledged that he would "never vote for a declaration of war which would mean sending American boys overseas"—a reflection of the public sentiment to remain out of the war, just as his eventual vote for the declaration of war reflected a profound change in public opinion by December 8, 1941.[63]

Pipes waged a spirited campaign and attracted attention from both the national Republican party and the national press, but in the end he was not successful.[64] Third District voters chose the Democrat to represent them in Congress.

60. U. S. G. Pettycrew to David W. Pipes, October 3, 1940, Jules Godchaux to Pierre Chastant, August 2, 1940, Pipes Collection; *Times-Picayune,* July 30, 1940.

61. *Morning Advocate,* September 16, 1940.

62. *Morning Advocate,* October 31, 1940; *Town Talk,* November 4, 1940.

63. *Morning Advocate,* October 31, 1940.

64. Dudley A. White to David W. Pipes, September 16, 1940, and *Washington, D.C., Sunday Star, New York Herald Tribune, Chicago Sunday Tribune, New York Times, Washington Times Herald, Baltimore Sun,* all July 21, 1940, clippings in Pipes Collection.

The campaigns in the Fourth and Fifth Districts were relatively tame. The Fourth District race drew five contestants: incumbent T. Overton Brooks and four challengers, three of whom (Henry O'Neal, James U. Galloway, and J. Frank Colbert) had supported Jones's gubernatorial candidacy.[65] The governor therefore remained neutral in the first Democratic primary but endorsed O'Neal over Brooks in the second, citing O'Neal's "ability, honor, and integrity," as well as his personal friendship with the new Speaker of the House, Sam Rayburn, who had replaced the late William Bankhead.[66]

In the face of the challenge first from four opponents and now from O'Neal, Brooks stressed the significance of his congressional experience and the importance of national defense during the deteriorating world situation. While he did not advocate active American involvement in combat, Brooks's stance accurately reflected public opinion in northwest Louisiana, which was somewhat stronger than opinion in the rest of the state in accepting possible American intervention in the war.[67]

He scored the Roosevelt administration for its failure to prepare the nation's defenses for any eventuality during the past eight years and belittled its catch-up efforts: "Stuffing money into our national defense system will not revitalize it overnight." He pledged his continued support for the nation's preparedness program, support for the "Dies Americanism Committee," adequate federal old-age pensions, and assistance "for the farmers and workingmen of Louisiana." His campaign slogan was "Defense to the Utmost," and campaign literature stressed that he was "At His Post of Duty."[68]

Fourth District voters decided to return a man of experience to Congress, as they elected Brooks despite the reformers' efforts in favor of

65. *Shreveport Journal,* May 31, June 5, 24, August 6, 16, 1940; *Shreveport Times,* August 6, 1940.

66. *Morning Advocate,* September 8, October 3, 1940.

67. *Shreveport Times,* September 9, 13, 19, 22, October 23, 1939, June 12, 14, 16, 24, 1940; *Congressional Record,* 76th Cong., 3d sess., 1940, vol. 86, pt. 16: 4062, 4211–12, 4622–23.

68. *Shreveport Journal,* July 18, 1940; *Shreveport Times,* August 6, 1940; *Congressional Record,* 76th Cong., 3d sess., vol. 86, pt. 17: A2550–51.

O'Neal. Brooks's friends evidently could not resist a bit of highjinks following his win. On the morning after their victory parade in downtown
Shreveport, groundskeepers at the Caddo Parish courthouse found a
stuffed effigy bearing the name "Sam Jones" hanging from a tree on the
courthouse square. Brooks continued to survive anti-Longite opposition
and remained in Congress until his death in 1961.[69]

The Fifth District race was even quieter than the Fourth. Even though
his five opponents included Lincoln Parish district attorney Truett Scar-
borough, and state senators Edward Gladney and D. Y. Smith, incumbent Newt V. Mills led in the first primary and defeated Gladney in the
second primary.[70]

The campaign for Louisiana's Sixth District seat in 1940 focused on
Sam Jones and the reform effort to overhaul the state. The race originally
drew four candidates: incumbent John K. Griffith; attorney Jared Young
Sanders, Jr., son of former governor Sanders; Sidney Bowman from
Hammond; and New Roads sugar businessman Allen Ramsey Wurtele,
a Republican. Sanders, scion of a family whose anti-Longism had included the elder Sanders's celebrated fisticuffs with Huey Long in the
lobby of the Roosevelt Hotel in New Orleans in late 1927, allied himself
firmly with Jones and the reformers in the congressional campaign.[71]
Griffith and Bowman attacked Jones and the reformers, while Wurtele
conducted an anti–New Deal crusade.

Sanders received widespread support from Jones leaders in the district,
and the governor issued a written endorsement. The Hammond Democratic Club backed Sanders for "carr[ying] the banner of decency and
honest government shoulder to shoulder with us in our recent fight for
the restoration of democracy in Louisiana."[72]

Sanders gratefully accepted this and other anti-Longite support. He
told a Sixth District Sam Jones rally in Baton Rouge that the main choice

69. *Morning Advocate,* October 16, 1940; *Congressional Directory,* 88th Cong., 1st sess.,
1963, 65.

70. *Times-Picayune,* July 23, 1940; *Morning World,* September 11, October 16, 1940.

71. *Morning Advocate,* August 20, 1940; *Hammond Vindicator,* July 5, 1940; *Congressional Directory,* 77th Cong., 1st sess., 1941, 43; Williams, *Huey Long,* 271–72.

72. *Hammond Vindicator,* August 9, 16, 1940; *Times-Picayune,* August 14, 1940.

in the race was between "those who believe in the graft and corruption of the past 12 years, and those who are for honesty and decency in government." He acknowledged that democratic government was under attack abroad, but also reminded his audiences that it was on trial "right here in the United States," referring to the recently exposed Louisiana Scandals. He cast an eye toward his plans as a lawmaker by also warning that the United States needed to be armed and trained now that only the British fleet stood between the New World and the Nazis.[73]

Representative Griffith began his campaign in absentia, with a political advertisement in which he maintained that "world conditions are such that it is necessary for Congress to remain in session and this prevents my returning home at this time to conduct a personal campaign." He stressed the importance of his membership on a "major committee" (Naval Affairs). "Local Democratic Friends" paid for another advertisement that asked voters to reelect him because "this is no time to play petty politics in National Affairs and there should be no change made in our Congressmen or Senators in Washington that would delay the preparedness program."[74]

Griffith also launched virulent attacks on both Jones and Sanders. He charged that the governor was "attempting to drive the people like cattle and to tell them how to vote" with his endorsement of Sanders. He criticized Sanders for alleged excessive absences during his previous congressional term.[75]

Bowman, the third candidate in the race, also waged an anti-Jones and anti-Sanders campaign. He denounced Sanders's absence on crucial congressional roll call votes and charged that Sanders had played only a small role in the Jones campaign. He assailed Sam Jones, who, he said, "has replaced dictatorship with autocracy." He remarked that the government-reorganization constitutional amendment, which was also on the ballot in the 1940 fall election, "does to the government of Louisiana what Hitler,

73. *Town Talk,* August 6, 1940; *Hammond Vindicator,* August 9, 16, 30, 1940; *Morning Advocate,* August 18, 1940.

74. *Hammond Vindicator,* August 23, 30, 1940.

75. *Morning Advocate,* September 4, 9, 1940.

Stalin, and Mussolini did to their countries."[76] Nevertheless, this association with the reformers turned out to be an asset for Sanders, who defeated both his opponents in the first Democratic primary.

The Seventh District campaign was no contest. Incumbent René L. DeRouen announced that he would not run for reelection because of poor health. The only candidate who qualified to run for the seat was Vance Plauché, a Lake Charles attorney who was also Sam Jones's friend, campaign comanager, and first head of civil service. Jones enthusiastically endorsed Plauché's candidacy, and he ran unopposed in both the primary and the general election.[77]

The Eighth District race was quite a bit livelier, featuring a Longite, an anti-Longite, and a genuine Long. The Longite was incumbent congressman A. Leonard Allen, brother of the late governor Oscar Allen, who had first been elected to Congress in 1936. The Long was Dr. George Shannon Long, Huey and Earl's elder brother, who had been a dentist and state representative in Oklahoma before moving back to Louisiana in 1934, originally to Monroe, and later to the small community of Dry Prong in rural Grant Parish.[78]

The reformers were represented by James B. Aswell, Jr. Aswell was the son of a former superintendent of education and Eighth District congressman who, along with Governor Newton C. Blanchard, had reformed the state's education system from 1904 to 1908. The younger Aswell had shown promise of a literary career during the 1920s when his short stories appeared in major magazines, including *Collier's*. He began a newspaper column, "My New York," and was the Broadway correspondent for the Central Press Association. Increasing difficulty in selling his material during the late 1930s, however, led to deep disillusionment with the American literary establishment and prompted his return to Natchitoches Parish in September 1938 to become a "Farmer-Writer," as he de-

76. *Ibid.,* August 31, September 1, 9, 1940.

77. *Times-Picayune,* July 19, 1940; *Congressional Directory,* 77th Cong., 1st sess., 43; John B. Fournet to Rene L. DeRouen, July 22, 1940, Fournet Papers, LLMVC.

78. *Town Talk,* July 5, September 6, 1940; *Congressional Directory,* 77th Cong., 1st sess., 43; *Congressional Directory,* 83d Cong., 1st sess., 53; Williams, *Huey Long,* 16, 22.

scribed himself. He was a campaign leader for Sam Jones in the Eighth District and became state director of publicity following Jones's election.[79]

Reformers joined in Aswell's effort to unseat Allen. Jones-Noe alliance forces throughout the district endorsed him, as did the governor himself. His campaign was at once anti-Longite and pro-preparedness. In his opening speech, a radio broadcast from Alexandria (the major city of the Eighth District), he recalled that Allen had "defended the regime of graft and corruption from every stump he could get hold of" in the recent gubernatorial campaign. He later dubbed Allen "the zero Congressman of the United States" because no bill he introduced had ever passed both the House and the Senate.[80]

In stressing his support for United States preparedness, Aswell referred often to the fall of the French. He remarked on the Fourth of July that "we must be tough in our determination to keep this island of democracy free in a world where chains clank and the marching feet of aggressors sound louder and louder." He compared Allen to the tired old politicians who had "lost" France: "France had too many Leonard Allens in office and we have too many in Washington."[81]

Aswell also relied on a network of "Junior Jim Aswell Clubs," organizations of young voters dedicated to electing a young man (Aswell was born in 1908, Allen in 1891, Long in 1883) to represent them. Club director Cecil Roberts remarked, "We are the ones to have to live under future governments [and] we want a young man who understands our needs to lay a strong foundation for that government."[82]

---

79. Rodney Cline, *Builders of Louisiana Education* (Baton Rouge, 1963), 14–16; Merritt Hubbard to Ann Watkins, October 28, 1929, Polly Hightower to James B. Aswell, Jr., December 12, 1927, H. N. Swanson to Aswell, December 9, 1929, Swanson to Carol Hill, January 13, 1930, Anne L. Young to Aswell, November 11, 1929, Mark Hellinger to Aswell, March, 1931, Aswell to Ann Watkins, January 15, 1935, Watkins to Aswell, January 8, 1935, H. N. Swanson to Aswell, July 31, 1933, rejection slips from *Ladies Home Journal,* April 4, 1930, *Cosmopolitan,* June 2, 1930, Aswell Voter Registration Certificate, all in Aswell Papers; *Morning Advocate,* June 23, 1942.

80. *Town Talk,* July 18, August 2, 5, 13, 27, 30, 1940

81. *Ibid.,* June 26, July 5, August 27, 1940.

82. *Ibid.,* July 17, 1940; Aswell to Cecil Roberts, September 12, 1940, Aswell Papers.

Incumbent Allen identified himself as "a consistent foe of un-Americanism, [who has] supported every move in Congress to stamp out un-American 'isms' and has always championed Congressman Dies," noting further that he had authored a bill to deport American Communist Party leader Harry Bridges. Although he continued to oppose active American intervention in the war, Allen defended his support of preparedness, and his patriotic stance led Major General O. R. Gellette, adjutant general of the Order of the Stars and Bars, to call upon all fellow Confederate veterans and their widows, children, and friends to vote for Allen because of "his fight against the sinister forces of foreign 'isms' which are now seeking to undermine and destroy our great nation."[83]

Though Allen's staff announced that he was too busy to campaign full-time in the district, he utilized a refinement of Huey Long's system of sound equipment mounted on trucks. By 1940, improvements in the quality of sound recording had made the live politician unnecessary. Allen used two trucks to broadcast tape recordings of his speeches. The *Town Talk* immediately recognized the long-range implications of this campaign device and commented, "If television could be hooked up to the new type broadcast trucks, a politician could 'visit' in person and carry on a campaign throughout his district or state and remain comfortable in his office all at the same time." (Louisiana had received its first look at television on September 11, 1939, when RCA set up special broadcasting and receiving equipment at the D. H. Holmes department store in New Orleans.)[84]

Despite his largely absentee campaign, Allen was renominated in the first Democratic primary, but only by a slim margin. He received 21,835 votes to Aswell's 17,013 and Long's 4,219. The seat remained largely in Longite hands for decades. Allen held onto it until 1952, when George Long was elected. Long, in turn, served until 1958, when he was defeated by Harold McSween. This break in Longite control was immediately repaired by Earl Long, who had just been elected to the seat when he died in 1960.[85]

83. *Town Talk,* July 16, August 1, 1940.
84. *Ibid.,* August 31, 1940.
85. *Town Talk,* September 11, 1940.

Overall, Governor Jones was pleased with the result of the 1940 congressional election. Reformers now occupied five seats. Moreover, the three incumbent Longites promised to cooperate with him "toward the upbuilding of a better and greater state and the securing of national recognition."[86]

The 1942 federal political season, Louisiana version, was a relatively quiet interlude between the major statewide campaigns of 1940 and 1944. The 1942 contests are notable, however, for the Old Regular's defection from their alliance with the reformers supporting Hale Boggs in the Second District; J. Y. Sanders's loss to James H. Morrison in the Sixth District; and Longite Allen J. Ellender's reelection to the United States Senate even though reformer E. A. Stephens attempted to unseat him.

Early speculation that former governor Noe would run for Ellender's Senate seat faded away in 1942 as federal investigators focused on Noe in the Win or Lose Oil Company tax evasion case. By 1942, moreover, Sam Jones and Noe had ended their alliance. Therefore, Stephens, a New Orleans businessman and former president of the New Orleans Dock Board, took up the reform banner in the Senate campaign.

Ellender and his allies' first reaction was to report that they had considered Stephens a suspicious character ever since Jones had named him to the dock board. They were joined in their attack by the *Farmer's Friend,* the newspaper of the Farmers' Protective Union and mouthpiece for James H. Morrison, which called Stephens a "pal and cohort of Hitler's No. 1 U.S. Agent Baron von Spiegel." About Stephens's assignment to the dock board, the paper commented, "This latest obnoxious appointment made by stupid Sam Jones will give the Nazis an inside track into the biggest and most important utility in the State of Louisiana."[87]

Edgar von Spiegel was the German consul in New Orleans until he was expelled along with other German diplomats by President Roosevelt in June 1941. Stephens replied to insinuations that his association with the German meant he supported the Nazi cause with the observation that as

86. *Morning Advocate,* November 7, 1940.
87. *Farmer's Friend,* n.d., clipping in Fournet Collection.

president of the dock board, he had treated von Spiegel with civility but had not developed a warm friendship with him. The reformers themselves were suspicious of the German as well. Governor Jones requested Secretary of State Cordell Hull to investigate the consul's activities as early as the summer of 1940.[88]

Ellender also played on the war issue. "This is no time for factional or personal politics," he said in his formal statement of candidacy. "I do not believe that anyone should turn . . . to personal political matters, but that we should all pull together." This belief, however, did not prevent him from launching an attack on Stephens for what Ellender termed his "foreign" birth, as a native of Virginia. Stephens responded by wondering publicly whether Mayor Maestri and Ellender, had they been alive in 1815, would have rushed to the Chalmette battlefield and shouted to Andrew Jackson, "Stop! You can't save our city and our nation! You are a foreigner from Tennessee!" Dr. George Long, in his statement endorsing Stephens, foreshadowed a memorable quip by Lloyd Bentsen in his 1988 vice presidential debate with Dan Quayle. Long remarked of Ellender, "I know the friends of Huey Long. I know the Huey Long program inside out, and I also know a hypocrite when I see one."[89]

The striking feature of the 1942 Senate race was its aura of "politics as usual." The war became at best a second-rate issue as the factions battled for the Senate seat amid charges and countercharges of corrupt activities.[90] Just as the reformers feared, Ellender retained the seat, thus signaling something of a Longite resurgence.

House of Representatives races in 1942 were generally lackluster. The *Times-Picayune* characterized the campaigns in the first Democratic primary as "dull." The elections resulted, however, in three changes in Louisiana's House delegation.

Anti-Longite Hale Boggs drew a major obstacle to his reelection when former congressman Paul Maloney resigned from his post as collector of internal revenue for Louisiana and announced that he would run for his

88. *Times-Picayune,* June 18, 1940; *States,* June 16, 1941.

89. *Morning Advocate,* July 22, August 19, 1942.

90. Becnel, *Senator Allen Ellender,* 115–21.

old seat in the House. In the ensuing campaign, Boggs stressed his unstinting support for the war effort and his successful efforts to bring military bases to the First District and charged that Maloney had done nothing during his years in Congress to prepare the country for the crisis of war. "The tide of history left him sitting on his little raft of petty, local politics," he remarked of Maloney's experience. Maloney countered by citing those years of service helping the country survive the depths of despair caused by the Great Depression as reason for the voters to return him to Washington. He was apparently successful in winning back at least some of the Old Regulars who had previously crossed over to support Boggs, as he defeated the incumbent (although by fewer than a thousand votes) to reclaim his place in the House.[91]

The Sixth District race featured James H. Morrison challenging incumbent J. Y. Sanders. Sanders opened his campaign in July with a ringing proclamation of his support for President Roosevelt's conduct of the war. Morrison, however, questioned Sanders's dedication to the interests of his constituents. "While our beloved people were beset with worries that their sons in the armed forces were given adequate equipment," Morrison fumed, "what was this Sam Jones rubber stamp doing? . . . little J. Y. Sanders was helping to author, support, and vote for a pension bill for himself . . . was securing for himself an X [unlimited gasoline] rationing card, and playing petty politics at the request and dictates of Gov. Jones." Sanders countered that he had not voted for a four-thousand-dollar pension for himself, and that statements to the contrary were "either malicious fabrications of a perverted intellect or they are the delusions of a diseased imagination."[92]

Morrison's platform was a mixture of pledges "to do everything possible to win the war as soon as possible," as well as "to support President Roosevelt's war policy 100%," and promises of jobs and benefits for the Sixth District. Sanders, in turn, objected to Morrison's promising to support the war in Congress when he had not served in the armed forces. "By his own actions and utterances," Sanders said, "he has branded him-

91. *Times-Picayune*, July 25, August 9, 12, September 2, 9, 11, 1942.
92. *Morning Advocate*, July 8, 12, 1942.

self an Isolationist, an Obstructionist, an Objector to Military Service in time of war, an advocate of the America First Committee, and the German Bund, and a sympathizer of [Burton K.] Wheeler, [Hamilton] Fish, and [Charles] Lindbergh."[93] These barbs, however, as well as Sanders's plea that voters not grant a draft exemption to "allergic-to-khaki" Morrison, failed, as he lost the election by the slim margin of 27,990 votes to 29,078 for Morrison.

Vance Plauché chose not to run for reelection in the Seventh District. State Representative William J. Dodd considered a campaign for the office, but the army draft called him into service and he chose not to ask for a deferment to run for Congress. Opelousas insurance man Henry D. Larcade subsequently defeated J. L. McHugh—who had Governor Jones's active support—for the post.[94]

The next congressional elections, in 1944, returned all Louisiana's members of the House of Representatives to Washington. The only lively campaign occurred in the Sixth District, where Congressman Morrison drew several opponents, the most prominent of whom were East Baton Rouge state senator H. Alva Brumfield and Tangipahoa Parish district attorney Bolivar E. Kemp, Jr. Morrison defeated Brumfield in the second primary.[95]

United States senator John Overton also faced a challenge when his term expired in 1944. He announced in March of that year that he intended to retire and return to his Alexandria home. James A. Noe declared his intention to run for the seat, but withdrew when his campaign failed to attract adequate support. Former governor Earl Long stated that if Overton did not run, then he would enter the race. For the reformers, E. A. Stephens declared his candidacy but Sam Jones revealed that he would return to private life at the end of his term as governor rather than run for the Senate seat. At the behest of "Democratic colleagues in Wash-

93. *Ibid.,* October 2, 4, 15, 1942.

94. William J. Dodd to John B. Fournet, March 10, August 21, October 2, 1942, Fournet Collection; *Congressional Directory,* 78th Cong., 1st sess., 43; *Morning Advocate,* October 15, 1942.

95. *Morning Advocate,* December 19, 1944.

ington" and "insistent demands from all political factions in the state," Overton changed his mind and proclaimed his candidacy for reelection.[96]

Overton based his campaign on his record of support for the war effort and his work to provide "several hundred million dollars" worth of flood control, navigation, irrigation, and reclamation projects to the state. He also revealed an uneasiness with the growth of the federal government.[97]

Despite his announcement during 1943 that he had been "stabbed in the back" by the Old Regulars who had planned to support James A. Noe in the 1944 Senate race, Overton received support from that organization as well as from Senator Ellender. He was also backed by some north Louisiana interests not normally associated with the Longites. The *Shreveport Times* maintained that if Overton should lose, it would likely leave north and central Louisiana without the one Senate seat they had customarily held.[98]

Overton's principal opponent was Stephens, loser to Ellender in 1942 and now a veteran of both the Jones and Davis gubernatorial campaigns. Stephens attacked Overton on the issues of his age, his Longite connections, and his opposition to Roosevelt's successful attempt to change the arms embargo at the beginning of the war in order to ship arms to Britain and France.[99]

Overton overcame the challenge posed by Stephens and two minor candidates and won reelection in the first primary. In a postmortem editorial on the race, the *New Orleans Item* found three reasons for Stephens's loss: Jones and Davis chose not to endorse him openly; many reformers voted for Overton; and late in the campaign, Stephens adopted a more liberal stance by endorsing the New Deal, thus causing some voters to consider him to be indecisive and insincere.[100]

---

96. John H. Overton to W. Scott Heywood, April 1, 1944, Heywood to Sam Jones, May 6, 1944, Jones to Heywood, May 12, 1944, Jennings-Heywood Oil Syndicate Records; *Morning Advocate,* May 12, 18, 24, July 6, 9, 23, September 21, 1944; *Item,* May 24, 1944; *Town Talk,* June 29, July 8, 1944; *States,* July 8, 1944.

97. *Morning Advocate,* July 7, 25, August 9, 1944.

98. *Ibid.,* July 27, August 16, 1944; *Shreveport Times,* July 30, 1944.

99. *Morning Advocate,* July 28, August 11, 1944; *States,* August 11, 1944.

100. *Morning Advocate,* September 21, 1944; *Item,* September 14, 1944.

*   *   *

The 1944 presidential and congressional races marked the end of federal elections in Louisiana during the World War II years. Several of these contests reflected the bifactional divisions within the state. The success of the reformers in the 1940 congressional elections, following on the heels of Sam Jones's displacement of the Longites in the executive branch, was the zenith of achievement for the anti-Longites on the federal level during the war years. But while voter displeasure with the Longites contributed to reform success in five districts that year, the reformers failed to hold their gains. Moreover, they failed to capture either of the state's Senate seats. The Longite faction thus remained strong, capable of reasserting its control of the state as it did in Earl Long's triumphant return as governor in 1948.

The war years also sowed the seeds of major discord in national politics that were to blossom during the later days of peace. The Democratic party in 1940 and 1944 beat back fledgling southern revolts by means of the political power, record of leadership, and overpowering personality of Franklin D. Roosevelt. By 1948, however, the South's anger at the Democratic party—by then well on its way to becoming ever less rural, conservative, and southern—could no longer be contained by President Harry Truman, and the party split apart.

7

Prep Schools for Boot Camp

Education in Louisiana during the war years faced unprecedented problems, assumed new responsibilities, and increased its emphasis on certain themes of the traditional curriculum. When the United States initiated national defense programs that included training thousands of soldiers in Louisiana army camps, children of the many soldiers transplanted for that purpose overran school systems designed to accommodate only the local population. The central Louisiana area, encompassing Camps Beauregard, Livingston, Claiborne, and Polk, experienced significant overcrowding. State superintendent of education John E. Coxe announced on January 7, 1941, that approximately six hundred more students were attending school in Rapides Parish than in the previous year and that the system expected about five hundred additional students by February 15. Small Pollock High School in neighboring Grant Parish experienced an increase of about one hundred students and expected about one hundred more within a few weeks. Nevertheless, Coxe promised that Louisiana would provide education for all children of soldiers stationed in the state.[1]

Educators, however, experienced problems fulfilling that promise. Massive federal aid programs that might have facilitated the absorption of the new students did not then exist. The major federal assistance program available during the early 1940s was a Works Progress Administra-

---

1. *Town Talk,* January 7, 1941.

tion program cosponsored by the State Department of Education, which provided nutritious lunches for underprivileged children.[2] The new need for expansion of facilities and faculty had no similar federal program to help the state meet it.

A specific difficulty brought on by the war was that the massive army training exercises known as the "Louisiana Maneuvers," conducted during 1941 and 1942, posed considerable danger to schoolchildren riding buses on roads crowded with military vehicles. Delays in opening schools in the maneuver area in turn created problems in completing the requisite number of school days as well as problems in accounting. The school boards preferred beginning teacher pay periods on the actual first day of classes, thus retaining control of payroll funds for an additional time, while the Louisiana Teachers' Association requested that pay periods begin on the day school would have normally begun. The State Board of Education resolved the dispute, ordering school systems in the maneuver area in 1941 to pay their employees on the same schedule they would have used if they had followed their normal calendars.[3]

The problems in transportation caused by wartime gasoline rationing were also felt by the school system. The State Department of Education in 1943 directed all parish superintendents to prepare maps for the routes of each school bus so that an adequate supply of war-rationed gasoline could be obtained.[4]

Another severe wartime shortage was, of course, that of personnel. Hundreds of teachers and other school employees either entered the armed forces or accepted higher-paying jobs in war-related industries. As a result, the state issued more than a thousand temporary teaching certificates between March 1941 and March 1942. These "Class T" certifi-

2. Jerry W. Valentin, "The WPA and Louisiana Education," *Louisiana History* 12 (fall 1969): 391–95.

3. Willoughby Aaron Sullivan, Jr., "The Development of the Louisiana Teachers' Association" (Ed.D. diss., Louisiana State University, 1968), 310; *Morning Advocate,* August 14, 1941; Louisiana Department of Education, Bulletin No. 460: *Official Proceedings, August 22, 1941.* Department of Education bulletins will hereinafter be cited as "Bulletin" with the appropriate number and title.

4. Bulletin No. 518: *Ninety-fourth Annual Report for the Session 1942–43,* 20.

cates were valid only for one year and were issued only to "applicants of high qualifications on recommendation of the superintendent." Regardless of that claim, Louisiana Teachers' Association leaders worried that the new teachers would be unqualified, that scholastic achievement in the state would drop, and that "the schools will be subjected to harsh and unjust criticism."[5]

In the midst of these dislocations and annoyances, Louisiana schools assumed additional functions in wartime society. Teachers, already under stress owing to increased class size, implemented rationing programs for scarce resources by enrolling students on ration lists and distributing ration books or commodities. They also encouraged their charges to buy war stamps and bonds to help finance the war effort.[6]

The Louisiana education system, along with other systems across the country, attempted to inculcate a strong awareness of national defense and a vigorous patriotism in its students. The *Times-Picayune* observed, "National defense will be an underlying theme of classes from kindergarten through college," and the observation proved correct. During the summer of 1940, representatives from the American Legion of Louisiana and the United Veterans Defense Council appeared before the Board of Education to request new programs for the schools. The American Legion requested a course on flag etiquette, and the Veterans Defense Council petitioned that one hour each week be set aside to educate students "that a national crisis now exists." The board approved the peti-

---

5. *Town Talk,* August 31, 1945; Sullivan, "The Development of the Louisiana Teachers' Association," 199; E. B. Robert, "The College of Education of Louisiana State University in the Present Emergency, March 4, 1942," in *The Life and Work of E. B. (Ted) Robert* (Baton Rouge, 1972), 214; "Minutes of the Executive Council, Louisiana Teachers' Association, May 24, 1941," *Louisiana Schools,* September 1941, 32; "Editorial Comment," *Louisiana Schools,* January 1942, 17; "Shortage of Teachers with Special Reference to Louisiana," *Louisiana Schools,* December 1942, 9.

6. *Town Talk,* January 22, February 4, 1942; Sullivan, "The Development of the Louisiana Teachers' Association," 311; Bessie Lawrence, interview by author, September 10, 1983; Thomas P. Southerland, "Rules and Regulations Enacted by Rapides Parish School Board since 1893 and Their Implications" (Ed.D. diss., Louisiana State University, 1960), 55–56.

tions, and directed an enthusiastic Department of Education to implement the program.[7]

The department quickly prepared a circular explaining the objectives of an "intelligent patriotism" program. Included were several specific goals for teachers. Depending on grade level, students would learn to understand and appreciate the meaning of the flag; to sing the national anthem and other patriotic songs; and to condemn "dishonesty, corruption, graft, and inefficiency in government" (an objective especially useful in Louisiana). They would hold mock constitutional conventions and learn that they would not be able to do so under a dictator, and would study the Magna Carta, the Declaration of Independence, and the Bill of Rights.[8]

Programs throughout the state emphasized the combined themes of defense and patriotism. Teachers at Ruston High School, for example, developed and taught a unit on national defense during 1941. Students learned about the army and navy, defense bases, diplomatic policy, and the role of industry in war.[9]

Decades after the war, Bessie Lawrence, a third-grade teacher at Buckeye High School in rural Rapides Parish during the 1940s, remembered the patriotic tenor of school life during the war years. The school day would begin with the Pledge of Allegiance and salute to the flag. The principal would often conduct assemblies around the flagpole in front of the school. The students would sing patriotic songs, and a faculty member, or occasionally a soldier, would speak on a patriotic theme, stressing the virtue of the democracy symbolized by the United States flag. "We taught them that's what men were fighting for. As long as it flew, we would be free, but if someone else took us, we would not be free."[10]

In New Orleans, teachers at Henry W. Allen Elementary School used the popularity of military subjects to encourage their students to read

7. *Times-Picayune,* August 26, 1941; Bulletin No. 438: *Official Proceedings, August 16, 1940,* 25–26, 28–29.

8. Bulletin No. 453: *Minutes of the Meeting of the State Board of Education, May 5 and 6, 1941,* 26–27.

9. Judith Crymes, "National Defense—A Project," *Louisiana Schools,* January 1942, 19, 32.

10. Bessie Lawrence, interview by author, September 10, 1983.

more energetically. They devised a system of military ranks in which students received "promotions" for reading certain books. Reading any ten approved books made a student a "second lieutenant" in the army or an "ensign" in the navy; two historical novels read promoted one to the rank of "first lieutenant" or "lieutenant j. g." After rising through the ranks by means of assigned reading, a student could complete the program by reading three "outstanding" plays and become a "general" or an "admiral."[11]

The new emphasis on patriotic observances in the public schools caused disagreement about the constitutional relationship between church and state. Controversy arose when A. J. Smith, principal of Evergreen High School in Avoyelles Parish, refused to exempt Jehovah's Witnesses attending his school from pledging allegiance to the flag during classroom exercises, even though doing so conflicted with their religious beliefs. Reverend Victor Blackwell of the denomination and Richard Cadwallader, a representative of the Louisiana League for the Preservation of Constitutional Rights, protested Smith's requirement to the Louisiana Board of Education. Attorney General Eugene Stanley advised board members that because they had approved the resolution requiring the observance, he could find no reason why they should not be the ones to enforce it. The board split on the issue. Most members stated that all students should salute the flag, but others suggested a compromise that would specifically exempt Jehovah's Witnesses from the requirement. The board deferred action on the question indefinitely, leaving parish superintendents and school principals to wrestle with the problem.[12]

In addition to the measures designed to inculcate patriotism in schoolchildren, the Department of Education developed plans for adult instruction about the national emergency, in response to a nationwide call by President Roosevelt and U.S. Commissioner of Education John W. Studebaker for development of forums focused on war-related issues. Louisiana programs included singing patriotic songs, reciting the Pledge of

11. *Times-Picayune/New Orleans States,* November 23, 1941.
12. Bulletin No. 453: *Minutes . . . May 5 and 6, 1941,* 31–33; *Town Talk,* January 8, 1941; *Morning Advocate,* April 9, May 7, 1941.

Allegiance, and discussing pertinent topics, including "The Local Community's Part in the Present Emergency," "Public Health and the War," "The Farm Family's Part in the Present Emergency," "Inter-American Friendship," and "The Bill of Rights."[13]

World War II also touched off a debate concerning the utility of education. Governor Jones asked educators to make schooling more practical. "The plain fact is that our boys and girls are not learning in sufficient numbers how to earn a living in their own bailiwicks," he complained. "Somehow, I can't escape from the notion that it is more important for a young man in the coastal parishes to know how to build a boat than to know Latin."[14] Although the governor might have overstated his case in order to be persuasive, he clearly believed that Louisiana should train its students for traditional farming, fishing, and trapping occupations, as well as for positions in the newer oil and chemical industries.

Not everyone in Louisiana agreed that public education should abandon its responsibilities for teaching the history and legacies of Western civilization and developing well-rounded intellects just for the purpose of imparting timely technical knowledge. John Edward Hardy, writing in the *Louisiana Municipal Review,* remarked, "All that the new war-time studies can provide is a knowledge of technique. The necessary development of the intellect must be accomplished by other means." If educators neglect to instill in students the qualities that empower them to use technical power justly, then "we are defeated though we conquer those nations which have appeared as the immediate incarnation of the forces of evil."[15] Hardy argued his case well, but modifications of the curricula to incorporate programs requested by the federal government tilted education in the direction of its vocational components.

Such vocational programs were designed to contribute to the war effort by improving industrial performance and increasing agricultural production. Schools provided industrial training under three plans. Plan

13. Bulletin No. 478: *Proposed Plan of Citizenship and Civilian Morale Education for Louisiana,* 1–2, 4–7.

14. *Morning Advocate,* August 12, 1941; *Times-Picayune,* October 21, 1941.

15. John Edward Hardy, "War-Time Proposals for High School Curricula Changes," *Louisiana Municipal Review,* March-April, 1943, 27, 42.

I (Trade and Industrial) established pre-employment refresher courses for people drawn from the rolls of the Louisiana State Employment Office and Works Progress Administration, as well as courses for people already employed. Plan I courses were devoted to such subjects as welding, machinery, electricity, sheet metal, automobile mechanics, and radio repair. Classes met when schools were not in regular use. By the end of the 1939–40 school year, 4,938 people were enrolled in courses offered under Plan I.[16]

Plan II (Vocational Education for Defense Workers for Rural and Non-Rural Youth) established courses specifically for persons between seventeen and twenty-five years of age just entering the industrial work force. Program A of Plan II provided training in the operation, care, and repair of tractors, trucks, and automobiles; metal work; woodworking; and elementary electricity. Program B provided more intensive training in motor mechanics, welding, machine shop, lathe operation, drill press operation, shaper operation, electrical work, sheet metal work, and radio repair. By the end of the 1939–40 school year, approximately ten thousand Louisianians were enrolled in Program A and twelve hundred were enrolled in Program B.[17]

Plan III offered education in three areas: agriculture, trade and industry, and home economics. These courses were tailored specifically to impart intensive training to youth engaged in NYA programs. Approximately four thousand of the five thousand National Youth Administration workers in Louisiana at the end of the 1939–40 school year were enrolled in some phase of Plan III.[18]

The home economics courses taught in Plan III included instruction in health and nutrition, home care of the ill, first aid, clothing, housing, consumer buying, and personal living. Students enrolled in the Trade and Industry section of the plan also received training in federal, state, or local

16. Bulletin No. 448: *Ninety-first Annual Report for the Session 1939–40*, 32–34, 41; Bulletin No. 473: *Manual for Vocation Training for Defense Workers for Administrators and Teachers of Vocational Training . . .* , 11; Bulletin No. 445: *Official Proceedings, January 3, 1941*, 17–19.

17. Bulletin No. 448: *Ninety-first Annual Report*, 34–35, 41.

18. *Ibid.*, 36, 42.

government offices in bookkeeping, filing, typewriting, manual and machine record keeping, and preparing statistical data.[19]

The war also altered the state's regular high school curriculum. Modifications occurred primarily in two areas: implementation of the voluntary "High School Victory Corps" program, and improvement in the vocational agriculture programs already in place in many schools.

The High School Victory Corps caused an extensive expansion in educational programs in participating schools because it required new emphasis in traditional subjects and introduction of subjects not generally taught in high school. The Victory Corps was originally intended for schools desiring an ROTC program but not possessing the necessary facilities. The United States Army provided a curriculum approved by the state Department of Education, and ROTC departments in colleges and universities trained instructors and sponsored high school units. The object of the Corps was to familiarize boys with army life and thus shorten the basic training period required for recruits.[20]

Courses in the first year of study covered military courtesy and customs of the armed services, infantry drill regulations, military sanitation and first aid, military history and policy, military organization, and rifle marksmanship. The second year of study included map reading, techniques of rifle fire, tactical training (as scout, observer, sentinel, listener, sniper, or messenger), automatic rifle and machine-gun fire, combat training, and infantry drill. In addition, the curriculum included lessons in the opposing philosophies of the Axis and Allied powers, patriotic attitudes, progress of the war, recognition of propaganda, global geography, and the wartime economy. Community service included participation in civilian defense, scrap drives, war stamp and bond drives, and conservation of community resources.[21]

Louisiana schools also helped develop future army clerks by providing training in army procedure and forms. The Department of Education

19. Bulletin No. 454: *Louisiana for Defense,* 37–41.

20. Bulletin No. 520: *Military Training and Leadership in High Schools of Louisiana (High School Victory Corps Program),* 1–2.

21. *Ibid.,* 3–5; Bulletin No. 496: *Wartime Education Curriculum Changes (Implementing the High School Victory Corps),* 14, 37, 40–57.

suggested that this course be ranked as a second-semester senior course worth one-half credit toward graduation, but warned that it would not substitute for a regular business course.[22]

Not all Louisianians initially favored the rush to turn the state's educational system into prep schools for boot camp. A coalition of parent-teachers' associations defeated a bill requiring compulsory military training for high school and college students introduced in the 1940 legislative session.[23] The Japanese attack on Pearl Harbor led critics to accept the inclusion of military subjects in Louisiana schools. Even then, however, the High School Victory Corps remained voluntary.

Louisiana adjusted its Vocational Agricultural Education program to provide instruction in producing specific crops deemed essential by the secretary of agriculture. The schools provided evening classes for out-of-school youth and adults, while high school students participated in vocational agriculture training during the regular school day.[24]

Instruction focused on how to increase production of milk, poultry, eggs, pork, beef, mutton, lamb, wool, soybeans, peanuts, and vegetables. Agriculture teachers also participated in scrap drives, taught how to preserve and can food, helped to develop cooperative school-community facilities for food preservation, and—because of the increased mechanization of agriculture caused by the agricultural labor shortage—stressed farm machinery care and repair in their farm shop facilities.[25]

In addition to training rural workers, the state Department of Education created emergency farm workers' schools to help prepare persons

22. Bulletin No. 511: *Pre-induction Training in Army Clerical Procedures,* 1–4.

23. *Item,* June 5, 1940.

24. John H. Mitchell, "Development of Vocational Agricultural Education in Louisiana" (Ph.D. diss., Louisiana State University, 1959), 202; S. M. Jackson, "Adjusting the Program of Vocational Agriculture to Meet the Needs of the War Effort," *Louisiana Schools,* December 1942, 12–13; S. M. Jackson, "The Part Rural War Production Training Will Play in the 1943 Food for Victory Program," *Louisiana Schools,* March 1943, 19.

25. Mitchell, "Development of Vocational Agricultural Education," 202–203; Bulletin No. 490: *Louisiana State Plan for Vocational Education to Carry Out the Provisions of Public Law No. 647 . . . ,* 32; Bulletin No. 518: *Ninety-fourth Annual Report for the Session 1942–43,* 77; *Morning Advocate,* August 2, 1943.

fourteen years of age or older for farm work. The students either had no farm experience or needed additional training. The program accepted both in-school and out-of-school students of both sexes.[26]

The principal educational organization for students of agriculture, the Future Farmers of America, suffered from declining membership during the war years. Many vocational agriculture teachers entered the armed services, and some departments closed for lack of qualified replacements. Membership in the Louisiana State University chapter of FFA dropped from 125 in 1939–40 to 0 in 1942, and the chapter was not reorganized until after the war. The other school-related organization for agricultural students, the 4-H Club, continued operations during the war years, even though it experienced the same problems as FFA: declining membership and shortage of sponsoring agents. Louisiana 4-H students, nevertheless, participated in numerous war-related scrap collection and bond sale drives.[27]

Modernization of Louisiana's educational system began during the war years because of reform movements within the state and as a response to national defense requirements. The major internal change that occurred was the addition of a required twelfth year for high school graduation. The Louisiana Teachers' Association worked for that goal for several years. Representative William J. Dodd, who was also state LTA president, criticized Superintendent Coxe and Governor Jones for not lobbying the requirement through the 1940 legislature, and the measure was finally enacted in 1944.[28]

A change in methods of instruction occurred during the war years as a result of the increased availability of visual media, primarily films. The armed services first discovered that films were useful in educating large numbers of people. Although visual aids had been a peripheral part of

26. Mitchell, "Development of Vocational Agricultural Education," 238, 246.

27. Frederick W. Williamson, *Origin and Growth of Agricultural Extension in Louisiana, 1860–1948: How It Opened the Road for Progress in Better Farming and Rural Living* (Baton Rouge, 1951), 230–31; *Agricultural Extension Annual Narrative Report (1944),* 1.

28. Weimer, "John Easterly Coxe," 21; Anthony Eugene Pacella, "A History of the Louisiana School Boards Association" (Ed.D. diss., Louisiana State University, 1977), 41; Bulletin No. 530: *Official Proceedings, April 10, 1944,* 25.

Louisiana education for some time, the war years brought them into far more classrooms than ever before. By 1945, the Department of Education had six depositories in the state from which schools could borrow films. Money to purchase films was scarce, but federal agencies, especially the Agriculture and War Departments, donated approximately 100 films to Louisiana schools prior to 1945, primarily on war-related subjects. The Education Department reported in 1943 that it owned 330 prints of 205 film titles. The Agricultural Extension Service also contributed films for use in classrooms. The new importance of educational media also affected the curriculum of teacher-training programs. The LSU College of Education added a new short course taught during the summers of 1941 and 1943, which covered the functions and use of audiovisual aids.[29]

The Department of Education experienced reorganization on two levels during the war years—by Governor Jones and by Education Superintendent John Coxe, who took office in 1940. The governor's reorganization was only temporary because the courts ruled it unconstitutional, but Coxe's revision survived longer. Former superintendent T. H. Harris had preferred a system of general-area supervisors. Coxe had served as head state supervisor of high schools until Harris dismissed him in early 1939. Elected to replace his former boss, Coxe instituted a system of subject-area supervisors. He also organized the department into three major divisions: Administration and Finance, Instruction and Supervision, and Higher Education.[30]

The war years also meant alterations for Louisiana's colleges and universities. War-related jobs or the armed services took many students, especially males, away from their studies—so many, in fact, that Southern University president J. S. Clark wrote in June 1943, "Our campus has almost developed the appearance of a female school." Enrollment at Louisiana State University dropped from 5,682 to 4,233 between June and

29. Pauline M. Rankin, "The Development of Educational Media in Louisiana" (Ph.D. diss., Louisiana State University, 1977), 62, 65, 72.

30. Weimer, "John Easterly Coxe," 9–21; Charles Edward Sutton, "Activities of the Louisiana State Department of Education on the Elementary School Level, 1940 to 1964" (Ph.D. diss., Louisiana State University, 1969), 61.

December 1942. Southeastern Louisiana College (now Southeastern Louisiana University) at Hammond enrolled 612 students in September 1940, its largest enrollment up to that time. At the beginning of the 1944 school year, however, only 331 students matriculated. The student population at Xavier University fell from 1,012 in 1939–40 to 510 in 1944–45. Other institutions of higher learning, both public and private, shared the experience of declining enrollment.[31]

Louisiana's colleges sought to replace regular students lost to the war effort with army recruits who needed specialized training. The Board of Education in April 1943 authorized colleges under its control to negotiate training contracts with the military. State colleges began a spirited competition among themselves to secure training programs for their campuses.[32]

Courses relating to war needs were added to the offerings. Louisiana Polytechnic Institute (now Louisiana Polytechnic University), Southwestern Louisiana Institute (now the University of Southwestern Louisiana), and Louisiana State Normal College (now Northwestern State University), launched military training programs. Southeastern Louisiana Col-

31. *Morning Advocate,* January 10, August 26, 1943; Charles Vincent, *A Centennial History of Southern University and A&M College, 1880–1980* (Baton Rouge, 1981), 148; Douglas Coughlin Marshall, "A History of Higher Education of Negroes in the State of Louisiana" (Ph.D. diss., Louisiana State University, 1956), 143; Leroy Ancelet, "A History of Southeastern Louisiana College" (Ph.D. diss., Louisiana State University, 1971), 75, 92; *Southeastern Louisiana University, Fifty Years: Foundation for the Future* (Hammond, La., 1975), 6–8; Oscar Hoffmeyer, Jr., *Louisiana College: Seventy-Five Years* (Pineville, La., 1981), 70; Louisiana Department of Education, *An Historical Sketch of Louisiana State Colleges* (Baton Rouge, n.d.), 40.

32. Bulletin No. 502: *Official Proceedings, April 5, 1943,* 62; Bulletin No. 519: *Official Proceedings, October 5, 1943,* 6–11; Bulletin No. 526: *Official Proceedings, January 11, 1944,* 12–14; Bulletin No. 518: *Ninety-fourth Annual Report for the Session 1942–43,* 23; *Historical Sketch of Louisiana State* 40; Florent Hardy, Jr., *A Brief History of the University of Southwestern Louisiana, 1900 to 1960* (Baton Rouge, 1973), 55, 102; Joel L. Fletcher to Allen J. Ellender, March 3, 1943, Gus Trahan to Ellender, March 3, 1943, Ellender Papers, AJE; James Domengeaux to Overton Brooks, March 2, 1943; Joel L. Fletcher to Brooks, March 4, 1943, Overton Brooks Papers, LLMVC.

lege acquired a Civil Aeronautics Authority training program. Two of Louisiana's private colleges, Centenary College and Louisiana College, acquired small air force programs. Southwestern Institute and Southern University offered agricultural refresher courses.[33]

Colleges for women also contributed to the war effort, but in other ways. The Sisters of the Academy of Holy Angels (later Our Lady of Holy Cross College) in New Orleans, for example, conducted air raid drills, sold defense stamps, and participated in Red Cross activities. Academy students constructed 326 garments for Red Cross distribution to soldiers.[34]

Louisiana college students adjusted psychologically to the grim realities of war in various ways. Some were apathetic, others adopted the new sense of patriotism, while still others saw in the threat to their country a reason to do well in their studies. Many enrolled in non-required mathematics and science courses and extracurricular first aid courses, or volunteered as air raid wardens. Major General Campbell B. Hodges, president of LSU, told students in February 1942 that "every man student at the University, down to and including every freshman man, will see service before this war is over." He therefore instituted compulsory physical education for every male undergraduate.[35]

While several other schools likewise made physical education compulsory and emphasized intramural sports to improve the physical condition of male students, the Board of Education voted on January 11, 1943, to discontinue all intercollegiate athletic contests involving the colleges under its control. The *Morning Advocate* applauded the board's action, noting that "to continue these sports and maintain their schedules in the

33. Gerard Banks to Overton Brooks, February 26, 1943, Brooks Papers; Ancelet, "History of Southeastern Louisiana College," 43; Walter M. Lowrey, *150: Centenary College of Louisiana Sesquicentennial, 1825–1975* (Shreveport, La., 1975), 21; Hoffmeyer, *Louisiana College*; Vincent, *History of Southern University,* 148–49.

34. Betty L. Morrison, "A History of Our Lady of Holy Cross College, New Orleans, Louisiana" (Ph.D. diss., Louisiana State University, 1976), 52.

35. Andrew W. Hunt, "The College Student and War Morale," *Louisiana Schools,* November 1942, 3, 38; *Morning Advocate,* February 24, 1942.

face of transportation shortages, and rapidly dwindling enrollments of eligible students is obviously impossible."[36]

The ban on intercollegiate athletics lasted only nine months. In October 1943 the board allowed resumption of the contests because a navy training program it had authorized in March (and which several colleges had obtained) required that enrollees have the opportunity to participate in college athletics. The guidelines for the reinstituted program, however, required that the number of events be held to "a reasonable minimum," that students not be absent from campus more than 48 hours for an athletic event, and that "no means of transportation requiring the use of rubber or gasoline shall be used for out-of-town trips by athletic teams, contestants, or spectators connected with any college unless OPA [Office of Price Administration] approves in advance."[37]

Peter Finney, the historian of LSU football, maintains that "beyond doubt, the backbone of American football in 1943 was the U.S. Navy with its famed preflight and physical training courses." He also recounts that some members of Coach Bernie Moore's 1943 LSU team reached the Orange Bowl that year only because Tiger fans saved gasoline rationing coupons to transport the team to Miami.[38]

Conditions of scarcity on Louisiana college campuses did not improve until after the war, when returning veterans created an abundance of students. The G.I. Bill, officially the Servicemen's Readjustment Act of 1944, provided veterans with educational assistance that increased college enrollments. Several institutions then established special guidance centers to help veterans select the proper studies and to help them obtain their federal education benefits.[39]

36. *Morning Advocate*, January 14, 1943; Bulletin No. 498: *Official Proceedings, December 16, 1942*, 4–5; Bulletin No. 499: *Official Proceedings, January 11, 1943*, 11–12; Hardy, *History of the University of Southwestern Louisiana*, 93; Lowrey, *150: Centenary College*, 23.

37. *Morning Advocate*, October 6, 1943; Bulletin No. 519: *Official Proceedings, October 5, 1943*, 66; Bulletin No. 526: *Official Proceedings, January 11, 1944*, 19–20.

38. Peter Finney, *The Fighting Tigers, 1893–1993: One Hundred Years of LSU Football* (Baton Rouge, 1993), 153–54.

39. Vincent, *History of Southern University*, 149; Ancelet, "History of Southeastern Louisiana College," 79; Frank James Price, *Troy H. Middleton: A Biography* (Baton Rouge,

*   *   *

While Louisiana's entire education system encountered problems and challenges during the war years, facilities for black students remained separate from—and decidedly unequal to—those for white students. In 1940–41 there were only forty-five public and ten private high schools for blacks accredited by the state. Fourteen parishes provided only elementary schools for their black students. The state department of education reported in 1941 that "the number of Negro educables in several of these parishes does not justify a high school." The report made no mention of the undeveloped potential in those parishes. Thirty-nine parishes employed black supervisors for their separate black schools, but the black administrators were subordinate to white administrators in their districts. Black education in Louisiana continued to focus almost entirely on vocational training: agriculture, home economics, and industrial arts. Some schools, however, provided academic courses for the students who needed them as a foundation for professional training.[40]

The state department of education recognized as early as 1940 that "neglect of the Negro and indifference to his home life, his health, his education, and his training for useful and gainful employment are detrimental to public welfare." Despite that recognition, the Louisiana Educational Survey Commission found in 1942 that the state had done little to improve black public education. The commission repeated almost exactly the same sentiment expressed by the Education Department two years earlier.[41]

The commission acknowledged, however, that improvement of black education would be difficult. Several parishes subsidized white education by expropriating money provided by the state for black teachers and schools. Black education could ill afford the loss. Louisiana in 1942 spent

---

1974), 298–302; Jack Stokes Ballard, *The Shock of Peace: Military and Economic Demobilization after World War II* (Washington, D.C., 1983), 48–49.

40. Bulletin No. 458: *Ninety-second Annual Report of the Session 1940–41,* 109–19.

41. Bulletin No. 432: *Ninetieth Annual Report for the Session 1938–39,* 14; Carleton Washburne, *Louisiana Looks at Its Schools: A Summary Report of the Louisiana Educational Survey* (Baton Rouge, 1942), 105.

$66 per year for the education of each white child but only $15.50 for each black child.[42]

The commission also asserted that black schools could do little to liberate their students from substandard home environments. Two- or three-room frame cabins frequently housed large black families with barely adequate shelter. Parents were often poorly educated sharecroppers who could provide no newspapers or books for supplemental learning.[43]

The schools themselves were equally deficient. About two-thirds were one-room buildings with several grades demanding the teacher's attention at the same time. School buildings usually resembled surrounding homes—wood frame structures heated by a wood stove, providing primitive toilet facilities at best, and surrounded by inadequate playground space. In addition, black schools were often staffed by teachers who were ill-trained and paid less than their white counterparts. Instruction and available textbooks (often castoffs from white schools) were geared to white values, and thus often failed to awaken the black pupil's interest in learning.[44]

Wartime problems notwithstanding, the number of blacks receiving at least the rudimentary education available in the state's black schools increased. By 1946, Louisiana provided 128 public high schools, 83 of which were state approved, for black students.[45]

The findings of the Department of Education and of the Louisiana Educational Survey Commission reflected a regional pattern. For generations, blacks in the South had been traditionally relegated to subservient roles in a society that was content to provide only substandard facilities for them, when it provided any facilities at all. But World War II changed relations between the races, both nationally and in the South in particular. Richard M. Dalfiume notes that the war marked the point at which blacks decided no longer to accept unequal treatment without protest.

42. Washburne, *Louisiana Looks at Its Schools*, 114–16.

43. *Ibid.*, 107–109; Bulletin No. 518: *Ninety-fourth Annual Report, Session 1942, 1943,* 50–56.

44. Washburne, *Louisiana Looks at Its Schools*, 109–14.

45. Marshall, "Higher Education of Negroes," 60.

"The dominant attitude in World War II came to be that the Negro must fight for democracy on two fronts—at home as well as abroad."[46]

Louisiana blacks, including black educators, joined in this fight. Eight black citizens of East Baton Rouge Parish asked the school board in May 1943 to begin adjusting salaries "so that white and black teachers with equal qualifications and equal experience would receive equal salaries." J. K. Haynes, president of the Louisiana Colored Teachers' Association, asked Governor Jones in June 1943 to persuade the Board of Education to equalize teachers' salaries in order to prevent more black teachers from leaving the profession for jobs in defense industries. Daniel E. Byrd, state president of the National Association for the Advancement of Colored People, also requested that Jones work for equalized salaries. He noted that despite the contention of the white Louisiana Teachers' Association that equalized salaries would mean lower salaries for whites because the state did not have sufficient funds to increase black salaries to match those of whites, no such event had occurred in any of the ten former slave states that had already equalized salaries. The governor replied that he agreed in principle, but a revised statewide salary schedule prepared by Superintendent Coxe retained disparate salaries for blacks and whites, a condition that continued throughout Jones's administration.[47]

Black educators filed several lawsuits during the war years in attempts to secure equal pay for teachers. The first of the suits, *McKelpin v. New Orleans School Board,* filed in June 1941, claimed that black teachers and principals in the system received uniformly lower wages than white employees possessing equal qualifications. The school board lost a motion to dismiss the case from the federal district court in 1942, and consented to eliminate salary differences based on race.[48]

In November 1944, the federal district court in Baton Rouge heard a

46. Richard M. Dalfiume, "The 'Forgotten Years' of the Negro Revolution," *Journal of American History* 55 (June 1968): 90, 95.

47. Petition, May 15, 1943; Daniel E. Byrd to Sam Jones, June 14, 1943; J. K. Haynes to Jones, June 15, 1943; "Meeting of Committee on Equalization of Teachers' Salaries," June 7, 1943; H. W. Wright to Jones, May 11, 1943, all in Jones Collection, HTML.

48. Leedell Wallace Neyland, "The Negro in Louisiana Since 1900: An Economic and Social Study" (Ph.D. diss., New York University, 1958), 95.

suit brought by Wiley Butler McMillon and two other Iberville Parish teachers. The plaintiffs charged that the parish school board had violated their rights to equal protection under the laws (as set forth in the Fourteenth Amendment to the United States Constitution) by maintaining separate pay scales for black and white teachers. Upon receipt of the original suit, the board instituted a new salary schedule based on education, experience, merit, and responsibility. Thurgood Marshall of New York, special counsel to the NAACP representing the plaintiffs, argued that the school board minutes showed the use of color classification in granting raises, and that the word *race* had not been eliminated in salary schedules until late 1944. Salary lists Marshall introduced revealed that white teachers in Iberville Parish received an average salary of $1,749 for a nine-month school year ($194.33 per month), while black teachers averaged $637 for seven or eight months ($91 per month for a seven-month year). The plaintiffs requested that the school board adopt a salary schedule based solely on education and experience, and equalize black and white salaries for the 1946–47 school year.[49]

For the time being, black educators failed to persuade either courts or the educational establishment to equalize salaries statewide. By 1944, black teachers' salaries had increased by more than 50 percent over the 1940 levels, but that increase occurred mainly because Orleans Parish, which employed 12 percent of the state's black teachers, had equalized salaries as a result of the *McKelpin* case. Black teachers waited until 1948 for equalized salaries to be established statewide, when Governor Earl Long made them part of the ambitious legislative program he introduced at the beginning of his first full term in office.[50]

Louisiana's public schools took on many additional responsibilities during the war. Superintendent Coxe reported to the Board of Education in 1942 that "in this supreme [war] effort, our educational forces have duties

49. *Morning Advocate*, November 28, 1944; Bulletin No. 548: *Official Proceedings, January 8, 1945, 66–68.*

50. Bulletin No. 543: *Ninety-fifth Annual Report for the Session, 1943, 1944,* 47; Sindler, *Huey Long's Louisiana,* 210.

as clearly defined as those of our soldiers." Louisiana's schools assumed those duties with changes in instructional method and in the curriculum. The greatest wartime deficiency of Louisiana's educational establishment was its failure to improve black facilities and standards, even though leaders of both races acknowledged that black education was substandard. Generations of inequality, however, had produced acceptance of substandard black education in Louisiana, the South, and the nation at large. The first stirrings of determined black protest occurred during World War II, but achievement of educational equality over the objections of conservative white southerners who adopted the strategy of "massive resistance" lay far in the future.[51]

51. Bulletin No. 480: *Wartime Education in Louisiana Schools,* 3; Numan V. Bartley, *The Rise of Massive Resistance: Race Relations in the South during the 1950s* (Baton Rouge, 1969), 340–45.

8

Working the Fields

Louisiana agriculture in 1939 and 1940 retained many of the aspects that had characterized it since Reconstruction. The state's farm population typically lived on farms comprised of fewer than fifty acres. Of the 150,007 farms in Louisiana in 1940, 12,508 consisted of fewer than ten acres, 62,989 of ten to twenty-nine acres, and 33,487 of thirty to forty-nine acres. The number of large farms (858 containing a thousand or more acres, for example) skewed the average farm acreage to just over sixty-six acres in 1940.[1]

Many Louisiana farmers in 1939–40 were still tenants. The United States Census Bureau, which attributes one "operator" to each farm, found that of the 150,007 farm operators in Louisiana in 1940, 52,936 were full owners, 7,376 were part owners, 528 were managers, and 89,167 were tenants (not quite 60 percent of the total). Within the ranks of tenantry, the share tenants (31,460) and sharecroppers (39,631) far outnumbered the 11,210 cash tenants, the 1,469 share-cash tenants, and the 5,406 tenants who farmed under other arrangements.[2]

Farmers in Louisiana in these years typically grew some cotton. Cotton acreage was reported on 114,291 farms. Cotton produced more farm income in 1940 than any other crop: $33,540,333 in cotton lint and an additional $6,333,126 in cotton seed. (Closest to cotton in value were cereal

---

1. *Seventeenth Census, 1950: Agriculture, Louisiana,* vol. 1, pt. 24, 3.
2. *Ibid.,* 4.

crops at $28,122,337.) Each farmer, however, produced only a few bales of cotton. While 9,210 farmers reported growing one bale of cotton or less in 1940, 14,011 reported one and one-half to two bales, 14,779 reported two and one-half to three bales, and 14,984 (the largest number in any category) reported three and one-half to four bales. From that point the numbers decline—13,706 farmers reported four and one-half to five bales, while only 16 reported over 500 bales.[3]

Louisiana farmers still depended on animal power. The 1940 census found only 6,937 tractors in the state. Mules and mule colts constituted the second most valuable category of livestock on Louisiana farms, second only to cattle and calves. Moreover, the value of all horses and colts, many of which were used as draft animals, was third.[4]

American agriculture by 1939 had survived almost two decades of severe depression. Farm prices, temporarily high because of abnormal demand and scarcity during World War I, had collapsed during the early 1920s. Gross agricultural income in the United States fell from $17.7 million in 1919 to $10.5 million in 1921. Louisiana agriculture shared in the bust. Per capita farm income in Louisiana fell from $332 in 1919 to $129 in 1921, and went on to fluctuate throughout the decade, always remaining less than $250. Then the Great Depression added its burden and per capita farm income sank to $80 in the bleak year of 1932. By 1933, however, early New Deal agricultural programs had initiated a weak recovery. Farm income reached a Depression high of $207 in 1937 before declining again to $153 in 1940. But then the next four years saw a dramatic rise: $230 in 1941, $360 in 1942, $476 in 1943, $497 in 1944, and $528 in 1945. A postwar boom lasted until 1948, when per capita income reached $752.[5]

President Roosevelt's New Deal wrestled with the problem of southern rural poverty throughout the 1930s, but none of the several programs succeeded in eliminating widespread deprivation on southern farms. De-

3. *Sixteenth Census, 1940: Agriculture,* 672, *Special Cotton Report,* 101.

4. *Seventeenth Census: Agriculture,* vol. 1, pt. 24, 6; *Sixteenth Census: Agriculture,* 672.

5. Arthur M. Schlesinger, Jr., *The Crisis of the Old Order, 1919–1933* (Boston, 1957), 105; J. P. Montgomery, *Agricultural Statistics for Louisiana, 1909–1957* (Baton Rouge, 1958), 9.

mand for agricultural produce during World War II accomplished what the New Deal had not—war needs substantially raised farm income by creating larger markets for expanded production. The primary reason for this growth is obvious: the world needed more food and fiber than the producing countries could supply, and Louisiana farmers shared in the rise in agricultural prices caused by this favorable condition.[6]

Production and prices were not uniformly high, however. Bad weather and insects, the bane of the farmer's existence, plagued the state. Drought and boll weevil infestation devastated the cotton crop in north Louisiana and east Texas in 1941, when cotton yields dropped to less than 25 percent of the normal harvest for the area. Mrs. N. E. Teagle of St. Maurice wrote to Senator Ellender that the 1942 crop year was no better: "It has been one of the turbelst years I have ever expearenced and I am 64 years old." New Deal relief agencies still in operation prevented the destitution that normally would have followed such a catastrophe.[7] In addition, late spring weather, combined with lack of labor, led to the smallest number of acres (930,000) planted in cotton in Louisiana since 1915.

The 1944 crop year also turned out badly. A hot, dry summer followed a late, wet spring, and both total acreage and average yield per acre declined in most areas. Fortunately for the farmers, however, prices increased slightly over 1943.[8]

Farmers expect bad weather and occasional poor harvests as a normal course of their business. The war years, however, brought an additional problem that was not successfully solved. As in most other areas of the economy, the tremendous demand of military mobilization and the opportunity for the relatively high wages and steady income of war-related

6. Paul E. Mertz, *New Deal Policy and Southern Rural Poverty* (Baton Rouge, 1978), 1–6, 253–62; Stephen D. Reiling and Fred H. Wiegmann, *Louisiana Agriculture: Economic Trends and Current Status, 1940–1977* (Baton Rouge, 1979), 22.

7. *Shreveport Times,* December 22, 1941; *States,* November 21, 1941; R. S. Wilds to Allen J. Ellender, October 9, 1941, G. J. Posey to Ellender, October 10, 1941, Max Cockerham to Ellender, October 10, 1941, Lon H. Law to Ellender, November 7, 1941, Grover B. Hill to Ellender, January 17, 1942, Mrs. N. E. Teagle to Ellender, December 17, 1942, Ellender Papers.

8. *Morning Advocate,* July 13, December 22, 1944; *Item,* April 2, 1945.

industry caused a shortage of farm workers. Louisiana farmers tried to solve their labor problems in two ways: mechanization of farming and recruitment of ex-farm labor or nontraditional farm labor.[9]

Mechanization of Louisiana agriculture had proceeded slowly before the 1940s. There were only 1,691 tractors on Louisiana sugarcane farms in 1930, but by 1945, the number had increased to 6,499. The labor shortage caused cane farmers to utilize machines whenever possible and affordable. The number of cane harvesters increased from 79 in 1942 to 124 in 1943, 192 in 1944, 329 in 1945, and 422 in 1946. In addition, county agents in the sugar-producing parishes reported 266 flame cultivators—used to replace hand hoeing of sugar crops—in use in 1945 and 313 in 1946.[10]

Mechanization of production of other crops lagged behind that of sugar. The first mechanical cotton picker did not appear in the state until the 1945 harvest season, when it was used on a plantation near Cheneyville in southern Rapides Parish. It performed well, even though rain caused a lengthy delay between defoliation and harvest, so that the machine gathered an inordinate amount of trash along with the cotton in its first use. True mechanization of cotton farming did not occur anywhere in America until after the war. Cotton planters during 1940–45 still relied almost as much on hand labor as had antebellum planters.[11]

Mechanization of rice harvesting lagged even further behind. The problem with rice was that successful mechanical harvesting required a moisture content in the grain well in excess of that needed for successful storage. While the use of tractors in planting and cultivating before World War II signaled the beginning of mechanization of rice production, mechanical harvesting devices could not be utilized until the development of modern grain-drying facilities during the postwar years.[12]

9. *U.S. House, Hearings Before the Select Committee Investigating National Defense Migration,* 77th Cong., 2d sess., 1942, pt. 28, 10857.

10. E. Carl Jones, "Mechanization on Large Sugar Cane Farms in Louisiana" (master's thesis, Louisiana State University, 1947), 17, 65, 79–80.

11. *Morning Advocate,* September 21, 1945.

12. David O. Whitten, "American Rice Cultivation, 1680–1980: A Tercentenary Critique," *Southern Studies* 21 (spring 1982): 22.

Although machines thus helped to fill some of the demand for farm labor, Louisiana agriculture still relied primarily on hand labor and animal power at the end of the war. The number of horses and mules on Louisiana farms decreased during the war years and the total number of tractors increased, but by 1945 only 8.8 percent of Louisiana farms were equipped with a tractor.[13] In addition, tractors often only supplemented, and did not completely replace, draft animals or hand labor on farms where they appeared during the war.

Therefore, farmers and the agricultural establishment sought to recruit farm workers from nontraditional sources. These sources included people who had never worked on farms before, many of whom received training at emergency farm workers' schools provided by the Louisiana Department of Education. High school students throughout the state also enrolled in the "Victory Farm Volunteers" to help harvest produce. In exchange for their work, the students received small payments—two cents per pound, for example, for picking snapbeans and between $1.50 and $3.00 per day (depending on individual ability) for digging Irish potatoes. School principals occasionally rearranged class schedules to allow students time to work in the fields; almost a thousand students in Terrebonne Parish alone helped to harvest the 1945 crop.[14]

Louisiana farmers also hoped to recruit former agricultural laborers who had migrated to towns seeking work during the Depression. If such workers proved reluctant to return to the farm, farmers hoped to force them back by removing the income from government sources that permitted them to remain in town. The Caddo Parish police jury, on December 11, 1941, unanimously approved a resolution calling upon the Works Progress Administration, the Shreveport City Council, and the Shreveport Chamber of Commerce to help guide "idle labor now on relief rolls" back to farms. Juror J. P. Fullilove attacked the "idleness of the city" and urged fellow jurors: "For God's sake, let's get these fellows back on the farms."[15]

13. W. D. Curtis, *Statistical Data and Trends in the Agriculture of Louisiana,* vol. 1 (Baton Rouge, 1947), 13.

14. Mitchell, "Development of Vocational Agricultural Education," 202; *Morning Advocate,* June 3, 1945.

15. *Shreveport Times,* December 12, 1941.

The next year, J. M. Crutcher, state WPA administrator, removed 2,600 farm workers from WPA rolls and, in addition, removed 7,600 persons from the "awaiting assignment" list and announced that they would not be considered for WPA payments while farm work was available. "The WPA will not be a party to such a labor shortage," Crutcher said, "but will do everything in its power to see that men of farming experience go back to the farms if the work is there for them."[16]

Louisiana farmers, however, were not desperate enough to accept unanimously the offer of Harry Itaya, an American citizen of Japanese descent who wrote to the *Shreveport Times* in 1943 from the relocation camp in Arkansas to which he had been transported. Itaya suggested that Japanese-Americans should be released from the internment camps and relocated on farms and plantations where they could grow crops for military and civilian use. Some Louisianians approved Itaya's proposal, calling it a "wise observance of our great American creed of life, liberty, and the pursuit of happiness," and "a concrete way to show that democracy is still alive in our country." Others adamantly rejected the suggestion. One person referred to his son in the military and wondered "what he would think if I stood by without opposing it and let this parish be filled with cheap Jap[anese] labor while he is risking his life fighting to free this nation of Jap[anese] rule and domination."[17] Louisiana's opinion, of course, remained a moot point. United States internment policy prevented any serious consideration of Itaya's suggestion.

While the searing memories of the surprise attack on Pearl Harbor prevented utilization of native Japanese-American labor, Louisiana farmers felt less hesitation about using German and Italian prisoner-of-war labor. As American troops participated in the North African campaign against German field marshal Erwin Rommel's Afrika Corps, captured German soldiers began arriving in the United States. The prisoners posed a problem to American authorities: where could they be safely interned for the duration of the war? In order to discourage escape or sabotage attempts, emergency wartime regulations decreed that camps could not be

16. *Times-Picayune,* February 28, 1942.
17. *Shreveport Times,* August 1, 1943.

located within about 170 miles of a coastline, within a 150-mile-wide "zone sanitaire" along the Mexican and Canadian borders, or near shipyards, munitions plants, or vital industries. Approximately two-thirds of the POW base camps (containing approximately three-fourths of the prisoners) were located in the southern and southwestern regions of the country. The United States government eventually yielded to pressure from the Louisiana Sugar Cane League and Louisiana members of Congress and allowed POWs to work in parishes bordering the Gulf of Mexico.[18]

Officials located the camps in southern areas for more than security reasons. Maxwell McKnight of the camp operations branch of the provost marshal general's office noted that the mild climate also appealed to army planners: "If you could have the prisons down South where the winters were milder, you had less of a problem with heat." Expenses for the screening and sanitation to shield POWS from southern mosquitoes partially offset the advantages of the warm climate, but did not stop construction of the camps. Mosquitoes could even be used to discipline POWs, as in an incident at Camp Wynne, Arkansas, where camp authorities ordered some POWs who refused an increased workload to stand out-of-doors naked for several hours exposed to the insects. Texas ranked first among southern states with thirty-three POW camps, while Arkansas and Louisiana tied for second with seventeen camps each.[19]

The United States treated its prisoners of war under the guidelines of the Geneva Convention of 1929. These provisions stipulated that prisoners of war other than officers could be required to work, but that the work could not be directly related to war operations and could not jeopardize the prisoners' health or safety. These restrictions did not preclude agricultural labor, so it proved acceptable as well as convenient to utilize prisoners of war to alleviate the shortage of farm workers. In the South, prisoners picked cotton, cut sugarcane, harvested tobacco and peanuts, cut pulpwood, and worked in fertilizer plants.[20]

18. Arnold Krammer, *Nazi Prisoners of War in America* (New York, 1979), 27–28.

19. Judith M. Gansberg, *Stalag: USA* (New York, 1977), 24; Krammer, *Nazi Prisoners of War,* 31.

20. Lt. Col. Lamar F. Peyton, "Treatment and Utilization of Prisoners of War by the United States during World War II" (master's thesis, Louisiana State University, 1973), 17;

Louisiana had first become involved with incarcerating enemies of the United States in late 1941, when the government sent Japanese, German, and Italian aliens to the quarantine station at Algiers. Then in 1942, the United States Army provost marshal general ordered the preparation of Camps Livingston, Polk, and Ruston to house enemy aliens and prisoners of war.[21]

Camp Livingston in Rapides Parish received its first installment of such prisoners, all Japanese men, in early June 1942. Newspaper reporters allowed into the camp in July wrote that authorities treated the prisoners well, as the United States had good reason to do, even though popular sentiment might have preferred otherwise. Because the Japanese government had not ratified the Geneva Convention accords, but only generally agreed to adhere to them, it was thus not bound to abide by the guidelines therein, including the ones regarding treatment of prisoners. American authorities could only hope that news of humane treatment Japanese prisoners received in this country would temper treatment of American captives in Japan.[22] This consideration became increasingly important after the fall of Corregidor and Bataan in May 1942 left thousands of Americans prisoners in Japanese hands.

German prisoners first reached Louisiana on July 9, 1943, when captured members of Rommel's Afrika Corps arrived at Camp Livingston, just north of Alexandria. Camp Livingston, along with nearby Camps Claiborne and Beauregard and Camp Polk near Leesville, had been primarily constructed as training camps for American inductees, but were also used to house POWs.[23]

Inquiries from farmers interested in employing POW labor began even as the German prisoners arrived in the state. Charles A. Farwell, educational director of the American Sugar Cane League, announced on July 3, 1943, that his association had explored the possibility of using Ger-

---

Matthew J. Schott and Rosalind Foley, *Bayou Stalags: German Prisoners of War in Louisiana* (Lafayette, La., 1981), 5–6; Krammer, *Nazi Prisoners*, 35, 90; Gansberg, *Stalag: USA*, 34.

21. Schott and Foley, *Bayou Stalags*, 2.

22. Peyton, "Treatment and Utilization of Prisoners of War," 19; *Town Talk*, July 14, 1942.

23. *Town Talk*, August 2, 1943.

mans to harvest the cane crop. Senator Ellender announced on July 8 that Louisiana would receive farm help from German and Italian POWs, but their use would be limited because of the Southern Defense Command prohibition against establishing a prison camp close to a coastline (which officials later lifted).[24]

By the height of the 1943 harvest season in October, more than 950 German prisoners worked on farms surrounding Camp Livingston and the subcamp established at Franklin specifically to provide laborers for the cane harvest. The army also permitted an expansion of camps and subcamps at various locations throughout the state to house workers near areas with farm labor shortages. Camp Claiborne received German prisoners from Camp Polk on November 4, Port Allen housed prisoners at a compound established at the parish fair grounds, and Lafourche Parish received several temporary camps to house workers beginning with the 1943 harvest. Subcamps at Rayne, Eunice, Jennings, Sulphur, and Welsh housed POWs used in the rice harvest. In 1944, Senator John Overton successfully requested a subcamp at Bastrop to house POWs whom area farmers wanted to help harvest the cotton crop.[25]

Farmers in areas with a shortage of farm labor worked closely with State Supervisor of Emergency Farm Labor Carl E. Kemmerly to establish the subcamps. Farmers contributed to the construction of the compounds, and then Kemmerly would contact army inspectors to certify that the facilities met Geneva Convention housing specifications, including the provision of kitchens and mess halls, sanitation facilities, water, and electricity. If the facility passed army inspection, army guards escorted prisoners to the site and maintained surveillance of the area. The expense of contributing to the construction of the compounds, plus the daily wage of $1.20 to $1.50 per day (usually 70 cents paid to the government for operating expenses of the compound and 80 cents paid to the

24. *Morning Advocate,* July 4, October 6, 1943; *Shreveport Times,* July 9, 1943.

25. *States,* September 29, 1943; *Town Talk,* October 19, November 5, 1943; *Morning Advocate,* December 16, 1943, November 3, 1983; Joseph T. Butler, "Prisoner of War Labor in the Sugar Cane Fields of Lafourche Parish, Louisiana, 1943–1944," *Louisiana History* 14 (summer 1973): 287; Joseph N. Lockwood, "The German Concentration Camp, Bastrop, Louisiana," *North Louisiana Historical Association Journal,* spring 1980, 34.

prisoner) for a minimum contingent of ten workers, meant that only substantial farmers or businessmen could afford POW labor.[26]

Louisiana farmers at all levels of income needed help from any source to harvest their crops. Not only had the armed services taken their workers, but war industries actively recruited farm workers with higher wages than they received on the farms. This activity began in 1942, when the boom in defense industries caused industrial labor shortages. P. Theo Landaiche, a St. Gabriel rice farmer, complained to Senator Ellender in January 1942 that several individuals who owned trucks facilitated the labor flight by using their vehicles to transport farm workers to defense industries in Baton Rouge. Representative Overton Brooks protested to Paul McNutt, chairman of the War Manpower Commission in Washington, that the WMC contributed to the drain of Louisiana's agricultural labor pool by placing advertisements in Louisiana newspapers offering jobs in both in-state and out-of-state industries. McNutt replied that the WMC and the United States Employment Service carried on their search for available workers nationwide, and no agency of the federal government had designated Brooks's congressional district in northwest Louisiana as a critical labor area in which they should refrain from recruiting workers.[27]

Thus industrial raids on the agricultural labor supply continued. Mark H. Brown, a Lake Providence lumber mill operator, complained in May 1943 that government contractors sent trucks to his area to transport labor to their construction sites for nonessential "grading, sodding, and beautifying" tasks, while makers of forest products and farmers lacked sufficient help. Furthermore, H. B. Naquin, a small-scale manufacturer of mechanical sugarcane harvesters, wrote to President Roosevelt that the giant Higgins Industries, which produced ships and other war imple-

26. Peyton, "Treatment and Utilization of Prisoners of War," 78; Butler, "Prisoner of War Labor," 178; *Louisiana Farm Bureau News,* May 1980, 1, 4; Schott and Foley, *Bayou Stalags,* 5.

27. P. Theo Landaiche to Allen J. Ellender, January 2, 1942, Louis Krielow to Ellender, February 24, 1943, Ellender Papers; Overton Brooks to Paul McNutt, May 2, 1944, McNutt to Brooks, May 12, 1944, Brooks to McNutt, June 23, 1944, Brooks Papers, LLMVC; *Congressional Record,* 78th Cong., 2d sess., vol. 90, pt. 10, A3345–46.

ments, depleted the available labor supply within "40 or 50 miles" in all directions by transporting workers from rural areas into New Orleans, and that "our sugar planters cannot compete with the prices that they are paying per day."[28]

Instructions issued by the WMC and the USES subsequently provided that individuals currently or recently employed in agriculture could not be referred to nonagricultural employment without prior consultation between the USES and a designated representative of the War Food Administration (usually a county agent of the State Agricultural Extension Service).[29] This provision proved to be ineffective, though, and relocation of agricultural labor continued to be a problem throughout the war.

Another effort to ease the labor shortage, this time by utilizing workers from the West Indies, was thwarted by geography, climate, traditional southern racial attitudes, and legalized segregation in the South. The governments of the United States and Jamaica agreed in 1943 that Jamaican workers could come to the United States, primarily to the destination of Camp Pontchartrain, adjacent to New Orleans. The extra labor was therefore tantalizingly close to Louisiana farmers. The Jamaican government, however, had agreed to send workers to the United States on two conditions: they had to return to Jamaica after the 1943 harvest season so they would not be exposed to a harsh North American winter, and they could not be used in the South. Some south Louisiana farmers asked Senators Ellender and Overton to prevail upon the federal government to seek changes in the original bilateral agreement. The War Food Administration subsequently asked the Jamaican government to extend the period of employment of its citizens in the United States and to allow their use in the Louisiana and Florida sugarcane fields, where the harvest season extended far beyond that of other crops. Despite pleas from Louisianians, however, the Jamaican government agreed to allow its citizens to remain in the United States over the winter of 1943–44 only with the

28. Mark H. Brown to Allen J. Ellender, May 15, 1943, H. B. Naquin to Franklin D. Roosevelt, June 15, 1943, Ellender Papers.

29. Paul V. McNutt to Allen J. Ellender, September 15, 1943, *ibid.*

provision that their employment be restricted to Florida, where the winters more closely matched those of the tropics.[30]

Failure to secure imported workers left the POWs as the only large pool of untapped labor. Their subsequent work in the fields of Louisiana brought them into close contact with many more Louisianians than would have occurred otherwise. The attitude of many citizens was more favorable toward the primary enemies, the Germans, than toward Italians, southern Europeans, or Asians. Black Louisianians, closely associated with the POWs in agricultural work, were of two minds about the prisoners: some blacks resented the competition for their work and the treatment some prisoners received, while others found satisfaction in seeing whites sharing their menial field work. Official attempts to discourage fraternization notwithstanding, hundreds of personal relationships developed between prisoners and both black and white residents.[31]

Louisiana's use of POW labor reached its peak during the 1945 crop year, after Germany's surrender but before the prisoners were repatriated. Many farmers and others who utilized POW labor in the forest industry feared continued agricultural labor shortages throughout the South after the war and wanted the government to keep the POWs for an extended period, but by 1946 POW labor had disappeared from the state.[32]

---

30. Charles A. Farwell to W. C. Kemper, July 31, 1943, Paul V. McNutt to Allen J. Ellender, August 17, 1943, September 14, 1943, Walter Godchaux to Farwell, August 2, 1943, Godchaux to Ellender, August 2, 1943, September 2, 1943, Wilson R. Buie to Ellender, August 28, 1943, Godchaux to Frank Wurzlow, August 23, 1943, August 30, 1943, Marvin Jones to Ellender, October 30, 1943, all in Ellender Papers.

31. Matthew J. Schott, "World War II Prisoners and Internees in Louisiana: A Lesson in Racial and Ethnic Stereotyping," (paper presented to the Louisiana Historical Association Annual Convention, March 25, 1983).

32. Schott and Foley, *Bayou Stalags*, 4; R. D. Crowell to Overton Brooks, January 28, 1944; E. A. Frost to Brooks, January 28, 1944; Q. T. Hardtner to Brooks, February 9, 1944, Brooks Papers; *Congressional Record*, 78th Cong., 2d sess., vol. 90, pt. 8, A825; Henry D. Larcade to Colonel Clifford S. Urwiller, February 19, 1945, *Congressional Record*, 79th Cong., 1st sess., vol. 91, pt. 10, A726–27; Goulden, *The Best Years*, 130.

*   *   *

In spite of the problems posed by bad weather and the agricultural labor shortage, Louisiana farmers continued to produce their three historic major staple crops: sugarcane, cotton, and rice, and each subdivision of agriculture responded to the challenge of war in its own way.

Louisiana sugar farmers, confined mainly to a 266,200-acre triangle with apexes in West Baton Rouge, Iberia, and Lafourche Parishes, produced an average of 4,800,000 tons per year from 1940 to 1944. The Sugar Act of 1937, originally scheduled to expire in 1940, was extended to regulate sugarcane production until 1944. This act authorized the secretary of agriculture to estimate the annual consumption requirements of the United States in December of each year, or at other times if necessary, and then allocate portions of the total to farmers in the sugar-producing areas of the country. It thus gave Secretary Wallace the power to manipulate the price of sugar through his authority to determine consumption requirements.[33]

In addition, an international agreement reached in 1937 between sugar-importing and -exporting countries allowed the exporting countries to produce sugar at high levels, thus in effect helping to hold down sugar prices. The international agreement formally ended in 1942, but the war caused new problems in the international sugar market before that date.[34]

After the war began, American sugar merchants, many of whom remembered the short supplies experienced during World War I, bought large quantities of sugar, even though Roosevelt and Wallace assured them that the American surplus of 800,000 tons would prevent shortages in the immediate future. Nevertheless, the buying spree caused Roosevelt to suspend all quota restrictions on September 11, 1939. He reinstated the quotas on December 26, 1939, but by then Louisiana sugar farmers had already planted a 1940 crop far in excess of any reasonable quotas. The

33. Reiling and Wiegmann, *Louisiana Agriculture,* 33; Rudolph Carrol Hammack, "The New Deal and Louisiana Agriculture" (Ph.D. diss., Tulane University, 1973), 242–43; Becnel, *Labor, Church, and the Sugar Establishment,* 34–35.

34. Murray R. Benedict, *Farm Policies of the United States, 1790–1950: A Study of Their Origin and Development* (New York, 1953), 399.

Department of Agriculture ruled, therefore, that farmers could harvest up to 110 percent of their share of the 1940 crop without deduction from their payments. Nature, however, had the last word on the 1940 cane crop, as adverse weather conditions destroyed much of it. In addition, Japanese expansion in the Pacific threatened United States imports from Hawaii and the Philippines. Therefore, the USDA, Secretary of State Cordell Hull, and Secretary of the Interior Harold Ickes agreed in April 1941 that all acreage restrictions should be lifted from sugar production. Marketing quotas remained, however, and were not lifted until after the attack on Pearl Harbor. After that attack, the government encouraged full production and distribution of sugar.[35]

On October 14, 1942, the Defense Supplies Corporation announced that it would reimburse United States refiners of Louisiana raw sugar for transportation costs they incurred in shipping raw sugar to refineries designated by the War Production Board instead of local refineries. The government hoped to keep the sugar supply distributed among all available refineries so that some would not be inundated while others lay idle. The Commodity Credit Corporation assumed responsibility for this program on December 16, 1942, and continued its reimbursement payments until 1946.[36]

The CCC also supplied assistance payments for harvest of the 1943 sugarcane crop. On October 11, 1943, it offered payment of 33 cents per ton of Louisiana standard sugarcane to be paid through the processors to the growers. An early freeze during the 1943 harvest season threatened to reduce the amount of sugar produced, so the CCC extended the payment program to include salvage operations for the freeze-damaged cane.[37]

These attempts to increase domestic sugar production aside, the United States and its allies produced less than they needed. This meant that U.S. consumers seldom received all the sugar they desired. Beginning in 1942, consumers received ration books that allowed them to pur-

35. Hammack, "The New Deal and Louisiana Agriculture," 255–61.

36. Earl B. Wilson, *Sugar and Its Wartime Controls,* vol. 1 (New York, n.d.), 65, vol. 2, 592–607.

37. *Ibid.*, vol. 1, 85–86, vol. 2, 608–12.

chase only a limited amount of sugar (originally slightly more than one-half pound per week, eventually falling to less than one-third pound per week), and then only within a carefully specified time.[38]

The staple crop covering the most acres in Louisiana during the war years was cotton, which averaged 995,000 acres per year during 1940–44. (Louisiana farmers grew corn on an average of 1.3 million acres during the period, but corn was not a staple crop grown primarily for sale. Instead, farmers generally used the corn as food for either themselves or their workstock.) Cotton production was widely spread over the state. A survey in 1945 found cotton on 61.3 percent of Louisiana farms, as opposed to sugarcane grown commercially on 6.51 percent and rice on 4.94 percent. All areas of the state except Jefferson, Plaquemines, St. Bernard, and Orleans Parishes produced at least some cotton during the war.[39]

Cotton was the historic crop of the South, and southern farmers could grow cotton well—so well, in fact, that they had repeatedly flooded the market during the 1930s, thus depressing prices. Because of the use of cotton lint in armament production, cotton became an important commodity during the war. Therefore, the Louisiana Agricultural Extension Service concentrated on improving the quality of the cotton produced. The USDA, however, recognized that huge stockpiles of surplus cotton precluded the need for production stimulation programs. The United States in March 1941 had a carryover of almost 12 million bales, and the carryover never fell much below 10.5 million bales at any time during the war.[40]

In 1941, Secretary of Agriculture Claude Wickard introduced a supplementary cotton program, which aimed to reduce the supply in two ways. The USDA paid cotton farmers to reduce their cotton acreage with stamps that could be used only to purchase cotton clothing at local stores participating in the program, and it paid farmers to grow vegetables on land taken out of cotton production.[41]

38. *Ibid.*, vol. 1, 87, vol. 4, 1321, 1351.

39. Reiling and Wiegmann, *Louisiana Agriculture,* 30; Curtis, *Statistical Data,* vol. 1, 9.

40. Hammack, "The New Deal and Louisiana Agriculture," 289; Williamson, *Origin and Growth of Agricultural Extension in Louisiana,* 222.

41. Hammack, "The New Deal and Louisiana Agriculture," 289.

The second part of this program met with little success. The payment to the farmers was a token $1.50 for a one-fourth-acre plot that had to be protected from livestock and had to grow at least six kinds of vegetables. A farm family could also receive a $3.00 payment for producing and storing three hundred quarts of frozen or canned food. Many farmers, accustomed to producing staple cash crops, disliked vegetable gardening and failed to understand the importance of family food production in diversified farm management. Despite admonitions from Georgia Farm Bureau president R. L. Wingate ("We cannot eat surplus cotton"), many cotton farmers throughout the South, including Louisiana, preferred to continue producing the crop they understood best. It should also be noted that it was not unprofitable to grow cotton during the war. The price of cotton on the New Orleans market reached 20.77 cents per pound, including government soil conservation payments, in January 1942. This was the highest cotton price since 1929.[42]

The third staple crop, rice, was planted on an average of 558,400 acres per year between 1940 and 1944. Rice was a crop of restricted acreage because it required the impervious subsoils found in southwest Louisiana, which were used to hold irrigation water to discourage weed growth. Southwest Louisiana produced 83 percent of Louisiana's total rice harvest during the war years, but Louisiana's share of the national rice market fell from 40.6 percent in 1939 to 28.6 percent in 1944.[43]

As for most other commodities, the U.S. government encouraged unlimited rice production and guaranteed prices. Loss of normal Asian supplies to Japanese expansion sharpened America's realization that it needed more domestic rice, and total plantings rose to the practical limit of 1.5 million acres across the country. Louisiana farmers harvested 88,690,000 bushels of rice, worth $147,819,000, between 1941 and 1944.[44]

42. *Ibid.,* 290; A. B. Curet, "Food Wins Wars, Too—So Pointe Coupée Parish Goes All Out for Victory," *Louisiana Municipal Review,* September–October 1942, 154–55; George Brown Tindall, *The Emergence of the New South, 1913–1945* (Baton Rouge, 1967), 704–705; *Times-Picayune,* January 23, 1942.

43. Reiling and Wiegmann, *Louisiana Agriculture,* 34–35; Whitten, "American Rice Cultivation," 21.

44. Hammack, "The New Deal and Louisiana Agriculture," 296–98.

Louisiana farmers also increased production of other crops during the war. They had grown soybeans for years, but primarily for making hay and forage and improving the condition of the soil. The federal government now called for more soybeans for vegetable oil production, and Louisiana's farmers responded. Soybeans remained a minor crop during the war, however, covering an average 31,800 acres annually between 1941 and 1944.[45]

Alongside the expansion of the various crops, the production of meat and meat products increased similarly. Swine, beef, poultry, egg, and milk production all expanded. The New Orleans market received 79,202,000 pounds of milk in 1940, 105,452,000 pounds in 1941, and 112,651,000 in 1942. Louisiana farmers produced about 10 million chickens in 1942 and improved egg production about 17 percent over the previous year. During the spring and summer of 1942, local farms supplied over one hundred railroad cars of eggs—over a million dozen—to an egg dehydration plant at Ruston in north Louisiana.[46]

Louisiana sweet potatoes also went to war. The B. F. Trappey family of Jeanerette had moved their agricultural canning operation to Lafayette shortly after 1930. There they developed a process for canning less-than-premium sweet potatoes, which had formerly been discarded, by packing them in a heavy sugar syrup that preserved both the shape and sweetness of the potato. By the beginning of World War II, the Trappeys had introduced the "candied yam" to much of the middle South. The Allied armed forces included the potatoes in their field rations, thus creating an unprecedented demand; the Trappeys responded by expanding their cannery, producing about 12 million pounds of canned sweet potatoes for the military before the end of the war. In addition, five plants in Louisiana—Trappey, Warriner Starch at St. Francisville, American Foods at Opelousas, Little and Company in Lafayette, and Frank Tea and Spice at New Iberia—produced dehydrated sweet potatoes. These plants in 1943 used

45. Reiling and Wiegmann, *Louisiana Agriculture,* 34–35; Williamson, *Agricultural Extension in Louisiana,* 229.

46. Williamson, *Agricultural Extension in Louisiana,* 225–27; *Shreveport Times,* July 7, 1942.

nearly one million bushels of raw potatoes. The entire production was purchased by the quartermaster corps.[47]

Louisiana forests likewise contributed to the war effort. As the United States shifted its national defense–preparedness program into high gear, the government became the country's largest lumber consumer. In September 1941 alone, the federal government ordered two billion board feet of lumber for the construction of cantonments. Southern pine timber producers supplied much of the need. Louisiana then had about 16,193,000 acres of forest land, about half in hardwood timber and the other half in pine.[48]

The federal government did not impose stringent controls on the forest industry, but industry trade groups organized lumber production. The Southern Pine Association, located in New Orleans, pledged its full support of the war effort, the government for its part accepted lumber of poorer grade than it had permitted before, and the timber industry boomed.[49]

By the end of 1945, Louisiana had produced 82 million board feet of timber in excess of its need, and 475 timber operators in the state had paid about $50 million to some forty thousand people working in the business. Timber producers in the state nevertheless struggled with shortages of labor, equipment, and transportation, as did timbermen in other sections of the United States. North Louisiana Soil Conservation District foresters noted at the end of the war that the heavier-than-normal cutting caused by war demand improved the north Louisiana timber stands by removing many weak "weed" trees of questionable value and thus leaving room for healthy trees to grow.[50]

47. *Morning Advocate,* May 27, 1944; J. Philip Dismukes, *The Center: A History of the Development of Lafayette, Louisiana* (Lafayette, La., 1972), 52–53.

48. James E. Fickle, *The New South and the 'New Competition': Trade Association Development in the Southern Pine Industry* (Urbana, Ill., 1980), 350; A. D. Folweiler, *Forest Land Ownership in Louisiana and Its Influence on Timber Production* (Baton Rouge, 1943), 9.

49. Fickle, *The New South,* 350–51; William G. Robbins, *Lumberjacks and Legislators: Political Economy of the Lumber Industry, 1890–1941* (College Station, Tex., 1982), 236–38.

50. *Shreveport Times,* August 26, 1945.

*   *   *

World War II caused much change in Louisiana farm demographics. Although the amount of land devoted to farming remained virtually the same—9,996,108 acres in 1939 (34.6 percent of the state's total area), and 10,039,657 acres in 1944 (34.7 percent of the total area)—the number of farmers declined from 150,007 in 1940 to 129,295 in 1945. The characteristics of the farm population changed noticeably, as more farmers obtained full or part ownership of the land they worked during the war. In 1940, 52,946 farmers owned their farms outright, and that number increased to 58,761 by 1945. The trend toward farm ownership cut across racial lines; the number of white full owners increased from 43,410 to 48,357, while the number of black full owners increased from 9,526 to 10,404. Overall, the number of farms operated by owners increased from 40.2 percent in 1940 to 50.4 percent in 1944.[51]

As may be expected, the number of farm tenants declined during the war years as agricultural workers bought the land they farmed, found jobs in war-related industry, or entered the armed services. The number of all classes of tenants fell from 89,167 in 1940 to 63,541 in 1945. The decline was greater among whites than blacks, with the number of white tenants deceasing by 14,524 to 11,102 blacks. The decline in tenantry occurred even for the poorest of Louisiana agricultural workers, the sharecroppers. In this category, the decline was greater for blacks than for whites, although at the end of the war there were still more black than white sharecroppers. The number of black sharecroppers declined by 8,438, and the number of white sharecroppers by 5,972.[52]

The scarcity of farm labor during the war years is illustrated by the decrease in the number of hired hands. In 1940, Louisiana farmers reported employing 56,712 hired hands. By 1945, that number decreased by 37,758, to a total of 18,954.[53]

The average age of Louisiana farmers rose during the war years, from 44.2 to 46.7 years in 1945. It is no surprise that the number of farmers in

51. Curtis, *Statistical Data*, 5, 7.
52. *Ibid.*, 5.
53. *Ibid.*, 14.

the "Under 35" age group dropped sharply, from 29 percent of the total number of farmers to 20 percent. The young farmers, of course, were most susceptible to the draft. Also, many of them felt less reluctant to leave the farm for industrial jobs. All other age categories of farmers increased their percentages of the total number of farmers during the war years.[54]

Statistics also reveal a slight trend toward larger farms. The "Under 30 Acres" classification declined from 50.3 percent of all Louisiana farms to 46.1 percent between 1940 and 1944, while all other classifications increased. The increases ranged from 1.3 percent in the "50–99 acre" classification to only .4 percent in the "180–259 acres" and "500 or more acres" classifications.[55]

The wartime prosperity brought many amenities to farm life. The number of trucks on Louisiana farms increased from 17,005 to 20,974 from 1940 to 1945, and the number of automobiles from 34,891 to 40,651. In addition, by 1945, 13.7 percent of farm dwellings reported running water, 24.4 percent received electricity, 48.7 percent were equipped with a radio, and 5 percent had telephone service.[56] All of these percentages were higher than they were in 1940.

Louisiana agriculture faced many challenges during World War II, which it met with varying degrees of success. Apart from the perennial problems of bad weather and insects, the labor shortage remained beyond the ability of Louisiana farmers to solve completely, although several human and mechanical substitutes were used effectively. Even in the face of these difficulties, however, the unprecedented worldwide demand for agricultural products brought Louisiana agriculture out of the economic doldrums of the 1920s and 1930s. While it stimulated Louisiana's agricultural economy, though, war demand failed to reorient it toward new crops. Louisiana farmers both before and after the war concentrated on growing their three traditional staple crops. Fortunately for them, the do-

54. *Ibid.*, 6.
55. *Ibid.*, 13.
56. *Ibid.*, 14.

mestic demand for those specific commodities—cotton, sugarcane, and rice—increased dramatically, because German naval attacks threatened to disrupt dependable trade routes and because Japanese expansion in the Pacific Basin and Asia eliminated traditional sources. Louisiana farmers, therefore, could vend their favorite crops in a seller's market and enjoy the attendant prosperity—while that market lasted.

9

Good-Bye to the Great Depression

During World War II, the South received about $4,442 million in federal funds for war plants, 17.6 percent of the national total. Louisiana received more of these funds than any other southern state except Texas—about $1,773,713,000. The South had also trained many recruits during World War I, and federal officials during the new war again sent thousands of new soldiers to the area for training. In addition, southern urban locations contained relatively large pools of workers needed in wartime industry. The South thus became an important region in the rush to mobilize the United States.[1]

Increased federal spending for war projects helped to bring Louisiana, the South, and the United States as a whole out of the Great Depression. The Works Progress Administration, the Civilian Conservation Corps, the National Youth Administration, and other agencies had brought hope and work during the decade of despair, and the programs remained popular when the war began. As late as 1939, the WPA remained a major employer in central Louisiana, sponsoring a nursery school in Alexandria, community centers in Grant, Natchitoches, Rapides, and Winn Parishes, archaeological expeditions in LaSalle and Avoyelles Parishes, the Historical Records Survey in ten parishes, a unit of the Veterans' Graves Regis-

1. Tindall, *The Emergence of the New South,* 699–700; *Morning Advocate,* January 30, 1945; David R. Goldfield, *Cotton Fields and Skyscrapers: Southern City and Region, 1607–1980* (Baton Rouge, 1982), 182–83.

tration Program, venereal disease control projects in Rapides, Natchitoches, LaSalle, and Concordia Parishes, and Vital Statistics Projects in
LaSalle and Rapides Parishes.[2]

Even though the WPA continued approving projects for Louisiana—
street construction and repair for Baton Rouge in March 1941 and statewide recreational facilities for soldiers in September of that year—its
labor force increasingly moved off WPA rolls and onto payrolls. The state
led all others in the percentage increase in private sector employment in
September and October 1940, with an increase of 141.8 percent. New Orleans WPA rolls reached their peak in April 1939, when the agency included 17,698 names on its rolls. By March 1942, only 6,489 names remained, and about 250 men per week were leaving those rolls as they
found work. By December 1942, when President Roosevelt ordered liquidation of the WPA, the Baton Rouge *Morning Advocate* thought that the
time had indeed come to issue a eulogy for that beneficial federal agency:
"For its purpose . . . the WPA was one of the soundest experiments of the
emergency relief era [but the] days of emergency employment are
gone—if not forever, at least until the war has been won."[3]

The National Youth Administration shifted the last phase of its work
in Louisiana to the war effort. NYA officials announced in July 1940 that
they planned to spend $1,271,038 in Louisiana during 1941 on projects
designed to prepare workers for industries expected to expand because of
national defense. In addition, the Civilian Conservation Corps during the
early 1940s oriented its program to the war effort. Some CCC workers,
for example, engaged exclusively in work on military reservations.[4]

The beginning of World War II in Europe brought an immediate

2. *Town Talk,* April 23, 27, 1940; William W. Breme, "Along the 'American Way': The
New Deal's Work Relief Programs for the Unemployed," *Journal of American History* 62
(December 1975): 636–52; Louisiana Department of Conservation, *Fifteenth Biennial Re-
port* (1940–1941), 59.

3. *Shreveport Times,* December 4, 1940; *Morning Advocate,* March 18–19, December 18,
1942; *Times-Picayune,* March 28, September 18, 1942.

4. *Times-Picayune,* July 2, 1940; *Town Talk,* January 9, 1941; *States,* July 2, 1941; Hubert
Humphreys, "In a Sense Experimental: The Civilian Conservation Corps in Louisiana,"
Louisiana History 5 (fall 1964): 347, 349–50, 367.

boom to the American economy as businesses rushed to stockpile materials and products that might become scarce. The boom collapsed after public consumption and exports failed to increase, but the American economy rebounded, albeit more slowly, in 1940.[5]

Louisiana's economy improved along with the nation's. Standard Oil Company in Baton Rouge began an expansion program, including facilities for the production of synthetic rubber, while Higgins Shipyards in New Orleans recorded banner profits in 1940. The federal government spent approximately $13 million to build training camps around Alexandria. The Louisiana Employment Service placed approximately 57,000 people in jobs, including 16,000 in work on the army camps alone. New passenger-car sales in the state increased from 27,882 in 1939 to 33,064 in 1940, and crude petroleum production increased from about 90 million barrels in 1939 to almost 102 million barrels in 1940.[6]

Retail sales in Baton Rouge during the 1940 Christmas season increased 25 percent over 1939 Christmas sales, and topped the 1929 record sales. Baton Rouge ranked seventh among United States cities in increased retail buying power in 1940, according to the Federal Reserve System report for the year. The National Industrial Conference Board found that earnings per person during 1940 increased in only three southern states: Virginia (to $408), Louisiana (to $390), and South Carolina (to $296). All three states stood above the 1929 levels of income per person, but their citizens were only relatively better off. Even the wealthiest southern state (Virginia) remained well below the United States average income per person ($546), and received less than half the earnings per person of the most affluent state in the Union (Connecticut, with $818 per person).[7]

The construction industry in Louisiana began to recover from the Depression even before the war started. The Federal Housing Administration reported that during the first week of March 1939 it accepted more

5. Eliot Janeway, *The Struggle for Survival: A Chronicle of Economic Mobilization in World War II* (New Haven, Conn., 1951), 146–48.

6. *Town Talk,* December 27, 1940.

7. *Morning Advocate,* December 28, 1940, March 8, 10, April 1, 1941.

mortgage loans for construction or improvement of private dwellings than during any comparable time period in its experience in the state. Following the federal government's decision to construct training camps in Louisiana, the building industry recovered even more, especially in central Louisiana with its concentration of war camps and influx of new residents. The value of building permits issued throughout the state grew 32.8 percent in 1939, declined 14.0 percent in 1940, increased 84.3 percent in 1941 (the height of the war-camp construction boom), and declined again in both 1942 and 1943.[8]

Industrial growth occurred throughout the state. While small manufacturers located plants in smaller towns, most of the industrial development occurred in the three major cities—Baton Rouge, Shreveport, and New Orleans.

Baton Rouge in 1940 boasted a population of 43,719. By 1945, its population numbered 110,000, much of that growth resulting from the city's industrial development. When the war began, Baton Rouge was already a major oil refining center, owing to the Standard Oil Company of Louisiana refinery.[9] During the 1940s, this refinery and other major industries located in Baton Rouge caused the city to become a vital cog in the nation's war machine.

The Standard Oil complex included the first catalytic cracking plant ever built, which contributed heavily to the production of badly needed 100-octane aviation fuel and also created by-products useful in making synthetic rubber. In addition, the complex housed an alkylation plant that made high-octane blending agents for aviation fuel, plants synthesizing both ethyl and isopropyl alcohol from petroleum, and plants that produced synthetic rubber. By June 1945 the refinery produced its one bil-

8. "Louisiana FHA Loans Lead the Nation," *Louisiana Police Jury Review,* April 1939, 57; *Town Talk,* May 7, 1940, January 1, 1941; *Louisiana Business Review,* March 1939, 15, January 1940, 16, January 1941, 16, January 1942, 18.

9. *Morning Advocate,* November 25, 1945; Mark T. Carleton, *River Capital: An Illustrated History of Baton Rouge* (Woodland Hills, Calif., 1981), 153–57; John L. Loos, *Oil On Stream! A History of the Interstate Oil Pipe Line Company, 1909–1959* (Baton Rouge, 1959), 3–7.

lionth gallon of high-octane aviation fuel, and the government estimated that it fueled one plane of every fifteen used in the war effort.[10]

Another high-tech industry in the capital city was aluminum. The Aluminum Company of America operated a plant in Baton Rouge that reduced bauxite ore to aluminum used in aircraft and other construction. By April 1944, the facility produced enough aluminum for two thousand fighter planes per month and employed approximately eight hundred persons.[11]

Baton Rouge also became a concentration depot for United States Army supplies in Louisiana. This project more than doubled the railroad trackage capacity in the Illinois Central Railroad yards. The *Morning Advocate* noted, however, that income from this source would obviously end with the war.[12]

Increased deposits in Baton Rouge banks, which set record levels during 1940, revealed the city's growing prosperity. At the end of 1940, Fidelity Bank and Trust Company reported deposits of $5,550,537 compared with $5,078,262 at the end of 1939. City National Bank reported $11,009,595 on deposit at the end of 1940, compared with $10,860,227 one year before. Louisiana National Bank reported $11,876,391 on deposit in 1940, compared with $11,250,811 the previous year. Growth in bank deposits continued throughout the war. In 1942, the three banks received an additional $15,378,778 in deposits.[13]

Shreveport was the center of wartime prosperity in northwest Louisiana. The Shreveport Chamber of Commerce sought with determination to bring defense industries, contracts, and army bases to that corner of the state. When President Roosevelt unveiled his "favored areas" for war industries and included Shreveport on his list, the chamber lobbied aircraft manufacturers to build a factory near the city. The chamber's board of directors instructed its recruiters to offer manufacturers free factory sites

10. *Morning Advocate,* June 1, 1945; W. B. Cotton, Jr., "Baton Rouge Refinery Converts Petroleum into War Materials," *Louisiana Municipal Review,* July–August 1943, 105–06.

11. *Morning Advocate,* March 24, 1942, April 16, June 2, 1944.

12. *Ibid.,* May 30, 1942.

13. *Ibid.,* January 2, 1941, April 1, 1943.

supplied by the city provided that the industry offered sufficient revenue to justify such a contribution.[14]

Even though the chamber of commerce failed to lure an airplane manufacturer to Shreveport and also failed in a prolonged effort to convince the federal government to build an army cantonment near the city, throughout the war it provided information on raw material priorities, labor relations, allocations, contract services, and other business information. It also actively sought small war contracts for area businesses.[15]

Several local businesses did receive such contracts, and so were able to contribute to the war effort. The J. B. Beaird Company, for example, employed approximately eight hundred people in 1943 to produce shell casing, tanks for the production of synthetic rubber and storage of high octane gasoline, landing barge anchors, and armored tank parts. The Brewster Company received raw steel tubing, which it finished into 250-pound bomb bodies and shipped to shell-loading plants.[16]

In an effort to complete the bomb-production capability of the area, the Shreveport Chamber of Commerce began lobbying the army ordnance department in 1940 for a munitions plant. The War Department replied that the requirements for munitions plants were rigid: sites must encompass at least six thousand acres, without any pipelines or oil or mineral leases, be served by two railroads and by highways, and preferably be located within twenty-five miles of a town of 100,000 population.[17]

Northwest Louisiana, however, did meet those requirements, and the War Department notified local officials in April 1941 that it intended to locate an ordnance plant at Minden, provided it could obtain sufficient land. By September, the acreage was acquired from 105 private landown-

14. Shreveport Chamber of Commerce Minutes, June 13, 1940, microform, Troy H. Middleton Library, Louisiana State University, Baton Rouge, La.

15. *Ibid.,* March 13, 15, May 8, November 6, December 11, 1941.

16. *Shreveport Times,* June 25, July 18, 1943; Viola Carruth, *Caddo 1000: A History of the Shreveport Area from the Time of the Caddo Indians to the 1970s* (Shreveport, 1971), 173; Allen J. Ellender and John H. Overton to Pat Beaird, August 26, 1941, Ellender Papers.

17. Shreveport Chamber of Commerce Minutes, August 8, 1940, February 13, 1941, July 10, 1941.

ers. Auctions in November and December disposed of some 600 dwellings and farm buildings.[18]

Costs of constructing the Minden Shell Loading Plant ran higher than original estimates, because contractors found that the site was too flat to drain properly without an extensive network of ditches and canals. In addition, they found the water table too high and the soil too unstable for construction without larger and heavier foundations than originally anticipated. Nevertheless, by 1943, the massive plant encompassed 16,025 acres and included 430 buildings.[19]

While many parts of Louisiana thus shared in the wartime industrial development, New Orleans remained the state's busiest area, producing a myriad of goods ranging from Liberty Ships to tents. Ships were manufactured by Louisiana Shipyards, Delta Shipbuilding Company, and Higgins Industries. Delta Shipbuilding launched its first Liberty Ship in May 1942 after working on it 242 days. Interestingly, by January 1943, improvements in construction techniques had cut the time necessary for Delta to build a Liberty Ship to slightly over 67 days.[20]

Consolidated Vultee Aircraft Corporation of Downey, California, also operated an aircraft production plant in New Orleans. One of the warplanes it built was the Consolidated Model 31, a "flying boat" ordered by the navy, powered by two thousand-horsepower Wright engines and capable of cruising at 160 miles per hour at high altitudes.[21]

Many small manufacturing plants in New Orleans produced other war matériel. Rheem Manufacturing Company made 105-millimeter shell casings, and the Neptune Boat and Davit Company built lifeboats. Edwin H. Blum manufactured 161,000 pairs of military trousers in 1944; by the same year, the Federal Fiber Mills had produced enough manila and sisal rope to encircle the globe. The Snider Poster Process Company

18. *Shreveport Times,* August 11, 1943; Allen J. Ellender to various radio stations in Shreveport, June 5, 1941, and Frank Wurzlow to various radio stations in Shreveport, July 11, 1941, Ellender Papers.

19. *Shreveport Times,* August 11, 1943.

20. *Morning Advocate,* April 8, 1941; *Item,* July 18, 1941; *Times-Picayune,* March 28, 1942, January 8, 1943.

21. *States,* July 11, 1943, October 5, 1944; *Item,* July 11, 1943.

made decals that eliminated hand-lettering of airplane instrument panels, the National Blow Pipe and Manufacturing Company constructed metal ammunition shipping containers, and the Crescent Bed Company built berths for Liberty Ships. The International Lubricant Corporation produced special greases ordered by the armed forces to keep their equipment running when exposed to sea water or extremes in temperature.[22] Other small plants produced numerous other goods.

The dominant war industry in the city was the manufacturing empire of Andrew Jackson Higgins. Higgins, a native of Columbus, Nebraska, had migrated to Mobile, Alabama, in 1906 and to New Orleans in 1910, where he entered the lumber business. That enterprise crashed in 1922, but Higgins recouped his fortunes as a shipbuilder. During 1930 and 1931, his boats set speed records on the Mississippi River from New Orleans to St. Louis. Eventually, he evolved a design that allowed his boats to jump logs and small spits of land without damaging vital components. From that design, he developed the Higgins Eureka, a 36-foot motorboat that could rush onto a beach without damage. Oil companies quickly adopted the boat for use in the marshes of Louisiana, the Amazon River basin, the Persian Gulf, and the Far East. Higgins's association with the armed forces began in 1936, when the army ordered from him two river-steamer inspection boats. The navy ordered its first landing boats in 1938, and he produced Eurekas for the United States, Britain, Finland, and Holland. By 1941 he was producing landing boats, ramp-type welded-steel tank lighters, and patrol torpedo ("PT") boats.[23]

In September 1940 Higgins's company employed four hundred pro-

22. *Morning Advocate,* August 12, 1941, December 31, 1944; *States,* January 19, 1945; Allen J. Ellender and John H. Overton to Robert S. Maestri, September 13, 1941, Ellender Papers.

23. "Higgins Is the Name," *Time,* May 4, 1942, 76, 78; McGuire, "Andrew Jackson Higgins Plays Presidential Politics," 274–75; A. A. Hoehling, *Home Front USA* (New York, 1966), 52; Jerry E. Strahan, *Andrew Jackson Higgins and the Boats That Won World War II* (Baton Rouge, 1994), 5–87; U.S. Senate, *Hearing Before a Special Committee Investigating the National Defense Program,* 78th Cong., 1st sess., 1943, pt. 17: 6999; *Morning Advocate,* March 25, 1941; *Times-Picayune,* August 24, 1941; *Shreveport Times,* October 24, 1943; Andrew J. Higgins to Allen J. Ellender, December 2, 1940, Ellender Papers.

duction workers. By 1941, he employed eighteen hundred workers and spent $700,000 monthly for Louisiana labor and products. By 1944, employees numbered about twenty thousand, blacks as well as whites, in seven different manufacturing units in New Orleans. In all, the company sold more than 14,000 combat boats of all types to the Allies. In September 1943, the United States Navy reported that the majority of its 14,072 vessels were either designed or built by Andrew Jackson Higgins.[24]

Higgins, like the more famous shipbuilder Henry J. Kaiser, used new production methods to build ships quickly. He also shared in the misfortunes common among American manufacturers during the war. He planned to operate a vast new shipyard built by the federal government in which he proposed abandoning traditional narrow shipways for larger ways accommodating several keels at once. A keel would be placed on rollers at the head of the way and eased toward the water's edge. Workers would construct the ship as the keel slid gradually toward the water. In 1942, however, the United States Maritime Commission canceled its order for two hundred Liberty Ships that he planned to construct at this yard because of the shortage of steel necessary to build both the ways and the ships.[25]

Higgins criticized the "dollar-a-year" men who ordered cancelation of his Liberty Ship contract for the proposed Michaud plant, but despite a rare agreement between Governor Jones and New Orleans mayor Maestri, both of whom peppered Washington with appeals to restore the contract, the Maritime Commission chose not to reinstate it.[26]

24. McGuire, "Andrew Higgins Plays Presidential Politics," 275; *Morning Advocate,* March 25, 1941; *Item,* May 22, 1944; Morton Sosna, "More Important Than the Civil War?" paper presented Southern Historical Association Annual Meeting, November 5, 1982.

25. "Crepe Hung in Louisiana," *Time,* July 27, 1942, 13, 74; Strahan, *Andrew Jackson Higgins,* 99–101; *Congressional Record,* 77th Cong., 2d sess., 1942, vol. 88, pt. 5: 6635–40; *Congressional Record,* 77th Cong., 2nd sess., 1942, vol. 88, pt. 10: A2983; Sam Jones to Allen J. Ellender, May 16, 1941, Ellender Papers; Sosna, "More Important Than the Civil War?" 11.

26. *Morning Advocate,* August 4, October 31, 1942; *Town Talk,* August 12, 17, 1944; *Congressional Record,* 78th Cong., 2d sess., 1944, vol. 90, pt. 10: A3541–45; Sosna, "More Important Than the Civil War?" 12; Hoehling, *Home Front,* 53.

Higgins then cast about for another war product to build at his huge Michaud site, and settled on airplanes. He first hoped to build the Curtiss C-76 Caravan all-wood troop transport, but the army canceled its plans for wooden airplanes. A complex series of negotiations with federal defense officials brought him a contract in 1942 for twelve hundred Curtiss C-46 Commandos, all-metal transports designed to carry paratroopers, light artillery, or freight. The plant built only one of these airplanes before the army canceled the contract in August 1944. Higgins then expanded production in the Michaud plant of a newly designed rescue boat sturdy enough to be dropped by parachute from high altitudes to airplane crash or shipwreck survivors. The Michaud plant also produced parts for the atomic bomb designed by FDR's top-secret Manhattan Project.[27]

Higgins's difficulty in obtaining and keeping war production contracts illustrates the vagaries of fortune experienced by businessmen who tied most of their industrial production to war contracts and thus depended upon the military's continuing need for specialized products. Changes in the military situation quickly made some items obsolete.

The center of wartime prosperity in the southwest portion of Louisiana was Lake Charles, which became an important petrochemical center. The city and Calcasieu Parish in 1921 began constructing a ship channel from Lake Charles to the Gulf of Mexico. By 1926, the channel and a newly opened port provided a convenient outlet to the Gulf. By 1931, the volume of goods passing through the port exceeded a million tons per year.[28]

Industrial development in Lake Charles began in 1933 with the opening of two factories. Mathieson Alkali Works invested $7.5 million, and Swift Packing Company $2.5 million, in their respective new plants. Calcasieu Parish also produced some 12 million barrels of oil annually by 1939, and about 25 million more barrels moved through the port. The availability of petroleum led Continental Oil Company in 1939 to con-

27. Strahan, *Andrew Jackson Higgins,* 147, 182, 230, 279.

28. Kathleen Collins, "Lake Charles Claims Rarest Port in the World," *Louisiana Heritage,* volume 2, no. 3, 13–14.

struct a vast $5 million complex including an oil refinery, a tank farm, and a pipeline to transport crude oil from large oil fields in the vicinity.[29]

The war brought an intensified development of the Lake Charles petrochemical industries. Mathieson enlarged the alkali plant in 1941. Cities Service Company built a high-octane gasoline refinery that by 1945 produced twenty-five thousand barrels per day. Firestone Rubber Company produced synthetic rubber at a factory financed by the Defense Plant Corporation, a division of the Reconstruction Finance Corporation created to finance the construction of defense production facilities and to stockpile strategic materials. The corporation also financed butadiene, ammonia, and magnesium plants in Lake Charles.[30]

Senator Allen Ellender lobbied intensely to convince the War Shipping Administration to use the port of Lake Charles for more rice shipments, especially those to Cuba and Puerto Rico, but met with little success. Ellender eventually had to report to his correspondents on the subject that the WSA would not promise to ship the entire 1943 Louisiana rice crop through the port, as its boosters wanted.[31]

For the central part of the state, wartime economic development stemmed from training United States Army troops. The training program included a series of massive maneuvers that brought thousands of soldiers into the area. The immediate stimulus to the economy was the construction of army posts in which inductees received basic training.

Central Louisiana's association with training camps had begun during World War I. Late in 1917, workers had completed Camp Beauregard north of Alexandria to train National Guard units from Alabama, Arkansas, Louisiana, and Mississippi. During the postwar demobilization,

29. Collins, "Lake Charles," 14–15; "Facts About Calcasieu Parish," *Louisiana Police Jury Review,* April 1939, 35; John W. Harrop, Jr., "Lake Charles—A Decade of Progress," *Louisiana Municipal Review,* September–October 1941, 140–41.

30. Collins, "Lake Charles," 15; *Morning Advocate,* June 15, 1941; *American Press,* December 2, 1941; *Shreveport Times,* May 27, 1944; *Item,* August 23, 1945.

31. E. S. Land to Allen J. Ellender, May 29, July 2, 1943, T. A. Smith to Alva P. Frith, July 8, 1943, Frith to Ellender, July 27, 1943, Ellender to Frith, August 5, 1943, Ellender Papers.

the army sold most of Beauregard's 5,200 acres, but retained a small area for a summer training ground for Louisiana National Guard units. Beauregard also became a Citizens' Military Training Camp. The CMTC program provided high school boys with thirty days' experience in military organization, management, discipline, instruction, athletics, recreation, and social contacts during their summer vacation.[32]

Camp Beauregard was shocked out of its peacetime inactivity by Adolf Hitler's stunning conquests of his European neighbors. The army worked on a military air field north of Beauregard in 1939, and in 1940 officials at the United States Army Fourth Corps Area, headquartered in Atlanta, Georgia, selected central Louisiana for army training maneuvers. The 1940 Louisiana Maneuvers began in May and eventually involved more than seventy thousand troops spread over Rapides, Natchitoches, Sabine, and Vernon Parishes. Foot soldiers cursed Louisiana's mud and heat, but the maneuver area pleased army officials so well that they returned in the autumn of 1940, and in 1941, 1942, and 1943.[33]

Besides bringing central Louisiana to the nation's attention, the maneuvers brought thousands of Americans from other regions into the area, where they were pleased to receive a warm welcome. The *Alexandria Town Talk* remarked, "The men in the ranks have taken to Alexandria as though it were their home—and have received a royal welcome." Never were they more welcome, of course, than when on leave they would storm into the city with money to spend. A warm weekend in early May 1940 brought such an influx. The *Town Talk* reported that "every roadside establishment in the local area was crowded with troop-

32. *Town Talk,* July 29, 1957; Jerry Purvis Sanson, "Cenla During World War II," *Alexandria Daily Town Talk, Centennial Edition,* April 8, 1983, 18; *The Peep Sight: Camp Beauregard, Louisiana, 1931* (n.p., 1931), 20–23; Elaine H. Brister, *Once Upon a River: A History of Pineville, Louisiana* (Baton Rouge, 1968), 124–30; Terry L. Jones, "Overview of Camp Beauregard History," *Camp Beauregard and Central Louisiana, 1940–1945* (New Orleans, 1994), 21.

33. Sanson, "Cenla," 18; "Extensive War Games in Louisiana," *Louisiana Police Jury Review,* April 1940, 67–68; *Town Talk,* March 25, April 8, 1940; Brister, *Once Upon a River,* 129–30; Christopher R. Gabel, "The 1940 Maneuvers: Prelude to Mobilization," *Camp Beauregard and Central Louisiana, 1940–1945,* 31–32.

ers . . . and while they were here there was a steady tinkle of cash drawers in every establishment where refreshments and sandwiches could be obtained."[34]

The 1940 maneuvers pumped large amounts of money into the central Louisiana economy. The troops engaged in the fall maneuvers, for example, received some $700,000 in pay and allowances. The total cost of these maneuvers was $1,826,200, or about $87,000 per day.[35] The portion of that money that found its way into the local economy whetted the area's appetite for more.

It had not long to wait. The 1941 Louisiana Maneuvers easily eclipsed the magnitude of those in 1940. Army officials sought to make the exercises as close to real battlefield experience as possible. They formulated a background scenario in which the "nations" of "Kotmk" (Kansas, Oklahoma, Texas, Missouri, and Kentucky, with its "capital" at Houston) and "Almat" (Arkansas, Louisiana, Mississippi, Alabama, and Tennessee, with its "capital" at Birmingham) prepared for battle as tensions escalated over failure to secure Kotmk navigation rights on the Mississippi River. Army planners obviously spent much time constructing this elaborate plan that even included a jeering slogan Almat troops could shout at Kotmk troops about Kotmk premier Kodunkis: "Kodunkis is the Bunkis."[36]

Preliminary maneuvers began in late May as the two "countries" deployed their troops to strategic locations as the "navigation conference" between their inland waterways commissions supposedly dragged on at Memphis. Troops arriving in central Louisiana early were acclimated to battle noises by recordings of dive bombers, machine guns, cannon, and the wail of gas-warning sirens broadcast over loudspeakers placed throughout the Beauregard practice range. The first skirmish of the maneuvers occurred on June 17, but full "hostilities" were not to break out until August. As the starting date neared, central Louisiana was inun-

34. *Town Talk,* May 6, 11, 1940; Chuck Saucier, "Saying Goodbye," *Cenla: The Magazine of Central Louisiana,* November–December 1992, 12.

35. *Times Picayune,* August 17, 1940; *Town Talk,* August 21, 1940.

36. *Morning Advocate,* August 3, 5–6, 1941.

dated with people. During the latter part of July, between three and four hundred military vehicles passed through Alexandria each day. Soldiers arrived by the thousands—about five thousand on July 30; ten thousand on July 31; and five thousand on August 1.[37]

These Louisiana Maneuvers of 1941 were the largest peacetime maneuvers in American history up to that time and constituted a landmark in the development of army strategy and planning for war because they proved the usefulness of tanks in modern warfare. The previous year's exercises had demonstrated the capacity of armored columns to overrun a defending army when General Joseph Stilwell commanded a blitzkrieg invasion of Louisiana just as Hitler's forces had done in order to slice through the Low Countries and France. The 1941 maneuvers further revealed the weakness of conventional defense against armored might as General George S. Patton confirmed that tanks could operate effectively even in the marshes of Louisiana. In addition, during the fall of 1941 the army learned about reconnaissance and troop supply problems encountered in battlefield conditions, and thus had several months to seek solutions to those problems before the United States entered the war.[38]

The maneuvers were important not only for the development of an effective United States fighting machine but also for the Louisiana economy. The army payroll for the last part of August was the largest processed in Shreveport up to that time—approximately $900,000 issued through Commercial National Bank. Alexandria merchants stocked their shelves in anticipation of heavy business, and they were not disappointed. Most of them remained open on Labor Day, and troops on holiday

37. *Morning Advocate,* May 5, 9, 30, June 6, 10, 17, 1941; *Town Talk,* July 30–August 1, 1941.

38. Kent Robert Greenfield, Robert R. Palmer, and Bell I. Wiley, *United States Army in World War II: The Army Ground Forces, vol. 1, The Organization of Ground Combat Troops* (Washington, D.C., 1947), 44–45; Barbara W. Tuchman, *Stilwell and the American Experience in China, 1911–1945* (New York, 1971), 208–209; Ladislas Farago, *Patton: Ordeal and Triumph* (New York, 1963), 161–65; Dwight D. Eisenhower, *Crusade in Europe* (Garden City, N.Y., 1948), 10–13; J. Lawton Collins, *Lightning Joe: An Autobiography* (Baton Rouge, 1979), 111–15.

crowded stores in the maneuver area, sometimes buying out an entire stock, especially of tobacco, candy, and refreshments. Theaters and restaurants experienced constant lines for seats, and some smaller store owners reported selling as much in a day as they normally sold in a year. One study of the maneuvers estimates that they were worth about $25 million to the state.[39]

The army descended upon central Louisiana again in 1942 and 1943 for maneuvers, but these exercises were much less extensive than the massive 1941 undertaking. Additional maneuvers planned for April 1944 did not occur because the army needed the scheduled units to bolster the forces then in training for the cross-Channel invasion of Europe.[40]

On the downside, the maneuvers contributed to the area's transportation problems throughout the war. The average vehicular traffic in the maneuver zone rose from 40,762 vehicles per day in 1940 to 95,023 in 1941. Louisiana requested $1,407,150 from the Public Works Administration in August 1941 to improve highway markings for nighttime driving, and in December 1941 presented the United States Public Roads Administration a bill for $2,014,689.30 to repair road damage in the maneuver area.[41]

Owing to bureaucratic red tape and shortages of labor and material, that damage was slow to be repaired. Many people experienced difficulty reaching their jobs, adequate supplies failed to reach rural stores, schoolbuses and mail carriers had trouble completing their rounds, doctors sometimes failed to reach their patients, and farmers found it difficult to bring their produce to market. The Public Roads Administration began

39. Viola Carruth, *Caddo 1000,* 173; *Town Talk,* August 29–September 1, 1941; G. Patrick Murray, "The Louisiana Maneuvers: Practice for War," *Louisiana History* 12 (spring 1972): 123.

40. *Morning Advocate,* August 2, 1942, February 2, 1943; *Town Talk,* August 3, 1942, February 1, 1943; *Shreveport Times,* August 31, 1943; Robert R. Palmer, Bell I. Wiley, and William R. Keast, *United States Army in World War II: The Army Ground Forces, vol. 2, The Procurement and Training of Ground Combat Troops* (Washington, D.C., 1948), 384, 470.

41. *Town Talk,* May 6, 1940, December 31, 1941; *Morning Advocate,* May 30, August 9, 1941; *Shreveport Times,* January 1, 1942.

repairs on February 1, 1942, and commandeered some engineer troops to assist in grading and hauling, but had only $400,000 available for its maintenance program.[42]

The maneuvers, to be sure, brought thousands of troops, the attention of the nation, and the excitement of "war" to Louisiana, but training camps constructed in the state contributed more steadily to the economy. The complex of camps around Alexandria originated at the end of the 1940 maneuvers, when U.S. Representative A. Leonard Allen and Governor Jones announced that the army planned to take over Camp Beauregard from the Louisiana National Guard. Jones and Louisiana National Guard commander Raymond H. Fleming had proposed to army officials in May 1940 that they use Beauregard as a training facility for National Guard troops, whom Congress was then considering calling into active service for one year. Congress approved the Guard bill on August 27, 1940, and work began almost immediately on Camp Beauregard.[43]

In September the army announced plans to construct two additional training camps in the area, one near Tioga, north of Alexandria (eventually named Camp Livingston), and one near Forest Hill, about eighteen miles southwest of Alexandria (Camp Claiborne). The need for still more facilities led to plans announced in October to construct a large training camp for an armored contingent of about ten thousand troops near Leesville in Vernon Parish, which became Camp Polk, the largest armored-force training camp in the United States. By April 1941, over thirty-two thousand troops were training in the camps around Alexandria.[44]

These camps, plus the Alexandria Air Base, Barksdale Field near Bossier City and its satellite locations, other air bases at Baton Rouge and

42. J. H. Anderson to Allen J. Ellender, December 31, 1943, J. G. Christiansen to Ellender, February 29, 1944, General Richard Donovan to Ellender, March 9, 1944, Lois Whittaker to Ellender, May 29, 1944, Thomas McDonald to Ellender, September 28, 1944, Ellender Papers; *Shreveport Times,* February 1, 1942.

43. *Town Talk,* August 21–22, 28, 1940; Isaac D. Chapman, "Louisiana's Natural Resources and National Defense," *Louisiana Conservation Review,* autumn 1940, 35.

44. *Morning Advocate,* October 20–21, 1940; *Item,* November 18, 1940; *Town Talk,* December 7, 18, 1940, January 3, 11, 21, 1941, July 29, 1957; *Times-Picayune/New Orleans States,* August 22, 1943; *Shreveport Times,* August 31, 1943.

New Orleans, and the coast guard base in New Orleans, provided both construction jobs and income from maintenance and service requirements. By October 1940 about 8,000 workers were building Camps Beauregard and Livingston. The number employed on these two projects grew to 36,857 in January 1941. In April 1941 construction employees at these two camps plus Camps Claiborne and Polk numbered about 80,000.[45]

Rapides Parish assessor Trent L. James established an employment headquarters at his office in the courthouse to secure work on the camps for unemployed citizens of central Louisiana. The U.S. House of Representatives found in 1941 that both residents and nonresidents of Louisiana worked in camp construction, the resident group consisting of citizens of Rapides and other parishes and the nonresident group of those brought into the state by construction companies or unions. The Louisiana State Employment Service directed many sugar workers into jobs at the camps after the short 1940 harvest season. Army camp construction paid as much as $1 per hour for an eight-hour day, six days per week; and many farm workers continued to hold these jobs rather than return to the uncertain income from farm labor.[46]

General Fleming had commented in August 1940 that placement of the training camps in the state would mean "the expenditure of millions of dollars more in Louisiana for the subsistence of men," and he proved to be correct. In November 1940 the army estimated that the costs of operating Camps Livingston and Claiborne would reach about $500,000 per day, and that they planned to use local suppliers for perishable and imme-

45. *Morning Advocate,* October 20, 1940; *Town Talk,* July 29, 1957; Lester C. Verigan, Jr., "Barksdale Air Force Base: Satellite Operations in Northwest Louisiana," *North Louisiana Historical Association Journal,* winter 1994, 16–19.

46. *Morning Advocate,* September 21–22, October 20, 1940; *Town Talk,* September 18, 1940, July 29, 1957; Chapman, "Louisiana's Natural Resources," 36; *U.S. House, National Defense Migration Hearings Before the Select Committee Investigating National Defense Migration,* 77th Cong., 1st sess., 1941, pt. 11: 4664–65; Mrs. L. J. Barrios to Allen J. Ellender, February 1, 1943; Julius Maillian et al. to Ellender, February 26, 1943, Paul McNutt to Ellender, March 19, May 3, 1943, L. M. Green to Ellender, March 23, 1943, Major General E. Reybold to Ellender, May 18, 1943, Ellender Papers.

diately expendable supplies (such as $12,000 per day for gasoline and $600 per day for stovewood) whenever possible. Louisiana farmers and suppliers therefore found a ready market for their goods at the army camps, even though they sometimes complained of army purchasing procedures that seemed unnecessarily stringent or complex.[47]

While much of Louisiana's economic development occurred in the form of industrialization in the cities, other areas of the state shared in wartime prosperity. The oil and gas industry experienced dramatic growth during the latter half of the 1930s. The value of Louisiana petroleum products doubled between 1935 and 1938, reaching slightly above $130 million by the end of that period. Spurred on by the national defense effort, oil operators drilled about two hundred holes in 1941 and discovered twenty-nine new fields. These new discoveries brought the state's known reserves officially to 925,972,000 barrels, third highest in the nation. Louisiana's production of crude oil rose from 214,888,995 barrels in 1940–41 to 275,709,168 barrels in 1944–45. Lack of labor and steel for oil field production caused the number of wells drilled during 1942 to drop to 137, but by 1943 approximately 7,300 wells spread over 46 parishes produced 8 percent of the entire United States output.[48]

A by-product of the increased industrialization was labor union conflicts. Louisiana labor troubles represented the larger labor problem that existed in the United States during the war. At that time, the labor union movement was split into the rival American Federation of Labor and Congress of Industrial Organizations. Each group increased membership in the South during the war years.[49]

47. *Town Talk,* August 22, 1940; *Item-Tribune,* November 24, 1940; Raymond Fleming to Roy Dibuono, October 28, 1940, Harry D. Wilson to Quartermaster Marketing Center, Chattanooga, Tennessee, May 13, 1941, Wilson to Allen J. Ellender, March 27, 1942, Jones Collection, HTML.

48. *States,* December 29, 1941; William G. Rankin, "The Conservation of Louisiana's Natural Resources," *Louisiana Police Jury Review,* April 1939, 54–55; U.S. House, *Petroleum Investigation (Crude Oil Prices and Extension of the Cole Pipe Line Act) Hearings Before a Subcommittee of the Committee on Interstate and Foreign Commerce,* 78th Cong., 1st sess., 1944, 137–38; Louisiana Department of Conservation, *Sixteenth Biennial Report* (1942–1943), 214; Department of Conservation, *Seventeenth Biennial Report* (1944–1945), 15.

49. F. Ray Marshall, *Labor in the South* (Cambridge, Mass., 1967), 225–27.

Unions made their advances despite a growing anti-union sentiment that equated unionism with dangerous radicalism. Some Louisianians shared this sentiment, even though the state remained friendlier than other southern states to the concept of unionism. By the summer of 1943, the AFL reported its organization of the Aluminum Company of America, DuPont Chemical, Copolymer, and Bell Telephone workers in Baton Rouge. In New Orleans, union contracts protected metal trades workers in marine repair shops, the Delta Shipyards, and Higgins Industries, as well as about five hundred office workers and an unspecified number of teamsters, who were members of new local chapters of their unions. The union cause was furthered by the Louisiana legislature when it refused to approve antilabor legislation (primarily "right to work" laws and other measures limiting strikes or regulating internal union affairs) similar to that enacted by neighboring states (including Texas, Arkansas, Florida, Alabama, and Mississippi) as part of an antiunion reaction in 1943.[50]

The United States labor union movement during the war years sought to preserve improvements it had obtained for workers since the New Deal went into effect in 1933. The Roosevelt administration wanted peace within the factories to ensure production of war materials to meet the emergencies of the 1940s. In exchange for agreeing not to stage strikes detrimental to war production (even though some walkouts occurred), the unions obtained support of "maintenance of membership" and protection of wages from the effects of inflation. A union could recruit enough new members to keep its membership at prewar levels, and the "Little Steel" formula pegged wages to the cost-of-living increase between January 1 and May 1, 1942.[51]

Despite this agreement, major strikes occurred in the coal, steel, and railroad industries, causing severe criticism of the labor union movement. Many Americans envisioned "greedy" unions endangering the lives of American soldiers by not producing the maximum number of armaments the factories could turn out. Many workers also resented the relatively

50. *Ibid.*, 225–26, 241–42.
51. Perrett, *Days of Sadness,* 264–65.

high fees they had to pay to join unions working on defense-related jobs.[52] Unions thus lived in an uneasy coexistence with individual members, newspapers, and officials ready to criticize their every perceived misstep and to curtail hard-won rights, at least for the duration of the war.

On May 11, 1942, the Louisiana State Federation of Labor passed a resolution urging all affiliated unions to adhere to a strict no-strike policy for the duration of the national emergency, but some Louisianians nevertheless remained critical of unionism. The resolution was simply not enough to quell the sentiments that had been brewing for months. As early as April 1941, Governor Jones had noted a growing antiunion attitude in the nation and the state, and told a state labor convention in Baton Rouge that "unless you keep first and primarily the confidence of the American people you stand in grave danger of losing all the things labor has won for itself in a bloody, uphill struggle over half a century."[53]

The month before, the *Baton Rouge Morning Advocate* had derided "greedy professional labor leaders" who were "winning some battles in America for Mr. Hitler" by "sabotaging the national defense program." A short while later, the newspaper railed against reports that jobs on the new airport under construction north of the city were reserved for union members, and that only about one-half of the construction jobs at Camp Polk were filled by Louisianians because of union membership requirements. On December 11, 1941, the Shreveport Chamber of Commerce approved a resolution that decried "unnecessary strikes delaying war preparation work" and called for legislation outlawing strikes in industry essential to warfare during the emergency period.[54]

A *New Orleans Times-Picayune* editorial of March 18, 1942, criticizing labor unions elicited comments both favorable and unfavorable. In a letter to the editor, Mrs. W. F. Russo reminded readers that her two sons in

---

52. Richard R. Lingeman, *Don't You Know There's a War On? The American Home Front, 1941–1945* (New York, 1970), 136–37; Roy Hoopes, *Americans Remember the Home Front: An Oral Narrative* (New York, 1977), 103.

53. *Congressional Record,* 77th Cong., 1st Sess., 1941, vol. 87, pt. 12: A3090; Sam Jones Address, April 7, 1941, Aswell Papers, LLMVC.

54. *Morning Advocate,* March 23, 27, 1941; Shreveport Chamber of Commerce Minutes, December 11, 1941.

the armed forces "are on duty 24 hours a day and $21 a month is the miserable sum they get," while labor unions clamored for increased wages at home. Another reader wrote that a proposal to pay "time-and-a-half" for overtime work would only be "the incentive for deliberate slowdowns which prevent the government from getting a fair output per worker at the established normal union wage scale." Carl Mitchell of Bogalusa, a self-styled "working man," condemned "selfish, greedy groups of so-called labor leaders who are destroying the influence of labor by taking advantage of war to promote a labor dictatorship." Defenders of labor in this episode included Mrs. Bertha T. North of Algiers, who wrote to the editors that "your lying, filthy editorial . . . should be condemned by every decent working man and woman in the city of New Orleans," and Henry Gegenheimer, who remarked that the newspaper attempted "through distortion of the facts, to assign to the laboring man the dubious role of profiteers, which said role seems to be the motive of the interests you seem to be serving."[55]

Union leaders tried to improve the image of their organizations in the state. In April 1942, state AFL president E. H. "Lige" Williams described recent attacks on organized labor as "well thought out." They reminded him, he said, "of the well-known Hitler plan to divide and conquer." Steve Quarles, president of the Central Trades and Labor Council of New Orleans, reminded Louisianians that union members had sons in the armed forces "just as are the sons of the manufacturers' association and the Chamber of Commerce of the United States," and added, "we are not profiteering in this crisis." Labor leaders in Winnfield reported to Representative A. Leonard Allen that they denounced press attempts to stampede Louisiana officials into precipitating antiunion action: "There is no more loyal and patriotic group in America than organized labor."[56]

Such encouraging words from labor leaders notwithstanding, Louisiana experienced several strikes during the war years. One of these occurred when a small group of workers walked off construction jobs at Camp Polk in April 1941 because they thought that negotiations between

55. *Times-Picayune,* March 18, 20, 26, 1942.
56. *States,* April 6, 1942; *Town Talk,* April 3, 1942.

union and government representatives were progressing too slowly. Their wildcat strike idled four hundred other workers until union officials ordered them back to work.[57]

Some two months later, even though Industrial, Pipefitters, Welders, and Helpers Union [AFL] business agent R. O. Middleton insisted that "no strike was called," workers established a picket line against Stone and Webster Construction Company, which was building an expansion of the Ethyl Gasoline plant at Baton Rouge. The unions demanded a "closed shop" and the discharge of workers who refused to join the unions. The dispute ended about two weeks later when Paul A. Rasmussun, president of the Baton Rouge Building Trades Council, announced that the Ethyl plant would reopen as a "union shop" with union members given preference in employment.[58]

In August 1941, members of Local 260 United Construction Workers Organizing Committee (CIO) struck at the Johns-Mansville Products Corporation plant in Marrero, idling about four hundred workers in a dispute concerning overtime pay. Also in 1941, both Louisiana Shipyards and Delta Shipbuilding Company faced strikes called to enforce demands for a closed shop. Garbage collectors and incinerator workers in New Orleans struck for higher wages during 1943.[59]

In April 1945, employees at the Cities Service Refinery in Lake Charles struck to protest recent rent increases in the privately owned Maplewood housing project for war workers. This strike was crucial because the Firestone Tire and Rubber plant next door depended on the refinery for a steady supply of butadine to make synthetic rubber. In response to the walkout, Governor Jones asked President Truman to take over and operate the refinery. Truman in turn ordered Interior Secretary Harold Ickes to seize the plant because interruption of its production would "unduly impede or delay" the war effort. The workers agreed to return to their jobs the next day, but continued striving for rent reductions in Ma-

57. *Morning Advocate,* April 5, 1941.

58. *Ibid.,* June 4, 1941; *States,* June 20, 1941.

59. *Times-Picayune,* August 19, September 27, 30, 1941; *States,* September 15, 1943.

plewood, requesting the Federal Housing Authority to take over the property.[60]

Louisiana's two bitterest strikes occurred early and late in the war. The first was a 1941 strike by the International Brotherhood of Electrical Workers (AFL) against Gulf States Utilities. The IBEW maintained that GSU refused to bargain collectively with it, and instead negotiated with the Gulf States Electric Employees' Association, a company union. GSU maintained that the National Labor Relations Board on May 10 had ruled that "the unit contended for by the brotherhood is inappropriate for purposes of collective bargaining" and that the IBEW was now illegally trying to force its recognition as the collective bargaining agent in defiance of the NLRB ruling.[61]

During the night of July 12–13, 1941, a power outage left large sections of Baton Rouge and the surrounding area in darkness. GSU officials maintained that the blackout had been caused by saboteurs who drained oil from a transformer at Oak Grove in Ascension Parish, causing it to explode. The officials also announced that the alleged saboteurs could be prosecuted under federal antisabotage acts that forbade disrupting the flow of electricity to the national defense effort, since in addition to the power supplied to local defense industries, the lines at Oak Grove fed electricity into the Tennessee Valley Authority system, which, in turn, supplied power for the manufacture of aluminum. GSU offered a five-hundred-dollar reward for information about the saboteurs and strongly implied that they were IBEW members.[62]

On July 20, Howard Colvin, southern regional director of the Labor Department Conciliation Service, announced that he had failed to settle the dispute between the IBEW and GSU. The Defense Mediation Board assumed jurisdiction over the case while police guarded company property. The NLRB issued the last ruling in the dispute in February 1942 when it held that GSU had not interfered with the right of its employees

60. *Morning Advocate,* April 13–14, 18–20, 1945; *Town Talk,* April 19–20, 1945.
61. *Morning Advocate,* July 11, 1941.
62. *Ibid.*

to organize and had not dominated the formation of the Gulf States Electric Service Employees' Association, which it held to be a labor union. The NLRB also recommended dismissal of charges brought against GSU by the IBEW.[63]

Louisiana's other major labor dispute occurred when Andrew Jackson Higgins experienced a bitter strike as the war drew to a close. In 1943, Higgins had portrayed a cozy relationship between labor and management at his New Orleans plants when he testified in Washington before the Senate Special Committee Investigating the National Defense Program (commonly known as the Truman Committee, after its chair, Harry Truman). Higgins had reported that his was an organized shop with his workers represented by the American Federation of Labor. He had added that when grievances arose, he called his business managers and the union leaders together "in a soundproof room" and settled the problem. When large rush orders for boats arrived, labor union bands helped him to boost workers' morale by providing patriotic music for pep rallies that he held to persuade his employees to work harder and complete such assignments. ("When the tears are running down their eyes, then I have the silver-tongued labor leader tell them what's expected of them. I ask them how they are going to do it, and we get along fine.") Unions also helped keep absenteeism low at the Higgins plants by detailing members to find out why an absent employee missed work.[64]

By late 1944, however, good feelings between management and labor at the Higgins yards disappeared in acrimonious charges and countercharges complicated by an attempt by the CIO to supplant the AFL as representative of the majority of Higgins workers. The dispute became public over the so-called Hot Ship episode. As the winter of 1944–45 approached, Great Lakes shipbuilders had about one hundred ships under construction, and the threat of delays caused by approaching winter weather prompted navy officials to request that the ships be completed in ice-free areas. Higgins agreed to finish building a portion of them. The

---

63. *Ibid.,* July 20, 22, 23, 1941, February 4, 1942.

64. *U.S. Senate, Hearing . . . National Defense Program,* pt. 17, 6999–7005; Sosna, "More Important Than the Civil War?" 10.

United States Maritime Commission, which was in charge of the project, classified the work as "new construction" and authorized Higgins to pay workers time-and-a-half for overtime work on the ships. But the unions declined to accept that rate; they declared the work to be ship repair or conversion and asked for double wages for working overtime. The commission refused to let Higgins pay the higher wage scale, and the unions responded by ordering their members not to work on the "Hot Ship." This prevented between thirty and fifty ships from being sent to Higgins for completion, and on November 30, 1944, he notified the unions that their contract would be canceled on January 1, 1945. The CIO muddied the situation when it filed for an election to determine which labor organization legitimately represented Higgins workers.[65]

Difficulties developed soon after the beginning of 1945. Higgins first sought to close his facilities, but announced that he would put his plants back in operation after the National Labor Relations Board ordered a collective bargaining election to determine whether his workers wanted to be represented by the AFL or the CIO.[66]

Trouble simmered at the Higgins plants throughout 1945. In June, about seven thousand members of the Building Trades and Metal Trades unions walked off their jobs, idling about five thousand additional workers, in protest of Higgins's having hired ex-servicemen to work at the plants without requiring them to join unions. Morris Gottesman, treasurer of Higgins Industries, subsequently announced that his office was preparing a list of names of striking workers eligible for the draft that he planned to send to Raymond Fleming, Selective Service director in Louisiana. A spokesman commented that union members would "rather fight the Japs than be browbeaten by Higgins."[67]

On June 5, the War Labor Board directed the strikers to return to work, but they refused. The next day, John P. Frey, international presi-

65. *Item,* November 1–2, 1945; Stuart S. Hellman to Allen J. Ellender, June 8, 1945, Stuart S. Hellman, *Background of Present Dispute Between Higgins Industries Incorporated and the American Federation of Labor* (n.p., n.d.), 3, Ellender Papers; Strahan, *Andrew Jackson Higgins,* 255–82.

66. *Morning Advocate,* January 6, 1945.

67. *States,* June 4–5, 1945; Hellman, *Background of Present Dispute,* 3.

dent of the Metal Trades Workers, directed the New Orleans local to resume work pending appeal of Higgins's decision to cancel their original contract. As long as the appeal was not settled, he maintained, the contract remained in effect. Local union officials added their approval of Frye's plea and recommended a fifteen-day return to work during which they hoped to iron out their differences with Higgins. The strikers, however, voted to remain off their jobs and did not return to work until July 13, after union leaders informed them that according to army and navy officials, the strike was depriving those branches of the armed services of badly needed war equipment. The strikers formally announced that they were returning to work because the armed services needed boats, not as a favor to Andrew Higgins.[68]

Higgins realized that reductions in war contracts as the war ended gave him new leverage in the situation. He announced during the first week of June that some fifteen hundred of the strikers would not be needed at his City Park plant, even if they voted to return to work. Treasurer Gottesman announced on August 16 that the company planned a $25 million reconversion from production of landing craft to production of boats for civilian use, but cancelation of Higgins's remaining $20 million in war contracts still meant that about two-thirds of its workers would be laid off, many of them permanently.[69]

In October, Higgins walked out of a Washington meeting with members of the NLRB and the unions, declaring that he could no longer work with the unions. On October 29, another work stoppage occurred at his plants. Union members claimed that Higgins had locked them out and declared an open shop. Higgins said that he knew nothing of such action; that while he had not received official notification of the strike, union members were not on their jobs; and that the CIO unions (which then claimed to represent a majority of Higgins workers, even though the election had not yet been held) called the walk-out because he had broken off contract negotiations with them. This strike proved the last straw for

68. *States,* June 6–7, 9, 12, 1945; *Morning Advocate,* June 6, 13, 1945; Strahan, *Andrew Jackson Higgins,* 272.

69. *Morning Advocate,* August 16–17, 1945; *Times-Picayune,* August 17, 1945.

Higgins. He announced that he planned to close his three remaining New Orleans shipbuilding plants, sell them to the highest bidder, and subcontract his remaining obligations to other firms. He would then devote his energy, he said, "to [a] crusade to see that men who want work can get it without paying tribute to anybody."[70]

Jack Rawls, vice president of the New Orleans Metal Trades Council, called the closures a "red herring." AFL spokesman William L. Donnels, joint chairman of the Metal Trades and the Building Trades Council, said Higgins had "the mind and spirit of an old-time plantation overseer." Higgins, however, remained adamant that he would not negotiate with the unions under prevailing conditions.[71]

He did hint, though, that he had not completely discounted continuing boat production in New Orleans under a different arrangement. Subsequently, he announced that he planned to liquidate all his holdings and carry on his operations with a new firm. Union leaders claimed this action was only an attempt to break the strike by means of questionable legality, but police protected prospective employees who lined up for the new jobs Higgins offered.[72] As it turned out, he was no more successful with the new company than he had been with the old, and continued labor disputes eventually forced final closure of Higgins's boat-building operations.

The war, then, had quite an impact on the Louisiana economy. Most basically, the war brought more people into the state. Then those people made money and paid taxes. The 1940 census found 2,363,880 people in Louisiana, while 1950 found 2,683,516, an increase of 13.5 percent. The population increase occurred primarily in the urban industrial areas and the training camp areas. Greater New Orleans, for example, grew by 64,463 (to 559,000) individuals between 1940 and November 1945; greater Shreveport grew by 17,775 (to 130,000) during the same years; while

70. *States,* October 29, 1945; *Item,* November 1–2, 5, 1945; *Morning Advocate,* November 2–3, 1945; Strahan, *Andrew Jackson Higgins,* 279–305.

71. *Item,* November 2, 1945; *Morning Advocate,* November 5, 1945.

72. *Morning Advocate,* November 6, December 1, 1945, January 8, February 2, 1946; *Item,* November 10, 29, 1945.

Baton Rouge grew by 75,281 (to 110,000); Alexandria and Pineville by 28,756 (to 60,119); and Lafayette by 5,790 (to 25,000).[73]

This sharp increase in population strained the ability of many areas to provide housing and basic services. Fresh groundwater use increased 10 percent from 1940 to 1943, to about 50 million gallons per day. Rental property in Alexandria became virtually unobtainable. By October 1941, 693 army personnel paid $31,497 in combined monthly rent in Alexandria. The number of gas meters in the city increased from 4,125 in 1941 to 6,142 in 1943. During the same period the number of electricity meters increased from 6,900 to 8,672 and the number of water meters from 5,500 to 6,237. Renters in many areas around army camps in central and north Louisiana complained of unjust rent increases as new workers and armed forces personnel began arriving in greater numbers and thus created unprecedented demand.[74]

The resulting increase in income and taxes was large. The United States Department of Commerce reported that the state's 1941 income broke the record levels of 1929. Combined incomes of Louisianians totaled $863 million in 1929, fell to $86 million by 1940, and shot up to $1,028 million in 1941. Louisiana received $7,655,654 from income taxes in 1941, $8,541,137 in 1942, $9,030,769 in 1943, $11,213,417 in 1944, and $11,464,000 in 1945. Total state revenue rose from $96,830,000 in 1939 to $145 million in 1945. Bank deposits topped $1 billion for the first time in October 1943.[75]

73. *States,* July 4, 1944; *Morning Advocate,* November 25, 1945; J. C. Maher, "Water Supplies and Louisiana's War Effort," *Louisiana Municipal Review,* January–February 1943, 8; T. A. Pittman to Warren M. Simon, January 2, 1943; Pittman to Jack Stewart, March 8, 1945, Fournet Papers, LLMVC; *Sixteenth Census, 1940: Population,* 435; *Seventeenth Census, 1950: Population,* vol. 1, 18.

74. *Town Talk,* November 28, December 31, 1940, October 1, 1941, July 11, 22, 1942, October 9, 1943, May 30, 1944; *Shreveport Times,* November 21, 1940; *Shreveport Journal,* December 10, 1941; Herman Colvin, "Alexandria Goes to War," *Louisiana Municipal Review,* January–February 1941, 4–5; Goldfield, *Cotton Fields and Skyscrapers,* 183–84.

75. *Shreveport Times,* July 20, 1942; *Times-Picayune,* October 16, 1943; *Louisiana Revenue Bulletin,* July 25, 1943, 8–9, January 25, 1944, 6–8, July 14, 1944, 6–7, July 1945, 1–15; *Financial Statistics of States: 1939 Louisiana,* vol. 1., no. 20 (Washington, D.C., 1941), 1; *State Government Finances in 1945: Louisiana* (Washington, D.C., 1946), 1.

Much of Louisiana's wartime prosperity, of course, stemmed directly from federal government expenditures. The state received $1,733,713,000 worth of war contracts issued between June 1, 1940, and October 1, 1944, out of the United States total of $205 billion. Some Louisianians, Governor Jones among them, hoped that the new industrialization would result in a more balanced economy, with less dependence on agriculture. The Louisiana Department of Commerce and Industry created a fifty-member economic development committee to help attract businesses to Louisiana in the postwar years. While it was more industrialized than ever before, however, Louisiana remained a predominantly rural state after the war. In 1945, 192,836 people worked on farms, while in 1947, only 132,464 people worked in manufacturing in the state.[76]

A composite index of Louisiana business activity using the activity of the average month of the period 1937–1939 as a base number of 100 reveals that the overall index stood at 105.2 in 1940, 130.3 in 1941, 179.3 in 1942, 205.0 in 1943, and 210.4 in 1944. The years of World War II thus marked Louisiana's return from the economic doldrums of the Great Depression—a fundamental shift in which employment offices quit attempting to find a job for every applicant and instead frantically sought a worker for every job.[77] And while the war did not completely industrialize Louisiana, it set the economy on the road to industrialization—a trend the state shared with the rest of the South.

76. *Morning Advocate,* March 10, 1941, January 30, May 6, 1945; Overton Brooks, "Louisiana's Part in the War," *Louisiana Police Jury Review,* April 1942, 12; *Seventeenth Census, 1950: Agriculture,* vol. 1, pt. 24, 4; *Census of Manufacturers, 1947: Statistics by States,* vol. 3, 251.

77. *Louisiana Business Review,* January 1942, 3, January 1943, 3, January 1944, 3, January 1945, 3; *Manpower Review,* May 1943, 16.

10

War Bonds, Scrap Drives, and No Mardi Gras

Military concerns and requirements intruded into Louisiana society and culture during World War II. The conflict moved people to unfamiliar locales, rearranged relationships within families, curtailed the freedom generally enjoyed by American citizens, removed many consumer goods from store shelves, altered traditional holiday themes, demanded money and scrap, and helped set in motion civil rights movements that gathered momentum in the ensuing decades. World War II, in short, affected almost every aspect of life in the Bayou State.

It was impossible to escape the war. Many Louisianians, whether they wanted to or not, witnessed the Nazi invasion of Europe at movie theaters. During the terrible spring of 1940, they tried to forget the threatening conflict by escaping to such movies as *My Favorite Wife,* starring Irene Dunn, *Gone with the Wind,* starring Clark Gable and Vivian Leigh, and *Typhoon,* starring Robert Preston and Louisiana native Dorothy Lamour. The newsreels shown at those movies, however, brought the war into the state's—and the nation's—visual consciousness. "GERMAN BLITZKRIEG in Holland and Belgium! War Bulletin! Europe Aflame! Paramount newsreel flown from war zone gives first graphic evidence of chaos of 1940!" read one sensational advertisement.[1]

The war also spawned changes in clothing styles throughout the coun-

---

1. *States,* January 25, 1940; *Times-Picayune,* May 16, 22–23, 1940.

try. Vests, cuffs, ruffles, and patch pockets disappeared to conserve cloth. The summer of 1940 also brought a boom in red, white, and blue costume jewelry—especially pieces featuring flags, stars, or American eagles.[2]

Other changes affected Louisiana society. Some civic and professional organizations curtailed their activities. The New Orleans Music Teachers' Association decided in 1943 to hold only one meeting per year for the duration of the war because members were too busy with other activities to attend regularly. Some debutantes in New Orleans abandoned traditional parties in 1941 in favor of civilian defense activities, in which they learned about air raid procedures, ambulance driving, and other skills useful in wartime. In New Orleans, then as now the state's premier "party town," patriotic observances often took the place of the glittering social events of other seasons. A case in point was a dinner in honor of Washington's birthday held by the city in February 1942. It attracted 449 people, including Mrs. Clair Chenault, wife of General Clair Chenault, a native Louisianian then in charge of American volunteers preparing China's air defenses against Japanese attack. Jimmie Noe, a sponsor of the dinner, announced that proceeds would be split between the Democratic National Committee and a fund he had created to finance a bomber for General Chenault.[3]

Providing entertainment for soldiers stationed in the state partially replaced normal means of recreation. Some young women joined the "military maids" and attended dances for soldiers one or two Saturday nights per month. The Young Men's Business Club in New Orleans scheduled picnics, athletic contests, and seafood dinners for visiting soldiers. Baton Rouge sponsored block dances and opened private homes to soldiers for a meal, and the local Elks Club and YMCA provided showers at a nominal five cents for soldiers traveling through the city. The Masons located a Masonic Service Center at Alexandria to furnish stationery, stamps, magazines, books, newspapers, games, and puzzles to soldiers. In Decem-

2. *Times-Picayune,* March 14, 1940; *States,* August 6, 1940; *Town Talk,* April 15, 1942; Perrett, *Days of Sadness,* 134–35.

3. Louis Panzeri and Carole Lawrence, *New Orleans Music Teachers' Association* (New Orleans, 1981), 9; *States,* December 18, 1941; *Times-Picayune,* January 30, February 24, 1942.

ber 1941, the first United Service Organization (USO) center in the United States opened at DeRidder; it housed an auditorium, showers, locker rooms, library, game room, and kitchen for soldiers at nearby Camp Polk. Recreation facilities, however, remained racially segregated, as did most of American society. Newspapers throughout the war reported activity schedules for white USO centers, with separate schedules for "Colored" USO centers, as they were known.[4]

Louisianians shared with other Americans an interest in reading during the war. The Louisiana State Library loaned about 1.3 million books in 1941. Technical books vied for readers' attention with books of inspiration, escape, and adventure. The most popular nonfiction books at the East Baton Rouge Parish Library in March 1945 were Wendell Willkie's *One World,* Robert Scott's *God Is My Co-Pilot,* Sumner Welles's *A Time for Decision,* Walter Lippmann's *U.S. War Aims,* Ernie Pyle's *Brave Men* and *Here Is Your War,* and Gordon S. Seagrave's *Burma Surgeon.* The most popular works of fiction were Frances Parkinson Keyes's *Crescent Carnival,* Lloyd C. Douglas's *The Robe,* Somerset Maugham's *The Razor's Edge,* and Betty Smith's *A Tree Grows in Brooklyn.*[5]

The war saw an increase in the number of marriages as men popped the question either to avoid the draft (which usually proved futile) or to marry before leaving for an overseas assignment. The number of marriages drifted upward throughout 1940, even before the United States entered the war. In Orleans Parish, marriages during the first quarter of the year lagged behind those for 1939, and approximately equaled the 1939 level by mid-1940. Then Congress passed the Selective Service Act in August. In October, 581 couples married in New Orleans, up from 283 in October 1939 and second in the records only to June 1920, when soldiers returning from World War I elevated the number of marriages to 628. In Rapides Parish, marriages more than trebled between 1939 and 1941, and especially increased after army troops arrived in the area during the last

---

4. *Morning Advocate,* May 28, July 7, 12, August 3, 9, 1941; *Item,* July 5–6, 1941; *Town Talk,* July 22, 26, December 1, 3, 1941; *American Press,* December 1, 1941; Shreveport Chamber of Commerce Minutes, April 10, 1941.

5. Perret, *Days of Sadness,* 138; *States,* June 3, 1942; *Morning Advocate,* June 10, 1942, March 4, 1945.

quarter of 1940. Whereas there had been only 889 couples married in the parish in 1940, 2,212 couples bought marriage licenses at the parish court-house in 1941. The number of marriages continued climbing in 1942 (to 3,766), then tapered off in 1943 (3,736) and decreased significantly in 1944 (2,693). Rapides clerk of court Julius F. Arial estimated that about one-third of the 1941 and 1942 licenses were issued to out-of-town couples, and that about one-half of all licenses issued between 1940 and 1945 were given to couples at least one member of which was a native of central Louisiana. Reverend E. J. Vallery of Pineville, known as the "Marrying Parson," performed about one thousand marriage ceremonies between 1940 and 1948. Many of these marriages during the World War II years united a groom from another state with a bride from Alexandria, Pine-ville, or some small town or community in central Louisiana.[6]

The crime rate in Louisiana fluctuated during the war. In 1942, Alex-andria, with its concentration of army troops, added twenty officers to its police force, which was also augmented by one hundred military police. The city court collected fines totaling $16,845 in 1940 and $36,452 in 1941, and the police made 4,746 arrests in 1940 and 5,963 in 1941.[7] Throughout the state, the crimes of arson, burglary, confidence games, possession of narcotics, and sexual offenses generally increased, while murder, man-slaughter, assault, embezzlement, forgery, kidnapping, counterfeiting, and felonious assault generally decreased.

Officials of the federal narcotics bureau in New Orleans reported that supplies of illegal drugs in the city dropped during the war, causing prices to skyrocket. As peacetime sources of these drugs—Japan, the Japanese-mandated Pacific islands, and the Balkans—became inaccessible, drug users paid exorbitant prices for inferior Mexican drugs. Marijuana ciga-rettes, available on the streets of New Orleans for the price of two for 25 cents before the war, sold for $1.50 each by 1945. A pack of marijuana cigarettes, which cost $3 before the war, rose to $15 when it chanced to

6. *Item-Tribune,* July 26, 1940; *States,* August 27, 1940; *Item,* November 1, 1940; *Town Talk,* December 2, 1941, January 2, July 1, 17, 1942, August 22, 1945; Brister, *Once upon a River,* 126.

7. *Town Talk,* January 7, September 13, 1941, February 5, 28, 1942; *Times-Picayune,* August 30, September 18, 23–26, 1941.

be available. The New Orleans community conducted an extensive anti-marijuana campaign during the spring of 1942. At that time, police officials suspected the existence of two marijuana cigarette factories and about one hundred street peddlers in the city. The street dealers worked crowded street corners, barrooms, night clubs, and poolrooms. Customers would approach a seller and ask either "Where's the boy?" or "What's that you're holding?" as a code to indicate that they wanted marijuana. Officials also reported that black users of marijuana outnumbered white users by about three to one, and that most users were men, primarily between the ages of 18 and 25. Heroin, once priced at $20 per ounce in New Orleans, cost $150 per ounce by 1945. The supply situation was so acute that some addicts forged prescriptions, broke into drugstores, or raided doctors' medical bags in order to obtain drugs, while others attempted to conquer their dependency.[8]

Gambling, especially in New Orleans and its suburbs, continued throughout the war, despite periodic ineffectual police raids. Such raids typically drove gambling underground for a few days until officials looked the other way again.[9]

The presence of various types of illegal activity in the state offended the sensibilities of several groups. The New Orleans Ministerial Union launched a massive crusade against gambling in 1944. In the same year, the East Baton Rouge Police Jury recognized "open and widespread gambling in the parish" and urged law enforcement agencies to enforce anti-gambling laws. Other groups deplored illegal activity and tried to use the war to reform American and especially Louisiana morals. The East Louisiana Baptist Association complained in October 1941 that beer was available to soldiers even in camps located in "dry" parishes and wards, that during the recent maneuvers, "Government trucks were used and men in uniform doing the delivering, and that protest by citizens was met with rough retort." The association protested "the action of the Army officials in delivering our soldiers over to the tender mercies of the brewers, whose sole purpose is to exploit them for their pitiful army wages." In 1942, the

8. *States,* January 24, 1945; *Item,* March 19–26, 1942.
9. *Morning Advocate,* September 5, 1944; *Times-Picayune,* September 18, 23–26, 1941.

First Baptist Church of Ashland protested the use of scarce sugar in the production of intoxicating liquors, and the Women's Missionary Union of Zion Hill Baptist Church in Winnfield urged prohibition of liquor sales and suppression of vice within specified zones around army camps and industrial or other strategic areas. The Louisiana Moral and Civic Foundation petitioned President Roosevelt to close "all night clubs and gambling halls in these United States . . . until one year after peace is declared." The foundation held that such places were nonessential to the war effort, caused absenteeism, used supplies of gasoline and rubber, absorbed money in profit that people could otherwise use to buy war bonds, and contributed to juvenile delinquency and the overall crime rate.[10]

Perhaps the most stringent suggestion for the suppression of alleged immoral activity came from the Winn Parish Baptist Association on November 16, 1942. It called upon Congress to close all establishments in the United States engaged in the manufacture, sale, or storage of alcoholic beverages, to place all "diseased" prostitutes in "concentration camps" to be treated as saboteurs and to conscript healthy prostitutes into the war industry; and to conscript all men with venereal disease along with all criminals and place them in a "foreign legion." The association further desired a declaration of a period of prayer throughout the country every night except Sunday at 9:00 P.M. U.S. representative Leonard Allen dutifully introduced this petition in the House, but it disappeared in the Military Affairs Committee.[11]

Wartime shortages affected almost every aspect of life in Louisiana. Cities reduced garbage pickups, many stores stopped delivering packages, and dairies reduced deliveries. State highway director W. Prescott Foster and superintendent of state police Steve Alford warned Louisianians not to loiter around the state's bridges. The state posted armed guards to protect these vital facilities. Transportation systems struggled to maintain schedules for increased numbers of riders. New Orleans beer drinkers

10. *Morning Advocate,* September 5, November 22, 1944, January 2, 1945; *Congressional Record,* 77th Cong., 1st sess., 1941, vol. 87, pt. 14: A5283–85; *Congressional Record,* 77th Cong., 2d sess., 1942, vol. 88, pt. 2: 1805; Perrett, *Days of Sadness,* 239–40.

11. *Congressional Record,* 77th Cong., 2d sess., 1942, vol. 88, pt. 7: 8896, 9186.

found their beer bottled in quarts by the New Orleans Brewers' Association in order to save scarce metal bottle caps. Sliced bread disappeared from store shelves in 1943 when the Office of Price Administration allowed bakers to stop slicing it in order to offset an increase in wheat prices without raising bread prices. Young people were not used to the task of slicing bread evenly, and many older people had donated their bread knives to scrap-metal drives, confident that they had no more use for them. This situation lasted from January through March, when federal officials announced that they would again allow bakeries to sell sliced bread because "the savings are not as much as we had expected."[12]

Paul Maloney, federal revenue collector in New Orleans, noticed a change of attitude among people paying their income taxes in 1941 and 1942. About 200 Louisianians made voluntary tax contributions in 1941 ranging from $1.50 to $1,000. The same feeling persisted into 1942. One individual return in that year included an extra $20 and a note: "I felt I owed something more than $3 to a government that's doing so much for me, and also upholding freedom in the world." Crowds waiting to pay taxes, silent and sullen in previous years, now talked openly of Hitler and the Japanese and expressed a militaristic outlook: "I want my money used to kill a regiment," one proclaimed.[13]

There was unstinting support for scrap collection, and there were rallies for war bond and stamp sales. These activities gave many people a place in the war effort. They may have been unable because of age, health, or sex to fight on the battlefield, but they could supply scrap to be recycled into war matériel, or provide funds for new supplies.

Collection drives began in Louisiana early in 1941, primarily to aid Britain and France. The "Bundles for Britain" chapter in Baton Rouge collected money and merchandise and made hospital gowns for shipment overseas. Shreveport patriotic societies collected old automobile license plates to provide scrap metal for England. Students at John McDonogh

12. *Town Talk,* March 23, 1942; *States,* April 2, June 11, 29, 1942; *Item,* June 8, 17, 1942; *Morning Advocate,* July 25, 1942, January 3, 28, March 9, 1943, February 27, 1944.
13. *Morning Advocate,* March 19, 1941; *Times-Picayune,* February 29, 1942; *Item,* March 12, 1942.

High School in New Orleans organized the British War Relief Club in March 1941, which collected old clothes, wool, silk, and cotton for quilts and air-raid covers, and raised money for British relief. After Pearl Harbor, the organization became the War Relief Club and widened its scope to "all countries helping to preserve democracy."[14]

Scrap drives for domestic use began with a campaign for aluminum during the summer of 1941. The *New Orleans Item* predicted accurately that the drive "will be small training for larger things later." Louisiana threw itself enthusiastically into this first of the nationwide scrap drives. In New Orleans, Mayor Maestri's aluminum committee met with principals of forty-five black schools to encourage participation by black schoolchildren, and about 25,000 students responded to the call. The posts of the Veterans of Foreign Wars and United Spanish War Veterans staged a parade to begin the aluminum drive in the business section of the city. Xavier University held a bazaar and charged one piece of aluminum per person as admission. In the Alexandria area, members of Rapides Parish 4-H Clubs collected scrap. Boy Scouts in Metairie, Pineville, Baton Rouge, and other areas served as collection agents. Edmund D. Davis, executive director of Louisiana's national defense council, reported in September that the state had collected 132,000 pounds of aluminum. New Orleans led with 53,000 pounds, followed by Shreveport with 20,306 pounds, Baton Rouge with 16,540 pounds, Alexandria with 16,407 pounds, and Lafayette with 16,102 pounds.[15]

Utilization of material previously thought worthless began in earnest after the Japanese attack on Pearl Harbor and subsequent United States entry into the war. Governor Jones appointed Oakdale businessman Parrish Fuller to lead the state's "Salvage for Victory" campaign in February 1942, and Louisianians were soon rummaging through attics, barnyards, and back lots for waste paper, rags, metal, and articles made of natural rubber to recycle for the war effort. Cooks began saving waste cooking

14. *Morning Advocate,* January 7, March 1, June 10, 1941; *Town Talk,* January 13, 1941; "The War Relief Club of the John McDonogh High School," *Louisiana Schools,* December 1942, 14–15.

15. *Item,* July 3, 1941; *Item-Tribune,* July 13, 1941; *States,* July 19, 1941; *Town Talk,* July 21, September 21, 1941; *Morning Advocate,* July 22, 25, 1941.

fats in the summer of 1942 because they could be used to produce glycerin for explosives.[16]

A massive nationwide scrap drive was conducted during the autumn of 1942. Fuller's staff enlisted Louisiana schoolchildren in the effort. Teachers and school administrators explained carefully to students the items they were to collect, and assigned each child a specific section of the community to canvass. They integrated the scrap drive into English classes by directing the students to write three letters in which they expressed in their own words the purposes of the drive and its uses in the war. Students then hand-delivered the letters to their parents and to the people living on either side of them. Schools offered war-stamp prizes to the students who collected the most scrap each week, and many schools also granted "military rank" to students based on the amount of salvageable material collected.[17]

On October 5, Louisiana's newspapers aided the drive by sponsoring an intensive house-to-house search for scrap metal throughout the state; the papers underwrote the expenses of the campaign and provided cash prizes for the most scrap collected in specified neighborhoods. The drive turned up a diverse assortment of objects. Shreveport mayor Sam Caldwell donated the city's old firebell. O. P. Ogilvie, publisher of the *Coushatta Citizen,* donated a complete press that had been retired from service in 1935. The drive also uncovered steamboat paddlewheels, abandoned cars, appliances, World War I helmets and bomb casings, and Civil War cannonballs, cooking pots, and swords. Louisianians responded so well to the scrap drive that, ironically, collectors ran out of storage space.[18]

Collection drives continued throughout the war. Alexandria's abandoned streetcar rails fell victim to the war in 1943, and the D-Day invasion of France spurred an increase of blood donations at the Red Cross collection center in New Orleans, for use by the armed forces. By 1944,

16. *Morning Advocate,* February 27, 1942; *Town Talk,* July 17, 1942.

17. Parrish Fuller, "Outline of Overall Plan for Enlisting School Children in the Collection of Scrap Iron, Rags, Rubber, Etc.," *Louisiana Schools,* September 1942, 10–11, 30; Merle Weigel to H. S. Weigel, October 23, 1942, H. S. Weigel and Family Papers, LLMVC.

18. *Shreveport Times,* September 19, October 5–6, 1942; *Morning Advocate,* October 4, 6, 11, 1942.

however, most scrap drives lagged behind projected goals because it was difficult to sustain patriotic zeal at a high level and because supplies of scrap dwindled. The *States* noted in July that from June 27 until July 18, New Orleans collected only about two ounces of waste paper per person. The *Morning Advocate* reported in August that previously unused tin cans could now be "detinned" at a new plant in Birmingham, Alabama, and urged people to salvage them. But by the end of the month Baton Rougeans had collected only enough tin cans to fill about one-third of one boxcar.[19]

Louisianians consistently supported the sale of war stamps and bonds, which the federal government sold in seven issues. The first issue, dubbed "defense" stamps and bonds, appeared in 1941. Members of the Alexandria chamber of commerce agreed to sell stamps in their stores to make them more available to the public. In New Orleans and Baton Rouge, delivery boys for the *Times-Picayune, States, Morning Advocate,* and *State Times* delivered stamps to their customers. Students at Tulane University held a "Blackout Ball"—featuring a one-minute "lights out" every fifteen minutes—in the school gymnasium and used the proceeds to buy defense stamps and bonds. From May to December 1941, Louisianians purchased over $11 million in savings bonds and $5,418,000 in stamps. In comparison, Mississippians purchased $7,090,000 in bonds and $3,259,000 in stamps during the same period.[20]

Louisianians continued buying war stamps and bonds during 1942, even before the first of the big war bond drives in the state during September of that year. The *Alexandria Town Talk* congratulated its readers for their continued orders for stamps and for asking for stamps in lieu of change when they made a purchase. The Morgan and Lindsey store in Amite created a "Defense Window" in 1942, displaying pictures of local residents in the armed services in an effort to boost bond sales. The

19. *Town Talk,* June 8, 1944; *Morning Advocate,* July 24, August 9, 31, 1944; *States,* July 26, 1944.

20. *Town Talk,* September 10, 1941; *Times-Picayune/New Orleans States,* November 23, 1941; *States,* November 26, 1941; *Morning Advocate,* January 18, February 21, 1942; *Times-Picayune,* December 12, 1941, February 8, 1942.

Shreveport Retail Merchants' Association sold $601,615 in bonds in July. The total sales in Caddo Parish that month reached $1,489,000.[21]

War bond drives in Louisiana closely followed nationwide practices: numerous newspaper advertisements extolled the patriotic and economic virtues of stamps and bonds; business, civic, and fraternal organization members assisted in bond sales; and celebrities visited and entertained at rallies, boosting war bond sales. Later drives often included appearances by members of the armed forces demonstrating equipment purchased with bond proceeds, and programs in both black and white schools to encourage schoolchildren to purchase war stamps.

The Shreveport Chamber of Commerce urged its members to buy as many bonds as they could afford and give their time and energy to bond drives. The Louisiana councils of the Knights of Columbus added war bond sales to their varied activities in support of the cause. Hollywood luminaries who came to Louisiana to sell bonds included Laraine Day, Andy Devine, Fred Astaire, James Cagney, Lucille Ball, Judy Garland, Mickey Rooney, Betty Hutton, Greer Garson, Robert Young, and Harpo Marx. During the Third War Loan Drive, a "Cavalcade of Stars" rally in New Orleans attracted over a hundred thousand people, each of whom had to produce a receipt for a bond bought during the current drive as an admission ticket.[22]

As the seemingly interminable rallies continued, the federal government attempted to further whip up patriotic fervor by staging military "invasions." Some six hundred soldiers invaded Canal Street in Infantry Day ceremonies to promote Fifth War Loan Bond sales in New Orleans. Richard W. Leche, Jr., described to his father a rally he attended at New Orleans City Park Stadium in 1942. Displays included jeeps, motorcycles, trucks, and howitzers; live demonstrations included flame throwers and tank destroyers. (A live demonstration of phosphorus grenades in New

21. *Town Talk,* April 14, 1942; Shreveport Chamber of Commerce Minutes, August 13, 1942; Merle Weigel to H. S. Weigel, June 28, 1942, Weigel Papers.

22. Shreveport Chamber of Commerce Minutes, April 8, 1943; Roger Baudier and Millard F. Everett, *Anchor and Fleur-de-Lis: Knights of Columbus in Louisiana, 1902–1962* (New Orleans, 1965), 351, 354; *Morning Advocate,* September 17, 26, 1942, June 13, 15, 1945; *States,* November 16, 1943; *Times-Picayune,* September 21, 1943.

Orleans in 1945 resulted in spectators receiving burns when one grenade landed too close to them.) Baton Rouge witnessed a staged invasion of the Louisiana State University football stadium during the Fifth War Loan Drive, and the Seventh War Loan Drive brought a mock air attack on Harding Field north of the city. Alexandria experienced an invasion by Higgins boats and Camp Livingston soldiers during the same drive.[23]

State War Finance Committee chairman Leon Tujacque announced in August 1945 that Louisiana had exceeded its quota in each of the war loan drives by the following amounts:[24]

Bond Drive	Louisiana Quota	Louisiana Sales
1	$8,250,000	$11,778,000
2	$50,515,000	$79,721,768
3	$123,000,000	$139,750,693
4	$96,000,000	$126,839,300
5	$126,000,000	$165,995,100
6	$110,000,000	$146,149,065
7	$112,000,000	$177,882,000

Louisianians also filled time left empty by the disappearance of traditional leisure activities by working in civilian defense. Louisiana, with its miles of unpopulated coastline, war production facilities, and concentration of training camps, was considered a prime target for enemy attack. The warning network for such attack established by the United States Office of Civilian Defense required citizen volunteers "of known probity" to scan the skies throughout the country for approaching enemy airplanes twenty-four hours a day. The effectiveness of this system depended on a close distribution of watchers so enemy aircraft could not slip through the network undetected. When that distribution was not possible because of the scarcity of population in Louisiana's coastal parishes, the Office of Civilian Defense called upon intracoastal bargemen, fishermen, trappers,

23. *Item,* June 15, 1944; Richard W. Leche, Jr., to Richard W. Leche, Sr., November 30, 1942, Leche Papers, LLMVC; *Morning Advocate,* June 16, 1944, May 31, June 18, 1945.
24. *Item,* August 20, 1945.

and oystermen, who knew the marshy coastal areas well. A Civil Air Patrol coastal patrol base also operated at Grand Isle from June 25, 1942, until August 31, 1943. Airplanes from the base patrolled the central Gulf coast on the lookout for German submarines. In other areas of the state, volunteers enrolled in the more common air warning system.[25]

Beginning in July, 1940, the National Defense Council of Louisiana, chaired by Colonel L. Kemper Williams, spearheaded defense efforts in the state. By 1942, over one hundred thousand Louisianians had participated in national defense work. Air-raid warden was the most popular job, while aircraft spotter was second. In general, Louisiana's urban areas and their surrounding parishes organized more thoroughly for Civilian Defense than did rural areas.[26]

Caddo Parish had one of the most organized defense programs, boasting by 1942 both the Shreveport Defense Council and the Caddo Parish Defense Council. Other parishes had one defense council, typically located in the largest town and usually open only part-time. In some rural parishes, especially away from the coast, civilian defense remained largely nonexistent, unless a parish happened to be home to a defense-related activity. Nevertheless, many of these parishes cooperated fully in other aspects of home front life.[27]

25. Col. R. Ernest Dupuy and Lt. Hodding Carter, *Civilian Defense of the United States* (New York, 1942), 22–27; Louis E. Keefer, *From Maine to Mexico: With America's Private Pilots in the Fight against Nazi U-Boats* (Reston, Va., 1997), 197–230; Sam H. Jones, "Civilian Defense in Louisiana," *Louisiana Police Jury Review,* April 1942, 20–21; Joseph W. Reid, Jr., "The Geography of Louisiana's Civilian Defense Organization I," *Louisiana Municipal Review,* March–April 1942, 44–45; Louisiana Department of Education, Bulletin No. 480: Wartime Education in Louisiana Schools, 12; Frederick J. Stielow, "Isolation and Development on a Louisiana Gulfcoast Island: Grand Isle, 1781–1962" (Ph.D. diss., Indiana University, 1977), 214; *Morning Advocate,* August 1, 1941; *Item,* December 8, 12, 1941; *Shreveport Times,* December 10, 1941, February 5, March 12, 1942; *Town Talk,* February 6, 1942.

26. Sam H. Jones, "Civilian Defense in Louisiana—A Review of 1942," *Louisiana Police Jury Review,* April 1943, 17–21.

27. Shreveport Chamber of Commerce Minutes, April 9, 1942; Joseph W. Reid, Jr., "Civilian Defense," *Louisiana Municipal Review,* May–June 1943, 68–69; Leonard B. Watt, Jr., "Lincoln Parish Prepares for 'Total War,'" *Louisiana Police Jury Review,* April 1942, 14–15.

The closest any combat came to reaching the state was a series of off-shore torpedo and depth charge incidents. At least three torpedoes struck and sank a United States cargo ship just as it entered the Mississippi River at 3:05 P.M. on May 12, 1942, thus bringing warfare to the lower Mississippi for the first time since 1862. In addition, a mysterious explosion, suspected to have come from a torpedo, damaged a jetty earlier that same day. Two more ships sank on May 13 at an unspecified location in the Gulf of Mexico, and survivors arrived in New Orleans and Key West, Florida, for treatment.[28] Even though the threat to American ships lessened after the 1942 rash of attacks, the sinkings brought the war dangerously close to home in Louisiana.

The state experienced no major espionage episodes during the war, but attacks on ships in the Gulf and the frightening rapidity with which Adolf Hitler's forces overran civilian populations in Europe left many Louisianians suspicious of any activity perceived to be friendly toward the Axis powers. Discovery of Nazi flags on flagpoles at Martin Behrman High School and at a playground in Algiers on May 24, 1940, led local citizens to form an "American Vigilance Committee" to investigate all un-American activity in the area. Baton Rouge was rocked in July 1940 by the discovery of four men digging under a wire fence at the DuPont Ethyl plant. The men escaped, leaving behind four sticks of dynamite and a mystery. East Baton Rouge sheriff Newman deBritten dispatched deputies and bloodhounds to the scene, but the men had disappeared into the night. This episode, occurring so close to a vital war plant—only one other plant in the nation, DuPont's facility at Wilmington, Delaware, produced the same tetraethyl high-octane leaded fuel—led state police to redouble their security measures.[29]

On at least two occasions, however, common occurrences caused flurries of unwarranted excitement amid the wartime anxiety. An unannounced flight of four airplanes alarmed Baton Rouge on the night of

28. *Shreveport Journal,* May 15, 1942; *States,* May 16, 18, 1942; *Item,* June 6, 1942; Stielow, "Grand Isle," 214–15; Thomas L. Karnes, *Tropical Enterprise: The Standard Fruit and Steamship Company in Latin America* (Baton Rouge, 1978), 217–18.

29. *States,* May 24, July 6, 1940; *Item,* July 6–8, 1940; *Morning Advocate,* July 6–9, 1940; Heleniak, *Soldiers of the Law,* 52.

September 9–10, 1940. Citizens jammed telephone lines reporting the flight as the airplanes faded away from view. Sheriff's deputies learned later that the planes were on night training maneuvers from Barksdale Air Force Base. In a different kind of scare, Alexandrians awakened on the morning of March 21, 1942, to find a fine yellow dust covering the ground. Speculation that the powder might be a poison or residue of a poison gas sprayed by enemy airplanes during the night caused a wave of concern until chemists from Camp Beauregard and Louisiana College confirmed that the yellow powder was simply spring pollen blown from trees by a strong March wind.[30]

The perception that the state was vulnerable to an enemy attack caused Louisianians to accept war-related disruptions of normal activity. Alcée Legendre, coordinator of civilian defense in the New Orleans area, announced on December 9, 1941, that his office was preparing for practice blackouts in the city. Attorneys for New Orleans discovered, however, that the city had no way to punish those who did not comply, so the city council approved a ninety-day jail term and one-hundred-dollar fine for anyone failing to comply with blackout orders. The Orleans Parish School Board canceled all night activities in the public schools to avoid any possible interference with the practice blackouts. New Orleanians rushed to hardware stores to purchase flashlights and candles, quadrupling normal demand for these items, and also created a run on guns and ammunition in local gun stores. New Orleans newspapers on December 15 published a full-page instruction sheet prepared by the United States Office of Civilian Defense informing people what action to take in the event of a real air raid: "1. Keep Cool 2. Stay Home 3. Put Out Lights 4. Lie Down 5. Stay Away From Windows." Also included were directions for handling an unexploded incendiary bomb if it happened to fall: "Spray a fine mist of water [over it]. Streams or buckets of water will make it explode."[31]

New Orleans held its first practice blackout on the night of March

30. *Morning Advocate,* September 10, 1940; *Town Talk,* March 21, 1942.
31. *Times-Picayune,* December 10, 15, 1941; *Item,* December 12, 18, 1941; *Times-Picayune/New Orleans States,* December 14, 1941.

6–7, 1942. Legendre proclaimed it "99%" effective, but reporters in an airplane circling the city reported that some automobile headlights remained on. In addition, lights shone along the wharves, as did streetlights along the waterfront, aircraft warning beacons atop the WWL radio transmitting tower, and the Mississippi River bridge navigation warning lights, all of which clearly outlined highly vulnerable locations. Baton Rouge followed with its first practice blackout on the night of March 31–April 1 and met with similar results, with the exception that officials ordered lights atop the state capitol, Mississippi River bridge, and WJBO radio tower to remain on. Soon after, however, the manager of executive buildings, Frank Grevemberg, ordered the spotlight illuminating Huey Long's grave extinguished for the duration of the war. The first statewide practice blackout did not occur until the night of February 5–6, 1943, almost 14 months after American entry into the war.[32]

World War II intruded upon daily life in Louisiana in mundane, personal ways as well. Consumers faced shortages and rationing of many commodities to which they were accustomed. The first shortage developed after the federal government announced its seizure of raw silk supplies for the national defense program as Japanese expansion threatened normal supply areas in Asia. American women clogged department stores as they stockpiled silk stockings, despite assurances that a new DuPont chemical plant would supply substitute nylon hose. Hosiery continued to be a scarce item during the war.[33]

Automobile owners faced the twin trials of tire and gasoline rationing. Tire rationing began in January 1942 in order to conserve supplies of rubber for military use. Gasoline rationing followed in the spring, both to conserve gasoline and to save tires by discouraging all but essential driving. Tire-rationing provisions were stringent. Parish ration boards could not issue a certificate authorizing an individual to buy a tire until inspection showed that the old tire was not safe at normal speeds, even if re-

32. *Item,* March 7, 1942; *Morning Advocate,* April 1, May 31, 1942; *Times-Picayune,* May 17, 1942; *Town Talk,* February 6, 1942.
33. *Morning Advocate,* August 5, 1941.

treaded and recapped. Furthermore, a certificate did not guarantee a tire. Each parish received a monthly allotment of tires, and people holding valid certificates often encountered great difficulty locating an available tire. Orleans Parish, with about 100,000 cars and trucks registered, received an allotment of 1,282 tires for January 1943. Scarcity led to theft, prompting citizens of Shreveport to form the Automobile Vigilante Society in March 1942. New Orleanians reported 823 tires stolen between December 1941 and August 1942, 159 in July alone.[34]

Gasoline and tire rationing caused other problems throughout the state. Workers sometimes had trouble obtaining sufficient gasoline to drive to defense or other vital jobs and had to plan their trips carefully. Ration boards urged compliance with the 35 miles-per-hour speed limit to conserve fuel and tires. The severe limitation placed on Louisiana motorists is revealed in the state's shipments of motor gasoline during November 1943, when it shipped 44,796 barrels. Only 9,437 barrels of this total were shipped for local demand.[35]

Gasoline rationing in a state that produced as much oil as Louisiana seemed pointless to many people. Governor Jones claimed that rationing would wreck the state's petroleum-based economy. The otherwise rebellious 1942 legislature agreed with him and sent President Roosevelt a resolution decrying the expected slump in oil and other business in the state. The *Baton Rouge Morning Advocate,* however, adopted a positive attitude toward gasoline rationing: the United States needed to conserve its rubber

34. *Town Talk,* January 2, 1942; *Times-Picayune/New Orleans States,* January 4, 1942; *Item,* March 3, 1942; *States,* August 10, 1942; L. E. Frazar and J. E. Brumfield to All Members of War Price and Rationing Boards [for] State of Louisiana, June 22, 1943, Sam Jones to W. Scott Heywood, December 28, 1943, Jennings-Heywood Oil Syndicate Records, LLMVC.

35. W. C. Heywood to Ray C. Martin, July 1, 1943, Heywood to Major B. A Hardey, October 12, 1943, Heywood to To Whom It May Concern, December 30, 1943, F. J. Gimble, Charles A. Clark, and W. Scott Heywood to All Motorists, May, 1944, Jennings-Heywood Records; Merle Weigel to H. S. Weigel, October 3, November 15, 1942, Weigel Papers; Minutes, Natural Gas and Natural Gasoline Committee District 3 Records, microform, Middleton Library, Louisiana State University, Baton Rouge, La.

supply, and moreover, "maybe the state will find some way to get along without depending on the motorist for such a large chunk of revenue."[36] Louisianians also experienced shortages of food supplies. They lined up at schools to register for sugar-rationing books that entitled them to purchase a limited amount of sugar within a specific time period. Sugar rationing continued to be a common reminder of wartime sacrifice. As late as May 1945, Baton Rougeans stocked up on sugar after hearing a rumor that allotments might be reduced.[37]

Various adaptations occurred in response to food rationing. Coffee, a mainstay of many Louisianians, became scarce. Merle Weigel of Amite wrote to her husband stationed in England of her surprise that refreshments at a recent club meeting in January 1943 included coffee, "even second cups." In February, she reported that the shortage had boosted afternoon tea consumption, but "I guess I'm just Southern enough that nothing can ever really take the place of coffee." In May, she reported that visitors often brought along their own coffee, butter, and sugar so they would not deplete their host's supply of rationed items. Ice cream virtually disappeared from store shelves. Mrs. Weigel wrote to her husband in 1943 that rationing "makes us very careful with our food—we can't waste it, and we can't make fancy desserts, pastries, etc.—but those are really unnecessary."[38]

Intermittent shortages of basic foods also plagued Louisiana during the war. Restaurants instituted "Meatless Tuesdays" in 1942, substituting fowl, animal organ meat, and egg dishes for traditional red-meat dishes. Abattoirs throughout the state closed in 1943 until the Office of Price Administration could establish slaughtering quotas. Louisiana existed on "short rations" and tight supplies of meat for much of the war. Restaurants reduced portion sizes early in 1943, and some began serving meat dishes only every other day. Shreveporters formed the Clean Plate Club

36. *Morning Advocate,* May 25, 28, June 2, November 27, December 4, 1942.

37. *Ibid.,* February 19, April 27, 1942, May 6, 1945; *States,* May 4, 1942; *Town Talk,* May 6, 1945.

38. Merle Weigel to H. S. Weigel, January 14, February 1, 7, April 8, May 3, 28, 1943, Weigel Papers.

to reduce waste. Officials at Charity Hospital in New Orleans announced in 1945 that a shortage in the hospital's rationing point allotment caused undesirable modifications in patient diets. OPA officials could offer little help during these shortages. New Orleans district director Gilbert J. Fortier reassured people in July 1945 that "there is still enough for all of us to eat," but also said that "not until after the war is over and the liberated peoples are self-sustaining will we be able to buy and eat as extravagantly as we did before Pearl Harbor."[39]

Less essential items also became scarce during the war. Chewing gum became a casualty in 1942, owing to scant supplies of both sugar and chicle, a major ingredient in gum and a product of South America temporarily displaced by war materials in intercontinental shipping. There was a dearth of seafood because fishing boats lacked adequate crews, fuel, and spare parts. Black pepper became scarce because suppliers and the OPA could not agree on an adequate price for it. Ice was limited in New Orleans during the summer of 1944 because of a labor shortage at the icehouse until the War Manpower Commission directed the U.S. Employment Service to scour the city for able-bodied workers. Metal license plates disappeared from Louisiana vehicles in 1943, being replaced by fiber plates to conserve steel. Louisiana also switched from requiring both front and rear plates to rear plates only.[40]

Some Louisianians sought ways to circumvent rationing requirements. Thieves broke into a safe in the rationing board office at the old state capitol in Baton Rouge in April 1944 and stole rationing coupons for gasoline, shoes, food, and sugar. Illegal markets for sugar, hosiery, and meat existed in the state. Revenue collector J. O. Fernandez reported in 1945 that eight individuals had admitted participating in illegal vending in New Orleans and paid $71,968.39 in taxes on an estimated $1,500,000 unreported profit for the past year. Some New Orleans consumers who banded together to oppose both illegal market activity and some grocers'

39. *Morning Advocate,* November 18, 1942, February 26, 1943, July 14, 17, 1945; *Town Talk,* February 4, 12, March 25, 1943, July 11, 1945; *Shreveport Times,* July 12, 1943; *States,* July 12, 1945.

40. *Item,* June 8, 1942, February 23, July 1, 4, 1944; *Morning Advocate,* February 3, 1943; *Shreveport Times,* October 1, 1943; *States,* December 1, 1943.

practice of charging more for items than the OPA allowed found that their grocers refused to sell groceries to them.[41] It is impossible to determine exactly how much illegal marketing occurred in Louisiana during the war, since the very nature of the enterprise means it leaves no paper trail or other evidence of its dimensions.

Another area of life that the war impinged upon was traditional holiday celebrations, which were now imbued with a patriotic flavor. Specifically American holidays provided even more reason for patriotic themes. This new tendency to make all holidays into quasi-patriotic celebrations was especially obvious at Christmastime.

During America's last peacetime Christmas, people had reflected on their good fortune to be living in a country still at peace. Many of them sought to symbolize this appreciation (and, incidentally, to celebrate the first prosperous Christmas for some of them since 1928) by making Christmas 1940 into a joy- and light-filled holiday. New Orleans Public Service, Incorporated (a utility that also wanted to sell more electricity) accurately reflected this feeling in an advertisement published early in December: "Christmas lighting now becomes the symbol of the freedom that shines in the heart of every American. That is your warrant for making the lighting of your tree and your home this year a ceremony to drive home this truth, that liberty and light go together."[42]

Other, more economically disinterested sources reflected the same opinion. The *Hammond Vindicator* asked its readers to turn on any lights they controlled for a Christmas Eve "Night of Light" "to show the light of liberty still in the United States." *Times-Picayune* editorial writers looked down Canal Street and rhapsodized that "one inevitably thinks of the blackouts in Europe and realizes that what is seen here is almost too good to be true."[43]

Sam Jones, however, raised the ghost at the banquet: "The only note of sadness in this Christmas," he said, "is the war in Europe." Indeed, the

41. *Morning Advocate,* April 1, 3, June 18, 1944, March 11, April 22, 1945; *Times-Picayune,* June 18–19, 1944, April 22, 1945.

42. *States,* December 11, 1940.

43. *Hammond Vindicator,* December 20, 1940; *Times-Picayune,* December 24, 1940.

news of December 25, 1940, portended darker days ahead. Some three hundred thousand Nazi soldiers invaded Rumania from Hungary as Hitler secured a Balkans base for his proposed spring offensive against Russia.[44]

The next Christmas, the "Pearl Harbor Christmas," was dominated by the Japanese attack in Hawaii and the awesome task that the United States now faced in the conflict. The *Lake Charles American Press* editorialized on the overriding bittersweetness of the day: "It is the opportunity to share Christmas one more time with those who are dear to us." The *New Orleans States* assured its readers that the Christ whose birthday they celebrated was undoubtedly on their side in the conflict, insisting that "[Christ] wouldn't have believed in the rule of the Hitlers and Mussolinis and their yellow and grinning Allies. He would have believed in the kind of rulers that are asking their people to never give up the fight until freedom is won."[45]

Despite the dark foreboding that clung to this Christmas, many people attempted to keep the ritual as normal as possible. Catholic and Episcopal churches held traditional midnight services, charitable organizations distributed gift baskets to the poor, and carolers serenaded their friends. But things were not the same. As the *New Orleans Item* commented, "The swelling notes of 'Oh, Say Can You See' mingle with tinkling 'Jingle Bells' . . . there is no peace on earth."[46]

The following Christmases continued the military emphasis. In 1942, the theme of the *Alexandria Town Talk*'s doll and toy fund, which collected money to purchase toys for poor children, was "Give Scrap to Kill a Jap and Bring Joy to a Girl or Boy." Citizens were to donate scrap metal to be sold for the war effort and the proceeds used to purchase dolls and toys.[47] An individual could thus be patriotic, militaristic, and philanthropic all at the same time.

---

44. *Morning Advocate,* December 23, 26, 1940; William L. Shirer, *The Rise and Fall of the Third Reich* (New York, 1960), 811, 822–23.

45. *American Press,* December 11, 1941; *States,* December 24, 1941.

46. *Item,* December 24, 1941; *States,* December 25, 1941; *Times- Picayune,* December 26, 1941.

47. *Town Talk,* November 11, 1942.

As the tide of war turned in favor of the Allies, Christmas celebrations acquired a more positive cast. The Christmas holiday did not return to normal, however, until the 1945 season brought the most joyous Christmas mood since Pearl Harbor.[48]

The New Year's holiday similarly gave Louisianians a pause to reflect on the conditions of the world. New Year's Day 1941 dawned on gloomy predictions about life in Louisiana for the next year. A. L. Wedgeworth, president of the Shreveport Chamber of Commerce, expected "a cessation of living for individual gain and the lighter things of life." Walter E. Jacobs, president of Shreveport's First National Bank, remarked, "It is going to be necessary to work harder and to make sacrifices that our generation has never known." But other Louisianians reflected a happier mood. The *Town Talk* remembered the years of economic want experienced during the Great Depression, and hoped that "the hardships and vicissitudes experienced in the past will not arise to plague and harass the people."[49]

Since the year 1941 brought not only a measure of economic recovery but also war in early December, New Year's celebrations welcoming 1942 were relatively subdued. As with the Christmas observances, many people realized that it might be their last holiday together for several years. Also, officials prohibited use of industrial whistles to welcome the New Year because they were also used as air-raid warnings and could cause a panic.[50]

Rain came with nightfall in Louisiana on New Year's Eve 1944, so the state quietly ushered in the year that proved to be the last of the war. New Year's Day 1946, however, saw a revived holiday celebration as Louisiana followed its first peacetime Christmas with a return to traditional New Year's Day activities.[51]

The holiday most publicly identified with Louisiana, Mardi Gras, was a war casualty. The last wartime Mardi Gras celebration occurred in

48. *Morning Advocate,* December 22, 1944, December 24, 1945.

49. *Shreveport Times,* December 29, 1940; *Town Talk,* January 1, 1941.

50. *States,* December 30, 1941; *Item,* December 30, 1941; *Times-Picayune,* December 31, 1941; *Shreveport Journal,* January 1, 1942.

51. *Morning Advocate,* January 1, 1945, January 1, 1946.

1941, and proved to be one of the largest, giddiest celebrations up to that time. Soon after the Pearl Harbor bombing, New Orleans carnival organizations announced that "because it would be inconsistent with the present status of the nation," there would be no Mardi Gras parades or balls in 1942; the celebration was thus canceled for the first time since 1919 and only the third time in history, the others being during the Civil War and during World War I. The School of Design, sponsor of the Rex Parade, asked its members for full 1942 dues to cover expenses already incurred in design and construction of 1942 floats, then assessed reduced "standby" dues for the rest of the war. The Harlequin Krewe held the only ball of the 1942 season, a dance in honor of fifteen hundred visiting servicemen. The theme of the ball was military—the occupation of Iceland.[52]

Mardi Gras Day, February 17, 1942, found the normal business-day crowd on New Orleans streets. The city celebrated by purchasing war bonds, over $150,000 worth on that day alone. New Orleans continued to use Mardi Gras to promote bond sales for the remainder of the war. The 1943 sale brought in about $1 million during Mardi Gras week. The 1945 season featured twenty costumed individuals selling bonds outdoors on Canal Street, and retail merchants throughout the city participated either by purchasing bonds or setting aside a small space in their establishments for bond sales. As the war was ending in August 1945, officials of the Mardi Gras krewes decided to hold the 1946 carnival season as usual.[53]

Other holiday observations acquired a military tinge. The New Orleans St. Patrick's Day parade was replaced by church services and bond sales rallies. Observers also commented on the seriousness of April 1, 1943: "perhaps [the April Fool] was too busy at his defense job, preparing to give the world's greatest hotfoot to those dignitaries Hitler, Mussolini, and Tojo." Easter became an even greater symbol of hope among Christians than it already had been in normal years. The *Baton Rouge Morning Advocate* commented in 1941, "Few years have needed Easter's promise

52. *Ibid.,* February 16, 1941; *Times-Picayune,* February 19–26, December 13, 28, 1941; Charles L. Dufour and Leonard V. Huber, *If Ever I Cease to Love: One Hundred Years of Rex, 1872–1971* (New Orleans, 1970), 191, 211.

53. *Times-Picayune,* February 18, 1942; *Morning Advocate,* March 14, 1943, August 19, 1945; *States,* February 13, 1945.

and hope more." While traditional trappings of Easter disappeared—the chocolate Easter bunny and candy eggs were casualties of sugar rationing, and a temporary downturn in egg production caused a shortage of eggs in 1943—the spirit of Easter remained strong throughout the war.[54]

The changes in holidays, diets, and freedom of movement proved to be temporary, but World War II also brought the beginnings of more permanent social change in Louisiana. Both blacks and women edged closer toward equal treatment during the war.

At the beginning of the war, African Americans were still experiencing the unequal treatment that had historically dominated race relations in the United States, but many students of the civil rights movement see the war years as the point at which blacks decided not to accept continued inequity without protest. During World War I, they had followed W. E. B. Du Bois's admonition to subdue racial grievances only to be subjected to lynchings, race riots, and continued discrimination during the 1920s and 1930s. As historian Richard M. Dalfiume observed, "The dominant attitude during World War II came to be that the Negro must fight for democracy on two fronts—at home as well as abroad.[55]

Black Americans had to overcome the effects of generations of unequal treatment in politics, education, and employment. Their secondary role in American life was revealed in a study completed during 1940. During World War II, the black population of the United States numbered about 12 million, with about 2.2 million between the ages of sixteen and twenty-four. Of these, at least 500,000 were unemployed. Moreover, the average black youth with a job worked 49 hours per week for $8.71, while the average white person of the same age group worked 44 hours per week for $15.17. In addition, 9.5 percent of black youth obtained semiskilled jobs, compared to 20 percent of white youths, and only 2 percent received skilled jobs, compared to 8 percent of white youth. It did blacks little good to hope for redress from the political system, for they

54. *States,* March 2, 16, 1942; *Item,* March 17, 1942; *Morning Advocate,* April 13, 1941, April 4, 7, 1943, April 1, 1945.

55. Dalfiume, "The 'Forgotten Years' of the Negro Revolution," 90–96.

had virtually no political voice. Ten states used poll taxes, head taxes, educational tests, or outright intimidation to deprive blacks of the right to vote, while fifteen states segregated public conveyances and places, and eighteen states provided segregated school facilities.[56]

World War II, however, gave black Americans a bit of hope for improvement of their lot. The labor shortage created opportunities for black workers to enter new occupations and establish themselves in recognized positions. Economic development set southerners on the course of acquiring more education and sophistication, which eventually helped to undermine traditional systems of race relations based on economic relationships in an agricultural society. The war provided blacks the opportunity to prick the conscience of white America by stressing the anomalous position their country had created for them: they were fighting for liberty in foreign countries and yet enduring an unequal status quo at home. As one black soldier commented, "If I've got to die for democracy, I might as well die for some of it right here and now."[57]

Black Americans responded to the same stirrings of patriotism as did other Americans, and their contributions to the war effort could be used as a foundation for future drives for equality. As Felton G. Clark, Negro Coordinator of the United States Civilian Defense program in Louisiana, remarked, "No better argument for the better integration of the Negro into the opportunities of American life and democracy can be given than the record of serving his country in a crucial hour as the present one."[58]

Various segments of black communities made concentrated efforts to focus attention on the war effort. The theme of the annual Parish

56. Al-Tony Gilmore, "The Black Southerner's Response to the Southern System of Race Relations," in *The Age of Segregation: Race Relations in the South, 1890–1945,* ed. Robert Haws (Jackson, Miss., 1978), 67–76; "Age: 19, Color: Negro, Occupation: None," *Look,* December 3, 1940, 20–22.

57. Dalfiume, "The 'Forgotten Years' of the Negro Revolution," 96; Gunnar Myrdal, *An American Dilemma: The Negro Problem and Modern Democracy,* vol. 1 (1944; reprint, New York, 1962), 409; Tindall, *The Emergence of the New South,* 716; Robert Higgs, "Race and Economy in the South, 1890–1950," in *The Age of Segregation,* ed. Haws, 90; Martha Byrd, "The Home Front—World War II," *American History Illustrated,* July 1979, 17.

58. *Times-Picayune,* December 23, 1941.

Achievement Day for rural black schools in East Baton Rouge Parish in 1941 was "home-school-community coordination for national defense." The Louisiana Colored Teachers' Association urged all black schoolchildren to buy at least one defense stamp per week for the duration of the war, and its members to join the payroll allotment plan to purchase war bonds. A report in 1944 indicated that blacks in New Orleans had bought $585,000 worth of bonds in the current drive, while blacks in Bogalusa, in St. John the Baptist Parish, and Ouachita Parish had bought $12,000, $5,000, and $2,500 worth, respectively. The Baton Rouge Negro Chamber of Commerce in 1944 pledged its support of the Community War Chest drive.[59]

Black Louisianians received some recognition from within the white establishment. In 1941, the *Monroe News-Star* remarked, "It is wise and right that both in the military services and in defense industries, broadening opportunities should be opening up for Americans of colored blood."[60]

Nevertheless, other Louisianians looked less benignly on the stirrings of progress within the black community. The *Town Talk* suspected that "fifth columnists" were at work among the black population, "spread[-ing] . . . theories of Naziism." E. A. Stephens, in his 1942 Senate campaign against Allen Ellender, raised the "black threat" issue, just as did other southern politicians engaged in difficult campaigns. Stephens charged that draft boards inducted more whites than blacks, thereby "depleting the white manhood in the South." The emerging situation, Stephens said, was intolerable: "We of the south cannot pour out our young manhood and leave our streets and roads populated by Negroes incited by northerners to seek social equality." Southern parents were willing to sacrifice their sons to protect the United States, he claimed, but "they must not pay for this patriotism by the loss of their dignity and the social balance that we know to be right and just."[61]

59. *Morning Advocate,* April 2, 1941, December 5, 1942, October 13, 1944, June 12, 1945; *Times-Picayune,* March 20, 1942.

60. *Monroe News-Star,* July 7, 1941.

61. *Town Talk,* July 27, 1940, August 10, 1942.

The specter of the "outside agitator" haunted thought about racial equality during the war. Charlton H. Lyons told fellow members of the Shreveport Chamber of Commerce that white men of the South should begin solving the problems associated with the "Negro question" before "outside agitators" attempted to settle those issues without proper knowledge of the South's social structure. In April 1943, the chamber asked Louisiana members of Congress and state officials to stop the Office of War Information from distributing a booklet recounting ("extolling" in the parlance of the chamber) black contributions to the war, claiming, "Distribution of such literature in the south tends to create racial unrest and misgivings, promote a feeling among the [N]egroes that the federal government desires social equality between the races." The *Shreveport Times* urged all Louisianians to close ranks to prevent racial unrest "regardless of any outside influences." In his retirement speech to Congress in 1944, James Domengeaux said that "except when aroused by self-seeking demagogues," southern blacks "were always assured of a security far surpassing in its real benevolence the bureaucratic schemes of modern days." The culprits, he said, were "self-seeking demagogues" who "lure [blacks] by false promises to hope for a status they know [they] can never attain."[62]

The Fair Employment Practices Commission, a federal organization, appeared to much of the white South to be the ultimate outside agitator. The Shreveport Chamber of Commerce contended that FEPC actions "had created ill will between races," and opposed further existence for the agency. Fifth District congressman Charles E. McKenzie called the FEPC a "fraud on American constitutional rights" that had "tried to make it appear that the South is a hot bed of prejudice and bigotry."[63]

The conservative reaction against the FEPC ultimately proved to be ineffectual. The South learned that the federal government would reinforce its new commitment to equality by granting or withholding federal

62. Shreveport Chamber of Commerce Minutes, April 8, July 8, 1943; *Shreveport Times,* June 25, 1943, April 5, 1944.

63. Shreveport Chamber of Commerce Minutes, June 8, 1944; *Morning Advocate,* August 16, 1943.

funds. Shreveport, for example, lost sixty-seven thousand dollars in federal funds for construction of a health center because the city refused to
meet the requirement that 12 percent of unskilled workers on the project
be black. Mayor Sam Caldwell angrily criticized "bureaucrats in Washington" for attempting "to cram the [N]egro down our throats." "We
have lost the health center," Caldwell said, "but thank God we have retained our respect and white supremacy. We are not going to be bribed by
federal funds to accept the [N]egro as our political or social equal."[64]

The tide of equality, however, was too strong to be stemmed. Southern
officials found that United States Supreme Court writs were applicable
throughout the South, even when they overturned traditional political
and social practices. In 1944, the Court ruled in *Smith v. Allwright* that the
Texas system of all white Democratic party primary elections, which effectively excluded blacks from voting, was unconstitutional. Political
leaders throughout the South were outraged, not least in Louisiana. Senator John Overton pledged, "The South at all costs will maintain the rule
of white supremacy." If white primaries would no longer be allowed,
"The [N]egro can be kept from the polls by educational qualification
tests." State senator Welborn Jack of Caddo Parish introduced a new
"white primary" bill in the 1944 session of the legislature, but the house
committee on elections sidetracked it with an unfavorable report. Committee members and members of the Davis administration thought that
present state laws were adequate to prevent black voter registration without conflicting with the Court ruling.[65]

While the ruling in *Smith v. Allwright* had the immediate effect of
strengthening the hand of southern conservatives, who began a rear-
guard struggle to preserve the virtual white monopoly of the ballot box,
it also opened the door for black voter registration. But that registration
proceeded slowly. Rapides Parish registrar of voters P. T. Haworth reported in August 1944 that seventeen blacks had registered to vote in the
parish—thirteen as Democrats and four as Republicans. Haworth re-

64. *Morning Advocate,* September 17, 1943.

65. *Shreveport Times,* April 4–5, May 7, 17, June 7, 1944; Alpheus Thomas Mason, *The
Supreme Court from Taft to Burger* (Baton Rouge, 1979), 190–92.

marked that no blacks had been registered to vote in the parish for twenty years, and that no one could remember any blacks ever having registered as Democrats. He further noted that he had disqualified about as many blacks as he had registered because they had not been able to complete the registration form "intelligently." The assistant registrar of voters in Tangipahoa Parish, Merle S. Weigel, reported to her soldier-husband in August 1944 that no blacks had attempted to register there yet, and added, "Of course, we don't intend to let any register, but don't want any trouble about it." The number of Louisiana blacks registered to vote did rise from 886 (.1 percent of the total number of registered voters) in 1940 to 7,561 (1 percent of the total number of registered voters) in 1946, but it was not until October 1964 that every parish in the state had at least one black on the voting rolls.[66]

Other racial barriers in the South were also tested during the war, especially by black soldiers used to the relatively freer societies in other areas of the United States. Buses, historically segregated in the South, became increasingly crowded as shortages of gasoline and tires for private automobiles caused more people to use them. Whites crowded into the rear seats of many buses, the seats normally assigned to blacks, thus causing blacks to stand in the aisles or to be left at the bus stop. Attempts were made to maintain traditional roles under those conditions. In one incident, two black soldiers from Camp Livingston attacked Alexandria bus driver L. J. Bell after he attempted to force them to move from the "white only" section of his bus, where they had found seats.[67]

Friction between the races occasionally erupted into violence. The major disruption in Louisiana occurred in January 1942 in Alexandria. Soldiers crowded into the city on January 10 after receipt of their pay-

66. William G. Carleton, "The Southern Politician—1900 and 1950," *Journal of Politics,* May 1951, 225; George Brown Tindall, *The Disruption of the Solid South* (Athens, Ga., 1972), 35; *Town Talk,* August 8, 1944; Merle Weigel to H. S. Weigel, August 11, 1944, Weigel Papers; Riley E. Baker, "Negro Voter Registration," *Louisiana Studies,* winter 1965, 338–39.

67. Tindall, *Emergence of the New South,* 716–17; Adam Fairclough, *Race and Democracy: The Civil Rights Struggle in Louisiana, 1915–1972* (Athens, Ga., 1995), 82; Merle Weigel to H. S. Weigel, March 11, 1943, Weigel Papers; *Town Talk,* November 14, 16, 1942.

checks. Black military police normally patrolled the black neighborhood centered on Lee Street, where most black entertainment establishments were located. On this day, however, a patrol of about sixty white military police entered the neighborhood and arrested a black soldier because of "disorderly conduct," and the "Lee Street Riot" began. Businesses along several blocks of the street sustained broken windows, and news reports indicated that approximately twenty-eight black soldiers were injured, including three to five who were shot and seriously wounded. One eyewitness later reported, "Bullets were whistling and bricks were flying. The Japs might as well have been attacking as far as I was concerned. I ducked." The official army investigation of the incident reported that a show of force might have been necessary following the initial arrest, but that civilian law enforcement officials, including Alexandria police and state troopers, along with some of the military police, "indulged in indiscriminate and unnecessary shooting." Persistent reports following the riot suggested that the toll of dead and wounded was much higher than the estimates originally reported.[68]

Even though African Americans experienced some measure of improvement in their social and economic condition, they remained trapped in a segregated society in Louisiana during the war years, just as they did in the rest of the South. Politically, they remained virtually powerless. The number of blacks registered to vote remained low, and thus no Louisiana politician thought it necessary to accommodate their needs. Some white politicians played on the fears of their constituencies, however, promising, if they were elected, not to allow the increased black representation to affect the state. Powerful public reaction against any attempt on the federal level to achieve a semblance of equality prevented the dissolution of the segregated society during the war years.

While blacks shared in the enhanced economic opportunities created by the war's demand for increased agricultural and industrial production,

68. *Morning Advocate,* January 11, 1942; *Town Talk,* January 12–13, 21, 24, 1942; Myrdal, *An American Dilemma,* vol. 1, 419, 421; Fairclough, *Race and Democracy,* 74–75; William M. Simpson, "A Tale Untold? The Alexandria, Louisiana, Lee Street Riot (January 10, 1942)," *Louisiana History* 35 (spring 1994): 133–49.

they did not break down all the barriers that had limited them in this sphere. Increased prosperity allowed many black tenants to become land-owners, but many more were left in tenantry at the end of the war. Demand for industrial workers brought black agricultural workers into higher-paying factory jobs, but many remained on farms. Those who ob-tained industrial employment remained workers and did not move up the employment scale.

Black education in Louisiana, one of the most visible symbols of the "separate but equal" society, experienced little improvement during the war years. A survey of Louisiana education ordered by the reformers after their 1940 victory revealed the inadequacies of black schools, and some white officials publicly recognized the state's problems with its sys-tem of black education, but a shortage of funds and lack of widespread popular support limited the improvements made in black education. The most impressive advancement of black educators during the war was equalization of black and white teachers' salaries in Orleans Parish. That limited victory left sixty-three other parishes with antiquated, unequal pay scales for black and white teachers with equal education and experi-ence, but it indicated that the old days of inequality were numbered.

While the World War II experience did not bring the widespread real-ization of a desegregated society in Louisiana, it awakened the modern resurgence of the quest for black equality. The comprehensive achieve-ment of that equality, though, lay well beyond the war years.

Another group also began edging closer to the mainstream of Ameri-can life during World War II. Women, customarily relegated to civic pur-suits, housework, or "women's jobs" in the workplace, took advantage of the labor shortage caused by the war to move into nontraditional employ-ment. They became stock board markers at the New Orleans office of Merrill Lynch, Pierce, Fenner, and Bean; they managed parking lots, drove taxicabs, welded and repaired aircraft, delivered newspapers, worked in machine shops, drove trucks, and managed stores, often re-placing men who had gone to war. In addition, more than four hundred Louisiana women applied to the Women's Auxiliary Army Corps Offi-cers School during the first week of open applications in 1942.[69]

69. *Item,* December 6, 1941, March 12, May 27, June 6, 1942; *Times-Picayune,* February 8, 1942; *States,* March 28, July 27, 1942; *Morning Advocate,* February 28, 1943; *Town Talk,*

The movement of women into nontraditional roles received a mixed reaction in Louisiana. The *Times-Picayune/New Orleans States* editorialized, "It would be foolishly optimistic to suppose that we shall be able to win this war by employing only a part of our human resources." The *Alexandria Town Talk* remarked of female war workers, "these women are not enslaved, but released. And they are regarded with new respect." Nevertheless, the same *Town Talk* editorial recognized the traditional conservative outlook and added, "It is surprising how they take to it. Especially so when it is remembered how inept with machinery women were always supposed to be."[70]

Louisiana women also edged closer to full participation in politics and government during the war years. Lucille May Grace held a statewide elected office as registrar of state lands. Other women expressed new interest in the traditionally male province of government. The League of Women Voters established chapters in Baton Rouge, New Orleans, Monroe, and Shreveport during the war years. Members corresponded with legislators and other officials about government policies they wished to influence, supported child labor and civil service legislation, and discussed national and international issues. Organizers, however, often found potential members reluctant to join an organization involved in the consideration of political issues because of the traditional view that a "lady" did not participate in government business. One League study recounts a voter service report from the Shreveport chapter that lamented the "general reticence of women, brought up in the Old South tradition, to undertake any work of this kind."[71] Nevertheless, the groundbreaking work performed by these chapters established foundations for later advances by women in Louisiana politics.

Many Louisiana legislators, also brought up in the Old South tradition, objected to a bill introduced in 1942 that would have eliminated the

---

July 23, 1942; Merle Weigel to H. S. Weigel, July 1, 1942, Weigel Papers; Cathy Thurlkill, "A Woman's Place Is in the War: North Louisiana Women's Contributions to World War Two, 1941–1945," *North Louisiana Historical Association Journal*, winter 1997, 51.

70. *Times-Picayune/New Orleans States*, February 22, 1942; *Town Talk*, May 25, 1942.

71. Gayle Rogers, "The Shreveport League of Women Voters and the Drive for Permanent Voter Registration in Louisiana," *North Louisiana Historical Association Journal*, spring–summer 1993, 75–79.

requirement that women register separately for jury duty. The bill was designed to replenish the supply of potential jurors, depleted by the large number of men away at war, by automatically including women as well as men voters on jury rolls when they registered to vote. The Louisiana Federation of Business and Professional Women's Clubs favored the bill, but it was defeated. One legislator spoke for many others when he suggested that women jurors would sometimes be required to hear unsavory testimony, from which southern womanhood had to be protected. The *Morning Advocate,* however, commented on the defeat of this bill, "We'll have more of this sadly comic business as long as the idea persists that women are, after all, much inferior to men and don't deserve an opportunity to prove that the holders of these opinions are wrong."[72]

Louisiana women who had entered the workplace during the war years gave a variety of reasons for their employment. Michelina LaCerva, Rosemary Jones, and Ruth Arcenaux, the first women hired at the Rheem Manufacturing plant in New Orleans, said, "We hope to turn out our work fast, so that the ones we love can blast the Japs." Significantly for later developments in the women's movement, Ruth Sanderson, a worker at the ordnance plant near Minden, reported, "That first check was the prettiest check I ever saw." Many other women who experienced the feeling of economic liberation created by a paycheck found it difficult to retreat from the workplace after the war ended. A job could also assuage the loneliness experienced by many women when their loved ones left for war. Merle Weigel wrote to her husband, "I'm so glad I have a job for it keeps me busy all day and when I get home at night I'm tired and can sleep."[73]

Indeed, loneliness became a daily companion for many women. Mrs. Weigel took on numerous war-related duties in lieu of her usual activities. She resigned from her bridge club, she wrote her husband, because "my heart is not in a bridge game when there are so many more useful things I can be doing." She volunteered for Red Cross bandage making

72. *Morning Advocate,* June 26, 1941, June 14, 17, 1942.
73. *States,* March 28, 1942; Thurlkill, "A Woman's Place," 53; Merle Weigel to H. S. Weigel, July 10, 1942, Weigel Papers.

and knitting, worked at the ration board office, and obtained a job first in an Amite drugstore and then as assistant registrar of voters in Tangipahoa Parish, all this in addition to being the single parent of two adolescent boys.[74]

Her numerous activities, however, did not completely fill her days: "When I go to the Post Office in the morning and don't get a letter from you I'm blue all day—and when I get one I'm 'pepped up' all the rest of the day," she wrote to her husband in June 1942. "Nothing seems right in any way since you are gone. I get so terribly lonesome for you," she wrote in September. Holidays caused especially acute loneliness. Various Christmastime letters included such sentiments as "I'd give so much to know where you are today and what you are doing"; "I dread [Christmas] without you with us"; and "It just seems like everything I go to do brings back memories of the many good times we've had together." Early one summer she wrote, "I've been praying for you all day to-day darling and wondering just where you are."[75] Loneliness, uncertainty, and adjustments to managing both a job and a home became constants in the lives of many women.

Like blacks, women retreated somewhat from their wartime gains during the late 1940s and 1950s. But these two groups did not forget their wartime forays into prosperity and equality. Their permanent acceptance into full-time participation in the American economy and culture would not come for some twenty years after the conclusion of the war.

74. Merle Weigel to H. S. Weigel, October 19, 27, November 30, 1942, *Amite Progress,* February 11, 1943, clipping, Weigel Papers.

75. Merle Weigel to H. S. Weigel, June 28, July 2, 4, August 6, September 9, 15, December 15, 21, 24, 25, 1942, June 6, 1944, Weigel Papers.

11

The End of World War II

Shortly after the United States entered World War II, its leaders began to consider the adjustments that would be necessary when the conflict ended to reconvert the country from a military power to a peacetime society. Many feared that another economic depression would occur when the demand for war materials ceased. New Deal experience with large-scale planning programs to meet social and economic emergencies, however, provided hope that with careful preparation, the country could escape major social and economic dislocation.[1]

In Louisiana, concern about an end-of-war recession appeared by mid-1941 and reflected a basic division among the state's interest groups, into those who thought that the federal government should continue spending on public improvement programs similar to those of the New Deal and those who feared that such a continuation of federal spending during the reconversion period would result in severe repercussions later. Governor Jones warned Louisianians in June that even though many of them had found jobs in new defense industries and thus were enjoying prosperity after the lean years of the Depression, the industrial production would probably decline after the war, and industrial workers should prepare themselves for the possibility of postwar unemployment. Shreveport mayor Caldwell, conversely, announced in December 1941 that he ex-

1. Ballard, *The Shock of Peace,* 15–19; Goulden, *The Best Years,* 9.

pected large federal expenditures on postwar programs to absorb many of the unemployed.[2]

The Truman administration's senior reconversion planner, John W. Snyder, thought that the end of the war would cause "an immediate and large dislocation of our economy," but vowed, "We will not manufacture a single shell, nor a single piece of equipment above absolute minimum military needs, for the purpose of reducing the shock of terminating war work."[3] Many Louisianians agreed with him.

The Shreveport Chamber of Commerce exemplified the conservative reaction against massive federal spending programs in January 1941 when it warned against "an orgy of spending" by the federal government after the war and decided to formulate a plan of reconversion for the local area. The subsequent Post War Readjustment Council Report called upon the United States Chamber of Commerce to initiate a nationwide program to "maintain capitalism or American free enterprise" while local chapters stood watch over the inevitable spending of federal money, and proposed that any federal project should benefit the local area economically—for example, by expediting traffic or commerce. The Shreveport chamber's postwar department conducted an industrial survey, promoted industrial development, and maintained a file of names of servicemen available for work after the war.[4]

The Louisiana Bankers' Association formulated its own postwar plans. The bankers sought to ease the return of veterans to the community (and increase bank profits) by establishing a committee on G.I. services to keep abreast of all benefit programs available to veterans, including those featuring government-guaranteed loans. The association held a series of G.I. meetings to explain those benefits to returning veterans.[5]

In the public sector, the Louisiana Department of Public Works urged police juries to establish planning boards, make an inventory of parish resources and facilities, and develop a three-pronged plan for their efficient

2. *Morning Advocate,* June 11, 1941; *Shreveport Times,* December 5, 1941.

3. Goulden, *The Best Years,* 92.

4. Shreveport Chamber of Commerce Minutes, January 8, 1942, January 13, 1944.

5. *Morning Advocate,* June 13, 1945; *Golden Jubilee: A Publication Commemorating the Louisiana Bankers' Association Golden Anniversary, 1900–1950* (Baton Rouge, 1950), 72.

use after the war. The plan was to include projects for the parish, including improvement of roads, bridges, and drainage systems; projects to be carried out by private corporations; and improvement projects for individual landowners. East Baton Rouge Parish called upon its citizens to suggest projects that would facilitate the return of veterans to civilian life, create wealth-producing jobs, and have a cultural dimension beneficial to the growth of the community.[6]

Governor Jones announced his plan for the postwar South in August 1943. He called for diversifying agriculture, industrializing the economy, and developing commerce by improving waterways, highways, railroads, and air transport facilities. He further entreated Louisianians to abandon their traditional one-party Democratic political allegiance, which, he thought, had "done nothing but maneuver us into a corner and further impoverish our people."[7]

Louisiana's master plan for postwar development, announced by Department of Public Works director DeWitt L. Pyburn in September 1944, included many of Jones's ideas, even though by then he had relinquished the governor's office to Jimmie Davis. The plan, clearly a creation of officials who had accepted the importance of government spending during the reconversion period, provided for the expenditure of approximately $500 million on a vast construction program that included armories, health centers and laboratories, hospitals, college buildings, farmers' markets, and airports, as well as improvement of state parks and the state's drainage system, and dock and wharf improvements at the port of New Orleans.[8]

Other Louisianians turned their attention to the diplomatic necessities of the newly configured peacetime world. The war years had witnessed a growing acceptance of the idea that the United States must assume a major role in international relations, an idea that was widely disseminated by editorial writers for the state's major newspapers between the be-

6. *Morning Advocate,* July 12, 1944; Gertrude Bouque, "Planning and the Postwar World," *Louisiana Police Jury Review,* April 1944, 16.

7. *Morning Advocate,* August 20, 1943.

8. *Ibid.,* September 17, 1944.

ginning of war in September 1939 and the Pearl Harbor attack in December 1941.[9]

The immediate international concern had been winning the war. The *Shreveport Times* had observed, "What we must do now is put our shoulder to the wheel of war and try to grind out victory so that we may have a chance to do something when the time for peace comes." Or, as the *Alexandria Town Talk* had remarked more succinctly, "Winning comes first."[10]

The golden days of peace, however, could only be preserved by the United States's participation in a postwar international organization, or so thought Louisiana newspaper editorial writers. The lesson of the United States's failure to join the League of Nations during the 1920s and 1930s haunted discussion of the similar period that would follow World War II. While contemplating the future, the *Monroe Morning World* editorialized in December 1941 that because the United States had not supported the League, "we are compelled to join with other nations and help fight and finance another world war in order to save ourselves."[11]

Although terribly costly in both money and lives, World War II gave rise to hope among editorial writers for continued international cooperation after peace had been established. The Baton Rouge *Morning Advocate* observed in January 1942 that "the allegiance which contributes . . . to the effective waging of war may well point the way to alliance in the world in peace when the war is over." The *Town Talk* speculated in February 1942 on the future of the "United Nations" (then only the name for the powers allied against the Axis), "Ties can be strengthened as we fight together for our ideals . . . close association in a big and righteous war should be in itself a power to hold the partners together on broad lines of common interest [in the postwar world]."[12]

Louisiana, along with the rest of the country, recognized a major turning point in the conflict as Allied armies gathered in England for the

9. Jerry Purvis Sanson, "Louisiana Reaction to the Beginning of World War II," *Southern Historian,* spring 1986; Sanson, "North Louisiana Press Opinion," 33–45.

10. *Shreveport Times,* July 23, 1942; *Town Talk,* March 6, 1942.

11. *Morning World,* December 26, 1941.

12. *Morning Advocate,* January 11, 1942; *Town Talk,* February 16, 1942.

cross-channel invasion of Europe during the early summer of 1944. Several mayors issued proclamations as early as the first week of May designating "D day," whenever it should come, as a day of devotion, and called upon churches to remain open and citizens to attend prayer services for Allied troops engaged in the invasion. Jimmie Davis's first proclamation as governor entreated Louisianians to pray for "spiritual protection, safety, and success" of American fighting forces on the day of the European invasion.[13]

News of the Allied invasion of Europe reached Louisiana on radio news bulletins broadcast at 2:32 A.M. on June 6, 1944. It was a day of mixed emotions—joy that the invasion at last had begun, and fear and concern for family members or friends who might be involved. J. E. McLaughlin, assistant pastor of St. Rita's Catholic Church in New Orleans, began a forty-hour prayer vigil at 4:00 that morning. Navy cadets at Tulane University heard the news at their 6:45 reveille and broke into cheers. Roman Catholic archbishop Joseph Francis Rummel issued a statement of support for the Allied troops, then paced in his garden in New Orleans, while mayor Maestri called upon citizens "to join in universal prayers for God's blessing upon our armed forces." In Alexandria, many residents stopped by churches throughout the day for a few moments of prayer. Governor Davis called a special joint session of the legislature for noon. Legislators and guests jammed the house chamber as Davis and Chaplain Edwin Olsen of Harding Field prayed for a successful invasion and the protection of Louisiana citizens involved.[14]

The Normandy beaches bought with such terrible cost on D day functioned as a foothold from which Allied soldiers pressed to liberate Nazi-dominated Europe. By the spring of 1945, many observers realized that Germany could not sustain the war effort much longer and looked forward with hope to a quick end to the war. The United States, however, had to endure one more trial before it savored a victory over the Nazis: President Franklin Roosevelt died at his Warm Springs, Georgia, retreat

13. *Town Talk,* May 4, 1945; *Item,* May 15, 1944.

14. *Item,* June 6, 1944; *States,* June 6, 1944; *Town Talk,* June 6, 1944; *Morning Advocate,* June 7, 1944.

on April 12. Lieutenant Governor J. Emile Verret articulated the feelings of many Louisianians in his remarks at a memorial service for Roosevelt held in New Iberia: "I personally had never seen or known the President, yet I personally feel that I have lost a friend." One unidentified New Orleans woman was in her yard on the afternoon of April 12 when her neighbor called to her to turn on her radio. The woman reported that before she reached her house, she overheard a report that Roosevelt had died: "I couldn't get up the steps. It was like a member of my family [had passed away]."[15]

Downtown New Orleans stores remained open during their usual business hours that night, but clerks reported small crowds who bought very little. People gathered around radios in department stores and hotel lobbies listening for details of the events in Warm Springs and the transfer of power in Washington. The Roosevelt Hotel closed its lounge and its restaurant for lack of business. A security guard at Pat O'Brien's night club reported that the crowd was "quiet and gloomy." The city's Catholic churches tolled their bells for five minutes beginning at 8:00 p.m. Mayor Maestri ordered all flags on city buildings lowered to half-staff. Officials closed public and parochial schools and all colleges and universities in the city. In Baton Rouge, Governor Davis ordered flags on all state buildings lowered, and declared April 15 an official day of mourning for Roosevelt. All state offices and many stores closed that day, as well as New Orleans's Stock Exchange, Cotton Exchange, and Board of Trade. Many people throughout the state attended memorial services for the late president.[16]

Even while it mourned the fallen leader, Louisiana welcomed the new president, Harry Truman. The *Morning Advocate* reminded its readers that while Roosevelt's place in history was unique, "there is always a place in the sun for others. The truly great are always needed and there is always a place for them."[17]

As Allied armies pushed close to Berlin in the spring of 1945, rumors

15. J. Emile Verret, "Eulogy," April 14, 1945, Verret Papers, DL; *Item*, April 13, 1945.
16. *Item*, April 13–15, 1945; *Times-Picayune*, April 14–16, 1945; *Morning Advocate*, April 13, 1945; *Shreveport Times*, April 13, 1945.
17. *Morning Advocate*, April 15, 1945.

of peace swept Louisiana and the rest of the United States beginning in March. Eagerness to confirm any hint of peace revealed the desperate longing to end the war. In late March, callers jammed the *Shreveport Times* telephone switchboard asking whether peace had finally come. The calls began after a local radio station promoted its news department by announcing that listeners should stay tuned for "the big news stories of the day."[18]

Peace rumors again swept through Louisiana in late April. Bars closed in Shreveport in accordance with agreements between owners and police attempting to curb excessive celebrating. Church bells pealed in Baton Rouge announcing the victory, but official denials of a peace settlement quickly scotched the celebrations.[19]

Ironically, Louisiana remained calm during the days preceding Germany's actual surrender. Peace rumors of May 5, 1945, brought no new round of celebrations because skeptics now demanded proof before believing that the end of the European war had come. They had not long to wait. Germany surrendered at 2:41 A.M., Monday, May 7, 1945 (7:41 P.M. Central War Time, May 6, in Louisiana). The state began its celebration of "Victory in Europe Day" even before President Truman officially announced the peace settlement at 8:00 A.M. local time, May 8. Churches throughout the state opened for prayer and meditation, businesses closed, shopkeepers nailed boards across vulnerable plate-glass show windows, and workers in the Whitney Bank Building and the American Bank Building in New Orleans sent showers of confetti fluttering down in an impromptu celebration. Old-timers remembered the Armistice Day rallies in the city following World War I as rowdier. The major reason for the relatively sober celebration was that only one phase of the war had ended. As one New Orleans policeman commented, "Bullets are still flying in the Pacific."[20]

During the months between the surrender of Germany and the surrender of Japan, Americans increasingly turned their thoughts to the con-

18. *Item,* March 17, 1945; *Shreveport Times,* March 28, 1945.
19. *Shreveport Times,* April 29, 1945; *Morning Advocate,* April 29, 1945.
20. *Morning Advocate,* May 9–10, 1945; *Town Talk,* May 8, 1945; *States,* May 7–8, 1945.

sumer goods that would be available at the end of the war. An informal survey conducted on New Orleans streets by *Item* reporters in August 1945 asked what items respondents would purchase for dinner in a grocery store fully stocked with prewar supplies. Eight people replied steak, two replied meat of any type, and one each replied vegetables and chicken. A Baton Rouge Chamber of Commerce survey of 2,585 persons asked, "What will be your first purchase after the war when there are plenty of things to buy?" The replies reveal the pent-up demand for consumer goods: the most popular reply was an electric washing machine, followed by automobiles, electric irons, kitchen stoves, electric refrigerators, radios, furniture, furnaces, electric mixers, and electric food freezers.[21]

Rumors of a peace settlement with Japan swept through Louisiana as early as August 10. Official confirmation that the Japanese had surrendered reached the state minutes after it was announced at 6:00 P.M., August 15, 1945. A spontaneous victory celebration immediately erupted. New Orleans witnessed the largest round of festivities since the 1941 Carnival. Confetti piled six inches deep on some downtown streets; stores and offices closed; church bells rang; boats in the harbor sounded their whistles; and shopkeepers again boarded up vulnerable windows. City police made only 107 arrests, however. In downtown Baton Rouge, crowds jammed Third Street within fifteen minutes of the announcement and filled the air with confetti and the noise of whistles, sirens, and bells. Governor Davis declared a two-day state holiday. Shreveport celebrated with closed stores and offices, joyous merriment, and much noise. The Alexandria business district filled minutes after the announcement. The *Town Talk* reported comments randomly heard on the streets: "Thank God, it's done"; "How soon do you think my husband will come home?" "Oh, Gee"; "I'm going to cry"; "Praise the Lord that it's over"; and most poignantly, "I wish my son could have lived to see this day."[22]

The federal government announced the end of gasoline rationing only

21. *Item,* August 1, 8, 1945; Goulden, *The Best Years,* 93–94.
22. *Item,* August 10, 15, 1945; *Morning Advocate,* August 14–16, 1945; *Town Talk,* August 14, 1945; *Shreveport Times,* August 15, 1945.

a few hours after the Japanese surrender, thus initiating another round of celebration on August 16. Many motorists shared the pleasure of one Baton Rougean who reported, "I immediately drove my car to a gas station and said 'fill it up,' something I haven't been able to do for a long time. I hope I never need those gas coupons again." One Baton Rouge station, which had sold about a thousand gallons of fuel per day during rationing, sold approximately six thousand gallons the day rationing ended. New Orleans motorists likewise rushed to the pumps, causing the president of the New Orleans Service Station Association to comment, "Everybody said 'fill 'er up' just for the pleasure of saying it."[23]

Even as the state celebrated the end of the war, however, many Louisianians were concerned about the unconventional new weapon that had precipitated the conclusion of the conflict. The astonishing power of the atomic bomb and the consequences of possible misuse of atomic technology concerned editorial writers throughout the state. Louisiana's reaction to the beginning of the atomic age mirrored the reaction of Americans everywhere. Regarding atomic energy, the *Alexandria Town Talk* asserted on August 7, "Lest it become the monster by which man with his own hands and mind destroys himself, it behooves us to examine carefully, even prayerfully, the use to which this Frankenstein is put, and the hands in which its secrets lie."[24]

The next day, the *Shreveport Times* noted that the further civilization progressed, the more it acquired the ability to destroy "vast chunks of the world." That same day, the *Item* reported, "One common reaction to [the atomic bomb] seems to be that it is very unfortunate for humanity that so terrible a weapon had to be invented. For at least a dozen of our acquaintances have expressed in varying terms the feelings that atom-cracking will destroy us all, if not the world along with us."[25]

The *New Orleans States* speculated on the possibility of outlawing the new weapon as "the answer to fears that another war will end civiliza-

23. *Morning Advocate,* August 15–16, 1945; *Item,* August 16, 1945; Goulden, *The Best Years,* 91.

24. Paul Boyer, *By the Bomb's Early Light: American Thought and Culture at the Dawn of the Atomic Age* (New York, 1985), 3–26; *Town Talk,* August 7, 1945.

25. *Shreveport Times,* August 8, 1945; *Item,* August 8, 1945.

tion. It seems to us that attempts to outlaw the atomic bomb are doomed to failure unless they can be approached through strong international controls of the very process involved in the manufacture of atomic power." The *Baton Rouge Morning Advocate,* meanwhile, asked, "How can any logical person argue that any effort no matter how great, on behalf of lasting peace, is not entirely justified?"[26]

The threat of atomic proliferation appeared to some observers even in the virtual afterglow of the wartime detonations. This danger, some thought, might even enhance the possibility of constructing a lasting peace. A cautionary editorial in the *Advocate* proclaimed, "by this frightful invention the strongest fortifications known to man can be crumpled like tinfoil, the deepest shelters can be blown open, and the very mountains toppled. We are now trying to establish machinery to keep a lasting peace. We had better make it work. This may be our last chance to avoid the pocalyptic [*sic*] destruction with which the science of war so long had threatened us."[27]

The end of the war, even though it brought unimagined fears and the brooding threat of atomic warfare, also brought the beginning of America's cultural reconversion to the luxuries of peace. Many Louisianians celebrated Labor Day 1945, the first peacetime holiday since Thanksgiving 1941, with short automobile trips fueled by unrationed gasoline. The telephone company assured Baton Rougeans that new telephones were on the way to fill the backlog of 33,186 orders for residential or business service. Scarce china, silver, and crystal appeared on store shelves and met a brisk demand. One New Orleans jeweler remarked that "victory brides" created much new demand, and that "many of our old customers are replenishing their stocks or changing their china and silver patterns. They've had to do without fine things for so long." Former servicemen crowded into the state's colleges. Long-awaited floor samples of new Frigidaire electric refrigerators appeared on October 31. Customers could only place an order, but stores promised, "Deliveries as Soon as Frigidaires Are Available." Applications for new trucks numbered about four hundred

26. *States,* October 29, 1945; *Morning Advocate,* November 29, 1945.
27. *Morning Advocate,* August 8, 1945.

for every vehicle brought into the state. The Baton Rouge USO held its closing ceremonies in January 1946.[28]

Formal postwar reconversion of the Louisiana economy started when the federal government began canceling war contracts soon after the Japanese surrender. Higgins Industries lost all its war contracts by August 16. Consolidated Vultee Aircraft announced that it would complete the airplanes on the assembly line but would begin no new construction. Rheem Manufacturing lost two of its three war contracts by August 16. The last ship left the Delta Shipbuilding ways in New Orleans on October 11, thus bringing to a close the World War II era of ship building in the city.[29]

The *Item* regretted the resulting loss of employment but argued that "efforts to prolong production at public expense, without need" would have proven even more costly. "Sudden increase in employment at unprecedented wages was an abnormal condition brought on deliberately to meet the abnormal demands of an abnormal situation. Now it is time to return to normal living." Senator Allen Ellender urged workers to "forget this holiday spree" of high wartime wages so that United States production costs could be lowered sufficiently to allow American products to compete in the international market.[30]

Many workers realized that the future might not be as exciting (or as profitable) as the recent past. An *Item* survey at the Consolidated Vultee plant elicited these comments: "Before the war, I was a seamstress, but I'll never go back to it. I'd rather starve"; "My husband's in the Pacific and I hope he'll be back soon. So, I'll keep house for him. However, I'll sure miss those rivets. Housekeeping will seem mighty dull now"; "I guess I'll go back to [accounting]. I know it won't pay as well, but I figured on that and will be satisfied."[31]

Louisiana in 1945 was not the same state that it had been in 1939 when the war began. While precise measurements of change are impossible to

28. *Morning Advocate,* September 2, 19, 27, 1945, January 10, 28, 1946; *States,* October 29, 31, 1945; *Item,* November 15, 1945.

29. *Item,* August 16, 1945; *States,* October 11, 1945.

30. *Item,* August 20, 1945; *Morning Advocate,* August 30, 1945.

31. *Item,* August 17, 1945.

determine specifically for 1945, the entire decade of the 1940s brought continued population growth to the state. Louisiana's population in 1950 numbered 2,683,516, an increase of 319,636, or 13.5 percent, over the 1940 total. Urban growth outstripped rural growth. The total urban population increased by 39.1 percent over the decade, while the rural population lost 4.6 percent from the 1940 total. The 1950 census found that Louisiana's population was now more urban (50.8 percent) than rural (49.2 percent). The basic configuration, however, was still recognizable. No new urban area emerged to displace New Orleans as the state's most populous city. The same areas that had been urban in 1940 remained urban in 1950, but they had grown rapidly. Increases in population during the decade included New Orleans by 15.3 percent, Shreveport by 19.6 percent, Alexandria by 29 percent, Monroe by 36.3 percent, Lafayette by 74.6 percent, Lake Charles by 94.6 percent, and Baton Rouge by a staggering 261.8 percent. By 1950 Baton Rouge threatened to displace Shreveport as the state's "second city." Louisiana ranked fifth in the South in population growth during the 1940s, Florida, Virginia, Texas, and North Carolina having grown even faster.[32]

Louisianians in 1950 were slightly better educated than they had been ten years before. In 1940, the median grade completed for white residents was 8.2. By 1950, that number had increased to 8.8. Blacks reported 3.9 as the median grade completed in 1940 and 4.6 in 1950.[33] The increase for both races, however, was small enough to be considered negligible.

The Census of Manufacturers, completed in 1947, documents the economic shift toward industrialization in Louisiana. The 1939 census had found 1,779 manufacturing establishments in the state, employing 70,453 workers and paying annual wages of $55,083,540. The 1947 survey found 2,389 manufacturing establishments, employing 132,464 workers at total wages of $309,871,000.[34]

George Brown Tindall, in his massive study of the New South, maintains that the southern states emerged from World War II with social and

---

32. *Seventeenth Census, 1950: Population,* vol. 1, 18.

33. *Ibid.,* p. viii.

34. *Seventeenth Census, 1950: Population,* vol. 2, pt. 18, *Louisiana,* 18–32.

economic conditions much different from those they had known in 1939 and that, furthermore, they had even more radical changes in store.[35] Indeed, Louisiana had experienced much change since 1939; events of the next six years affected political considerations, the economy, and virtually every other aspect of life on the Louisiana homefront. But World War II served merely to trigger many transformations. The forces it unleashed would come to fruition only in the succeeding decades.

35. Tindall, *The Emergence of the New South*, 731.

BIBLIOGRAPHY

PRIMARY SOURCES

Archival Collections

Center for Regional Studies, Southeastern Louisiana University, Hammond, La.
  James H. Morrison Collection.
Cline Room, Magale Library, Centenary College, Shreveport, La.
  Petroleum Administration for War, Natural Gas, and Natural Gasoline
    Committee District 3 Records.
Archives and Manuscripts Collection, Dupre Library, University of Southwest-
  ern Louisiana, Lafayette, La.
  J. Emile Verret Papers.
Allen J. Ellender Archives, Allen J. Ellender Library, Nicholls State University,
  Thibodaux, La.
  Allen J. Ellender Papers.
Special Collections, Howard-Tilton Memorial Library, Tulane University, New
  Orleans, La.
  T. Hale Boggs Papers.
  William Walter Jones Collection of the Papers of Sam Houston Jones.
  deLesseps Story Morrison Papers.
Louisiana and Lower Mississippi Valley Collections, Louisiana State University
  Libraries, Baton Rouge, La.
  James B. Aswell, Jr., and Family Papers.
  Overton Brooks Papers.
  Dennis Daugherty Collection.
  John B. Fournet Papers.
  Jennings-Heywood Oil Syndicate Records.
  Richard W. Leche Papers.
  Charlton Harvard Lyons, Sr., Papers.
  David C. Pipes Papers.

H. S. Weigel and Family Papers.

T. Harry Williams Papers.

Microform Room, Troy H. Middleton Library, Louisiana State University, Baton Rouge, La.

Shreveport Chamber of Commerce Minutes, microfiche copy.

Richard W. Norton Memorial Library, Louisiana College, Pineville, La.

Keatchie-Mt. Lebanon Collection.

Interviews

Davis, Jimmie. Interview by Gus Weill. Louisiana Public Broadcasting, April 9, 16, 1984.

Jones, Sam Houston. Interview by Dennis Daugherty. Tape recording, May 6, 1970. Dennis Daugherty Collection, Louisiana and Lower Mississippi Valley Collections.

Jones, Sam Houston. Interview by James M. Godfrey. February 1977. Typescript. Louisiana State University Oral History Collection.

Lawrence, Bessie. Interview by author. September 10, 1983.

Long, Earl. "Last of the Red-Hot Poppas: Interview with Earl Long." Phonograph recording. Baton Rouge: News Records, Inc., 1961.

Long, Russell B. Interview by Gus Weill. Louisiana Public Broadcasting, January 9, 16, 1984.

Morrison, James H. Interview by author. May 13, 1982.

United States Government Documents

Census Reports

Census of Manufacturers, 1947: Vol. 3: *Statistics by States.*

Financial Statistics of States, 1939. Louisiana. Vol. 1, no. 20.

Sixteenth Census, 1940: Agriculture. Vol. 2, pt. 2.

Sixteenth Census, 1940: Agriculture. Special Cotton Report.

Sixteenth Census, 1940: Population. Vol. 1.

Seventeenth Census, 1950: Agriculture. Vol. 1, pt. 24.

Seventeenth Census, 1950: Population. Vol. 1.

Seventeenth Census, 1950: Population. Vol. 2, pt. 18.

State Government Finances, 1945: Louisiana. Vol. 1.

Congressional Directories and Congressional Record

Congressional Directory. 77th Cong., 1st sess., 1941.

Congressional Directory. 78th Cong., 1st sess., 1942.

Congressional Directory. 83d Cong., 1st sess., 1953.

Congressional Directory. 88th Cong., 1st sess., 1963.

Congressional Record. 76th Cong., 3d sess., 1940. Appendix, Vol. 86, pts. 16, 17.

Congressional Record. 77th Cong., 1st sess., 1941. Vol. 87, pts. 12, 14.

Congressional Record. 77th Cong., 2d sess., 1942. Vol. 88, pts. 2, 5, 7, 10.

Congressional Record. 78th Cong., 1st sess., 1943. Appendix, Vol. 89, pt. 12.

Congressional Record. 78th Cong., 2d sess., 1944. Appendix, Vol. 90, pts. 8, 10.

Congressional Record. 79th Cong., 1st sess., 1945. Appendix, Vol. 91, pt. 10.

Congressional Hearings

U.S. Congress. House. *Hearings Before the Select Committee Investigating National Defense Migration.* 77th Cong., 2d sess., 1942, pt. 28.

———. *National Defense Migration Hearings Before the Select Committee Investigating National Defense Migration.* 77th Cong., 1st sess., 1941, pt. 11.

———. *Petroleum Investigation (Crude Oil Prices and Extension of the Cole Pipe Line Act): Hearings Before a Subcommittee of the Committee on Interstate and Foreign Commerce.* 78th Cong., 1st sess., 1944.

U.S. Congress. Senate. *Hearing Before a Special Committee Investigating the National Defense Program.* 78th Cong., 1st sess., 1943.

Other Federal Publications

The Classification Process, Special Monograph No. 5, Vol. 2: *Selective Service System.* Washington, D.C.: United States Government Printing Office, 1950.

Employment Security Review, July 1942.

Greenfield, Kent Roberts, Robert R. Palmer, and Bell I. Wiley. *United States Army in World War II: The Army Ground Forces.* Vol. 1: *The Organization of Ground Combat Troops.* Washington, D.C.: Historical Division, Department of the Army, 1947.

Manpower Review, May, 1943.

Palmer, Robert R., Bell I. Wiley, and William R. Keast. *United States Army in World War II: The Army Ground Forces.* Vol. 2: *The Procurement and Training of Ground Combat Troops.* Washington, D.C.: Historical Division, Department of the Army, 1948.

Louisiana Government Documents

Legislative Journals and Calendars

Acts Passed by the Legislature of the State of Louisiana at the Regular Session, 1940.

Acts Passed by the Legislature of the State of Louisiana at the Regular Session, 1942.

Acts Passed by the Legislature of the State of Louisiana at the Extraordinary Session, 1942.

Acts Passed by the Legislature of the State of Louisiana at the Regular Session, 1944.

Acts Passed by the Legislature of the State of Louisiana at the Extraordinary Session, 1945.

Calendar of the House of Representatives of the State of Louisiana at the Tenth Regular Session . . . 1940.

House Calendar, Seventeenth Extraordinary Session, 1942.

Official Journal of the Proceedings of the House of Representatives of the State of Louisiana at the Tenth Regular Session, 1940.

Official Journal of the Proceedings of the House of Representatives . . . at the Eleventh Regular Session . . . 1942.

Official Journal of the Proceedings of the House of Representatives . . . at the Seventeenth Extraordinary Session . . . 1942.

Official Journal of the Proceedings of the Senate . . . at the Tenth Regular Session . . . 1940.

Official Journal of the Proceedings of the Senate . . . at the Seventeenth Extraordinary Session . . . 1942.

Senate Calendar of the State of Louisiana, Tenth Regular Session. . . .

State Government Reports

Agricultural Extension. *Annual Narrative Report.* 1944.

Committee to Consider Changes in the Powers, Duties, and Responsibilities of the Governor. *Report, May 11, 1966.*

Department of Conservation. *Fifteenth Biennial Report.* 1940–1941.

———. *Sixteenth Biennial Report.* 1942–1943.

———. *Seventeenth Biennial Report.* 1944–1945.

Department of State Civil Service. *Report.* 1943–1944.

Louisiana Business Review.

Louisiana Crime Commission. *Report to the Legislature, May 11, 1942.*

Louisiana Revenue Bulletin.

Washburne, Carleton. *Louisiana Looks at Its Schools: A Summary Report of the*

Louisiana Education Survey. Baton Rouge, Louisiana Educational Survey Commission, 1942.

Louisiana Department of Education Bulletins

No. 432. *Ninetieth Annual Report for the Session 1938–1939.*

No. 438. *Official Proceedings of the State Board of Education, August 16, 1940.*

No. 445. *Official Proceedings of the State Board of Education, January 3, 1941.*

No. 448. *Ninety-first Annual Report for the Session 1939–40.*

No. 453. *Minutes of the Meeting of the State Board of Education, May 5 and 6, 1941.*

No. 454. *Louisiana for Defense.*

No. 458. *Ninety-second Annual Report for the Session 1940–41.*

No. 460. *Official Proceedings of the State Board of Education, August 22, 1941.*

No. 473. *Manual for Vocational Training for Defense Workers. . . .*

No. 478. *Proposed Plan of Citizenship and Civilian Morale Education for Louisiana.*

No. 480. *Wartime Education in Louisiana Schools.*

No. 490. *Louisiana State Plan for Vocational Education. . . .*

No. 496. *Wartime Education Curriculum Changes (Implementing the High School Victory Corps).*

No. 502. *Official Proceedings of the State Board of Education, April 5, 1943.*

No. 511. *Pre-induction Training in Army Clerical Procedures.*

No. 519. *Official Proceedings of the State Board of Education, October 5, 1943.*

No. 520. *Military Training and Leadership in High Schools of Louisiana (High School Victory Corps Program).*

No. 526. *Official Proceedings of the State Board of Education, January 11, 1944.*

No. 530. *Official Proceedings of the State Board of Education, April 10, 1944.*

No. 543. *Ninety-fifth Annual Report for School Year 1943–1944.*

No. 548. *Official Proceedings of the State Board of Education, January 8, 1945.*

Other Louisiana Government Documents

Address by Governor Jimmie H. Davis Before the Joint Session of the Legislature, May 15, 1944. Baton Rouge: Louisiana House of Representatives, 1944.

Roster, Members and Officers. Constitutional Convention, State of Louisiana, of 1921. . . . Baton Rouge: Ramires-Jones Printing Co., 1921.

Louisiana Newspapers (1939–1945 except where noted)

Alexandria Daily Town Talk.

Baton Rouge Morning Advocate.

Hammond Vindicator (1939–1941).

Lafayette Daily Advertiser.

Louisiana Farm Bureau News (May 1980).

Mansfield Enterprise (September 5, 1940).

Monroe Morning World.

Monroe News Star (July 7, 1941).

New Orleans Catholic Herald.

New Orleans Item.

New Orleans Item-Tribune.

New Orleans States.

New Orleans Times-Picayune.

New Orleans Times-Picayune/New Orleans States (combined Sunday edition).

Progress (1939–1940).

Shreveport Journal.

Shreveport Times.

Books

Behrman, Martin. *Martin Behrman of New Orleans: Memoirs of a City Boss.* Ed. John R. Kemp. Baton Rouge: Louisiana State University Press, 1977.

Collins, J. Lawton. *Lightning Joe: An Autobiography.* Baton Rouge: Louisiana State University Press, 1979.

Eisenhower, Dwight D. *Crusade in Europe.* Garden City, N.Y.: Doubleday & Co., 1948.

Gallup, George, and Saul Forbes Rae. *The Pulse of Democracy.* New York: Simon & Schuster, 1940.

Harris, T. H. *The Memoirs of T. H. Harris, State Superintendent of Public Education in Louisiana, 1908–1940.* Baton Rouge: Bureau of Educational Materials and Research, College of Education, Louisiana State University, 1963.

Hebert, F. Edward, and John McMillan. *"Last of the Titans": The Life and Times of Congressman F. Edward Hebert of Louisiana.* Lafayette, La.: Center for Louisiana Studies, University of Southwestern Louisiana, 1976.

Howell, Roland Boatner, Sr. *Louisiana Sugar Plantations, Mardi Gras and Huey P. Long: Reminiscences of Roland Boatner Howell, Sr.* Baton Rouge: Claitor's Publishing Division, 1969.

Irey, Elmer L., and William J. Slocum. *The Tax Dodgers: The Inside Story of the*

T-Man's War with America's Political and Underworld Hoodlums. New York: Fireside Press, 1949.

Long, Huey P. *Every Man a King: The Autobiography of Huey P. Long.* New Orleans: National Book Company, 1933.

The Peep Sight: Camp Beauregard, Louisiana, 1931. N.p., n.d.

Roosevelt, Franklin D. *The Complete Presidential Press Conferences of Franklin D. Roosevelt.* Vol. 15 (1940). New York: DaCapo Press, 1972.

————. *Public Papers and Addresses of Franklin D. Roosevelt.* 1940 vol. *War—and Aid to Democracies.* Comp. Samuel I. Rosenman. New York: Macmillan, 1941.

Robert, E. B. *The Life and Work of E. B. (Ted) Robert.* Baton Rouge: Bureau of Educational Materials and Research, College of Education, Louisiana State University, 1972

Sam Jones' Report to the People. December, 1943.

Truman, Harry S. *Memoirs of Harry S. Truman.* Vol. 1, *Year of Decisions.* Garden City, N.Y.: Doubleday & Co., 1953.

Wilson, Earl B. *Sugar and Its Wartime Controls, 1941–1947.* Vols. 1, 2, and 4. New York: Statistical Press, n.d.

SECONDARY SOURCES

Books

Ballard, Jack Stokes. *The Shock of Peace: Military and Economic Demobilization after World War II.* Washington, D.C.: University Press of America, 1983.

Bartley, Numan V. *The Rise of Massive Resistance: Race Relations in the South during the 1950s.* Baton Rouge: Louisiana State University Press, 1969.

Bass, Jack, and Walter DeVries. *The Transformation of Southern Politics: Social Change and Political Consequence since 1945.* New York: Basic Books, 1976.

Baudier, Roger, and Millard F. Everett. *Anchor and Fleur-de-Lis: Knights of Columbus in Louisiana, 1902–1962.* New Orleans: Louisiana State Council, Knights of Columbus, 1965.

Becnel, Thomas A. *Labor, Church, and the Sugar Establishment: Louisiana, 1887–1976.* Baton Rouge: Louisiana State University Press, 1980.

————. *Senator Allen Ellender of Louisiana: A Biography.* Baton Rouge: Louisiana State University Press, 1995.

Benedict, Murray R. *Farm Policies of the United States, 1790–1950: A Study of Their Origin and Development.* New York: Twentieth Century Fund, 1953.

Billington, Monroe Lee. *The Political South in the Twentieth Century*. New York: Charles Scribner's Sons, 1975.

Blum, John Morton. *V Was for Victory: Politics and American Culture during World War II*. New York: Harcourt Brace Jovanovich, 1976.

Bolner, James, ed. *Louisiana Politics: Festival in a Labyrinth*. Baton Rouge: Louisiana State University Press, 1982.

Boyer, Paul. *By the Bomb's Early Light: American Thought and Culture at the Dawn of the Atomic Age*. New York: Pantheon, 1985.

Brinkley, Alan. *Voices of Protest: Huey Long, Father Coughlin, and the Great Depression*. New York: Alfred A. Knopf, 1982.

Brister, Elaine H. *Once upon a River: A History of Pineville, Louisiana*. Baton Rouge: Claitor's Publishing Division, 1968.

Burns, James MacGregor. *Roosevelt: The Soldier of Freedom*. New York: Harcourt Brace Jovanovich, 1970.

Calhoun, Milburn, ed. *Louisiana Almanac, 1995–96*. Gretna, La.: Pelican Publishing Co., 1995.

Camp Beauregard and Central Louisiana, 1940–1945. New Orleans: Louisiana National Guard, 1994.

Carleton, Mark T. *Politics and Punishment: The History of the Louisiana State Penal System*. Baton Rouge: Louisiana State University Press, 1971.

―――. *River Capital: An Illustrated History of Baton Rouge*. Woodland Hills, Calif.: Windsor Publications, 1981.

Caro, Robert A. *The Years of Lyndon Johnson: The Path to Power*. New York: Alfred A. Knopf, 1982.

Carruth, Viola. *Caddo 1000: A History of the Shreveport Area from the Time of the Caddo Indians to the 1970s*. Shreveport: Shreveport Magazine, 1971.

Carter, Hodding, *et al.*, eds. *The Past as Prelude: New Orleans, 1718–1968*. New Orleans: Tulane University, 1968.

Christman, Henry M., ed. *Kingfish to America: Share Our Wealth, Selected Senatorial Papers of Huey P. Long*. New York: Schocken Books, 1985.

Clay, Floyd Martin. *Coozan Dudley LeBlanc: From Huey Long to Hadacol*. Gretna, La.: Pelican Publishing Co., 1973.

Cline, Rodney. *Builders of Louisiana Education*. Baton Rouge: Bureau of Educational Materials and Research, College of Education, Louisiana State University, 1963.

Conaway, James. *Judge: The Life and Times of Leander Perez*. New York: Alfred A. Knopf, 1973.

Curtis, W. D. *Statistical Data and Trends in the Agriculture of Louisiana.* Vol. I. Baton Rouge: Louisiana Agricultural Extension Service, 1947.

Dallek, Robert. *Franklin D. Roosevelt and American Foreign Policy, 1932–1945.* Oxford: Oxford University Press, 1979.

Daniels, Jonathan. *The Man of Independence.* New York: Lippincott, 1950.

Davis, Forrest. *Huey Long: A Candid Biography.* New York: Dodge Publishing Co., 1935.

Deutsch, Hermann B. *The Huey Long Murder Case.* Garden City, N.Y.: Doubleday & Co., 1963.

Dismukes, J. Philip. *The Center: A History of the Development of Lafayette, Louisiana.* Lafayette, La.: City of Lafayette, 1972.

Dodd, William J. ("Bill"). *Peapatch Politics: The Earl Long Era in Louisiana Politics.* Baton Rouge: Claitor's Publishing Division, 1991.

Donahoe, Bernard F. *Private Plans and Public Dangers: The Story of F.D.R.'s Third Nomination.* Notre Dame: University of Notre Dame Press, 1965.

Dufour, Charles L., and Leonard V. Huber. *If Ever I Cease to Love: One Hundred Years of Rex, 1872–1971.* New Orleans: School of Design, 1970.

Dupuy, Col. R. Ernest, and Lt. Hodding Carter. *Civilian Defense of the United States.* New York: Farrar and Rinehart, 1942.

Fairclough, Adam. *Race & Democracy: The Civil Rights Struggle in Louisiana, 1915–1972.* Athens, Ga.: University of Georgia Press, 1995.

Farago, Ladislas. *Patton: Ordeal and Triumph.* New York: Ivan Obolensky, 1963.

Fickle, James E. *The New South and the "New Competition": Trade Association Development in the Southern Pine Industry.* Urbana, Ill.: University of Illinois Press, 1980.

Finney, Peter. *The Fighting Tigers, 1893–1993: One Hundred Years of LSU Football.* Third edition. Baton Rouge: Louisiana State University Press, 1993.

Folweiler, A. D. *Forest Land Ownership in Louisiana and Its Influence on Timber Production.* Louisiana Bulletin No. 377. Baton Rouge: Louisiana State University, 1943.

Gansberg, Judith M. *Stalag: USA.* New York: Thomas Y. Crowell Co., 1977.

Garson, Robert A. *The Democratic Party and the Politics of Sectionalism, 1941–1948.* Baton Rouge: Louisiana State University Press, 1974.

Golden Jubilee: A Publication Commemorating the Louisiana Bankers' Association Golden Anniversary, 1900–1950. Baton Rouge: Louisiana Bankers' Association, 1950.

Goldfield, David R. *Cotton Fields and Skyscrapers: Southern City and Region, 1607–1980.* Baton Rouge: Louisiana State University Press, 1982.

Goulden, Joseph C. *The Best Years, 1945–1950.* New York: Atheneum, 1976.

Haas, Edward F. *DeLesseps S. Morrison and the Image of Reform: New Orleans Politics, 1946–1961.* Baton Rouge: Louisiana State University Press, 1974.

Hair, William Ivy. *The Kingfish and His Realm: The Life and Times of Huey P. Long.* Baton Rouge: Louisiana State University Press, 1991.

Hamby, Alonzo L. *Beyond the New Deal: Harry S. Truman and American Liberalism.* New York: Columbia University Press, 1973.

Hardy, Florent, Jr. *A Brief History of the University of Southwestern Louisiana.* Baton Rouge: Claitor's Publishing Division, 1973.

Havard, William C., ed. *The Changing Politics of the South.* Baton Rouge: Louisiana State University Press, 1972.

Haws, Robert, ed. *The Age of Segregation: Race Relations in the South, 1890–1945.* Jackson: University Press of Mississippi, 1978.

Heard, Alexander, and Donald S. Strong. *Southern Primaries and Elections, 1920–1949.* University, Ala.: University of Alabama Press, 1950.

Heleniak, Roman. *Soldiers of the Law: Louisiana State Police.* Topeka, Kans.: Josten's Publications, 1980.

Hoehling, A. A. *Home Front U.S.A.* New York: Thomas Y. Crowell Co., 1966.

Hoffmeyer, Oscar, Jr. *Louisiana College: Seventy-Five Years.* Pineville, La.: Louisiana College, 1981.

Hoopes, Roy. *Americans Remember the Home Front: An Oral Narrative.* New York: Hawthorn Books, 1977.

Howard, Perry H. *Political Tendencies in Louisiana.* Rev. ed. Baton Rouge: Louisiana State University Press, 1971.

Humphrey, Hubert H. *The Political Philosophy of the New Deal.* Baton Rouge: Louisiana State University Press, 1970.

Janeway, Eliot. *The Struggle for Survival: A Chronicle of Economic Mobilization in World War II.* New Haven: Yale University Press, 1951.

Jeansonne, Glen. *Gerald L. K. Smith, Minister of Hate.* New Haven: Yale University Press, 1988.

———. *Leander Perez, Boss of the Delta.* Baton Rouge, Louisiana State University Press, 1977.

———. *Race, Religion, and Politics: The Louisiana Gubernatorial Elections of 1959–60.* Lafayette, La.: Center for Louisiana Studies, University of Southwestern Louisiana, 1977.

Johnson, Donald Bruce. *The Republican Party and Wendell Willkie.* Urbana, Ill.: University of Illinois Press, 1960.

Kane, Harnett T. *Deep Delta Country.* New York: Duell, Sloan & Pearce, 1944.

————. *Louisiana Hayride: The American Rehearsal for Dictatorship.* Reprint. Gretna, La.: Pelican Publishing Co., 1971.

Karnes, Thomas L. *Tropical Enterprise: The Standard Fruit and Steamship Company in Latin America.* Baton Rouge: Louisiana State University Press, 1978.

Keefer, Louis E. *From Maine to Mexico: With America's Private Pilots in the Fight against Nazi U-Boats.* Reston, Va.: COFU Publishing, 1997.

Krammer, Arnold. *Nazi Prisoners of War in America.* New York: Stein & Day, 1979.

Kurtz, Michael L., and Morgan D. Peoples. *Earl K. Long: The Saga of Uncle Earl and Louisiana Politics.* Baton Rouge: Louisiana State University Press, 1990.

Leighton, Isabel, ed. *The Aspirin Age, 1919–1941.* New York: Simon & Schuster, 1949.

Lindsey, Coleman. *Elections in Louisiana.* Baton Rouge: Louisiana Department of Education, 1940.

Lingeman, Richard R. *Don't You Know There's a War On? The American Home Front, 1941–1945.* New York: G. P. Putnam's Sons, 1970.

Litton, G. Dupre. *The Wizard of Winnfield.* New York: Carlton Press, 1982.

Loos, John L. *Oil on Stream! A History of the Interstate Oil Pipe Line Company, 1909–1959.* Baton Rouge: Louisiana State University Press, 1959.

Louisiana State Department of Education. *An Historical Sketch of Louisiana State Colleges.* Baton Rouge: N.p., n.d.

Lowrey, Walter M. *150: Centenary College of Louisiana Sesquicentennial, 1825–1975.* Shreveport: Centenary College Alumni Association, 1975.

Luthin, Reinhard. *American Demagogues: Twentieth Century.* Boston: Beacon Press, 1954.

Malone, David. *Hattie and Huey: An Arkansas Tour.* Fayetteville, Ark.: University of Arkansas Press, 1989.

Marcus, Sheldon. *Father Coughlin: The Tumultuous Life of the Priest of the Little Flower.* Boston: Little, Brown & Co., 1973.

Marshall, F. Ray. *Labor in the South.* Cambridge, Mass.: Harvard University Press, 1967.

Mason, Alpheus Thomas. *The Supreme Court from Taft to Burger.* Baton Rouge: Louisiana State University Press, 1979.

McCaughan, Richard B. *Socks on a Rooster: Louisiana's Earl K. Long.* Baton Rouge: Claitor's Book Store, 1967.

Mertz, Paul E. *New Deal Policy and Southern Rural Poverty.* Baton Rouge: Louisiana State University Press, 1978.

Miller, Merle. *Plain Speaking: An Oral Biography of Harry S. Truman*. New York: Berkley Publishing, 1974.

Montgomery, J. P. *Agricultural Statistics for Louisiana, 1900–1957*. Baton Rouge: Louisiana State University, Agricultural Experiment Station, 1958.

Moscow, Warren. *Roosevelt and Willkie*. Englewood Cliffs, N.J.: Prentice-Hall, 1968.

Myrdal, Gunnar. *An American Dilemma: The Negro Problem and Modern Democracy*. Vol. 1. Reprint. New York: Harper & Row, 1962.

Opotowsky, Stan. *The Longs of Louisiana*. New York: E. P. Dutton & Co., 1960.

Panzeri, Louis, and Carole Lawrence. *New Orleans Music Teachers' Association, 1905–1980*. New Orleans: New Orleans Music Teachers' Association, 1981.

Parker, Joseph B. *The Morrison Era: Reform Politics in New Orleans*. Gretna, La.: Pelican Publishing Co., 1974.

Perret, Geoffrey. *Days of Sadness, Years of Triumph: The American People, 1939–1945*. New York: Coward, McCann & Geoghagan, 1973.

Phillips, Cabell. *The Truman Presidency: The History of a Triumphant Succession*. New York: Macmillan, 1966.

Price, Anne. *To Commemorate the 50th Anniversary of the Louisiana Capitol, 1932–1982*. Baton Rouge: State Times and Morning Advocate, 1982.

Price, Frank James. *Troy H. Middleton: A Biography*. Baton Rouge: Louisiana State University Press, 1974.

Range, Willard. *Franklin D. Roosevelt's World Order*. Athens, Ga.: University of Georgia Press, 1959.

Reiling, Stephen D., and Fred H. Wiegmann. *Louisiana Agriculture, Economic Trends and Current Status, 1940–1977*. Baton Rouge: Louisiana State University, Center for Agricultural Sciences and Rural Development, 1979.

Robbins, William G. *Lumberjacks and Legislators: Political Economy of the Lumber Industry, 1890–1941*. College Station, Tex.: Texas A&M University Press, 1982.

Robertson, Minns Sledge. *Public Education in Louisiana after 1898*. Baton Rouge: Bureau of Educational Materials and Research, College of Education, Louisiana State University, 1952.

Rutland, Robert. *The Democrats from Jefferson to Carter*. Baton Rouge: Louisiana State University Press, 1979.

Schlesinger, Arthur M., Jr., ed. *The Coming to Power: Critical Presidential Elections in American History*. New York: Chelsea House, 1972.

————. *The Crisis of the Old Order, 1919–1933*. Boston: Houghton Mifflin Co., 1957.

————. *The Politics of Upheaval.* Boston: Houghton Mifflin Co., 1960.

Schott, Matthew J., and Rosalind Foley. *Bayou Stalags: German Prisoners of War in Louisiana.* Lafayette, La.: N.p., 1981.

Sherrill, Robert. *Gothic Politics in the Deep South: Stars of the New Confederacy.* New York: Grossman, 1968.

Shirer, William L. *The Rise and Fall of the Third Reich.* New York: Simon & Schuster, 1960.

Sindler, Allan P. *Huey Long's Louisiana: State Politics, 1920–1952.* Baltimore: Johns Hopkins Press, 1956.

Sobel, Robert, and John Raimo, eds. *Biographical Directory of the Governors of the United States, 1789–1978.* Vol. 2: *Iowa–Missouri.* Westport, Conn.: Meckler Books, 1978.

Southeastern Louisiana University, Fifty Years: Foundation for the Future. Hammond, La.: Southeastern Louisiana University, 1975.

Strahan, Jerry E. *Andrew Jackson Higgins and the Boats That Won World War II.* Baton Rouge: Louisiana State University Press, 1994.

Sutton, Charles E., Charles L. Foxworth, and Robert E. Hearn. *Louisiana's Story of Public Education.* Ruston, La.: Bureau of Educational Research and Publications, College of Education, Louisiana Tech University, 1971.

Theodoulou, Stella Z. *The Louisiana Republican Party, 1948–1984: The Building of a State Political Party.* New Orleans: Tulane University, 1985.

Tindall, George Brown. *The Disruption of the Solid South.* Athens, Ga.: University of Georgia Press, 1972.

————. *The Emergence of the New South, 1913–1945.* Baton Rouge: Louisiana State University Press, 1967.

Tuchman, Barbara W. *Stilwell and the American Experience in China, 1911–1945.* New York: Macmillan, 1971.

Tulane Studies in Political Science. New Orleans: Tulane University, 1956.

Vincent, Charles. *A Centennial History of Southern University and A&M College, 1880–1980.* Baton Rouge: Southern University, 1981.

Weill, Gus. *You Are My Sunshine: The Jimmie Davis Story.* Waco, Tex.: Word Books, 1977.

Williams, T. Harry. *Huey Long.* New York: Alfred A. Knopf, 1969.

————. *Romance and Realism in Southern Politics.* Baton Rouge, Louisiana State University Press, 1966.

Williamson, Frederick W. *Origin and Development of Agricultural Extension in Louisiana, 1860–1948: How It Opened the Road for Progress in Better Farming and Rural Living.* Baton Rouge: Louisiana State University, Division of Agricultural Extension, 1951.

Zinnman, David H. *The Day Huey Long Was Shot: September 8, 1935.* New York: Ivan Obolensky, 1963.

Articles

"Age: 19, Color: Negro, Occupation, None." *Look,* December 3, 1940.

"America Needs to be Bombed." *Louisiana Municipal Review,* July–August 1942.

Angers, Bob, Jr., "Sam Houston Jones: Reform Governor." *Acadiana Profile,* October–November 1971.

Angers, Trent. "The Three Faces of Dudley LeBlanc." *Acadiana Profile,* second quarter, 1977.

Baker, Riley E. "Negro Voter Registration in Louisiana, 1879–1964." *Louisiana Studies,* winter 1965.

Basso, Hamilton. "The Death and Legacy of Huey Long." *New Republic,* January 1, 1936.

Bouque, Gertrude. "Planning and the Postwar World." *Louisiana Police Jury Review,* April 1944.

Breme, William M. "Along the 'American Way': The New Deal's Work Relief Programs for the Unemployed." *Journal of American History* 62 (December 1975).

Brinkley, Alan. "Huey Long, the Share Our Wealth Movement, and the Limits of Depression Dissidence." *Louisiana History* 22 (spring 1981).

Brooks, Davy. "A Turn of Events: Earl Long and the Louisiana Gubernatorial Elections of 1940 and 1948." *Southern Historian,* spring 1984.

Brooks, Overton. "Louisiana's Part in the War." *Louisiana Police Jury Review,* April 1942.

Bugea, James, Carlos Lazarus, and William T. Pegues. "The Louisiana Legislation of 1940." *Louisiana Law Review,* November 1940.

Butler, Joseph T. "Prisoner of War Labor in the Sugar Cane Fields of Lafourche Parish, Louisiana, 1943–1944." *Louisiana History* 14 (summer 1973).

Byrd, Martha. "The Home Front—World War II." *American History Illustrated,* July 1979.

Caldwell, S. S. "Address." *Louisiana Municipal Review,* May–June 1940.

Carleton, William G. "The Southern Politician—1900 and 1950." *Journal of Politics,* May 1951.

Chapman, Isaac D. "Louisiana's Natural Resources and National Defense." *Louisiana Conservation Review,* autumn 1940.

Collins, Kathleen. "Lake Charles Claims Rarest Port in the World." *Louisiana Heritage,* vol. 2, no. 3, n.d.

Colvin, Hermann. "Alexandria Goes to War." *Louisiana Municipal Review,* January–February 1941.

Corley, Dawson. "Huey's Capitol Idea." *Louisiana Life,* January–February 1982.

Cotton, W. B., Jr. "Baton Rouge Refinery Converts Petroleum into War Materials." *Louisiana Municipal Review,* July–August 1943.

"Crepe Hung in Louisiana." *Time,* July 27, 1942.

Crown, James C. "Louisiana's David." *New York Times Magazine,* March 3, 1940.

Crymes, Judith. "National Defense—A Project." *Louisiana Schools,* January 1942.

Curet, A. B. "Food Wins Wars Too—So Pointe Coupée Parish Goes All Out for Victory." *Louisiana Municipal Review,* September–October 1942.

Dakin, M. G. "Louisiana Tax Legislation of 1940." *Louisiana Law Review,* November 1940.

Dalfiume, Richard M. "The 'Forgotten Years' of the Negro Revolution." *Journal of American History* 55 (June 1968).

Davis, Jimmie. "Country Music Is Part of the People." *Louisiana Heritage,* summer 1969.

"Defense Program Casts Louisiana in Leading Role." *Louisiana Police Jury Review,* April 1941.

Dixon, Margaret. "Governor Earl K. Long." *Baton Rouge Morning Advocate,* May 9, 1948, magazine section.

Dodd, W. J. "Address by President W. J. Dodd." *Louisiana Schools,* November 1941.

Dutton, Tom. "Sam Houston Jones: Louisiana's Liberator." *Christian Science Monitor Magazine,* April 27, 1940.

Editorial Comment. *Louisiana Schools,* January 1942.

Edwards, Edwin W. "The Role of the Governor in Louisiana Politics: An Historical Analysis." *Louisiana History* 15 (spring 1974).

"Extensive War Games in Louisiana." *Louisiana Police Jury Review,* April 1940.

"Facts about Calcasieu Parish." *Louisiana Police Jury Review,* April 1939.

Fournet, J. J. "A Message from President Fournet." *Louisiana Police Jury Review,* April 1939.

Fuller, Parrish. "Outline of Overall Plan for Enlisting School Children in the Collection of Scrap Iron, Rags, Rubber, Etc." *Louisiana Schools,* September 1942.

Gay, Edward J., Jr. "Louisiana Housing Legislation: Urban and Rural." *Louisiana Municipal Review,* January–February 1941.

Haas, Edward F. "New Orleans on the Half Shell: The Maestri Era, 1936–1946." *Louisiana History* 12 (summer 1972).

Hamby, Alonzo L. "The Liberals, Truman, and FDR as Symbol and Myth." *Journal of American History* 56 (March 1970).

Hardey, B. A. "Major Hardey Looks Ahead at the 'Golden Age of Louisiana.' " *Louisiana Conservation Review,* spring 1940.

Hardy, John Edward. "War-Time Proposals for High School Curricular Changes." *Louisiana Municipal Review,* March–April 1943.

Harrop, John W., Jr. "Lake Charles—A Decade of Progress." *Louisiana Municipal Review,* September–October 1941.

"Higgins Is the Name." *Time,* May 4, 1942.

Hood, John T., Jr. "History of Courts of Appeal in Louisiana." *Louisiana Law Review,* April 1961.

Humphreys, Hubert. "In a Sense Experimental: The Civilian Conservation Corps in Louisiana." *Louisiana History* 5 (fall 1964).

Hunt, Andrew W. "The College Student and War Morale." *Louisiana Schools,* November 1942.

Hyneman, Charles S. "Political and Administrative Reform in the 1940 Legislature." *Louisiana Law Review,* November 1940.

Jackson, S. M. "Adjusting the Program of Vocational Agriculture to Meet the Needs of the War Effort." *Louisiana Schools,* December 1942.

———. "The Part Rural War Production Training Will Play in the 1943 Food for Victory Program." *Louisiana Schools,* March 1943.

Jeansonne, Glen. "Challenge to the New Deal: Huey P. Long and the Redistribution of National Wealth." *Louisiana History* 21 (fall 1980).

———. "Partisan Parson: An Oral History Account of the Louisiana Years of Gerald L. K. Smith." *Louisiana History* 23 (spring 1982).

Johnson, Alva. "The Camera Trapped Them." *Saturday Evening Post,* June 15, 1940.

———. "Louisiana Revolution." *Saturday Evening Post,* May 11, 1940.

———. "They Sent a Letter." *Saturday Evening Post,* June 22, 1940.

Jones, Sam H. "Civilian Defense in Louisiana." *Louisiana Police Jury Review,* April 1942.

———. "Civilian Defense in Louisiana—A Review of 1942." *Louisiana Police Jury Review,* April 1943.

———. "Will Dixie Bolt the New Deal?" *Saturday Evening Post,* March 6, 1943.

Kurtz, Michael. "Earl Long's Political Relations with the City of New Orleans." *Louisiana History* 10 (summer 1969).

———. "Government by the Civics Book: The Administration of Robert F. Kennon, 1952–1956." *North Louisiana Historical Association Journal,* spring 1981.

"Legislation of 1940." *Louisiana Schools,* September 1940, 22–23.

Lockwood, Joseph N. "The German Concentration Camp, Bastrop, Louisiana." *North Louisiana Historical Association Journal,* spring 1980.

"Louisiana FHA Loans Lead the Nation." *Louisiana Police Jury Review,* April 1939.

"Louisiana's Governor-Elect." *Louisiana Police Jury Review,* April 1940.

McGuire, Jack B. "Andrew Jackson Higgins Plays Presidential Politics." *Louisiana History* 15 (summer 1974).

Maher, J. C. "Water Supplies and Louisiana's War Effort." *Louisiana Municipal Review,* January–February 1943.

"Minutes of the Executive Council." *Louisiana Schools,* September 1941.

"Mourners, Heirs, Foes." *Time,* September 23, 1935.

Murray, G. Patrick. "The Louisiana Maneuvers: Practice for War." *Louisiana History* 12 (spring 1972).

O'Connor, Stella. "The Charity Hospital at New Orleans: An Administrative and Financial History, 1736–1941." *Louisiana Historical Quarterly* 31 (January 1948).

Powell, Alden L. "Your Democracy Is in Your Hands." *Louisiana Municipal Review,* September–October 1943.

Pradillo, A. E. "Louisiana's Governor 'Sells' Middle West." *New Orleans Port Record,* October 1943.

Rankin, William G. "The Conservation of Louisiana's Natural Resources." *Louisiana Police Jury Review,* April 1939.

Reid, Joseph W., Jr. "Civilian Defense." *Louisiana Municipal Review.* May–June 1943.

———. "The Geography of Louisiana's Civilian Defense Organization I." *Louisiana Municipal Review,* March–April 1942.

"Rights Restored to Police Juries." *Louisiana Police Jury Review,* April 1941.

Robison, Daniel M. "From Tillman to Long: Some Striking Leaders of the Rural South." *Journal of Southern History* 3 (August 1937).

Rogers, Gayle. "The Shreveport League of Women Voters and the Drive for Permanent Voter Registration in Louisiana." *North Louisiana Historical Association Journal,* spring–summer 1993.

Sanson, Jerry Purvis. "Cenla During World War II." *Alexandria Daily Town Talk, Centennial Edition,* April 8, 1983.

———. "Louisiana Reaction to the Beginning of World War II." *Southern Historian,* spring 1986.

———. "North Louisiana Press Opinion and the Beginning of World War II." *North Louisiana Historical Association Journal,* fall 1980.

Saucier, Chuck. "Saying Goodbye." *Cenla: The Magazine of Central Louisiana,* November–December 1992.

"Schism among Long's Political Heirs." *Literary Digest,* September 28, 1935.

"Shortage of Teachers with Special Reference to Louisiana." *Louisiana Schools,* December 1942.

Simmons, George E. "Crusading Newspapers in Louisiana." *Journalism Quarterly,* December 1939.

Simpson, William. "A Tale Untold? The Alexandria, Louisiana, Lee Street Riot (January 10, 1942)." *Louisiana History* 35 (spring 1994).

Snyder, Robert E. "Huey Long and the Presidential Election of 1936." *Louisiana History* 16 (spring 1975).

Thurlkill, Cathy. "A Woman's Place Is in the War: North Louisiana Women's Contribution to World War Two, 1941–1945." *North Louisiana Historical Association Journal,* winter 1997.

Valentin, Jerry W. "The WPA and Louisiana Education," *Louisiana History* 12 (fall 1968).

Verigan, Lester C., Jr. "Barksdale Air Force Base: Satellite Operations in Northwest Louisiana." *North Louisiana Historical Association Journal,* winter 1994.

"The War Relief Club of John McDonough High School." *Louisiana Schools,* December 1942.

Watt, Leonard B., Jr. "Lincoln Parish Prepares for 'Total War.' " *Louisiana Police Jury Review,* April 1942.

Whitten, David O. "American Rice Cultivation, 1680–1980: A Tercentenary Critique." *Southern Studies* 21 (spring 1982).

"The Whole People." *Acadiana Profile,* October–November 1971.

Wilkins, S. A. "Dodd College: A Brief History." *North Louisiana Historical Association Journal,* summer 1980.

Theses and Dissertations

Ancelet, LeRoy. "A History of Southeastern Louisiana College." Ph.D. dissertation, Louisiana State University, 1971.

Banta, Brady Michael. "The Regulation and Conservation of Petroleum Resources in Louisiana, 1901–1940." Ph.D. dissertation, Louisiana State University, 1981.

Barr, Mortimer. "The Louisiana Public Service Commission." Master's thesis, Louisiana State University, 1941.

Bolding, Gary Arnold. "Efforts to Develop New Orleans as a World Trade Center, 1910–1960." Master's thesis, Louisiana State University, 1966.

Daugherty, Denny. "From Log Cabin to Governor's Mansion." Senior thesis, Louisiana State University, 1970.

Field, Betty Marie. "The Politics of the New Deal in Louisiana." Ph.D. dissertation, Tulane University, 1973.

Gordon, Richard Lawrence. "The Development of Louisiana's Public Mental Health Institutions, 1735–1940." Volume 2. Ph.D. dissertation, Louisiana State University, 1978.

Hammack, Rudolph Carrol. "The New Deal and Louisiana Agriculture." Ph.D. dissertation. Tulane University, 1973.

Jones, E. Carl. "Mechanization on Large Sugar Cane Farms in Louisiana." M.A. thesis, Louisiana State University, 1947.

Marshall, Douglas Coughlin. "A History of Higher Education of Negroes in the State of Louisiana." Ph.D. dissertation, Louisiana State University, 1956.

Mitchell, John H. "Development of Vocational Agricultural Education in Louisiana." Ph.D. dissertation, Louisiana State University, 1959.

Morrison, Betty L. "A History of Our Lady of Holy Cross College, New Orleans, Louisiana." Ph.D. dissertation, Louisiana State University, 1976.

Neyland, Leedell Wallace. "The Negro in Louisiana since 1900: An Economic and Social Study." Ph.D. dissertation, New York University, 1958.

Pacella, Anthony Eugene. "A History of the Louisiana School Boards Association." Ed.D. dissertation, Louisiana State University, 1977.

Peyton, Lt. Col. Lamar F. "Treatment and Utilization of Prisoners of War by the United States during World War II." Master's thesis, Louisiana State University, 1973.

Rankin, Pauline M. "The Development of Educational Media in Louisiana." Ph.D. dissertation, Louisiana State University, 1977.

Sanson, Jerry Purvis. "The Louisiana Gubernatorial Election of 1940." Master's thesis, Louisiana State University, 1975.

Southerland, Thomas P. "Rules and Regulations Enacted by Rapides Parish School Board since 1893 and Their Implications." Ed.D. dissertation, Louisiana State University, 1960.

Stielow, Frederick J. "Isolation and Development on a Louisiana Gulfcoast Island: Grand Isle, 1781–1962." Ph.D. dissertation, Indiana University, 1977.

Sullivan, Willoughby Aaron, Jr. "The Development of the Louisiana Teachers' Association." Ph.D. dissertation, Louisiana State University, 1968.

Sutton, Charles Edward. "Activities of the Louisiana State Department of Education on the Elementary School Level, 1940 to 1964." Ed.D. dissertation, Louisiana State University, 1969.

Weimar, Charles E. "John Easterly Coxe, Louisiana Educator." Ed.D. dissertation, Louisiana State University, 1974.

Other Secondary Sources

Long, Russell. Remarks. War and Politics Symposium, Louisiana State University, April 27, 1979.

Mills, Gary, and Grady McWhiney. "Jimmie Davis as a Figure of Continuity in Country Music." Paper presented to the Louisiana Historical Association Annual Convention, March 25, 1983.

Peoples, Morgan. "The Sunshine Governor from Jackson Parish." Paper presented to the Louisiana Historical Association Annual Convention, March 25, 1983.

Schott, Matthew J. "World War II Prisoners and Internees in Louisiana: A Lesson in Racial and Ethnic Stereotyping." Paper presented to the Louisiana Historical Association Annual Convention, March 25, 1983.

Sosna, Morton. "More Important Than the Civil War? The Social Impact of World War II on the South." Paper presented at the Southern Historical Association Annual Meeting, November 5, 1982.

INDEX

AFL. *See* American Federation of Labor (AFL)

Agricultural Extension Service, 181, 200, 204

Agriculture: mechanization of, 5–6, 193; sugar industry, 140–46, 157, 158, 193, 200, 202–204, 210; in Democratic platform, 141; and New Deal, 144, 191–92; and education, 179–80; cotton production, 190–91, 192, 193, 198, 204–205, 210; size of farms, 190, 208, 209; farm ownership, 190, 208; tenant farmers, 190, 208, 270; gross agricultural income in U.S., 191; and livestock, 191, 194; per capita farm income, 191; farm workers, 192–201, 208; rice production, 193, 198, 204, 205, 210, 221; and Victory Farm Volunteers, 194; POW labor for, 195–99, 201; West Indies labor for, 200–201; and blacks, 201, 208, 270; corn production, 204; meat and meat products, 206; soybean production, 206; sweet potato canning, 206–207. *See also* U.S. Department of Agriculture (USDA)

Alcohol, 244–46

Alexandria: industry in, 6; and military, 222–26, 241, 251, 268–69; population of, 238, 285; scrap drives in, 247, 248; war stamp sales in, 249; staged military invasions at, 251; wartime defense scare in, 254; race riot in, 268–69; segregation in, 268; victory celebration in, 281

Alford, Steve, 57, 96, 245

Allain, James S., 33

Allen, A. Leonard, 3, 152, 162–64, 226, 231, 245

Allen, George, 142

Allen, Oscar K. "O.K.," 12, 15, 29, 78, 162

Aluminum Company of America, 215, 229

American Democratic Association, 76

American Federation of Labor (AFL), 228–29, 231–35, 237

American Sugar Cane League, 142, 157, 197–98

Angola. *See* Louisiana State Penitentiary

Anti-Longites: and impeachment of Huey Long, 1–2; governors elected by, 3, 23; and 1939–40 gubernatorial campaign, 23, 28–29, 43, 52–53; and 1942 mayoral election, 81; and social programs, 103; and 1943–44 gubernatorial election, 121–22; and 1940 congressional elections, 154, 160–62, 170; and 1942 congressional elections, 166–67

Appleby, Paul, 144

Arcenaux, Ruth, 272

Arial, Julius F., 243

Army: black soldiers in, 150, 268–69; and Louisiana Maneuvers, 172, 222–26; training for, 172, 178–79, 180, 182, 184, 213, 214, 221–28; and High School Victory Corps, 178–79; Baton Rouge as depot for, 215; and Higgins ships, 218; payroll for, 223, 224; entertainment for soldiers, 241–42; women in, 270

Army camps, 171, 197, 213, 214, 221–22, 226–28